JON

MICAH

NAHUM

HABAKKUK

ZEPHANIAH

9.99

JONAH, MICAH, NAHUM, HABAKKUK, ZEPHANIAH

John L. Mackay

Christian Focus

© John L. Mackay
ISBN 1 857 92 392 8

Published in 1998
as part of the Focus on the Bible Commentary series
by
Christian Focus Publications
Geanies House, Fearn, Ross-shire
IV20 1TW, Great Britain.

Cover design by Donna Macleod.

The main scripture version used is the New International Version
(NIV), © International Bible Society, 1973, 1978, 1984. Published
by Hodder and Stoughton. Other versions referred to are the Authorised Version (AV), the New American Standard Bible (NASB),
and the New King James Version (NKJV)

The sections on Jonah, Micah and Nahum were previously
published in 1993 as *God's Just Demands*.

CONTENTS

PREFACE

It is not easy to know God. What is more, it can be uncomfortable to live knowing God. But knowing God is essential. 'Now this is eternal life: that they may know you, the only true God, and Jesus Christ, whom you have sent' (John 17:3). We must avoid the danger of corrupting our knowledge of God by substituting a human caricature of what God should be like for the revelation he has given in Scripture of what he really is. It is easy to be influenced by the ideas that exist of God as well-intentioned, undemanding, ready to accept us and give us what we want, and happy to make do with whatever we can scrape together to offer him of our time, resources and affection. Such a sentimental picture is plausible because it is effectively shaped by our sinful, human ideas, and lets us go on living as we please.

The five books of Scripture that are studied in this commentary act as an effective antidote to diminishing God by bringing him down to the sort of being we find it easy to live with. There is no doubt that the only true God is one who does abound in love (Jonah 4:2), delights to show mercy (Mic. 7:18), and rejoices over his redeemed people with singing (Zeph. 3:17). But we have to learn that God's love and his concern, which encompass even a heathen city (Jonah 4:11), are only one aspect of his character. We must also know him as the one who 'will not leave the guilty unpunished' (Nah. 1:3). We have not really grasped who God is until we realise that living with him has to be done on his terms, not ours. As the Creator of all, he has the right to demand how we live. As the Judge of all, he will exercise his right to demand that we account for what we have done. Knowing God as he really is leads us to acknowledge his just demands on us.

This is seen at various levels in these prophetic books. In Jonah, there is the matter of the personal demand made on the prophet. God requires individual obedience, even when the task is one which we do not understand, or with which we are out of sympathy. Disobedience merits God's judgment and wrath. There is also the divine demand for obedience from Nineveh. The pagan city at the heart of a great empire was not exempt from God's requirements and scrutiny, for he rules over all the kingdoms of mankind. If Nineveh had not changed her ways, she would have been engulfed by divine judgment.

In Micah, the focus is on the LORD's demands on his own people of Judah. They had been the recipients of God's favour, and he had

7

entered into covenant with them. They were the ones whose lives should have been a living expression of their allegiance and gratitude. But they were not, and so Micah summoned them to consider and amend their ways which were out of alignment with God's covenant demands. If they did not repent, God would justly punish them. That would not, however, be God's last word about his chosen people. After they had been punished for their rebellion, God would again extend mercy to them.

In Nahum, the demands of God's justice fall on Nineveh. Well over a century had elapsed from the days of Jonah, and Nineveh had reverted to its former cruelty. In the destruction that overwhelmed the once proud and self-confident city, there is a solemn reminder to all the nations of the earth that God will demand that they answer for their conduct before his judgment seat.

Habakkuk approaches the matter of God's just demands from a different angle. We find the prophet agonising over the fact that he cannot understand the way in which God acts to procure justice on earth. He knows God cannot tolerate evil and treachery, and yet he is raising up the merciless Babylonians to punish his people for their sin. Habakkuk is assured that eventually God will intervene to punish and overthrow the oppressor of his people. He is enjoined to wait with the confidence of a patient faith, for then he will see that whatever puzzles and seeming inequities God's justice throws up in this life, all the earth should be respectfully silent before the holy and sovereign God until he resolves the difficulties that have been encountered.

Like Micah, Zephaniah is acutely aware of the evil and corruption that prevailed in his day. He presents a stark picture of the coming reality of the great day of the LORD to shock the indifferent out of their spiritual lethargy. If all the nations are expected to fall under the scrutiny of the universal Judge, how can his own people possibly think they are going to be exempt. But Zephaniah also presents another side to the exercise of divine justice. It is designed not only to punish those who are obstinately wicked, but also to reclaim and purify. Beyond the impending outpouring of wrath there is a picture of God's provision for his people a provision which is shown to extend beyond the remnant of Israel. The blessings of divine restoration are presented to allure the wayward people back to the paths of covenant loyalty before it is too late to escape the just sentence on their misdeeds.

All humanity and every aspect of human conduct are subject to the requirements that God imposes on it. We have a fatally flawed view of him if we suppose that he is unaware of our behaviour or indifferent to it. There is no ultimate evasion of his just demands on us. Since all have sinned and failed to live up to the demands of God (Rom. 3:9-23), the final destiny of humanity would inevitably have been one of eternal punishment, had not God spontaneously and graciously provided a remedy. Salvation is possible only because God has permitted the penalty of his judgment to fall on a substitute, his own Son. He paid the price in the place of his people. It is only in this way that the demands of God's justice could be met and salvation provided for fallen humanity. Eternal life involves not only knowing and acknowledging God's just demands, but also knowing Jesus Christ, whom the Father sent, as the one who can effectively deal with the situation that arises when we fail to meet those demands.

Outline of Major Events

BC

853 Battle of Qarqar: Assyria meets coalition of western forces, including Ahab of Israel.

780-755 *Ministry of Jonah.*

773-754 Ashur-dan III of Assyria. Time of Assyrian weakness.

745-727 Tiglath-Pileser III of Assyria. Resurgence of Assyrian power.

722 Fall of Samaria. End of Northern Kingdom of Israel.

715-690 *Ministry of Micah.*

701 Sennacherib of Assyria threatens Jerusalem.

696-642 Reign of Manasseh. Period of Assyrian domination and religious apostasy in Judah.

663 Capture of Thebes in Egypt. Height of Assyrian power.

655-635 *Ministry of Nahum.*

640-609 Josiah rules in Judah. Period of religious reform.

630-625 *Ministry of Zephaniah.*

612 Fall of Nineveh. Rise of Babylonians.

610-600 *Ministry of Habakkuk.*

605 Battle of Carchemish in which Babylon routs Egypt and becomes dominant power in the Middle East.

586 Fall of Jerusalem.

KINGS OF ISRAEL	KINGS OF JUDAH	KINGS OF ASSYRIA
Omri 885-874	Uzziah 792-740	Shalmaneser III 858-824
Ahab 874-853	Jotham 750-731	Shamsi-Adad V 824-810
Ahaziah 853-852	Ahaz 735-715	Adad-nirari III 810-782
Joram 852-841	Hezekiah 729-686	Shalmaneser IV 782-773
Jehu 841-814	Manasseh 696-642	Ashur-dan III 773-754
Jehoahaz 814-798	Amon 642-640	Adad-nirari V 754-745
Jehoash 798-782	Josiah 640-609	Tiglath-pileser III 745-727
Jeroboam II 793-753	Jehoahaz 609	Shalmaneser V 727-722
Zechariah 753	Jehoiakim 608-598	Sargon II 722-705
Shallum 752	Jehoiachin 598-597	Sennacherib 705-681
Menahem 752-742	Zedekiah 597-586	Esarhaddon 681-669
Pekahiah 742-740		Ashurbanipal 669-626
Pekah 752-732		Ashur-etil-ilani 626-623
Hoshea 732-722		Sin-shum-lishir 623
		Sin-shar-ishkun 623-612
		Ashur-uballit 612-608

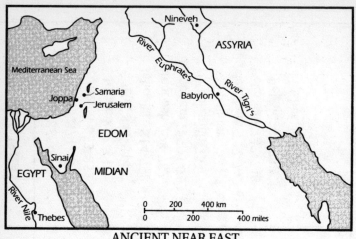

ANCIENT NEAR EAST

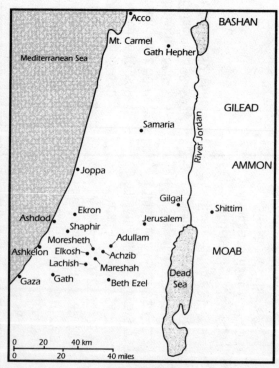

PALESTINE

JONAH

Overview

Jonah is different from the other eleven works that have been gathered in the collection we know as the Minor Prophets. It alone does not principally consist of the messages delivered by a prophet. The book of Jonah is a narrative, and has many resemblances to the narratives about Elijah and Elisha recorded in the Books of Kings. Indeed, Jonah was their successor. Elijah's ministry came to an end in 847 BC, and Elisha's ministry can be dated around 850-795 BC. Jonah was probably a younger contemporary of Elisha, who outlived him. Little information is given about the date of his ministry, but his visit to Nineveh seems to fall in the period 780-755 BC.

Like the narratives about Elijah and Elisha, the miraculous features prominently in the book of Jonah. This has led many to challenge its historicity. Undoubtedly it is not written as modern history. It omits many names and facts that we would have expected to be included. But they were not relevant for the purposes of the narrator. We may compare this with the number of times in Kings when the specific monarch with whom Elisha is dealing is left quite unnamed (2 Kgs. 5,7). The same terse narrative style is found in both places, focusing on what the narrator wants to emphasise as the point of the story. But such compactness and selectivity do not make Jonah unfactual, any more than the presence of miracles does — unless we have previously decided that miracles cannot happen anyway. Those who adopt that perspective are going to have trouble accepting most of Scripture, which prominently displays God's power not only in creating, but also in superintending his creation.

We shall also note that, apart from the miracles, there are other features of the narrative that have led many to question the historicity of Jonah. But there are more than adequate explanations that may be advanced to counter such doubts. There is no good reason to suppose that this book is a fable or a parable. It is undoubtedly a story that can teach us much, but that is because it really happened. It is not due to the fertile imagination of some masterly storyteller. Since there is no formal indication of the author of this book, we cannot be certain who it actually was, but much of the information must have come from Jonah himself, and it may well have been written by him, or someone very close to him.

The main purpose of the book was to stir Israel up to consider the character of the LORD whom they professed to serve, and to examine the nature of their relationship to him. That was why the story was written and included in the canon of Scripture. Jonah's mission to Nineveh was divinely designed to make Israel jealous, as the LORD displayed how he could bless a heathen nation. As is brought out in the concluding verse (4:11), Jonah himself had to learn about God's concern for all mankind, whether Jew or Gentile. But though Jonah is a short book, its teaching is not confined to one theme. Jonah's own experience was a much-needed warning against disobedience, as well as a display of divine grace claiming and restoring the sinner, even as he defiantly tries to evade God's command.

The chapter divisions correspond with the structure of the book. There are two sections, chapters 1 and 2, and chapters 3 and 4, both of which have a similar pattern. They begin with the prophet receiving the LORD's commission and his reaction to it (1:1-3; 3:1-4). The consequences of the prophet's actions are then related (1:4-16; 3:5-9): first the storm caused by his disobedience; and then when he obeys God and brings his message to Nineveh, the repentance displayed in that city. Both 1:17 and 3:10 are transitional verses that bridge between what has gone before and what follows, by relating how the LORD intervenes sovereignly in the situation to save. Jonah's reaction to this is then related: in the first instance, his own gratitude at being saved (chapter 2), but later his hostility at the LORD's relenting towards Nineveh (4:1-4). This leads into a final section (4:5-11) where the LORD acts to straighten out the prophet's attitudes and thinking.

Jonah 1:1-3: I Must Get Away From This!

The story of Jonah is narrated simply and effectively. Details we might want to know about are omitted because they would only divert attention from what should be grasped. This terse style is found right from the start, where in the first three verses we are introduced to Jonah (1:1), told of his commission (1:2), and of his disobedience (1:3). The story of the runaway prophet who feels he must get away from the LORD's command matches in its breathless style the breathlessness Jonah must have experienced when he arrived at Joppa. To appreciate all that is being said we have to look at it more slowly.

The word of the LORD came to (*verse 1*) is a phrase found over 100 times in the Old Testament to describe what took place when the LORD spoke to one of his prophets. Generally it is followed by the message they were authorised to deliver to the people in the name of the LORD.

This is found, for instance, at the beginning of the prophecies of Joel and Micah. But there are also passages, such as this, where what is related is a set of instructions to the prophet himself, as, for example to Elijah in 1 Kings 17:2; 21:17. It is the LORD's initiative that gets the story of Jonah started, just as it is the LORD's hand that determines the outcome.

The prophet who receives the LORD's message is named as **Jonah son of Amittai**. Some have felt that because the name Jonah means 'a dove', and Amittai is connected with the Hebrew word for 'truth' or 'truthfulness', an allegorical interpretation of the book is justified. This, however, is being too fanciful. Hebrew names nearly always meant something (just as Brown or Smith do), and Jonah here is just a name. We are told he is Jonah son of Amittai, because he is a real person about whom more is known from 2 Kings 14:23-27.

Jonah's prophetic ministry coincided with the reign of Jeroboam II (793-753 BC), who ruled over the northern kingdom of Israel. It had broken away from Judah after the death of Solomon (931 BC), and its subsequent history was marked by spiritual decline and apostasy. First of all, a debased worship of the LORD using idols and a non-Levitical priesthood had been established in the north, but by the time of Elijah's ministry (around 860-847 BC) the land had degenerated to outright worship of the Canaanite god, Baal. Though this threat had been dealt with by Elijah, and also by Jeroboam II's great-grandfather, Jehu (2 Kgs. 10:18-29), the official religion of the northern kingdom continued to be corrupted by idolatry and paganism. This was still true under Jeroboam II (2 Kgs. 14:24).

But Jonah was given an extraordinary message regarding Jeroboam's reign. It was going to be a time of prosperity and national success (2 Kgs. 14:25). This was not a reward for Jeroboam's piety, or that of his people. It was rather a gracious initiative from the LORD. Because of their disloyalty, he had been punishing his people through foreign invasion from both Syria (Aram) and Assyria, but now, seeing their desperate circumstances — they were on the point of being wiped out — 'he saved them by the hand of Jeroboam' (2 Kgs. 14:26-27). Repeated defeat before their enemies had not brought the people to their senses, and unfortunately granting a predicted time of blessing was to fail also. The people did not recognise their good fortune as coming from the LORD (Hos. 2:8). But knowing that it was Jonah who had brought the message of the coming period of prosperity helps us to understand his thinking in connection with the altogether different message he is commanded to relay in this book.

2 Kings also provides us with the information that Jonah came from Gath-Hepher (2 Kgs. 14:25; see Map II). In Joshua 19:13 this village is identified as being in the territory of Zebulun, and it probably lay a few miles north of Nazareth. Jonah was the only Old Testament prophet we know about from Galilee (John 7:52), and he is the only Old Testament prophet to whom Jesus compares himself and his ministry (Matt. 12:39-41; Luke 11:29-32; see on 1:17).

In the book of Jonah, however, it is not to his own nation that the prophet has to deliver his message — at least that is how it appears initially. We do have to remember that he wrote this book for them, so what he was doing affected them too. However, what the LORD says to him is **"Go to the great city of Nineveh"** (*verse 2*). In fact it begins with 'Arise!', a word that the NIV does not translate. It is used not just of getting to one's feet, but also of responding speedily to a matter that is presented as urgent. The task that the LORD is assigning to Jonah is one that requires immediate action.

Now Nineveh was in northern Mesopotamia, on the east bank of the river Tigris, opposite the modern city of Mosul (see Map). While it was not the capital of Assyria in Jonah's day, it was a major centre with royal palaces where the king would on occasion stay. It was a large and wealthy city, benefiting from Assyria being the major power in Mesopotamia. Its size and importance are mentioned again in 3:3 and 4:11. Jonah was being ordered to go to a major pagan metropolis.

Assyria had spread its power throughout the Near East. Already there had been various contacts with Israel. Assyrian records tell us that in 853 BC Ahab king of Israel joined an alliance of western states that fought against the Assyrian king Shalmaneser III at Qarqar. Assyrian records again tell us that in 841 Jehu paid tribute to Shalmaneser III of Assyria. Also in 796 Jehoash paid tribute to Adad-nirari III, who was conducting a series of campaigns in the west, evidently in an attempt to keep the area under his control.

There are other instances of Old Testament prophecies against foreign nations (see on Zeph. 2:4-15), but the prophet did not ordinarily travel to the foreign land to deliver it. The messages against the foreign nations had as their primary function reassuring God's own people of his watchfulness over their affairs and his readiness to act appropriately against those who harassed them.

But here Jonah is to go to Nineveh with a message. **Preach against it, because its wickedness has come up before me**. It is a denunciation of the city from the God who rules all. It proceeds on the basis of the LORD being the one to whom all nations are accountable. Whether they acknowledge him or not, he is 'the Judge of all the earth' (Gen. 18:25), and is taking official cognisance of what they are doing. When he decides to act in the matter, it is inevitable that judgment will engulf the city.

Nineveh was a major centre of the Assyrian Empire. As the Assyrians had increased their zone of influence through the ancient world, they had became renowned for their cruelty and rapaciousness (see on Nah. 3:1). Already this feature of Assyrian power had become so notorious that it called for specific divine intervention. There is no indication that the message to be sent would call for repentance, but that is an inevitable inference. When God warns people of his impending judgment, it is with the aim that they will respond in time and be saved. 'If at any time I announce that a nation or kingdom is to be uprooted, torn down and destroyed, and if that nation I warned repents of its evil, then I will relent and not inflict on it the disaster I had planned' (Jer. 18:7-8).

But what was the reason for God giving this commission to Jonah? One of the lessons of the book is that God's ways are beyond ours, and that his actions are not constrained by our understanding of what is going on. Our capacity to understand and approve does not set the standard to which God has to adhere.

Still there is more to it than that. Fitting it in with the divine programme outlined in 2 Kings enables us to see that if Jonah had carried out the commission when it was originally given to him, then it would have fulfilled a very important role in God's dealings with his covenant people — namely provoking them to respond to him. This was one aspect of the LORD's procedure in dealing with his people's waywardness and desertion of him. As early as the time of Moses, such circumstances had led him to say, 'I will make them envious by those who are not a people; I will make them angry by a nation that has no understanding' (Deut. 32:21). To rebuke them for their ingratitude, the LORD would make his own people envious of the blessings he had bestowed on others (Rom. 10:19-21; 11:14).

In this respect we can see an element of continuity between Jonah's ministry and that of his immediate predecessors, Elijah and Elisha. They too had been used to bring divine blessing to outsiders. Elijah had been ordered to go to Zarephath in Sidonian (Phoenician) territory, and had provided food for a widow and her family and restored her son to life (1 Kgs. 17). Elisha had cured Naaman the Syrian of his leprosy (2 Kgs. 5). Such facts did not sit comfortably with the small-minded view of the scope of divine blessing held by the Jews of our Lord's day (Luke 4:24-30). It is quite likely that Jonah and his generation considered themselves to have an exclusive right to the LORD's favour.

The LORD was blessing Israel with respite from their enemies, but this was so that they would return to him. It would not have been long after this that the LORD would send Amos and Hosea to Israel to condemn them for their ingratitude and lack of response. Jonah's ministry presumably took place earlier in Jeroboam's reign, and was designed to urge them back to the LORD, by showing how Nineveh would respond to the blessing bestowed on it (Matt. 12:41; 11:20-24).

But matters did not develop in such a straightforward fashion. Having received his urgent commission, one would have expected the narrative to have continued, 'And Jonah arose and went to Nineveh.' That's the way other prophets responded (e.g. Elijah, in 1 Kgs. 17:9-10), and it's the way Jonah will respond eventually too (3:3) – but first there's a rather surprising detour. **But Jonah ran away from the LORD and headed for Tarshish** (*verse 3*). That was in the opposite direction. To get to Nineveh, Jonah would have had to travel north and then east. We are not sure where he was when he received the command. Presumably it was in the Northern Kingdom, though perhaps not at his home town of Gath-Hepher. Had he been there, the port he could have reached soonest would have been Acco, which lay further north than Joppa (see Map II). It is likely that he was in the south of the land, not far from the capital, Samaria.

The location of Tarshish is uncertain. The word means a 'refinery' or 'smelter', and was used of a number of sites around the Mediterranean where Phoenician traders had gone to find metals. The most probable situation for it is in what is now southern Spain, near the mouth of the Guadalquivir. Scripture views it as a distant and remote place (Ps. 72:10; Isa. 66:19). Jonah's choice is thus seen to be of somewhere as far as possible from the city to which he had been directed to go.

Two questions are raised by this. (1) Why did Jonah not want to obey the command? (2) Did he really expect to change anything by running away?

(1) We are not told at this point the reasons for Jonah's disobedience. That remains until later (4:2). But his response does not seem to have been motivated by the personal danger involved. Undoubtedly taking

an unpopular message to Nineveh was no easy matter, but Jonah's attitude later on (1:12; 4:3,8) does not suggest that he was particularly afraid of death. Jonah did not want the LORD to spare Nineveh. He understood the conditional nature of the command given to him. It was opening up the possibility of a positive response from the people of Nineveh, and that would mean that the enemies of his people – and the enemies of God – would be blessed. Jonah's problems were primarily theological. Having already been the means of delivering a message of prosperity to his own people, he did not want to be party to a revival of Assyrian fortunes. They were pagan and had already shown their hostility to the LORD. They were only worthy of judgment. God should preserve the line of distinction between his own people whom he blesses and others who rejected him and should be rejected.

(2) As regards how his running away would solve his problems, there may have been an element of unthinking, irrational response, induced by guilt. He knew he was in the wrong and, like Adam and Eve trying to hide from the presence of the LORD among the trees of the garden (Gen. 3:8), he just wanted to avoid the one he had offended. It is unlikely that Jonah really believed he could find somewhere that the LORD's writ did not run. He himself will shortly confess (1:9) that the LORD is God of heaven and earth. He never doubted that, or believed that one could escape the scrutiny of God (Jer. 23:24). As chapter 2 shows, Jonah was conversant with the Psalms, and would have known the words of David, 'Where can I go from your Spirit? Where can I flee from your presence?' Even settling 'on the far side of the sea' would not suffice (Ps. 139:7,9).

Why run away then? The key is in the phrase which may be literally rendered 'Jonah arose to flee to Tarshish from the presence of the LORD'. 'The presence of the LORD' was something particularly associated with the land of promise. It was there God had been pleased to reveal himself to his people. Being there before the LORD was the place of the prophet's duty. Going somewhere else, away from the LORD's land and people, Jonah might well have been hoping that he would have escaped from this commission. It was not that he thought himself indispensable in carrying out God's purposes. Rather he thought that by getting out he would not have to witness what would happen when what was envisaged came to pass through some other prophet.

The story continues with the first of three mentions of Jonah 'going down', that chart the prophet's disobedience: *going down to Joppa* (1:3), *going down below deck* (1:5), *going down into the depths* (2:6).

The course of disobedience is downwards until the LORD intervenes. **He went down to Joppa, where he found a ship bound for that port. After paying the fare, he went aboard and sailed for Tarshish to flee from the LORD.** Joppa does not seem to have been conquered by Israel during Old Testament times, and so in a sense by going there Jonah would already have half-escaped. The ship going from Joppa would have been Phoenician. It is a measure of his desperation to get away that he resorted to going by sea. The Hebrews were not naturally sailors. The repetition of the phrase 'to Tarshish away from the presence of the LORD' re-emphasises Jonah's intention to be quit of the LORD's service.

Study Guide

These study questions are designed to assist individual reflection on the significance of Jonah for today. They may also provide useful starting points for those leading discussion groups. The Biblical references indicate passages of Scripture of relevance to each topic, but we may not always have a complete or final answer to what is asked.

Study questions: Jonah 1:1-3

verse 2: What role should patriotism play in the Christian's behaviour? (Rom. 9:1-5; 10:1; Gal. 3:28; 6:10)

Are unbelievers used by God today to stir up the church to renewed obedience? (Matt. 5:46-47; 1 Cor. 5:1; 6:6)

verse 3: What does Scripture teach about God's presence and knowledge? (Ps. 139:7-12; Jer. 23:23-24; Heb. 4:13)

Do these divine attributes have the same significance for the believer and the unbeliever? (Job 34:21-22; Pss. 11:4-5; 17:3)

Jonah 1:4-6: It's Not That Simple

So far Jonah has been allowed to go on his way unhindered. No doubt he thought it favoured his scheme that he found a ship going where he wanted. But now the LORD is no longer content to be a passive spectator of Jonah's disobedience and rebellion. The repetition of 'LORD' at the end of 1:3 and the beginning of 1:4 (they are successive words in the original) strongly emphasises the change that comes about through his intervention.

Then the LORD sent a great wind on the sea (*verse 4*). It is not the ordinary word for 'send' that is used, but a word meaning 'throw', or 'hurl', that is later used of the cargo being thrown into the sea (1:5) and Jonah also (1:15). The LORD whom all things serve (Ps. 119:91) hurled a wind at the sea. The divine control of the sea was a constant theme of Israel's praise (Pss. 24:2; 33:7; 89:9). The mythology of surrounding nations viewed the sea as a primeval force which had to be placated, but Israel asserted that the LORD had created the sea and as Creator he exercised rightful lordship over it. 'He spoke and stirred up a tempest that lifted high the waves' (Ps. 107:25). That is what happens here. **And such a violent storm arose that the ship threatened to break up**. It was no chance occurrence that engulfed Jonah, but the sea at the LORD's bidding acts as his instrument of punishment to find out and discipline the reluctant prophet.

But Jonah was not on his own. His guilt brought awesome consequences on others. Our actions impinge on the lives of others, 'for none of us lives to himself alone' (Rom. 14:7). There is no reason to suppose the 'great storm' was so localised that only one ship was involved, but it is on that one ship the story focuses. **All the sailors were afraid** (*verse 5*). The fear of the sailors is one of the themes of this chapter. It moves on from the natural reaction to their peril (as in Ps. 107:26-27), to an awe-stricken bewilderment at the revelation of Jonah's impiety (1:10), and then to wonder and dread as they recognise the LORD's power (1:16). Their reaction may have been intensified because of the unexpected nature of the storm. Generally there was a closed season for ocean-going voyages in the Mediterranean, when storms were likely to occur (Acts 27:9-12). So the seamen would have known that this storm was exceptional not only from its great ferocity, but also by its being out of season.

The crew would probably have been principally Phoenician. The Phoenicians were of Canaanite descent, and occupied roughly the area of modern Lebanon. They were renowned for their maritime activities, trading extensively around the Mediterranean coast, and founding many settlements, the most famous of these being Carthage, which later became the great enemy of Rome. This widespread activity no doubt meant that their ships also recruited crew from the other peoples they encountered.

Aware that this was no ordinary storm, **each cried out to his own god**. Although they were polytheists believing that there were many gods, the heathen often considered themselves to be worshippers of one guardian deity in particular, perhaps the god of their own nation, or birthplace, or one to whom they attributed their past good fortune.

Such a patron deity would be expected to accord special favour to his or her own devotees, and would be approached for help in difficult circumstances. Even in pagan thought there remained a consciousness of powers higher than humanity.

But they did not just engage in prayer. **And they threw the cargo into the sea to lighten the ship**. No doubt a trading ship left port heavily laden. It is a measure of their desperation that they were prepared to jettison the cargo, and probably also any spare tackle — the word in Hebrew is quite general. By getting rid of it 'from upon them', the ship would ride higher in the water, and so perhaps they would escape being swamped.

There was, however, one man on board who was quite unaware of all this frantic activity. The story moves back in time to pick up what Jonah had done. **But Jonah had gone below deck, where he lay down and fell into a deep sleep**. This had happened before the storm arose. Jonah had arrived exhausted after his hurried departure to Joppa and, not wishing to be drawn into conversation with anyone, had found a quiet spot in the ship, probably the sleeping quarters below deck. Physically and spiritually worn out by his experience, he had fallen into a more than ordinarily deep sleep (Gen. 15:12; 1 Sam. 26:12). The movement of the boat seems to have kept him asleep rather than wakening him up. It was not a matter of detachment from the ship's plight or indifference to his own spiritual situation. Quite the opposite. Jonah is totally drained by the course of action he has adopted and by the anxiety and inward tension that has come upon him as a result.

The captain went to him (*verse 6*). It may be that when the seamen had gone below decks to take up the cargo to throw it out, they had come upon their unusual passenger and reported it to the captain, or perhaps the situation had become so serious that the captain himself is helping to shift the cargo. The captain's words are reported tersely, but we should not think of them as brusque. At this point he had no reason to suspect that Jonah was the cause of all his troubles. **How can you sleep?** is a question of amazement that at a time of obvious danger someone could be in such a deep sleep. **Get up and call on your god! Maybe he will take notice of us, and we will not perish**. There is an ironic twist to the narrative. The prophet who had been commanded to 'rise ... call against Nineveh' (1:1, literally) is now exhorted to 'rise, call on your god', from whom he was running away! The captain was expressing his own theology. Certain that the storm had a supernatural origin, perhaps this stranger's god was the one behind it all. He does

not assume that this or any other god would unquestionably listen to
the prayer of a devotee. After all, the heathen gods were known to act
capriciously on occasion, and so might well not be prepared to
intervene to prevent the disaster that the captain saw looming. But he
expected that every individual had his own god, and no possible source
of assistance could be overlooked.

We are not told that Jonah complied with the captain's frantic
request. As the narrator is careful to point out the importance of prayer
(1:5,14; 2:1-2; 3:8; 4:2), we are probably justified in taking this as a
significant omission. It wasn't just being roused out of a deep sleep to
face a terrific storm and a heaving ship that made Jonah queasy and
befuddled. He who disobeys the LORD has disrupted his fellowship
with him, and his prayer life cannot but be affected. The accusations
of his own conscience which he was suppressing would have shrivelled up any prayer before it could be uttered. This is the prophet who
wants to get away from the presence of the LORD, and to approach him
in prayer was not possible without repentance. Jonah's silence and his
general conduct at this point contrast sharply with that of Paul in
similar circumstances (Acts 27:21-26) because one was walking in
God's way while the other had set his face against him. The disobedient prophet cannot act as an effective witness to the LORD, while his
rebellion lasts.

Study questions: Jonah 1:4-6
verse 4: Is seeing God as the one who controls the elements and the
weather an outmoded way of perceiving things? (Job 36:26-33; 38:22-
30; Ps. 147:8, 15-18; Matt. 5:45; Acts 14:17)

verse 5: If 'perfect love drives out fear' (1 John 4:18; Rom. 8:15),
how can 'fear' be used to describe a proper Christian attitude? (2 Cor.
5:11; Phil. 2:12; 1 Pet. 1:17; 2:17; Rev. 14:7; 19:5)

verse 6: Under what circumstances does God not answer prayer?
(Prov. 1:23-28; Isa. 1:10-15; 59:1-2; Jer. 11:9-11; 14:10-12; Zech.7:8-
14; Jas. 4:3)

Jonah 1:7-10: Found Out
The scene switches back on deck. The sailors have thrown the cargo
overboard, but the situation remains dire. They have been forced to the
conclusion that the extraordinary storm has not arisen by chance. Their
pagan background would have led them to attribute it to the action of

the gods, one of whom must be offended. They are unaware of having given offence themselves, and therefore take action to find out who it is that is responsible. **Then the sailors said to each other, "Come, let us cast lots to find out who is responsible for this calamity"** (*verse* 7). 'Lots', originally 'little stones', were made from various materials, and probably shaped like dice. They were used in a variety of procedures throughout the ancient east in divination, trying to ascertain the mind of the gods. The lots probably were used in pairs. Each had faces of dark and light colour. If both fell to expose a dark side, a negative answer was being returned; if light faces were revealed, a positive answer; and if there was one light and one dark, no answer was being given.

Use of lots was not just a pagan practice. Although divination in general was forbidden to Israel (Deut. 18:10-11), the casting of lots was permitted in certain circumstances. It was probably not viewed as an attempt to pry into the future, but rather as a way of bringing one's conduct into conformity with the will of the LORD. Lots were used to allocate the territory of the tribes at the Conquest (Josh. 18:6,8,10), to assign the duties of workers in the Temple (1 Chr. 24:5,31; 25:8; 26:13-16), and to choose the scapegoat (Lev. 16:9-10). There were also occasions on which lots were used to obtain divinely guaranteed knowledge about what had happened in the past. When Jonathan ate food contrary to Saul's command, this was found out by use of lot (1 Sam. 14:42). Lots had probably also been used earlier to uncover Achan as the one who had caused Israel's defeat at Ai (Josh. 7:14-18). But it was always acknowledged that the success of the procedure depended on God. 'The lot is cast into the lap, but its every decision is from the LORD' (Prov. 16:33).

It is a similar procedure the sailors employ here. **They cast lots and the lot fell on Jonah**. An answer is given because of the LORD's overruling. He exposes his runaway prophet as the cause of the storm.

Up to this point it is difficult to assess just how much Jonah was prepared to admit to himself. Doubtless he was inwardly troubled because of his disobedience. However, he was no doubt still justifying his behaviour to himself, that it was right not to want to have anything to do with the strange attitude and plan of God regarding Nineveh. It is not certain that he had yet associated the storm with his personal action. But when the lot indicated him as the party responsible for the storm, he must have re-assessed the situation.

The agitated seamen fire a barrage of questions at Jonah. **So they** asked him, "Tell us, who is responsible for making all this trouble for us?" (*verse 8*). The lot has convinced them that Jonah holds the answer to their questions, but they are uncertain if it is Jonah himself who is at fault. **What do you do?** This may also be understood as, 'What are you doing here?' **Where do you come from? What is your country? From what people are you?** These should not be understood as some sort of immigration questionnaire. They were religiously loaded questions. The gods of the heathen were generally deities who were worshipped in specific localities. Knowing Jonah's origins would help them decide which god to pray to, if Jonah were the cause of their troubles. Their questions are quite unlike those that Joshua asked Achan after he had been found out by lot (Josh. 7:19). Their concern is not for Jonah or his relationship with his God, but for their own safety.

As the later parenthesis in 1:10 makes clear, the whole of Jonah's answer is not recorded here. It is just his central confession of faith that is given. **He answered, "I am a Hebrew and I worship the LORD, the God of heaven, who made the sea and the land"** (*verse 9*). Israelites generally identified themselves to others as Hebrews (Gen. 40:15; Exod. 1:19; 3:18), and in certain texts the term is used specifically to distinguish between native Israelites and others (Deut. 15:12). It may not have been such an obvious corollary to say 'and I worship the LORD', because by Jonah's time there was much mixed worship in the land. Undoubtedly Jehu had turned the nation back from the outright paganism which had been the target of Elijah's protests during the reign of Ahab. But the worship of Israel was still syncretistic, an amalgam of worship of the LORD and worship of Baal.

Jonah refers to the LORD as 'the God of heaven'. This title is one that had occurred from earliest times (Gen. 24:3,7), but it became more commonly used in the post-exilic period as the Jews tried to communicate to others the transcendence of their God (Ezra 1:2; Neh. 1:4-5; Dan. 2:18). The name *Yahweh*, rendered as 'the LORD', was a personal name, and would not have meant much to people from other nations. It had to be explained that he was not a god of a certain city, or people, or land. As God of heaven, he is supreme (including being supreme over other gods) and his rule extends everywhere. Jonah also confesses that his God was the Creator who had made the sea and the land (Ps. 95:5), and who therefore was in control of what was happening to them as the tempest raged all around them (Ps. 135:6).

In the telling of the story, it is significant that the word Jonah uses to describe his relation to the LORD, 'worship', is literally 'fear'. This is a common Old Testament term for the true reverence that ought to characterise the worshipper of the LORD (Prov. 1:7), who perceives his exaltation and holiness. It is used here to contrast with the fear felt by the sailors (1:5,10,16). Theirs began as a genuine terror of the circumstances in which they found themselves. But though Jonah's confession of the LORD as his God is orthodox, is it genuine? It could only be a formal confession of loyalty while he was disobedient. (In this there is a parallel with the situation of Israel which professed loyalty to the LORD, but did not match it with obedience. No doubt those for whom this book was written were meant to see that.) The prophet had lost sight of the reality of the God whom he professed to follow. The sailors, however, progress from fear of the storm, to a great fear of what they have become involved in, to a fear that leads them to worship the LORD.

This terrified them (*verse 10*) is literally 'the men feared a great fear'. It was a reaction that exceeded what they felt in the face of the storm that engulfed them. The parenthetical explanation, **They knew he was running away from the LORD, because he had already told them so**, does not refer back to the beginning of the voyage, but to the present interrogation. The narrator is condensing. Jonah had made a complete confession of his situation to the sailors, and by now they know as much as we do. It is therefore with bewilderment and horror that **they asked, "What have you done?"** They could not take in the full dimensions of what Jonah had revealed to them. Rather than expressing a desire for more information, their question was an exclamation of consternation at the enormity of what Jonah had done – something he himself had hitherto failed to grasp.

Though Jonah's conduct had been defiant and rebellious, there is much to be admired in the way he now conducts himself. There is no suggestion that he tries to evade the issue at stake, or to play down his own role. Confronted with the enormity of what he had done and its consequences, he openly acknowledges his fault and admits responsibility.

Study questions: Jonah 1:7-10

verse 7: Are there circumstances where the use of lots might still be legitimate? (Acts 1:26)

What conditions would have to be satisfied before such a procedure is used? (1 Cor. 10:31; Eph. 4:1,29; Col. 3:17) *verse 9*: When may a confession of faith be correct and orthodox, and yet be sadly deficient? (Isa. 29:13; Ezek. 33:31; Matt. 15:8; Mark 7:6; Acts 8:13-21; Jas. 2:14-26)

When we realise we have sinned, what should we do? (Lev. 26:40; Ps. 32:5; Prov. 28:13; 1 John 1:9-2:1)

Jonah 1:11-16: The Drastic Solution

While the sailors' interrogation of Jonah was proceeding, **the sea was getting rougher and rougher** (*verse 11*). They had identified the source of the problem, but more needed to be done to resolve the situation. It was not a problem that the seamen could solve for themselves. In pagan religions it was imperative that each god was approached in the way specified by him — and especially so if the god was angry. They did not know about the worship of Jonah's God, and **so they asked him, "What should we do to you to make the sea calm down for us?"** Jonah, as a prophet of the LORD, was the one who could inform them how to deal with the situation, but they expect that action will have to be taken with respect to Jonah himself. If nothing is done, the storm is going to destroy them all.

"Pick me up and throw me into the sea," he replied, "and it will become calm" (*verse 12*). Jonah's reply is in effect to tell them to surrender him to his God from whom he had been fleeing. He is acknowledging that the LORD would not let him go, and that the sea was acting as the LORD's agent to catch and punish him. Jonah has no doubt that what has happened has been his fault. **I know that it is my fault that this great storm has come upon you.** If it is the LORD seeking him out to punish him, then the matter can only be concluded by that punishment coming upon him, and he acts to avoid others being drawn to their doom along with him. He uses the same word 'throw' as had occurred previously in 1:4 for the LORD sending a great storm, literally 'throwing' it, and in 1:5 for the sailors ineffectually throwing the cargo overboard to lighten the ship. Throwing Jonah into the sea will bring the storm to an end, for the LORD's complaint was not against the ship and its crew, but against his prophet. He is the one who has to face the consequences of his rebellion.

The seamen, however, were not immediately willing to adopt the course of action proposed by Jonah. The consideration shown by the heathen sailors to Jonah after he has confessed his rebellion contrasts sharply with Jonah's subsequent attitude towards Nineveh (4:1). **Instead, the men did their best to row back to land** (*verse 13*). It would seem that Jonah's open behaviour had made an impression on them, and they felt that the drastic course of action he was recommending would be liable to expose them to even greater troubles, as 1:14 indicates. It may be that the storm had arisen not long after their departure from Joppa, so that to row back to land was not a course of utter despair. No doubt they had already tried to do so, but despite their previous lack of success, they try again, because they want to get rid of Jonah, but not in the way he had suggested. The LORD, however, thwarted their expedients. **But they could not, for the sea grew even wilder than before**. What conditions were like by this time is unimaginable, for hitherto they had been extraordinarily serious.

Then they cried to the LORD, "O LORD, please do not let us die for taking this man's life" (*verse 14*). They had been afraid to follow Jonah's indicated course of action, because they were uncertain how the LORD would respond. **Do not hold us accountable for killing an innocent man**. 'Innocent' does not indicate that they felt Jonah was being accused unjustly. It is rather a recognition that they did not constitute a court of justice, and therefore had no right to put any to death. They do not want to be held accountable for shedding innocent blood. This was a serious matter in other lands as well as in Israel (Deut. 21:1-9).

For you, O LORD, have done as you pleased. This introduces a key theme in the book — the sovereignty of the LORD, and his right and ability to act, quite apart from the desires and wishes of man (3:9; 4:11). The sailors are arguing that the LORD had caused the storm and placed them in the circumstances in which they found themselves, and therefore no punitive sanctions should be inflicted on them.

Then they took Jonah and threw him overboard (*verse 15*). Having presented their case to the LORD, they act as had been suggested. **And the raging sea grew calm**. The simplicity of the statement serves to bring out the suddenness and completeness of the change. It provided them with an awe-inspiring example of the power of the LORD (Ps. 107:25; Mark 4:41).

At this the men greatly feared the LORD (*verse 16*). Their fear of the storm and of the circumstances now changes to a fear of the LORD (1:5,10). It is not suggested, however, that they became monotheists, and worshipped the LORD exclusively (see on 3:5). **They offered a sacrifice to the LORD and made vows to him**. They now took his reality and power into their reckoning. Their sacrifice could have been only of a most minimal sort on board a ship where the cargo, and probably also any superfluous tackling, had been jettisoned. It may be that they waited until they got to land, because sacrifice would ordinarily have been offered at a temple through a priest. Probably when they got back to land, they would have found in Israel a shrine to Yahweh at which to present their offering. The vows would have been regarding the making of future offerings to the LORD. Their new respect for the LORD would not be a one-off matter. They committed themselves to on-going expressions of thankfulness for their deliverance.

Study questions: Jonah 1:11-16

verse 14: What responsibilities do we have regarding the preservation of life? (Gen. 9:6; Exod. 21:12-14; Mark 8:2-3; Acts 27:10-11, 31-36)

How may we reconcile our knowledge of human actions with Scripture's teaching regarding God's sovereign control over events on earth? (Pss. 75:6-7; 115:3; Dan. 4:17, 25, 35; 1 Cor. 1:28; Phil. 2:12-13)

verse 16: What considerations should be taken into account in making vows, that is, promising to God to do something, or to follow some particular course of conduct in future? (Prov. 20:25; Eccl. 5:4-6; Acts 5:4; 18:18; 21:23)

Jonah 1:17: The LORD's Salvation

While the narrative about the sailors was being rounded off, Jonah had, as it were, been left in the sea. The next section of the book (1:17-2:10) tells us how the LORD rescued the prophet and how Jonah responded. We are undoubtedly meant to be interested in what became of Jonah, but the emphasis in the narrative is on what the LORD did to save him, rather than simply on Jonah. This is true not only in what Jonah says in his prayer (2:2-9), but also in the two statements (1:17; 2:10) that bracket the prayer. We are taught that salvation comes from the LORD alone and he bestows it graciously, not because we deserve it. The LORD who is the Creator of all is the one who controls his creation, not just in a general way, but even in directing the activity of each individual part.

But the LORD provided a great fish to swallow Jonah (*verse 17*). We are not told how long Jonah was in the water after being thrown overboard, but his rescue does not seem to have been immediate, given the references to drowning in the following prayer (2:5,7). The LORD did not leave his servant to the fate that seemed to have overtaken him, but provided the means of his rescue. The word 'provide', or 'appoint' is a key term in the book. It is used again at 4:6,7,8 to convey the idea of the determinative and particular control that the LORD has over every aspect of his created realm. A related word is used in Psalm 147:4-5: 'He determines the number of the stars and calls them each by name. Great is our Lord and mighty in power; his understanding has no limit.' There is no reason to suppose that the LORD created some new, special animal to rescue Jonah. Rather he so directed one of his creatures that it was in the right place at the right time, and acted in the specific way that he required. The miracle is the exercise of power that the LORD alone can command (Ps. 103:19).

The LORD rescued Jonah by means of 'a great fish'. The Hebrew word is not specific, and the word used in Matthew 12:40 is similarly indefinite, 'a huge fish' or sea creature. Jonah presumably never saw it, except from an inside angle, and so it is difficult to see how it can be positively identified. Certain species can, of course, be ruled out because it would be impossible for a man to enter their stomachs.

The fact that **Jonah was inside the fish three days and three nights** — and survived — has proved an obstacle to many as regards the historicity of the narrative. At this point, they argue, we obviously enter the realm of fiction. Hundreds of years after Jonah a story has been made up around him to teach later generations important spiritual lessons. In the same way as with the parables of Jesus, it is argued that we are not meant to ask, *Did this really happen?* but, *What am I being taught?*

It is possible to attempt to make what happened to Jonah more plausible by gathering records of incidents in which individuals have been swallowed by fish and survived for longer or shorter periods. Such an approach generally does not achieve its objective, because in Jonah's case the problem lies deeper than the facts. The fundamental problem is an unwillingness to concede the possibility of the miraculous, of God acting in his creation and shaping its destiny. Miracle is taken to be synonymous with non-historical, non-real. Such an approach is antagonistic to the veracity and integrity of Scripture where there is no hesitation in ascribing such control to God. That is indeed one of the lessons of the book of Jonah. The LORD is the one who 'appoints' as he sees fit.

To treat the book of Jonah as a parable or fable is unsatisfactory. Unlike the parables of Jesus, there is no indication in the text that it was originally intended to be understood in this way. What is more, Jesus himself had no doubts about the historicity of Jonah and the events of this book. 'For as Jonah was three days and three nights in the belly of a huge fish, so the Son of Man will be three days and three nights in the heart of the earth' (Matt. 12:40). It is incongruous and demeaning to the significance of his work that the comparison should be with some fictional character and event. The three days and three nights are equally real for both. The phrase seems to imply three full days and nights, with the extended period involved emphasising the significance of the event. The New Testament use of the phrase, however, indicates that it may be a way of describing part of one day, the whole of the next, and into a third day, rather than seventy-two hours precisely.

Jonah was being punished for his sin. There is no doubt that his rebellion against the task assigned him by God deserved to be punished, and was worthy of death. While it is improbable that Jonah was a swimmer, he could conceivably have been rescued in some other way — clinging to a piece of driftwood, or swept ashore by some gigantic wave. But that was not what the LORD had determined. He wished Jonah's punishment to be as close as could be to that of dying without actual death. Because of this Jesus was able to draw out the parallel with his own death, involving the punishment for sin, and also the fact that after the experience there was a resurrection to come. This was to give his followers a frame of reference and hope when they came to grapple with the reality of the cross.

But it is unlikely that the incident spoke in this light to the contemporaries of Jonah. They were not in a position to say that Jonah's experience paralleled what the Messiah to come would have to undergo. That awaited the definitive interpretative word of Jesus himself. At the same time, various truths that are brought out in the incident would have been accessible to them: for instance, the heinousness of rebellion against God, death as the appropriate penalty for this, the fact that God is able to rescue from death, and that his grace and salvation are capable of offsetting even the most atrocious of sins. Indeed these were lessons that Jonah and his contemporaries were expected to learn from the prophet's experience.

It may be that an otherwise puzzling reference in Hosea's prophecy reflects on Jonah's experience. Hosea's ministry began around 755 BC, not long after these events. 'Come, let us return to the LORD. He has torn us to pieces but he will heal us; he has injured us but he will bind up our wounds. After two days he will revive us; on the third day he will restore us, that we may live in his presence' (Hos. 6:1-2). The use of 'two' and 'third' may not originate in the gnomic language of wisdom sayings, but in what Jonah himself had experienced. What more could Israel, which like the prophet had been disobedient, hope for when afflicted for her sin, than that the LORD would extend to her the same favour he had so wonderfully shown to his prophet?

Study questions: Jonah 1:17
verse 17: Why did God perform miracles? (Exod. 4:2-9; Matt. 11:2-5; John 11:40-42; 20:30-31; Rom. 15:18-19)

What parallels exist between Jonah's experience and Christ's? (Matt. 12:39-41)

Jonah 2:1-10: The Grateful Prophet

With the sea having grown calm, the pace of the narrative relaxes also, and we have this extended account of Jonah's reaction to what happened to him. The authenticity of Jonah's prayer has often been questioned. It has not seemed to be in the right place. How could a prayer for thanksgiving be uttered before he was on land?

That would be to misinterpret the significance of the fish in a way that Jonah did not. Half-drowned though he was, he knew it was a pledge of ultimate deliverance. He had been in the water floundering, under the water about to drown. He felt himself abandoned by God. But being swallowed by the fish changed that. It did not remove all the physical difficulties he was in, but it certainly did ameliorate them — he could now breathe. He had no hesitation in recognising the hand of God at work in the miraculous provision made for him. If God in his mercy had not abandoned him, and had provided him with this measure of respite, then he could have hope for what the future had in store for him.

It was in these circumstances that we find it recorded, **From inside the fish Jonah prayed to the LORD his God** (*verse 1*). The narrator wants us to grasp that it was '*his* God' he prayed to. Although he had been acting in disobedience, his faith has once more asserted itself and directs his thought and action.

What is recorded for us in 2:2-9 is in poetry. Its many references to the Psalms reflect Jonah's knowledge of Scripture. Rather than being an artificial composition from various sources as some have suggested, it is the natural utterance of someone well-versed in Scripture.

While he was meditating upon the strange providence of God that had brought him into this unusual situation, Jonah naturally employed words and phrases he had often previously heard — and no doubt used himself — but now in his affliction he finds a new 'depth' to them.

The prayer has an introduction summarising the whole experience (2:2), followed by three stanzas (2:3-4, 5-6, 7-9) each of which starts afresh from the horrendous ordeal Jonah has just undergone.

He said, "In my distress I called to the LORD, and he answered me" (*verse 2*) sets out the theme of this prayer. It recalls a previous prayer of Jonah at the time when he had been in the water, expecting imminent drowning. His call is not necessarily a reference to a shout of a drowning man. It relates to what he was thinking within himself, and expressing to the LORD. He is able to record that his prayer for help had been heard. The LORD had provided for him in his distress by sending the great fish within whose belly he now lay. God's answer is what faith confidently expects in situations of distress, and it is not disappointed (Pss. 18:6; 118:5; 120:1).

The second part of 2:2 restates the matter in similar words in the parallel manner characteristic of Hebrew poetry. **From the depths of the grave I called for help, and you listened to my cry.** The reciprocal nature of prayer and the divine response is emphasised by the similarity between the Hebrew words for 'I called for help' and 'you listened'. 'From the depths of the grave' is literally 'from the belly of Sheol' (NIV margin), the place of the departed.

The use of the phrase does not imply that Jonah actually died. Sheol is frequently used hyperbolically (Pss. 18:5; 30:3; 86:13). Here Jonah uses it to convey how he felt while struggling in the water. The dire prospect facing him was that of joining the dead. But God not only heard his cry of anguish; he responded by providing for him in his need.

In 2:3-4 Jonah recounts his experience in greater detail. **You hurled me into the deep** (*verse 3*). It is a mark of Jonah's faith that he is able to see his experience as under the determining hand of God (Ps. 39:9-10). It had been the sailors who had hurled him into the deep (1:15), but Jonah recognises that in this matter they were merely the instruments of God, doing his bidding. What has come upon him is the just punishment he deserved at the hand of God for his disobedience.

He had begun to sink **into the very heart of the seas** (the plural bringing out the boundless nature of the waters), **and the currents** (literally, rivers) **swirled about me; all your waves and breakers**

swept over me. The last clause recalls the words of Psalm 42:7, where the figure was used in a spiritual metaphor. The experience of drowning was often used metaphorically in the Psalms (88:7; 69:1-2,14-15) and elsewhere (e.g. Lam. 3:54, 'The waters closed over my head, and I thought I was about to be cut off') to indicate a situation of great distress and impending demise. But in these other passages drowning is one of a number of metaphors employed to bring out the dire situation being experienced. It is only in the prayer of Jonah that drowning is referred to so extensively, because here of course it is not a metaphor, but relates to the real situation Jonah had been in.

I said, 'I have been banished from your sight' (*verse 4*) tells of how Jonah felt when he was struggling in the water. 'Said' covers inner speech, that is, thought, and not just what is spoken aloud. He felt permanently isolated from God (Ps. 31:22). Was not this what he had desired when he set out to go to Tarshish away from the presence of the LORD? But now he is experiencing what it is like to live without the sense of God's favour and presence, he has revised his estimate of how tolerable such a situation is. Such banishment from the presence of God is the just punishment of those who rebel against him (2 Thess. 1:9), but Christ underwent it (Mark 15:34) so that death's sting might be drawn for his people (1 Cor. 15:54-57).

In his affliction and distress he calls upon the LORD (Ps. 34:6; Hos. 5:15), which is the response of recovering faith. The words **Yet I will look again towards your holy temple** are better understood without the quotation marks of the NIV. They relate not what Jonah thought in the turmoil of his anticipated drowning, but rather on his expectation in the stomach of the fish after he had been swallowed. His distress caused his hope to increase, not to diminish. His affliction became a source of good to him as he realised that the LORD had intervened to rescue him, and that he could be confident that this meant there was a future role for him. The phrase does not signify seeing the temple as one who has travelled to it, but turning to it in prayer as the place where the LORD had specially shown his favour to his people, presencing himself with them there, accepting sacrifice, and above all answering prayer (1 Kgs. 8:30).

In 2:5-6 Jonah again recounts his traumatic experience and the salvation the LORD had extended to him. **The engulfing waters threatened me** (*verse 5*), or 'waters were at my throat' (NIV margin). His sensation was of one trapped and unable to breathe. **The deep** (the unfathomable ocean) **surrounded me; seaweed was wrapped around**

my head. He emphasises the peril of imminent death that he had been in. He had sunk so deeply into the water that he had been trapped by the weeds on the ocean floor. Evidently some time had elapsed before the fish had swallowed him.

To the roots of the mountains I sank down (*verse 6*). The mountains were thought of as extending out under the sea. This is then a way of describing the floor of the sea. 'Sank down' is literally 'went down'. It is the last of the three downward movements in Jonah's rebellion: *down to Joppa* (1:3), *down into the ship* (1:5), *down into the sea*. **The earth beneath barred me in for ever**. Most modern commentators take 'earth' here to be a special usage for 'underworld', with the imagery drawn from the bars used to close a city gate. The phrase would then be similar in origin to the 'gates of death' (Isa. 38:10) or 'gates of Hades' (Matt. 16:18), and would indicate that Jonah thought he had been trapped by death. Alternatively, the description may be of the rocks at the bottom of the sea trapping him in.

Again, however, Jonah is able to recount that what had seemed to be his fate was averted by the action of the LORD. **But you brought my life up from the pit, O LORD my God**. It was divine intervention alone that served to extricate Jonah from death. This reverses the downward movement of Jonah's rebellion by 'bringing up, causing to go up' that the LORD alone can supply from the 'pit', a term for the 'grave', or 'realm of the dead'.

In the third and final section of the prayer, Jonah again starts with the perilous situation he had been in: **When my life was ebbing away** (*verse 7*). It is a picture of weakness or fainting overtaking his life-force, as it turns in on itself, ready to expire. **I remembered you, LORD**, or, more literally, 'I remembered the LORD', not just in a general sort of way. This time he does not dwell on the details of his drowning experience, but rather on the response that was elicited from him. The LORD whose commands he was trying to forget was now remembered by him as the one who was able to save. **And my prayer rose to you, to your holy temple**. In a thought similar to 2:4, Jonah refers either to the Temple in Jerusalem as the place where God condescended to reveal himself, or the heavenly temple to which it corresponded.

Jonah then contrasts his experience in a time of danger with those whose religion was pagan. It may be that this reflects his recent dealings with the sailors, but more probably it comes out of the apostasy of the many in Israel who had espoused idolatry. They and Jonah had both rebelled, but the backsliders in Israel had not yet realised the folly of their conduct. **Those who cling to worthless idols forfeit the grace that could be theirs** (*verse 8*). The sense of 'the grace that could be theirs', which is one word in the original, is disputed. It could indicate the mercy they might receive from God. Others translate it as 'forsake their own Mercy' (NKJV), finding a direct reference to deity. Those within Israel who had abandoned the LORD for Baal worship, if they kept on in that, would not know the LORD's gracious help towards them. Alternatively, it might be a statement about their own loyalty, rather than the LORD's. Those who engage in idolatry no longer display the true loyalty that they should show to the covenant king.

Jonah sets himself over against a false response. **But I, with song of thanksgiving, will sacrifice to you** (*verse 9*). This is how the sailors had responded to deliverance given to them, and it was also the right way for those in Israel who experienced the LORD's blessing. But the sacrifice would not be just once. **What I have vowed I will make good**. This probably refers to on-going acts of worship; not just a thanksgiving that is offered once, but a total attitude that moulds and shapes a life. In Jonah's case it is virtually an expression of repentance and return to the LORD. The vow of future worship and obedience was what would condition his life from henceforth. The concluding **Salvation comes from the LORD** is an acknowledgement of what the LORD has done for Jonah. It implies that he alone could have done it; salvation is his prerogative. It also sets the scene for the prophet's new obedience. He has now to grapple with the full implications of this reality. This is the breath of new obedience, rather than a specific resolve. Jonah still had problems that would have to be worked out, but he now realised running away was not going to be the way to find an answer.

The narrative then reverts to prose, and simply states **And the LORD commanded the fish, and it vomited Jonah onto dry land** (*verse 10*). We do not know where, but presumably it was in Palestine. If the ship had not gone far when the storm arose, it would perhaps have been near the starting point of the voyage. Once again it is the LORD's sway that holds in the realm he has created. The mercy shown to Jonah removes his right to complain about mercy shown to others.

Study questions: Jonah 2:1-10
verse 1: What part does recognising our relationship with God play in returning to him? (Luke 15:18)

Have there been times when Scripture has 'come alive' for you in a special way?

verses 4 and 7: What is the Christian experience corresponding to looking towards the temple? (Heb. 4:14-16)

verse 9: What place should thanksgiving have in our lives? (Luke 17:16; Eph. 5:4,20; Col. 2:7; Heb. 13:15)

Jonah 3:1-4: Sent Again

The story begins all over again. This section (3:1-4) parallels the narrative of Jonah's original commission in 1:1-3, but now the ending is different. It is not Joppa Jonah goes to, but Nineveh as he had been told. His obedience, however, is not yet whole-hearted, as chapter 4 will show. But he did go.

It is a measure of God's magnanimity that we read, **Then the word of the LORD came to Jonah a second time** (*verse 1*). The expression used corresponds to that found in 1:1. The runaway prophet is privileged to hear God speaking to him once more. He has paid the penalty of his earlier disobedience and is again enjoying fellowship with God (Luke 15:32). He is not debarred from further service. The LORD who had saved Jonah still has a mission he wants him to carry through.

We are not told how long elapsed between 2:10 and 3:1. It is improbable that it happened as soon as Jonah reached the shore. He would have been physically and emotionally drained by all that he had gone through, and he would no doubt have been given a suitable interval to recover. It is, however, unlikely that a lengthy period of time was involved. The command to go to Nineveh is still, as in 1:2, one of considerable urgency.

"Go to the great city of Nineveh and proclaim to it the message I give you" (*verse 2*). 'The great city' refers primarily to its size, but overtones of its political influence and the grandeur of its buildings are not lacking. The magnitude of this strategic city is again emphasised in the following verse. To it Jonah is required to deliver the divine message and nothing else. A prophet's mission was not one where he had liberty to say what he wanted. It was God's message alone that his messenger may proclaim in the divine name (1 Kgs. 22:14; Jer. 1:7; 23:28; John 7:16; 12:50; 2 Cor. 2:17).

Jonah obeyed the word of the LORD and went to Nineveh (*verse 3*). What a change from last time! This is the chastened and renewed Jonah, acting in compliance with the divine injunction. He has considered his ways and resolved to walk in obedience, and so he hastens to

obey the divine command (Ps. 119:59-60). 'Arise! Go!' (3:2, literally), and now 'Jonah arose and went'. His actions are 'in accordance
with the word of the LORD', not what he himself thought would be for
the best.

Again, the narrator omits details we might want to be informed
about: how long did the journey take, how did Jonah travel - by foot
or by donkey, what route did he follow, what difficulties had to be
overcome to get to Nineveh. About these nothing is said, because they
were inessential to the story. We must therefore pay greater attention
to what is added, presumably because the narrator felt this could not
be missed out. **Now Nineveh was a very important city**.

The idiom employed here is literally rendered 'Nineveh was a city
great to God'. The same phrase is used of Gibeon (Josh. 10:2), though
it was not physically a large place. The greatness referred to would thus
be of status, rather than size. That it was 'great to God' may convey the
idea of a superlative, 'very important', as in the NIV translation.
However, it may well go beyond that.

What is being emphasised is that the city was of significance and
importance in God's sight: God cared about it. That theme will be
developed later (4:11). But we need to grasp it now to understand what
is going to occur.

Because it is said that 'Nineveh *was* a very important city', the
conclusion has often been drawn that the city no longer existed when
the book was written, otherwise it would have been 'Nineveh *is* a very
important city'. But that need not be implied by the Hebrew usage. In
looking back to the past, the narrator is emphasising what was true
when Jonah was there, and is not saying anything about conditions in
his own day. The phrase has no implications for the time of composition of the book.

The further description given of the city has also been obscure to
translators: 'a city of going of three days'. One way of understanding
it is as a description of the physical size of Nineveh. It is improbable
that it meant that it took three days to travel round its circumference.
No ancient city was that large. It is often suggested that the reference
is not just to the city proper, but to the much larger surrounding
'metropolitan district'. That approach is backed up by what is said in
Genesis 10:11 where its origins are associated with Nimrod who
moved up from Babylon to build four cities, Nineveh, Rehoboth Ir,
Calah, and Resen. It seems that these four cities are there collectively
called 'the great city', and that might explain the use of the term here

in Jonah as referring to the administrative area centred on Nineveh, but containing other towns also.

The 1978 edition of the NIV adopted another possibility: 'It took three days to go all through it.' This looked at the matter not from the angle of travelling round the perimeter of the area involved — which would have been as strange a way of describing a city's size in the ancient world as it is now — but of visiting every part of it. That fits in with the idea of Jonah moving extensively through the city, preaching at various points in it so that his message would be extensively known.

There is another way in which the phrase may be understood. The rendering now found in the NIV, **a visit required three days**, while still leaving open the previous possibility, also permits the phrase to be taken as a reference to the customs of Eastern etiquette. While Nineveh was not the capital of Assyria at this time, it was an important city in which there would be a standard procedure for receiving foreign visitors. As the Assyrians were highly superstitious, foreign visitors would cover not just political emissaries. Prophets would be accorded an equal, if not greater, status. A proper visit could not be hurried. The day of arrival would be followed by the day of formal presentation of one's message to the appropriate authorities, followed by the day of departure. What we are being told then is that Nineveh was not a small town where a visitor might begin to speak unannounced, but a royal city where the due protocol had to be followed. The significance of this is to emphasise that God's gracious warning was being extended to a truly major city.

On the first day, Jonah started into the city (*verse 4*). It is not at the outskirts of Nineveh that he proclaims the message, nor is it after one day's travel into the town. There is no mention made of the second or third day, presumably because of the immediacy of the response. He began his first day's activities, and — then we are not told precisely how far into the first day, but the implication is not too far — **he proclaimed: "Forty more days and Nineveh will be overturned"**.

This is a message of impending doom. 'Overturn' is somewhat ambiguous. It can be used of all sorts of turning and change from the physical destruction of the cities of the plain (Gen. 19:21,25,29) to emotional transformation, 'My heart is changed within me' (Hos. 11:8). Here, however, in the context of a message of warning, its meaning is quite clear. What is more, the destruction is in the near, not the distant, future. Although 'forty' is found in the measurement of

various critical periods in Scripture — the rain at the start of the flood
(Gen. 7:12), the period of testing in the wilderness (Ps. 95:10), the
temptation of Jesus (Matt. 4:2) — it seems here just to indicate a short
definite period, as we might say 'a month' or 'thirty days'. What is
going to happen to Nineveh is not going to be long postponed.

There are a number of interesting questions that may be explored
in connection with Jonah's message.

(1) Is this all that he said? It seems unlikely. The terse style of the
narrative has demonstrably led to condensation in many places (1:10;
4:2), and that seems probable here also. Certainly the knowledge the
king shows of the grounds of divine condemnation in 3:8 suggests that
Jonah clearly told them why this judgment was impending.

(2) Did Jonah tell them about his own experience? From the book
of Jonah itself there is nothing to prove this. In the New Testament,
however, Jesus clearly says, 'This is a wicked generation. It asks for
a miraculous sign, but none will be given it except the sign of Jonah.
For as Jonah was a sign to the Ninevites, so also will the Son of Man
be to this generation' (Luke 11:29-30). There is an increasing tendency
to interpret the sign of Jonah in this passage not as pointing to one who
had survived drowning, but to one who came with a prophetic message
from God. Jesus would then be like Jonah in that both presented the
word of God, but neither would be a miraculous sign, for no sign would
be given to that generation (Mark 8:12), only the proclamation of the
truth of God.

Such an understanding of Luke 11:29-30 is unsatisfactory in that it
implies there are two different meanings for 'the sign of Jonah' in
Jesus' teaching. Matthew 12:39-40 clearly identifies Jonah's being
three days and three nights in the belly of a huge fish as constituting
the sign which Jesus' own experience will parallel. This must also be
the meaning intended in Matthew 16:4 and Luke 11:29-30. It is not the
message that they both bring that Jesus refers to, but himself and Jonah
as persons. Although 'will' in 'so also will the Son of Man be to this
generation' (Luke 11:30) might be a logical future, it is more convinc-
ing to take it as a real future, referring to something that Jesus was not
yet at the time of speaking, but would be thereafter. What he and Jonah
had supremely in common was that both would undergo a death-
experience connected with God's judgment on sin, and both would
have a miraculous deliverance from death by the power of God. That
would constitute the sign to be given to their generation.

It is thus the case that when Jonah preached in Nineveh, we are not to think of him as only uttering the words, 'Forty more days, and Nineveh will be overturned.' The main theme of his message was God's impending judgment on sin, so as to stir up the Ninevites to the gravity of their situation. But he also informed them about his own experience of the consequences of disobeying God, and of how God's power can save from even the most extreme circumstances. In this way we can see that the message Jonah eventually brought to Nineveh went further than that announced in 1:2. Originally the emphasis had been on divine displeasure with the conduct of the Ninevites. Now it became one of imminent punishment, but with the prophet himself as a living example of God's willingness and power to save.

Study questions: Jonah 3:1-4
verse 1: 'The LORD disciplines those he loves' (Prov. 3:12). What should we learn from this? (Job 5:17-18; Ps. 119:67; Heb. 12:4-13; Jas. 1:12; Rev. 3:19)

How are we to use renewed opportunities for service? (2 Chr. 33:10-16; Isa. 1:16-19; Matt. 21:28-32)

verse 4: What word of warning has the church to bring to the world today? (John 16:8-11; Acts 2:30; 3:19; 17:30; 26:20; 2 Tim. 2:25-26)

Jonah 3:5-10: Nineveh's Repentance
As before (1:16), Jonah temporarily fades from the narrative, while attention is focused elsewhere. The preaching of one man is blessed by God to bring the heathen city to repentance (3:5). The impact of his proclamation is felt at the highest level in the land, and the king not only abases himself but makes public humiliation official policy (3:6-9). Such a genuine and general repentance does not go unnoticed by God, and the threatened disaster is averted (3:10).

The Popular Response (3:5). **The Ninevites believed God** (*verse 5*). A truly astonishing response! So much so that many have doubted if it actually occurred. They argue that if such a major city of the ancient world had indeed turned to the LORD, then some record of it would have survived. That is, of course, just what has happened, and the record is before us in Scripture. That there have not been found any secular records bearing on this event is not too surprising. If Jonah's mission is dated between 780 and 755 BC, then few records have survived from that troubled period of Assyrian history. Those that have reveal many internal problems. For instance, each year from 765-759 BC has a note

of an outbreak of plague, or of a revolt in some city of the land, or —
and this would probably have seemed worst to the superstitious
Assyrian mind — an eclipse of the sun.

Throughout the first half of the eighth century BC Assyria was
threatened by powerful tribes from the north, particularly by the
kingdom of Urartu, near the Caspian Sea, and her zone of influence
contracted considerably. It was not a matter of dominating an empire
that was the objective of public policy, but the security of the
traditional Assyrian homeland itself. It may be that the upheavals and
sense of impending catastrophe were influential in predisposing the
Ninevites to accept Jonah's message when it was brought to them.

But what is meant by they 'believed God'? Because faith and
repentance are like two sides of a single coin, answering this is linked
to the question of the nature and genuineness of their repentance, as
testified to in the New Testament (Matt. 12:41; Luke 11:32). If there
was a widespread, deep and genuine turning to the LORD, why did this
not have a substantial impact on the subsequent history of Nineveh?
The troubled nature of the times may explain why there is no contemporary Assyrian record of the 'revival' at Jonah's preaching. So too
would the probable suppression of any records of such an 'outlandish'
aberration by subsequent generations of Assyrian scribes, who would
evaluate matters from their pagan standpoint. But how could the
spiritual impact of such a revival have degenerated so swiftly as to
warrant Nahum's scathing indictment of Nineveh a century later? The
impact of Jonah's revival would undoubtedly fade, but if it had been
genuine, would not the history of Assyria from 745 BC on, when its
fortunes were restored, have been affected by it?

To cope with these genuine difficulties, it is suggested that the faith
described in 3:5 is something less than conversion to monotheism and
acceptance of the faith of Israel. Elsewhere the Old Testament opens
up the possibility of an awareness of God and his demands on the part
of non-Israelites (Gen. 20:11; 39:9; 42:18). Nebuchadnezzar (Dan.
3:28-30) and Cyrus (2 Chr. 36:22-23) displayed such an attitude of
reverence towards Yahweh, but without abandoning their polytheistic
world-view. That also seems to have been the sailors' reaction in 1:16.
What has happened here is more than an acceptance of the accuracy of
Jonah's prediction. The Hebrew term used indicates a trust in God as
the sender of the message. It may be significant that it is 'God' that is
used here, and not the covenant name *Yahweh*, rendered 'the LORD' in
the NIV. They accepted what Jonah was saying, and were prepared to

rest in the veracity of the god — presumably they identified him as one, if not the chief, of their pantheon — on whose behalf he was speaking.

Such an interpretation may also fit 3:10 and the New Testament references to the repentance of the Ninevites. Although it is possible for an individual to humble himself before the LORD, and yet not abandon his evil ways, as seems to have been the case with Ahab (1 Kgs. 21:25-29), what the Ninevites experienced was real, and measured up to the amount of light accorded them. They did not ignore the warning sent to them, and so God looked with favour upon the change that took place. That is why Jesus used them to warn the Jews of his day. 'The men of Nineveh will stand up at the judgment with this generation and condemn it; for they repented at the preaching of Jonah, and now one greater than Jonah is here' (Matt. 12:41; Luke 11:32). The men of Nineveh are competent witnesses to be called on the day of judgment to testify against those who have ignored the warnings given them. Even in Jonah's day, the response of the Ninevites should have acted as a spur to the covenant nation to respond to God's warnings (see on 1:2).

That the repentance of the Ninevites, though real, did not last, is not surprising when we consider the history of the chosen people themselves. Though being privileged with far greater light, their loyalty to the LORD frequently proved ephemeral. It is not at all impossible to suppose that the passage of ten to thirty years in a pagan environment meant that the changes which had occurred in Nineveh became a thing of the past.

It is clearly pointed out that their new perception of God and of themselves profoundly altered the behaviour of the people of Nineveh. **They declared a fast, and all of them, from the greatest to the least, put on sackcloth**. The outward affliction of their bodies by abstaining from food and wearing coarse, uncomfortable garments, was associated with times of grief. Sackcloth was thick, coarse cloth, often made from goat's hair, and usually worn only by the poor (1 Kgs. 21:27; Neh. 9:1-2; Isa. 15:3; Dan. 9:3-4; Joel 1:13-14). They adopted an outward posture to reflect their genuine conviction on hearing Jonah's message regarding their sinfulness. It is emphasised that this reaction was not just on the part of a few, but was widespread in the city, affecting all classes of people.

The Royal Decree (3:6-9). It was therefore not surprising that news of what was happening in the city came to the palace. There would have been royal residences in the city, as it was an old one of considerable size — but in fact it is not precisely stated that the king was there. Indeed the term 'king of Nineveh' is often objected to as being an anachronism, introduced by a later writer, unfamiliar with the terminology uniformly used elsewhere, 'king of Assyria'. But two factors mitigate such a challenge. 'King of Samaria' is used on occasions in the Old Testament (1 Kgs. 21:1; 2 Kgs. 1:3) as well as the customary 'king of Israel', and here where the emphasis is on the city itself, and not the whole empire, this may have been a natural variation. Alternatively, if Jonah's visit to Nineveh occurred at some point in the period 780-755 BC, at that time there was considerable reduction in Assyrian territory, and it may well be an accurate description of the current political realities in the reign of Ashur-dan III (773-755 BC).

The king shared in the general reaction. **When the news reached the king of Nineveh, he rose from his throne, took off his royal robes, covered himself with sackcloth and sat down in the dust** (*verse 6*). 'The news' may be of the reaction going on in the city, or just of the contents of Jonah's message, for prophecies regarding the welfare of the state would have been relayed to him without delay. The king too is convicted of the wrong that has been perpetrated, and humbles himself. His royal robes would have been costly and grand. Sitting on the ground is the posture of humility and self-abasement. It may also have been in the open-air for all to see.

What the people had already spontaneously initiated is now formally and officially approved by the king. **Then he issued a proclamation in Nineveh: "By the decree of the king and his nobles: Do not let any man or beast, herd or flock, taste anything; do not let them eat or drink"** (*verse 7*). The issuing of a joint decree is something that was common later on in Persian times, and may indicate that the weakness of the king at the time of Jonah's visit was such that he ruled jointly with a council of nobles. The fast is extreme, being extended to include animals, both cattle and sheep. The 'them' in 'do not let them eat or drink' refers to the animals, because the word for 'eat' is literally 'pasture', or 'graze', which of course applies only to animals. Again, the evidence we have for such a custom of involving animals in times of public humiliation and mourning only comes from a later Persian period, but there is no reason to suppose that this widespread and deep-felt reaction to Jonah's proclamation could not have led to such a decree earlier on. **But let man and beast be covered with sackcloth** (*verse 8*). All are to express their sorrow and grief at the situation in which they find themselves by donning sackcloth.

The response that is enjoined upon the people goes beyond the physical. Prayer is required (cf. 1:6; 1:14; 2:2). **Let everyone call urgently on God**. The situation is so dire that they must not be half-hearted in approaching the God who has given them this warning of impending doom. Such prayer is in contrast to the situation of the sailors earlier when each called on his own deity. Moral amendment is also required. Only a radical change will make a difference. **Let them give up their evil ways and their violence**. These are the words of the king of Nineveh, not Jonah, but they seem to require that Jonah's message be more than the words of 3:4. He also told them why divine judgment was impending upon them. 'Violence' refers to any infringement of human rights and not only physical harm. Nineveh throughout its history had an altogether justified reputation for rapacious behaviour (Nah. 2:11-12; 3:19). Here it is recognised as being wrong, and they are called to turn from their evil ways.

But it is not viewed as being automatic that their repentance will lead to divine forbearance, and that their turning will induce a divine turning. Just as the pagan captain and his crew had recognised the sovereignty of divine action (1:6, 14), so too do the king and his nobles. **Who knows? God may yet relent and with compassion turn from his fierce anger so that we will not perish** (*verse 9*). The same thought is captured in Joel 2:14: 'Who knows? He may turn and have pity and leave behind a blessing.' The repentant recognise that they have no case to argue for acceptance. Their future well-being is dependent solely on divine grace. Yet, though their grounds for hope are faint, they are not totally without foundation, for why else would God have sent Jonah with his message of warning?

Divine Reprieve (3:10). The narrator then adds an authoritative comment to interpret for us what has happened. **When God saw what they did and how they turned from their evil ways, he had compassion and did not bring upon them the destruction he had threatened** (*verse 10*). There is a play on words in the original here that is often found in the Old Testament. The same word may be used to describe moral 'evil' or 'sin', and also 'calamity' and 'disaster'. Indeed the one is often the outcome of the other when God acts in judgment. So here their '*evil* ways' would have resulted in the evil of *destruction*, had not God responded graciously to the acceptance given to his message and decided to act otherwise. They proved the genuineness of their repentance by their deeds (Acts 26:20). It is not their pious actions or prayers that merit forgiveness.

These two verses (3:9-10) and also the phrase 'a God who relents from sending calamity' (4:2) present a problem as regards what is being said about God. The word the NIV translates as 'with compassion' (verse 9) and 'he had compassion' (verse 10) is in many other translations rendered by 'relent' (as the NIV does in 4:2) or 'changed his mind'. It is not only a matter of feeling sorrow or pity; it also indicates an altered determination as to how to act. Indeed, the AV used 'repent' to render this word. Now, however, repentance is only used of turning away from what is wrong and sinful, and there is no suggestion that what God had been about to do was anything other than executing just and proper judgment on the sin of Nineveh. But there is still a problem: how can it be said that God relents, or changes his mind? If we say this, are we not diminishing God by making him appear arbitrary or indecisive? Can God relent and still be the unchanging one?

The Old Testament does not hesitate to affirm both that God is unchanging, and that he can and does alter his attitude towards people and his way of dealing with them. It is interesting to find both these truths stated in the one chapter of Scripture, 1 Samuel 15. In verse 11, the LORD tells Samuel, '*I am grieved* that I have made Saul king, because he has turned away from me and has not carried out my instructions,' while a little later Samuel says to Saul, 'He who is the Glory of Israel does not lie or *change his mind*; for he is not a man, that *he should change his mind*' (1 Sam. 15:29). The words in italics all render the same basic word, which is also that found in Jonah 3:9-10; 4:2.

There is no ultimate inconsistency between the two modes of expression. When God is said to change his mind, matters are viewed from our human perspective. It appears to us that there has been a change in God, but what has in fact changed is our human conduct. Saul was no longer the man he had once been, but was persistently disobedient. The Ninevites here have also changed their conduct, but in the opposite direction, away from their evil ways. God would have been inconsistent if his attitude towards them had remained the same despite the change in their behaviour. God is consistently against sin. There is no variation in his loathing of it, or in his determination to punish it. That is a constant feature of God's character.

When God announces that his judgment is about to fall upon the sinful, it is a statement of what will inevitably happen if they continue on their present course. But it is a conditional statement. It is intended to alert the wayward and bring them to repentance. If that occurs, then God responds appropriately to the changed circumstances. 'If at any time I announce that a nation or kingdom is to be uprooted, torn down and destroyed, and if that nation I warned repents of its evil, then I will relent and not inflict on it the disaster I had planned. And if at another time I announce that a nation or kingdom is to be built up and planted, and if it does evil in my sight and does not obey me, then I will reconsider the good I had intended to do for it' (Jer. 18:7-10). Even though God in his omniscience knows that a change on the part of the nation will take place, it does not compromise his truthfulness to announce the inevitable outcome of its present course of conduct, *if persisted in*. Though it may not be explicitly stated, the announcement of impending disaster is conditioned on continuing disobedience, just as enjoyment of the blessings of God's covenant is conditioned on obedience. The just judgment of God takes into account the attitude and situation of those to whom his demands are addressed. It is only because God does respond in this way that the sinner who believes in Jesus can come to know divine acceptance.

The judgment of God is always just. Four generations had to pass before the iniquity of the Amorites reached full measure (Gen. 15:16), and the LORD brought the Israelites back into Canaan to execute his judgment on them. Nineveh too already had a black history of idolatry and oppression, but the change that took place at Jonah's preaching showed that they were not yet so spiritually blind and hard as to warrant national overthrow. Their response averted, at least temporarily, their extermination. Because they had trembled at his word and become truly contrite, God was pleased to turn aside the disaster that would otherwise have engulfed them (Isa. 57:15; 66:2).

That such a response should result from one man's preaching in a pagan environment like Nineveh constitutes a perpetual source of encouragement whenever and wherever the gospel is preached.

Study questions: Jonah 3:5-10

verses 5 and 6: Are outward religious acts valid on their own? (Isa. 58; Joel 2:12-13; Matt. 6:16-18)

Should fasting have a role in the life of New Testament believers? (Mark 2:18-20; Acts 13:3; 14:23)

verse 10: Is God inconsistent when it is said that he 'relents'? (Jer. 18:7-10; 31:18-20; Ezek. 18:27-32; 33:12-20; Luke 15:20)

Jonah 4:1-4: The Furious Prophet

Having brought the story to a conclusion as far as the Ninevites were concerned in 3:10, the narrator now turns to consider Jonah's reaction to the LORD's reprieve of Nineveh. In the structure of the book this chapter parallels chapter 2, which set out Jonah's response to the deliverance granted to him by God. But now we do not hear a song of joyful praise. Jonah did not want Nineveh reprieved and he is furious with God.

But Jonah was greatly displeased and became angry (*verse 1*). The first clause is literally, 'It was evil to Jonah a great evil,' continuing the play on the word 'evil' found in 3:10. The prophet's attitude is that the lack of calamity coming upon Nineveh was itself a calamity. He displayed the discontent of a faith that lacked understanding. His reaction is described in a very strong fashion. It goes beyond mere irritation to fury. Jonah is burning with rage — violently angry with the way God has acted in showing compassion. In this he shows that he still did not appreciate the sovereignty of divine grace. Though he had obeyed God and gone to Nineveh, it was not as one who was completely in harmony with God. He had still a lot to learn.

Now it is easy to assess Jonah's behaviour at this point as petty, churlish and mean-minded. Indeed, his attitude is far from being commendable. But we should not write off the prophet too readily. For one thing, the LORD does not punish him, but rather treats him with patience and concern, so as to bring him to realise what is wrong. This is not the disobedient prophet, running away from his divine commission, but the perplexed prophet, obeying without understanding. Until we grasp the measure of Jonah's perplexity as to why God was so slow to act in judgment against evil and evildoers, we should not be quick to condemn him.

We notice that he acts in faith and sets out his problem before God. He is arguing with God; he is opposing what God has done; but he is not doing so by turning his back on God. **He prayed to the LORD** (*verse 2*). This is not the only place where Old Testament prophets express their difficulty in understanding what God is doing (Jer. 12:1; 15:18; 20:7).

Jonah first of all reveals what his problem had been all along. **O LORD, is this not what I said when I was still at home?** He presents it as a matter of 'my word' against the LORD's word, and he rather thinks his own was better. He does not specifically identify what he had said, but it seems to have been the case that in his own country he had expected that bringing a warning of judgment to Nineveh would result in a display of divine compassion. **That is why I was so quick to flee to Tarshish**. Jonah is concerned to justify himself and not God. His prayer is all about 'I', 'me', 'my' – six times in the NIV, nine times in the Hebrew of 4:2-3. He still thinks he was right – but right about what?

Several possible explanations of Jonah's complaint do not seem valid. It was not that he himself was going to suffer loss of face through bringing a word of judgment that did not come to pass, as if he had been a false prophet. The people's own consciences had smitten them with the truth of the accusations made against them. Nor is it necessarily the case that he saw Nineveh as the future harriers and destroyers of his people. They had already had contact with Israel on three occasions (see on 1:2), and they were a formidable military power at the height of their empire. But if the historical setting of Jonah has been rightly judged, Nineveh at this point was not a threat to anyone, and there seems no reason to credit Jonah with a knowledge of what the future held in terms of a revival of Assyrian power.

There seem to be two aspects to his complaint. There was a genuine desire to see Nineveh punished. It was all right for the LORD to save Jonah when he was being judged for his disobedience, but it was not right for mercy to be extended to the enemies of God's people. The God of salvation was to confine his mercy to one people, and not to extend it to foreigners. Jonah, though presumably aware of all the faults that could be found in Israel, did not want to see divine blessing extended elsewhere. Instead of showing the Ninevites favour, as he had to Jonah and Israel, God should have punished them. Jonah could not see how God could be concerned about any other people for their own sake.

But it was not just xenophobia. Jonah had a real problem grasping how it was that the LORD could act in this way. He had forgotten just how undeserving Israel itself was. God's grace had not been extended to it on account of some merit in Israel (Deut. 7:6-8). There was no way divine compassion could be channelled only along the routes approved or understood by human reasoning. Ultimately divine grace towards sinners cannot be understood. It does not have a reason. It simply reflects the way God is.

Jonah had a first rate theoretical knowledge of God. He is able to cite a fine confession just as he had done in 1:9. His problem is still that of living out that confession in practice. **I knew that you are a gracious** (outside any and every covenant relation) **and compassionate** (linked with understanding and love as a mother to her child) **God, slow to anger and abounding in love** (covenant loyalty),

a God who relents from sending calamity. This confession picks up the words of Exodus 34:6, 'the compassionate and gracious God, slow to anger, abounding in love and faithfulness', which had played a major role in determining Israel's perception of the LORD (Exod. 32:14; Nah. 1:3; Num. 14:18; Neh. 9:17; Pss. 86:15; 103:8; 145:8; Joel 2:13). Joel 2:13 may well be the source of the last clause, 'who relents from sending calamity'. (For a discussion of 'relents', see on 3:10.) This was the very God whose compassion Jonah himself had recently experienced in being rescued from drowning. But he still did not understand. He still found fault with God for saving those he felt to be beyond the circle of redemption. He was angry with God for acting in a way that he, Jonah, did not understand or approve. At root Jonah was finding fault with God for being the way he is.

With **Now, O LORD** (*verse 3*) he turns to the substance of his petition. **Take away my life, for it is better for me to die than to live**. A similar request had been made by Elijah after he had failed to turn the land back to the LORD (1 Kgs. 19:4). Elijah did not expect to see results from his zeal and activity on behalf of the LORD; Jonah had. Elijah felt he was no better than his fathers. He had failed God, and desired to be taken away. Jonah is speaking out of a sense of personal affront. The LORD has failed to live up to his expectations, and he petulantly wants no more of it. Is there an element of despairing challenge? 'Once you showed Elijah there was a deeper purpose in living. Have you a similar message for me?'

But the LORD replied, "Have you any right to be angry?" (*verse 4*). 'Are you right to be angry?' A question to bring him to see the error of his position and get through to him despite his being worked up with his bad temper. 'Is your anger justly kindled?' This is a challenge to Jonah to get his thinking straight. This twice repeated question (here and in 4:9) sets out one of the major themes of the book. Has Jonah, as the representative of a people chosen by God for no merit on their part, a people favoured by God even when they go astray, as a prophet who in his disobedience has personally known the saving hand of God in his life, any valid grounds for objection if God out of his mercy shows compassion to others also? The answer is obviously that man has no right to challenge God on the way he extends his mercy.

Study questions: Jonah 4:1-4

verse 1: How should we react when favour is shown to others? (Luke 15:25-32) *verse 3*: What should we do when we find ourselves out of step with God? (Ps. 119:11,18,34; Prov. 3:5)

verse 4: Are we ever right to be angry? (Exod. 32:19; Mark 3:5; Eph. 4:26-27, 31; Jas. 1:19-20)

Jonah 4:5-11: The LORD's Concern

Jonah was furious with the LORD for showing compassion to the repentant Ninevites. Once again he is at odds with God, and again we see the LORD's gentleness and compassion towards his angry prophet. The LORD seeks to cajole him into accepting the love that motivates the divine actions by providing him with an object lesson in divine sovereignty (4:5-8). He then repeats his inquiry about whether Jonah's attitude can be justified (4:9). The concluding divine speech contrasts Jonah's attitude and the LORD's, arguing from what Jonah felt towards the plant that had been provided to shade him to how God is rightly concerned about human and animal life. The narrative ends with a question. We are not told how Jonah responded. What matters is how we respond. Do we grasp the greatness of God's love? Are we eager that others enjoy it?

The Object Lesson (4:5-8). **Jonah went out and sat down at a place east of the city** (*verse 5*). It is difficult to decide when Jonah did in fact leave Nineveh. It could have been at the end of the three day period mentioned in 3:3, or later just before the forty days (3:4) had expired, or it might even have been after the completion of the forty days. A solution depends on our conclusion as regards when it would have been obvious that the judgment he had warned of had been averted by the repentance of the Ninevites. The statement of 3:10 is the narrator's inspired comment upon what happened, and in the light of his technique of finishing one matter before proceeding to the next even if that disrupts the temporal sequence, it is difficult to draw any conclusions from it as regards the order of events.

The most plausible scenario seems to be that when it was obvious that there was widespread repentance among the people, Jonah realised that this would lead to the exercise of divine compassion. He then uttered the words of 4:1-4 in the city probably not long after the end of the three days. He subsequently went outside to wait and see what would happen, and during that period the LORD challenged him. This makes sense of a number of features of the terse narrative. The picture of him waiting for judgment to fall even after the forty days have elapsed is far-fetched. That he is found 'at a place east of the city' fits in with him having gone through it from the west over a short period of time.

There he made himself a shelter, sat in its shade. The hot climate would have made waiting in the open an uncomfortable experience. To shade himself from the sun, Jonah made a makeshift shelter. Wood is a scarce commodity in Mesopotamia, and it would probably have been with stones or mud bricks that Jonah constructed the shelter. At best a few bits of shrub might have been used for the roof. The area would not have been uninhabited and it would have been easy for him to get food and water from local people.

Jonah **waited to see what would happen to the city** may not imply that he doubted the genuineness of the repentance of Nineveh. There were instances where punishment followed, even though there had been repentance, most notably in the death of David's child even after he had confessed his sin in connection with Bathsheba (2 Sam. 12:13-18). If the Ninevites were placing their hopes in a 'Who knows?', so too could Jonah. Despite the contrition of Nineveh, God might not disappoint him and might still bring destruction upon them.

It was not just Jonah's attitude towards Nineveh that was uncomfortable. Even with his shelter, it would have been far from pleasant out under the sun. **Then the LORD God provided a vine and made it grow up over Jonah to give shade for his head to ease his discomfort** (*verse 6*). The name used 'LORD God' is unusual. Although found in Genesis 2-4, it is not frequent elsewhere, and seems here to mark a deliberate change from LORD to God. LORD is the covenant name of God who has acted in mercy towards his people. This is particularly shown by his compassionate treatment of Jonah despite his fuming and reluctance to accept what God has done. The use of 'God' here and in 4:7-9 points to his action as the supreme ruler of all. He provides (see on 4:7) as he sees fit and as he alone can.

The plant provided is similar to the 'great fish' of 1:17. There is no necessity for supposing that either were newly created species. Although we do not know the precise type of fish or plant, the lesson being taught is God's control over all that he has created. Perhaps the plant was a gourd or a vine. Although several species are known to be fast growers, this one sprouted at an unprecedented rate. Its broad leaves would have provided shelter in the sweltering eastern heat, making a more effective roof for the structure than any Jonah had been able to construct. **And Jonah was very happy about the vine**. The

LORD's action brought him relief in his situation, alleviating its discomfort. Perhaps it also caused Jonah to think that his self-appointed surveillance of the city would bear fruit after all. Had the LORD come round to his prophet's way of thinking? Was this a token of divine approval of what he was doing?

But at dawn the next day (*verse 7*), after only one day in which Jonah enjoyed the benefits given to him by the shade of the plant, **God**, the Creator, the one with power to act over what he has made, **provided a worm**. 'Provide' is the same word that is used in 1:17 of the fish, in 4:6 of the vine, in 4:7 of the worm, and in 4:8 of the wind. God exercises a comprehensive and effective control. Be it a small worm, or a large fish, they are directed as he sees fit. Now, however, the purpose behind it is not relief, but destruction. **Which chewed the vine so that it withered**. The miracle is again to be found in the control exercised over creation. The plant does not wither in some unnatural way, but through divine oversight of a natural phenomenon. It happens precisely when and how God has determined.

When the sun rose, God provided a scorching east wind, and the sun blazed on Jonah's head so that he grew faint (*verse 8*). Again God's control is seen in that the situation in which Jonah finds himself is aggravated by the divinely summoned scorching wind. This dry, hot wind which withers green growth, and causes considerable physical distress, is a well-known phenomenon in the area — but it is under God's control and serves his purpose. Jonah at once feels the effect of the plant's death, and begins to suffer from sunstroke. **He wanted to die, and said, "It would be better for me to die than to live."** The words are identical to 'It is better for me to die than live' (4:4). If the provision of the plant had eased Jonah's lot and his bad temper somewhat, the situation was now reversed. He was back into his old mood again, and wishing he were dead. He speaks on the basis of common humanity, and challenges God's right to destroy.

The Repeated Inquiry (4:9). In a repetition of what happened in 4:3, **But God said to Jonah, "Do you have a right to be angry about the vine?"** (*verse 9*). Again the words are identical, 'Have you any right to be angry?' This repetition emphasises the link between the two sections of the chapter and prepares the way for the inferences that are drawn. Jonah's anger is now focused on the loss of the vine, and what has happened to it. **"I do," he said. "I am angry enough to die."** He felt he was being victimised by what had happened to him. Jonah was

sure he was right in what he considered should have happened to
Nineveh. Not only was God wrong in what he had done to the city, but
also in what he had done to the prophet.

The Challenging Question (4:10-11). It is the LORD who speaks,
reflecting a change in emphasis from the Sovereign who has in his
control all he has created, to the covenant God who deals in mercy with
his people. He remonstrates with Jonah and seeks to bring him to see
the folly and small-mindedness of his position. **But the LORD said,
"You have been concerned about this vine, though you did not tend
it or make it grow. It sprang up overnight and died overnight"**
(*verse 10*). 'Concern' is a feeling which goes out towards one in
trouble. It is often translated 'pity', but is more than a sympathy,
because it moves on into action taken to assist the other party. It reflects
the attitude of the Messianic king towards the weak and the poor (Ps.
72:13), though the word is used most often in a negative context, such
as the divine pronouncement, 'I will allow no pity or mercy or
compassion to keep me from destroying them' (Jer. 13:14). Concern
would have led to sparing them, as here.

Jonah was concerned about a mere plant, that had come and gone.
He had not had to take any trouble to grow it or tend it, but now that
it is dead, he is so stirred up that he would have been prepared to go to
great lengths to preserve it. If Jonah felt in such a way about a plant,
then how can he be critical of God's attitude towards Nineveh? The
force of the argument is from the lesser to the greater, and the intensity
of Jonah's reaction is being employed as a lever to give him insight into
the LORD's attitude. If he is unwilling to accept this insight, he will be
in a self-contradictory position.

**But Nineveh has more than a hundred and twenty thousand
people who cannot tell their right hand from their left** (*verse 11*).
To justify his concern, the LORD points out the size and significance of
Nineveh (see on 1:2; 3:3). Usually the 120,000 are taken to be children,
leading to estimates of the total population around 600,000. Archae-
ology suggests that figure may be on the high side for the city, though
not if the surrounding district is included. It is possible that those 'who
cannot tell their right hand from their left' is an idiomatic expression,
not for some early stage of human development, but for lack of ability
to discriminate between courses of action. The figure of 120,000
would then be for the total population ('people') of the city, who are
described as being unable to reach a considered and informed decision.

Nowhere does Scripture suggest that being outside Israel deprives people of knowledge of right and wrong. They are untaught, and while this does not make them innocent, it provides grounds for dealing with them gently. The addition **and many cattle as well** is probably not due to some Eastern pre-occupation with cattle as a source of wealth, but rather relates to Jonah's attitude towards the plant. If the plight of the Ninevites does not arouse him, perhaps the prophet who was concerned about the plant, would show concern about the animals that would be lost if a Sodom and Gomorrah style conflagration engulfed the city. It is urging Jonah to review his scale of priorities.

We are not told about how Jonah responded, for it is the reality of the LORD's compassion that is the dominant theme. **Should I not be concerned about that great city?** Although the question comes first in the verse in the Hebrew, the NIV puts it last to prevent what can sound like an anti-climax to us by ending the book with 'cattle'. The reader of the book of Jonah in every generation is being left with a testing question to grapple with. How do we perceive the grace of God? Does the example of the concern of 'God our Saviour, who wants all men to be saved and to come to a knowledge of the truth' (1 Tim. 2:3-4) provide the pattern for our concern?

Study questions: Jonah 4:5-11

verse 6: How should we react to the blessings God bestows? (Ps. 103:2,10; Isa. 63:7; Luke 17:18; Eph. 5:20; 1 Thess. 5:18)

verse 11: Can we set bounds to God's love? (Isa. 45:22; Ezek. 18:23; John 3:16; 1 Tim. 2:3,4; Tit. 2:11; 2 Pet. 3:9)

MICAH

Overview

A prophet — and a 'minor' one at that — writing in the closing years of the eighth century BC may at first appear a remote and distant figure. How can what he said then possibly be relevant to us today? But as we study Micah's prophecy, we become quickly aware of uncomfortable parallels between his situation and ours.

Western civilisation has abandoned its Christian foundations. In Micah's day, Judah had abandoned its religious heritage. There was indeed an outward willingness to worship the LORD (6:6-7), but Micah anticipates our Lord's test in Matthew 12:33-35, and examines the fruit present in society — and there is little to commend it. Violence was used to seize property (2:2) and to waylay passers-by (2:8). Justice was perverted (3:9). Commercial trickery and deceit were prevalent (6:10-12). Family life was distorted (7:5-6). Micah exposes the moral and social evils that prevailed in his day, and traces them to their source. The religious spokesmen of his day no longer spoke the truth (2:11; 3:11). Pagan practices had become prevalent (5:12-14).

It is the reality of the LORD's judgment upon all this that Micah brings out. He uses the example of Samaria, the capital of the Northern Kingdom, Israel, and its fate as a warning to Jerusalem and Judah (1:5-9). He is unsparing in his denunciation of those who are misusing their power in the land (2:1; 3:2-3, 9-10). He speaks as one who knows what the outcome of their behaviour inevitably will be, but yet he speaks in the hope that his words of warning will serve to turn them from disaster, as in measure they did (see comments on 3:12).

But though judgment was postponed by repentance, Micah knew that it would only be for a while, and that the people of Judah would revert to their old ways. The LORD would chastise his people for their rebellious ways, and yet his judgment would not be his final verdict on them. Three times Micah presents the future hope for a remnant who will be preserved by divine grace. On the first occasion, it is only a brief glimpse of this deliverance that we have (2:12-13). The second time, in chapters 4 and 5, it takes on a clearer outline, and we are introduced to the Ruler from Bethlehem, through whom the LORD will accomplish his people's deliverance. The third expression of hope closes chapter 7, and is designed to lead us to exclaim 'Who is like the LORD?', as Micah declares his faith in the one who will be true to his covenant commitment and redeem his people despite their unworthiness.

Micah 1:1: Introductions are important

When we read Micah, or one of the other prophets, we are often so eager to get to the 'real message' later on in the book that we pass over the introduction quite quickly. But we should not be in such a hurry. When Micah was writing down the message, he had already been preaching for quite a number of years. He was guided by the Holy Spirit to put this title at the beginning of his book, and it gives us four important starting points to help us appreciate and understand what follows.

(1) *The Divine Message.* The first thing the title tells us is that this is **the word of the LORD**. The prophets often employ this phrase, especially in the titles or superscriptions of their works (Jer. 1:2; Hos. 1:1; Jonah 1:1), to describe what is being said. But the fact that it is frequently used should not blind us to the astonishing claim that is involved in it. The message that follows is not to be attributed to the insight of human genius. It is rather a word **that came**. This message was revealed by divine initiative. Micah does not ask for any credit for having thought it up. What he claims is that it is **the vision he saw** (Isa. 1:1; Nah. 1:1). Here he uses a word that may refer not just to a vision, but also to a message perceived in other ways, for example, by hearing. But it was a message given to Micah, and he then in his preaching and writing relayed the information that had been entrusted to him by the LORD. This name when in small capitals stands for Jehovah, or Yahweh, the personal name of the covenant God of Israel. He was speaking to his people, and Micah was the herald proclaiming the message of the sovereign king.

(2) *The Divine Messenger.* The title also identifies for us the individual who received God's word, **Micah of Moresheth**. The name Micah was a very common one, and means 'Who is like the LORD?' In this or a longer form, Micaiah, it is used of fourteen men in the Old Testament. After Micah, perhaps the best known of them is another prophet, who lived more than a hundred years earlier (1 Kgs. 22; 2 Chr. 18).

We would have expected Micah to introduce himself in the usual way by telling us who his father was. Instead he tells us that he came from the Judean country town of Moresheth. It is most probably the same place as Moresheth Gath, mentioned in 1:14, which lay south west of Jerusalem, about halfway to the Mediterranean Sea (see Map

II). Since Micah would not have been known in his hometown as Micah of Moresheth, we may deduce that he became used to introducing himself in this way as he went to other parts of the country during his prophetic ministry. Much of it was probably in Jerusalem, where he was certainly well remembered a hundred years later (Jer. 26:17-19). This passage also indicates that Micah's message, if not Micah himself, was known to King Hezekiah (715-686 BC), and his ministry (no doubt along with that of his better known contemporary, Isaiah) played a role in the reformation that occurred under Hezekiah. Micah was thus one whose ministry was blessed in his own day, and was remembered much later on.

We know no more about Micah and his personal background than this. Sometimes he records his thoughts and personal feelings for us. But he does not tell us how or when God called him to be a prophet, or precisely when and where he delivered his various messages, or any of the other information we might have liked to know about him. We are not to be taken up with his personal circumstances. What matters is that he is the one through whom the LORD spoke, and still speaks.

(3) *A Time of Crisis.* The title does, however, tell us that it was **during the reigns of Jotham, Ahaz and Hezekiah, kings of Judah**, that Micah received his message. This is vital information for us. It enables us to locate Micah's message historically, as we have indeed already begun to do. In this way we can better understand what God was saying through his prophetic herald to the people of his own day. But, more importantly, when we see similar circumstances occurring today, it allows us to work out what God's message is for us. He does not change. His attitude to man's behaviour and his remedy for man's situation have always been the same. It is therefore not only legitimate but also necessary for each generation to apply the word of the LORD to its own time. In that way our perception of what is happening around us will be improved, and it may be that we will respond in time to the warnings that God's word still conveys to us.

The reigns of Jotham (750-731), Ahaz (735-715) and Hezekiah (715-686) of Judah were years which saw the collapse of the political strength that had been built up earlier in the century both in the northern kingdom of Israel under Jeroboam II (793-753) and in the southern kingdom of Judah under Uzziah (792-740). During their reigns the weakness of surrounding nations and their own friendly attitude towards each other had permitted them to extend the territory of their kingdoms so that together they ruled over almost all that David and Solomon had once controlled at the peak of Israel's influence. But by Micah's day there had been a considerable change in the international situation. The energetic and very competent Tiglath-Pileser III (745-727) had come to the throne of Assyria. The northern kingdom had been weakened by internal dissension after Jeroboam's death, and came increasingly under Assyrian control, culminating in the destruction of the capital city, Samaria, in 722 after an unsuccessful rebellion.

Judah was spared the same fate because Ahaz had been following a pro-Assyrian policy and was willing to pay substantial tribute. Although Hezekiah was out of sympathy with his father's policy, for the first part of his reign he made no open moves to break Judah's status as a tributary state. He did, however, try to tackle the internal problems of his kingdom.

But it was not just a period of political tension and upheaval that Micah lived through. There was also an economic and social revolution. The heyday of Uzziah had brought much wealth into the land, but it was not evenly distributed. The rich got richer, and invested their wealth in land, undermining the traditional pattern of rural life, and creating many social problems. As they selfishly pursued their own interests, they thought nothing of exploiting the poorer classes. There was also an erosion of standards in the religious life of the nation. Idolatry was openly fostered by Ahaz, and even those who claimed to worship the LORD became satisfied with the external aspects of worship without a true heart engagement. Prophets, priest and rulers condoned the prevalent materialism and religious superficiality. Micah was commissioned by the LORD to expose these conditions and to call for a return in the life of the nation to the standards of behaviour towards one's neighbour which God's covenant had laid down.

(4) *The Two Capitals.* The final piece of information conveyed in the introductory title is that Micah's message was **concerning Samaria and Jerusalem**. Mentioning the capital cities rather than the kingdoms of Israel and Judah is unusual, and perhaps reflects Micah's perception as a countryman that the declining standards in the nation had spread from the centre outwards. Although his message was for all the inhabitants of the land, it was addressed in a special way to those in positions of influence, and particularly in the capital. Although he begins by recording an early message about Samaria, most of the book focuses on the south. By the time Micah came to write down his

message Samaria had already fallen, but its fate served as an example for Jerusalem and Judah in Hezekiah's day. Indeed, through the messages sent to these two capital cities and their nations long ago, God still addresses us and warns us about our behaviour and responsibilities. An outward show of religious activity does not satisfy him, if it is not matched with a true concern for all the requirements of his word (Matt. 7:21-23). Those whom the King invites to enjoy the inheritance he has procured for them are those whose allegiance to him has been practically expressed in their actions towards the citizens of his kingdom (Matt. 25:34-40). Micah's message is concerned with the application of these principles of God-honouring living.

Micah 1:2-7: Where Judgment Begins ...

Micah starts the record of his prophetic ministry by going back over the earliest messages he had received from God. He returns to the closing years of the reign of Jotham, the king of Judah who died in 731 BC. This was before the northern kingdom of Israel had been wiped out by the Assyrians, who captured its capital city of Samaria in 722/21 BC. But it was already a time when the Assyrians were making their presence felt in Syria and Palestine (2 Kgs. 15:29).

Micah is, however, looking behind the human actors on the international political scene. They were only doing what God had ordained should occur. Micah has been shown how the hand of God, the judge of all the earth, will work. He is concerned to emphasise the reality of God's judgment, both on the nations (1:2) and on God's chosen people (1:5-7). Micah wants to puncture the complacency of those who feel they have a secure relationship with God, but who in reality are living as rebels against him. Unless they mend their ways, they will be the first to experience God's wrath.

Micah's message begins with the summons **Hear** (*verse 2*). The summons is repeated at 3:1 and 6:1, and serves to indicate the three main divisions of the book. The prophet is acting as a court-usher requiring all interested parties to pay attention to the actions of **the Sovereign LORD** as he comes in judgment. Three truths are emphasised.

(1) The LORD is not just a god of one people. He is Lord of all. **Peoples, all of you**, and **earth, and all who are in it** are his rightful subjects who should listen to him and obey (Ps. 49:1). The title Adonai is used twice (once translated 'Sovereign' by the NIV, and once as 'the

Lord') to emphasise the universal dominion of the LORD, Israel's God (Hab. 3:19; Zeph. 1:7). He is not a local deity, such as the heathen imagine, but one whose sway extends to every individual on earth, whether or not they are prepared to acknowledge him.

(2) There is also a warning conveyed to those who would suppose that God is distant, and so call into question the reality of his knowledge of what is on earth, and of his desire to intervene in judgment. He is described as **the Lord from his holy temple**. This combines his transcendence and his immanence. The 'holy temple' refers to his heavenly dwelling place, as in Psalm 11:4 and Habakkuk 2:20 (compare also Jonah 2:7). But he is not just introspectively absorbed in the praises of the seraphim. He observes and examines what people are doing, and 'from' serves notice that in his own good time he will openly and decisively intervene in the affairs of earth.

(3) The summons issued here is so that he **may witness against you**. Now at first this may seem awkward because the rest of the chapter describes judgment against Samaria and Jerusalem, not the other nations of the world. But Micah will later return to the theme that the destiny of all nations is inextricably linked with that of Israel and Judah (4:1-4; 5:7-9; 7:10), and that God will judge the nations (5:15; 7:16-17). Now they are being called on to watch and learn. This is what will ultimately be held against them. If judgment begins with the house of God (1 Pet. 4:17-18), then are those who do not acknowledge the Sovereign LORD going to be exempt? What is going to befall God's people is not some arbitrary and inexplicable act, but part of the total reality of divine judgment, which will sweep away all that opposes him.

The next two verses (1:3-4) describe the impending arrival of God in judgment using the language of theophany, as is found elsewhere (e.g. Judg. 5:4-5; Pss. 18:7-15; 68:7-8; Isa. 64:1-2). Attention is demanded. **Look! The LORD is coming from his dwelling place** (*verse 3*), that is, his holy temple mentioned in 1:2, and **he comes down**. This probably implies that his action is going to be based on close examination of the evidence (Gen. 11:5; 18:21). **The high places of the earth** may just be part of the general picture. As God descends from heaven, the first place he comes into contact with is the mountain tops (Amos 4:13). However, 'high places' were frequently thought of in ancient times as places of security from the enemy (Ps. 61:2; Obad. 3). Now in a reversal of human expectations, they are the first to experience God's presence in judgment. Also, 'the high places' were the sites of the Canaanite worship of Baal. When the LORD **treads** on them and destroys them, he exposes the impotence of the pagan deities whose shrines were there.

The presence of God affects all the earth from the highest mountains to the depths of the valleys. We are probably to take the first and third lines of 1:4 together, and the second and the fourth. The picture is one where **the mountains melt beneath him** ... **like wax before the fire** (Pss. 68:2; 97:5; Nah. 1:5; Hab. 3:6) and **the valleys split apart**... **like water running down a slope**, as when a violent rainstorm washes all before it down the valley. This is a graphic description of the tremendous forces unleashed when the LORD comes to judge the earth. Nothing escapes the impact of his presence. The awesome reality will be completely realised only on the final day (2 Pet. 3:10), but it is anticipated in every prior intervention of God in judgment in the affairs of men.

One aspect of this situation as it affected Micah's original audience in Jerusalem must be noticed. They had been used to hearing of God going forth to rescue them and judge their enemies (e.g. Judg. 5:4-5; Ps. 68). Micah's message would not then have struck them at first as being one of condemnation for them, but rather one of encouragement: was this not God intervening on their behalf as he had done of old? But Micah is using a technique also found in Psalm 50 and Amos 1 and 2 to communicate with a spiritually complacent nation, who are sure of themselves and unaware of the breakdown in their relationship with God. He speaks at first in terms that are familiar and comfortably remote. It seems as if God's anger is directed elsewhere, then he says, 'It's you I am talking about! Not them!' In this way Micah seeks to puncture their self-satisfaction and overcome the defences they have erected against criticism.

The true focus of the prophet's message need not even have become obvious at the beginning of 1:5, when it is said that **all this is because of Jacob's transgression, because of the sins of the house of Israel** (*verse 5*). 'Jacob' and 'Israel' were descriptions involving some ambiguity. They were originally religious terms rather than political, and referred to the whole covenant people. But after the division of the kingdom at the end of Solomon's reign, Israel also became the designation of the northern kingdom. Jacob also was used as a poetic equivalent for the north (Isa. 9:8; Amos 6:8; 7:2) as well as for the whole covenant people. It would be easy for those in Jerusalem to have supposed that Micah was talking about the sin of their northern neighbours. 'Transgression' or rebellion refers to positive acts that are contrary to the LORD's requirements and in defiance of his authority. The connotation of 'sins' is more negative, indicating rather failure, default, not matching up to the standards of God's law. The religious degeneracy of the northern kingdom and its consequences are clearly spelled out in 2 Kings 17:1-23.

Micah then asks questions to trace these faults back to their source. **What is Jacob's transgression?** Literally it is 'Who is Jacob's transgression?' Sin never exists apart from sinners and Micah's question is as much about the identity of those involved as it is about the nature of their misdemeanours. His rhetorical question **Is it not Samaria?** emphatically locates those responsible as being in the capital city. It is from the attitudes of those in government and in the ruling classes of Samaria that evil influences have spread through the land. Those who should have been nourishing the life of the nation have instead been poisoning it. Next Micah turns to probe the state of the south. We might have thought he would ask, 'What is Judah's sin?' But perhaps in another attempt to startle the complacent into thinking about their situation he introduces an unexpected question. He identifies their sin by saying, **What is Judah's high place?** A 'high place' was a Canaanite sacred site, originally on a mountain top, as being in some way nearer to the gods, but later on an artificial elevation on lower ground. **Is it not Jerusalem?** Micah is implying that if you go up to Jerusalem what you will find there is not the true temple of the LORD, but, just as in Samaria, something that has been distorted and debased through the influences of Canaanite worship, and amounts to nothing more than a pagan shrine. Even though Jotham was one who did what was right in the sight of the LORD, he, like many pious kings before him, had been unable to remove the high places (2 Kgs. 15:34-35). Later under Ahaz, things were to become much worse, with child sacrifice (2 Kgs. 16:3) and the erection of a pagan altar in the temple (2 Kgs. 16:10-16). One of the reforms of Hezekiah's reign was to remove the high places (2 Kgs. 18:4).

To this point Micah himself has been speaking of what he has seen and knows about as the LORD's prophet. But now he moves on to declare the LORD's verdict against his rebellious people, and does so by citing the LORD's own words. It is not on Jerusalem that judgment is first pronounced. The North had led the way in abandoning the LORD, and it will be the first to experience God's wrath.

Therefore (*verse 6*) makes it evident that the overthrow of Samaria is not arbitrary, but the fully justified consequence of her misbehaviour. Consequently the LORD declares, **I will make Samaria a heap of rubble**. The picture is not just of a mound of stones, recognisably once a city, but rather of 'a heap of the field' (AV). It will be so obliterated that it will become just like the heap of stones a farmer gathers out of his way in a corner neglected, uncared for, unnoticed. Samaria was situated in good country for growing vines, and that is what the site will again become, **a place for planting vineyards. I will pour her stones into the valley and lay bare her foundations**. It had been 'set on the head of a fertile valley' (Isa. 28:1,4), and its demolition will involve the stones of its buildings being tossed down the slope till the site is levelled.

But it will not just be that the houses and city walls will be destroyed. It is significant that the aspect of Samaria's fall that is particularly singled out for comment is that **all her** stone **idols will be broken to pieces** (*verse 7*). They were the reason for the LORD's devastating judgment. **All her temple gifts will be burned with fire; I will destroy all her images**. Whatever adorned Samaria's temples will be burned.

Since she gathered her gifts from the wages of prostitutes, as the wages of prostitutes they will again be used. 'Prostitution' is probably best taken to refer to idolatrous worship (as in e.g. Exod. 34:15; Deut. 31:16). The precious articles that adorned the temples of Samaria had been gifts from those who engaged in false worship there. When the city is overthrown, these treasures will be carried off by the enemy to adorn the temples of their own gods.

It is worth noticing that Micah here clearly exposes the flaw in Samaria as being religious corruption and idolatry. Micah is often, and not without reason, cited as a prophet of the poor, standing out against the social injustices of his day. But this initial message directed principally at the northern kingdom shows us clearly that he understood evil practices to be outward evidence of the inner corruption of a heart estranged from God. Oppression and injustice are the symptoms of a much deeper spiritual malaise, for it is out of what is stored up within them that men speak and act (Matt. 12:35).

Study questions: Micah 1:1-7

verse 2: Notice how important hearing and listening are when the word of God is spoken. What sort of hearing is not really hearing at all? (Matt. 15:10; Mark 4:9-12; Luke 8:18; Rev. 3:6) *verse 4*: How useful is it to approach spiritual matters indirectly? (2 Sam. 12:1-14; Ps. 50; Amos 1,2; Acts 17:16-33)

verses 5 and 6: What precautions should we observe in trying to learn from what has happened to others? (Luke 13:1-5; Phil. 15)

Micah 1:8-16: ... And Where It Ends

When others are struck by disaster, our feelings of relief at not being personally involved frequently prevent us from learning the lessons the tragedy could teach us. Micah is determined that Judah should learn from the experience of Samaria. He records his own reaction of grief and distress to the calamity about to overtake the northern section of God's people to induce his hearers in the south to be affected in the same way (1:8-9). He then goes on to tell of calamity encircling Jerusalem itself (1:10-16). The South had no reason to expect immunity from the LORD's judgment. As he had already indicated at the end of 1:5, they too were involved in practices similar to those in the North. So Micah seeks to press home the example of Samaria as a warning to the people of the South. (This was also done by his prophetic contemporary Isaiah, compare Isa. 10:11.) As we shall see, Micah emphasises the danger they are in by returning three times to focus on Jerusalem, at the end of each of the three parts of this section, in 1:9, 12, and 16.

In the previous section (1:6-7) it had been the LORD himself who spoke, but now Micah records his own reaction to the situation of which he has been informed. **Because of this** (*verse 8*) refers back to the message of judgment he has just delivered about Samaria, and its implications for Jerusalem. He therefore says, **I will weep and wail**. These words refer to the dirges and laments of the mourning rites that were customary at eastern funerals, where no restraint was placed on open expression of grief and sorrow. So devastated is Micah by the judgment which he knows is surely coming on Samaria, that he already presents himself as a mourner at the funeral of the Northern Kingdom.

To **go about barefoot and naked** were also open signs of distress, as when David ascended the Mount of Olives weeping and barefoot as an expression of his grief (2 Sam. 15:30). 'Naked' here, and on other occasions in Scripture, probably means not wearing the usual outer garments. Micah's actions seem just to have been those of a mourner, and not a pictorial representation of one going into captivity, as is the case in Isaiah 20:2.

He also says, **I will howl like a jackal and moan like an owl**, or more probably an ostrich. Ostriches were then found in the wilderness areas of the Near East and were often hunted. The reference here is to their harsh, doleful cry. The long drawn out nocturnal howl of a jackal is well known. These two animals are also linked together in Job 30:29 in a context of mourning and affliction.

In this, Micah shows himself to be like the other prophets of the LORD. They were never detached commentators on the social and religious scene of their day. Even though they had solemn warnings to deliver to unrepentant sinners, they did not let this harden their love for the people to whom they spoke. Isaiah 22:4 records how the prophet did not wish to be consoled when he considered the destruction the LORD would bring upon his people. Jeremiah in particular is not afraid to reveal the intensity of his grief over the people's sin (e.g. Jer. 8:21; 9:1). So too Micah here. It is still the case that those who present the warnings of the gospel to an unrepentant generation must do so lovingly and not harshly.

Micah makes clear that there are two reasons for his grief: the situation in Samaria, and the situation in Judah. He says for her, that is, Samaria's, **wound is incurable** (*verse 9*). There are two views about what constituted the 'wound' of Samaria.

(1) Some take it as the sin and rebellion that had struck a mortal blow at Samaria's national life. Micah is also overwhelmed with grief 'for' (not translated in the NIV) **it has come to Judah**. The same rebellious attitude against the LORD had already spread south to Judah, and not just in a marginal way. **It has reached the very gate of my people, even to Jerusalem itself**. The area immediately inside the city gate was the centre of the community where people met, the market was held, and the elders administered justice. So Jerusalem the centre of the life of the kingdom had been corrupted, and the situation in the south was desperate.

(2) In the light of 1:13, however, it may be preferable to understand the reference to Samaria's wound to be that caused by the LORD's punishment of his rebellious people. Then what Micah describes is the spread to the South of judgment such as the North had already experienced. The rendering of the NIV footnote 'He has reached the very gate of my people' presents a similar picture: the Assyrian king with his armies, acting as the instruments of the LORD's judgment, enter Judah and besiege the capital. In the years following the fall of Samaria they did make a number of incursions into Judah, culminating in 701 BC when Sennacherib overran the area and Jerusalem barely escaped (2 Kgs. 18:13-16). Micah would then be speaking of Jerusa-

lem as 'the gate of my people', the heart of the southern kingdom, reached but not overrun by the enemy.

Micah was not himself from the capital but from one of the smaller towns of Judah. Although critical of much that went on in Jerusalem, he does not let that blind him to the repercussions that will affect the whole land if the capital falls. He speaks with intense personal involvement and concern. He talks of the whole population as 'my people'. Neither his personal origins nor his loyalty to the LORD prevent him from identifying with them. What happens to them involves him, and already their condition was causing him grief.

In the next section (1:10-12) the theme of mourning continues to dominate. Micah cites words from David's lament over Saul and Jonathan (2 Sam. 1:20), **Tell it not in Gath** (*verse 10*). The site of Philistine Gath — the name itself is common, meaning 'wine-press' — is not yet definitely identified, and it is uncertain if it still existed in Micah's day. The saying had, however, probably become a proverb, implying that the enemies of God should not be given the opportunity to vaunt themselves over a calamity that had struck Israel. Indeed the command, **Weep not at all**, seems to imply that the disaster Micah sees coming will be so great that there will not be the time or opportunity for shedding tears.

The footnotes of the NIV, however, alert us to a feature of this passage: Micah repeatedly plays on the meanings of the names of the towns he mentions and on similarly sounded words in Hebrew. Perhaps it was suggested to him by the similarity in sound that exists between 'Gath' and the Hebrew word for 'tell'. It is not of course usually possible to convey this in an English translation. Even if it could be done successfully, this sort of literary technique is alien to us, and it is very doubtful if the effect on us would be to reinforce the solemnity of the message as it would have done for Micah's audience.

On the basis of the Septuagint, the ancient Greek translation of the Old Testament, there is another NIV footnote to 1:10, suggesting that instead of 'Weep not at all' there was originally one of these word-plays between a place name 'Acco' and the Hebrew word for 'weep'. 'Weep not in Acco' would then have substantially the same meaning as 'Tell it not in Gath', that is, a warning against carrying their weeping into the Phoenician city of Acco, which lay north of Mount Carmel (see Map II). But it is very difficult to see why Acco would have been chosen as a typical foreign city. At least Gath was mentioned in the proverb, and was also situated very close to the other towns Micah mentions. This alternative is therefore not very likely.

Micah now goes on to mention a number of other towns or possibly villages. Many of their names occur only here in the Old Testament, though they would undoubtedly be known to the people of Jerusalem Micah was addressing. So far as we can tell they were located in the Shephelah, the fertile low foothills on the edge of the Mediterranean coastal plain, which was where his hometown of Moresheth was (see Map II). Although Micah is now describing the disaster that will come upon Judah, he still makes it somewhat distant from Jerusalem, so that the impact of the end of 1:12 is intensified. Micah seems to have selected these particular places because of the opportunity their names gave for word association that would fit his message. They do not seem to occur in any particular order, and their haphazard listing may perhaps have added to the picture of confusion he is describing.

At the end of 1:10 Micah mentions **Beth Ophrah** (or, Bethleaphrah). Its location is unknown, but it seems unlikely that it was the same place as Ophrah in Benjamin near Bethel (Josh. 18:23; 1 Sam. 13:17). The name means 'house of dust', and so in the picture of disaster, its inhabitants are commanded to **roll in the dust**, a way of displaying extreme anguish (Josh. 7:6; Job 16:15; Ezek. 27:30).

Shaphir (*verse 11*) is of uncertain location, possibly south-east of the Philistine city of Ashdod. Its name means 'pleasant' or 'beautiful', but its inhabitants are to undergo a reversal of what such a name involves as they **pass on in nakedness and shame** (Isa. 20:4; 47:2-3; Nah. 3:5). They are being led off as slaves, stripped of their clothes and exposed to their captors' taunts.

Zaanan, the next place mentioned, may perhaps be the same as Zenan (Josh. 15:37), in which case it was located somewhere near Lachish. Its name sounds like the Hebrew word for 'come out', but again the situation is reversed. **Those who live in Zaanan will not come out**. We are not certain why. Are they to be besieged? or, Are they to experience a loss of nerve and be unwilling to come out to fight? or, Is it that they will be captured and slaughtered so that they are unable to come out and escape? At any rate, their fortunes will belie the name of their town.

It is even less certain what is being said at the end of 1:11 about Beth Ezel, which means 'house of nearness', and which has been tentatively located south-west of Hebron. Perhaps its name implies that it is a helper, or a place of refuge, but **Beth Ezel is in mourning**. Its cries of lamentation bear witness that it too is going to be engulfed in the disaster, and so **its protection is taken from you**, presumably from the inhabitants of the land who might have sought refuge there.

Maroth is yet another site that has not been located, but its name means 'bitterness', and so, unlike the last three places, it will in the impending disaster experience a fate corresponding to its name. **Those who live in Maroth writhe in pain, waiting for relief** (*verse 12*) which will not come.

The reason why there is no relief is that the **disaster has come from the LORD**. Literally, it has 'come down', and in that there is a reference back to the LORD's own coming down in 1:3. What is happening is no accident. It is the judicial intervention of their covenant LORD whom they have spurned, and consequently there can be no relief. The invading forces through whom the LORD will punish his people have reached **even to the gate of Jerusalem**. It may mean that the city itself will be under siege and so unable to help others. This in fact happened during Hezekiah's reign, when in 701 BC he and his army were trapped in Jerusalem by the Assyrian forces of Sennacherib — 'like a bird in a cage' as the Assyrian annals relate. In this second mention of Jerusalem (see also 1:9), Micah is emphasising that, just as the centre of national life had become spiritually corrupt, so the threat of divine retribution looms over it too.

In the third section of this lament (1:13-16) Micah again plays upon the names of places in the Judean foothills. Lachish had for centuries been a major fortress town. It lay about 48 kilometres (30 miles) south-west of Jerusalem, and therefore close to Micah's hometown of Moresheth. Lachish is similar in sound to the Hebrew word for a 'team' of war horses used to pull a chariot. But the command **You who live in Lachish, harness the team to the chariot** (*verse 13*) seems ironic. Its purpose is not fighting, but escape. It is uncertain how Lachish was **the beginning of sin to the Daughter of Zion**, a poetic reference to the population of Jerusalem (see on 4:8). We do not know of any major pagan shrine at Lachish. The **transgressions of Israel were found in you** may refer to their abandoning the LORD as their source of confidence and instead seeking security through political alliances and military strength, with which Lachish was of course very much associated. It was this secular outlook on life that Isaiah challenged in King Ahaz. 'If you do not stand firm in your faith, you will not stand at all' (Isa. 7:9; see also 2 Kgs. 16:5-9).

Therefore (*verse 14*), as a consequence of this pinning her hopes in the wrong place, when her military strength has failed her, Lachish

will give parting gifts to Moresheth Gath, the fuller name of Micah's hometown, 10 kilometres (6 miles) north-east of Lachish. Moresheth sounds like the Hebrew word for 'betrothed', but the gift Micah envisages is not the dowry customarily paid by the bride's father to the bridegroom. It is rather tribute paid by the land to the conqueror (2 Kgs. 16:8; 18:14-16) as he deports the inhabitants of Moresheth to a distant land . **The town of Aczib** was only a few miles from Moresheth, and in the coming tragedy it **will prove deceptive to the kings of Israel**, living up to the meaning of its name, 'deceptive'. It will not give the help it had promised to the royal house. Since Aczib was in the south, Israel must refer to the covenant people as a whole. The help expected would have been to the kings of Judah, not those of the north.

Mareshah was another important fortress town, lying between Aczib and Lachish. It is related in sound to the Hebrew word for 'inheritance' or 'possession', often one taken by conquest, and so Micah again brings out part of what will be involved in God's coming judgment by saying, **I will bring a conqueror against you who live in Mareshah** (*verse 15*). The 'conqueror' would be the Assyrians (Isa. 7:17; 10:5-6). The 'I' here is undoubtedly God, and indicates that though Micah has not set out this passage as direct divine speech, there can be no doubt that what he is relating has been revealed to him by God. So close did the prophets feel themselves to be to God, and so much did they associate all that they had to say with what had been revealed to them, that they often did not formally mark the transition from what was their description of the message or vision given to them and what was direct divine speech (1:6).

Then, as an indication that he is coming to the end of this section, Micah picks up a theme he had used at the beginning of it in 1:10, by again looking back to David's day. It was to the cave of Adullam that those who were in debt or discontented with Saul's rule had gathered (1 Sam. 22:1-2). Now **he who is the glory of Israel will come to Adullam**, another fortress town in Micah's home territory, east of Aczib. Again, 'Israel' here is not a reference to the Northern Kingdom, but to the covenant nation, whose glory may have been the king, or more probably the nobility of the land as a group. The nation's fortunes will be so strikingly reversed that it will be the highest in the land who have to tread the malcontents' path as they seek refuge in Adullam.

Then, for the third time, Micah focuses on Jerusalem, in effect resuming from 1:13 the personification of the city as Daughter of Zion. He addresses the city as a woman whom he urges to go into deep

mourning for the loss of her children. **Shave your heads in mourning**
(*verse 16*). Despite the injunction of Deuteronomy 14:1 against
shaving the front of their heads for the dead in the manner of the
Canaanites, the plucking out or shaving off of hair seems to have
remained a common expression of deep anguish over the loss of close
relatives (Isa. 22:12; Jer. 7:29; 16:6). Here Jerusalem is to mourn **for
the children in whom you delight**, with more than a hint that they had
been doted over. **Make yourselves as bald as the vulture** is a clear
reference to the pale, down-covered head of the griffon vulture. Notice
that the people of Jerusalem are being urged by Micah to engage in this
mourning immediately, not in the day when disaster strikes. He
presented himself to them as a mourner, and they were urged to join
him. If they accepted Micah's word as being truly from God, they
would become as sure as he was that the calamity of judgment would
ensue. **For they will go from you into exile** was one aspect of the curse
of the broken covenant, which had long since been announced (Deut.
28:41) and would soon be fulfilled (2 Kgs. 17:6). If the people accepted
the reality of their sin, then they would have acknowledged the
righteousness of God's threatened judgment, and that would have
been the first step on the pathway to restoration.

Micah has set before his people the inevitable outcome of their
rebellion against God. Out of an intense and compassionate concern
for the good of his fellow countrymen, such as Paul also would display
(Rom. 9:1-3; 10:1), Micah has been pleading with them in tears to
recognise the gravity of their situation. An evident and genuine
sympathy for the plight of those addressed is still necessary in the
presentation of the gospel.

But this section does not simply instruct us to consider the warnings
addressed to us by others. We are also to pay attention to what is
happening to those around us. Jerusalem had been shown what would
happen to the towns and villages around her. Though Micah has so far
only prophesied of the disaster as coming to the gates of Jerusalem,
that was not to be misinterpreted. There were no exceptions then or
now. The message is still the same, 'Unless you repent, you too will
all perish' (Luke 13:5).

Study questions: Micah 1:8-16

verse 8: What function does showing oneself to be affected by the
situation of the impenitent have in presenting the gospel to them? (Jer.
9:1; Luke 13:34-35; Rom. 9:2; 2 Cor. 11:29)

verse 10: Why would Micah find the attitude of the LORD's enemies a critical feature of the coming judgment upon his people? (Pss. 25:2; 35:25; 42:10; 89:50; 119:94,95. See also comments on 4:11.)

Micah 2:1-11: The Fitting Punishment

So far Micah has been concerned with piercing the complacency of his audience in Jerusalem — by making them see that they are the ones who are under threat from the LORD's judgment. Though that judgment will come upon them through enemy invasion, it will not just be the outcome of forces at work on the international political scene. The LORD determines the destiny of the nations, and he does so with particular reference to the situation of his own covenant people. The primary reason for the catastrophe that was to come on them was not political weakness, but their disobedience against the LORD. The nation had no respect for God and this had shown itself in its abandonment of his standards for living.

Micah points the finger at those who have been the chief beneficiaries of the new wealth that had come into the country with the economic recovery under Uzziah. In 2:1-5 he castigates their behaviour and announces God's condemnation of it. Then in 2:6-11 he lets us overhear a conversation between himself and other prophets who were condoning the current situation and providing a cover of religious respectability for it.

Woe! (*verse 1*) is a cry of grief originally used at funerals, but often employed by the prophets as a threatening introduction (see on Hab. 2:6; Nah. 3:1). Micah does not point directly to those he is speaking about, or name them. He rather describes them, and lets those whom the cap fits wear it. His description also makes clear that divine punishment is not arbitrary or capricious. He clearly spells out the reasons for God's intervention against **those who plan iniquity**. 'Iniquity' frequently refers to the abuse of power so as to cause trouble and thus bring harm on one's fellows (Hab. 1:3). It was no sudden temptation they had given in to. Their behaviour was deliberate and sustained. They **plot evil on their beds**, where as often in Scripture (Pss. 4:4; 36:4; 63:6) they are pictured as apart from the hustle of everyday life and alone with their thoughts. But this is no time of pious meditation for them. These people are so intent on amassing wealth that they spend sleepless nights devising schemes to satisfy their desires (Prov. 4:16), and then **at morning's light they carry it out**. They are so eager to carry out their plans that they can hardly wait for daylight to come (Hos. 7:6). What is more, **it is in their power to do it**. Wealth had flowed into the land in the days of Uzziah, but it had been concentrated in the hands of a few, and they were using it for their own selfish ends. They were in positions of influence, where they ensured that no obstacle was allowed to stand in their way.

The newly rich had more money than they could immediately spend. About the only investment opportunity that then existed was in real estate, in fields and houses. **They covet fields and seize them, and houses, and take them** (*verse 2*). Isaiah, who was a contemporary of Micah, talked about those who added house to house, and joined field to field till there was no space left for anyone else (Isa. 5:8). The smallholders of Israel were being bought out or evicted. The rich used violence to acquire property from those who would not sell to them. They were utterly unscrupulous in achieving what they wanted to the extent that **they defraud a man of his home**. As a countryman, Micah had witnessed the enormous social problems caused by the loss of the traditional small family farm and the creation of these large estates. The social structure of Judah was becoming increasingly polarised by the growing number of rootless, dispossessed farmers.

But Micah was not just concerned that the gap between the rich and the poor was widening, and about the cruelty and injustice that had attended it. He saw it as fundamentally a religious problem. The condition of society reflected an alienation in heart from God. Micah says, 'They covet', deliberately using the language of the tenth commandment (Exod. 20:17). Their outward actions sprang from an inward disregard for God's law. He also speaks of their defrauding **a fellowman of his inheritance**. The people of Israel had been taught by Moses that the land belonged to the LORD and he had entrusted it to them in their tribes and families. It was not to be permanently transferred to others (Lev. 25:23). Naboth's attitude toward his vineyard was a clear example of fidelity towards this covenant requirement (1 Kgs. 21). But now there was a whole class of oppressive Ahabs, trampling upon all the statutes that the LORD had laid down for his people.

Therefore, the LORD says (*verse 3*) introduces the divine word of judgment on such a situation. One problem that affects our interpretation of these verses is the identity of **this people**, or 'this family'. The word is used in Amos 3:1 to refer to the whole nation, and it may be taken in the same way here, so the ridicule of 2:4 is uttered against all Judah. But, more probably, 'this people' is the class of rich oppressors.

God's treatment of them is going to match their own behaviour. To offset their plans (2:1), God says, **I am planning**. They plotted 'evil' in 2:1, and so now God plans **disaster**. It is in Hebrew the same word, which can refer to calamity or to moral evil. This word-play is frequently used by the prophets to show that the calamities the LORD brings on his erring people are not arbitrary, but in response to their wrongdoing. The disaster **from which you cannot save yourselves** will be like a yoke put on an animal's neck so that it could pull a plough or a cart. No matter how the animal twisted and struggled it could not rid itself of the yoke. In the same way they will be unable to escape the coming punishment. **You will no longer walk proudly**. 'Walk' embraces every aspect of their conduct. Their total life-style has been characterised by pride towards God and their neighbours. God's judgment measures up to their offence and brings their haughtiness to an end. **It will be a time of calamity**, using the same word as is translated 'disaster' earlier in the verse. The same principle still applies. 'Do not be deceived: God cannot be mocked. A man reaps what he sows' (Gal. 6:7).

In that day (*verse 4*) when the disaster God is planning comes, unspecified **men will ridicule you; they will taunt you with this mournful song**. 'Ridicule' is literally 'take up a proverb' (see on Hab. 2:6). Here the singing of a song of lamentation is in deliberate contrast to what had previously prevailed. **We are utterly ruined; my people's possession is divided up**. It may be that these words had been first sung to describe the situation of those dispossessed by the rich and powerful. **He takes it from me! He assigns our fields to traitors**. The form of the word rendered 'traitors' makes it unlikely that it refers to foreign enemies. Rather it describes those from within the covenant community who had violated God's requirements. Now in the day of God's intervention in judgment against the land, the prosperity of the landowners is reversed. Those who sang first of themselves now turn the words in bitter derision against those who had oppressed them.

Micah then addresses a further explanation to the rich as a group. **Therefore you will have no one in the assembly of the LORD to divide the land by lot** (*verse 5*). When Israel occupied Canaan, the land was divided between tribes by lot (Josh. 18:8-10). Micah looks forward to the day when God will convene the sacred assembly of the people for the purpose of redistributing the land. Those who have violated his covenant requirements will then have no representative or descendant in the assembly of the people. Because of their sin the LORD will no longer recognise them as his, and they will have no portion in the restored land.

In the next section (2:6-11) Micah shows that the rich oppressors were not isolated in the community. They had their supporters. Micah spoke as a prophet of the LORD, but there were others who also claimed to be prophets speaking in the name of the LORD. They, however, presented a different message.

It is not the usual words for 'prophesy' and 'prophet' that are to be found in 2:6,11. Probably the word used here could have ambivalent overtones, not unlike the use of 'preach' in English, as in 'Don't preach at me.' The false prophets wanted to silence Micah and those who agreed with him (their command is addressed to more than one person), and so, **"Do not prophesy," their prophets say. "Do not prophesy about these things"** (*verse 6*). Micah's message was too critical of the influential groups on whom they depended for their livelihood for them to be comfortable. Similar opposition to prophetic warnings are recorded elsewhere (Isa. 30:10; Amos 2:12; 7:10-13). The other prophets were sure **disgrace will not overtake us** (compare 3:11). They were relying on the fact that they were God's covenant people, but without realising that such status required obedient covenant living. The message of the prophets of affluence accepted and reinforced the prevailing optimism that there would be no end to their prosperity, for God would remain with them, no matter what.

It is difficult to be certain who is speaking in 2:7. Some take the first part of the verse to continue the words of the false prophets as they recall the covenant blessings of the house of Jacob and emphasise the goodness of God's promises. 'Such things' as the disaster and judgment Micah was prophesying could not possibly come from their God. Their theology seems to have arisen from a partial acceptance of divine revelation, grasping the promises but de-emphasising the obedience that the LORD required and would reward (Deut. 5:32-33). The NIV, however, presents the first part of 2:7 as Micah's own words. He is trying to prick the conscience of the covenant people, and so says to them, **Should it be said, O house of Jacob: "Is the Spirit of the LORD angry? Does he do such things?"** (*verse 7*). God does not wish to be angry with his people and to utter threats against them because of their misconduct. That is not how he wants to act towards his people. There ought to be no need for such things to be said, nor would there be talk about God's anger and judgment if only his people's loyalty towards him went beyond lip-service and involved a real commitment to the lifestyle his covenant demanded of them.

The use of 'my' in 'my words', referring to the LORD, indicates that
a divine address begins in the second part of 2:7, and it continues to the
end of this section. **Do not my words do good to him whose ways are
upright?** Since what the covenant LORD says to his people tells them
how to behave, it ought to be a source of good, bringing blessing to
those who uprightly observe what is required. But that has not been the
case with Judah. **Lately my people have risen up like an enemy**
(*verse 8*). Within their own land they have acted like marauding troops
returning from battle. The only thought on their mind was to pillage
and plunder. **You strip off the rich robe from those who pass by
without a care.** Unsuspecting travellers have fallen foul of their desire
to snatch all that they can.

Their despicable behaviour has extended to women and children
also, quite contrary to covenant statutes, Exod. 22:22-24 (also Deut.
27:19). **You drive the women of my people from their pleasant
homes** (*verse 9*). For 'drive', see 'be emptied' (Zeph. 2:4). This picks
up a theme that was mentioned in 2:2 also. The action of the oppressors
was destroying the fabric of family life in the land, and not just the
current generation. **You take away my blessing from their children
for ever.** 'My blessing', or 'my glory', may refer to God's majestic
deeds on behalf of his people, and probably here points specifically to
the portion of his land allotted to each family and intended to be handed
down from one generation to the next. The rich are grabbing this land
and so preventing the children from enjoying a privilege that should
have been theirs.

The commands that are found next are addressed not only to the rich
oppressors but also to their sympathisers, those who have condoned
and joined in their covenant violations. They thought they were providing
additional security for themselves as they built up their grand estates.
But the certain verdict of God's judgment comes to them in the words
Get up, go away! (*verse 10*). The victors are themselves divinely
evicted. **This is not your resting place.** Canaan had been given to God's
people as a place of physical rest, and also as the place where they
could enjoy fellowship with him (Deut. 12:9; Ps. 95:11; Heb. 4:8-9).
But though the land had been ideally suited to their needs, now **it is
defiled, it is ruined, beyond all remedy** by their breaches of covenant,
and so they will not be permitted to remain in it. They had broken the
covenant, and so they were not permitted to remain in possession of the
blessings of the covenant (Deut. 30:18; Josh. 23:15-16).

In 2:11, Micah returns to the theme of 2:6 — the false prophet. This technique of reverting to a previous theme has already been used in 1:15, looking back to 1:10, to indicate the end of a section of a speech or writing, and to a certain extent it prepared Micah's hearers for a change of subject in 2:12. The LORD presents a hypothetical, but not impossible, set of circumstances. **If a liar and deceiver comes and says** (*verse 11*). The false prophet is described as a 'liar', literally one 'walking with/in wind and falsehood'. There is no substance to what he says, and so he is a 'deceiver'. But when such a person comes and presents a picture of material prosperity and indulgence (Isa. 56:12), **I will prophesy for you plenty of wine and beer**, then **he would be just the prophet for this people!** God no longer calls them 'my people', but stands apart from them. They would readily acclaim such a person as a true prophet. Those who give people a pleasant message that fits in with what they want to hear are always given a ready reception (Jer. 5:31).

This section stands as a permanent indictment of the misuse of wealth. Scripture does not condemn material blessings, but it recognises very clearly the dangers that ensue when the 'love of money' comes to dominate a life (1 Tim. 6:10). James, in the New Testament, criticises just as strongly as Micah the way in which the rich abuse their economic power to oppress others (Jas. 5:1-6). This need not be just a matter of individual conduct. When we live in a land of relative affluence, we must consider how it is that we behave towards communities and nations that are less prosperous. The temptation to pursue a course of action which is to our advantage just because we have the power and economic muscle to do it (2:2) must always be resisted. Might does not make right. Rather 'do not withhold good from those who deserve it, when it is in your power to act' (Prov. 3:27). The rich — the individual and also the community — are to do good, to be generous and willing to share (1 Tim. 6:18).

We must also watch how it is that we form our opinion of ourselves. There are always those who will flatter the rich. 'Men praise you when you prosper' (Ps. 49:18), and especially if they think some of that prosperity might come their own way. It is only in the light of the searching standards of God's word that we may truly assess our conduct. We must take care that our lives are not spent just storing up things for ourselves, without considering where we stand in relation to God (Luke 12:21,34).

Study questions: Micah 2:1-11

verse 1: What dangers does Scripture associate with wealth and material prosperity? (Deut. 8:17; Job 31:24-25, 28; Pss. 49:6-7; 52:7; Ecc. 4:8; Luke 8:14; Rev. 3:17)

What attitude should be adopted towards wealth and possessions? (Prov. 3:9-10; Matt. 25:27; 1 Cor. 16:2; 2 Cor. 8:2)

How may power be misused? (Luke 3:12-14; 19:8; Jas. 5:1-6)

verse 2: What are the consequences of coveting? (Ps. 39:6; Prov. 1:18-19; Eph. 5:5) How may we guard against them? (Matt. 6:33; Phil. 4:10-13; Jas. 4:2)

verse 6: How may we test the claims of those who say they are bringing the word of God? (Deut. 13:1-5; 18:17-22; Matt. 7:15-23; 2 Tim. 3:8; 4:3-4)

Micah 2:12-13: The LORD At Their Head

There is now a sudden switch in the theme of Micah's message, from judgment to hope. There are other passages in the Old Testament, such as Psalm 13:5 and Hosea 1:10, where hope suddenly brightens a previously dark scene, but it seems improbable that Micah would have relayed these words to the people of Jerusalem immediately after the message of condemnation that precedes them in the text. That would have been to endorse the approach of the prophets who were opposing him, for they promised peace and security from the LORD no matter how the people behaved.

It will not do, however, to argue that 3:1 is the natural continuation of 2:11, and that therefore these two verses have been misplaced. The problem is solved when we recognise that this is not the order in which Micah proclaimed his message in Jerusalem probably in the earlier years of Hezekiah's reign, around 710 BC. Rather the order is a feature of the way he later wrote up the substance of his prophetic ministry, perhaps in the aftermath of Sennacherib's invasion of 701 BC. Each of the three main sections of his prophecy (chapters 1-2, 3-5, and 6-7) were similarly structured: first exposure of sin, then judgment, and after that restoration and blessing. This arrangement underscored that while judgment would undoubtedly come from the LORD upon his erring people, it was never going to be his last word on their destiny. Before 701 BC, Micah had given such encouragement to those in Judah who were loyal to the LORD, and who were perplexed as to what would follow the devastation foreshadowed in chapter 1 or the threatenings of 2:10. Later, in writing up his message, he continued the same theme, because he realised that though conditions had temporarily improved, the repentance professed by Judah was superficial. There still lay ahead an even more severe time of judgment through which the faith of those who were the LORD's would have to be sustained. We too may learn from this bright glimpse of the salvation of God to look beyond whatever darkens the immediate prospects of God's people to the time 'when the day dawns and the morning star rises' (2 Pet. 1:19).

The details of the passage have proved difficult to interpret even for those who accept that they are found in the right place. Some, following the lead of Luther and Calvin, have considered that the transition from judgment to blessing is too sharp to be allowed, and have argued instead that what is presented here is the LORD gathering his people to lead them into judgment. But this does not easily fit in with the picture at the end of 2:13 'the LORD at their head'. The tone at that point is one of victory rather than of impending punishment.

But if this is a scene of deliverance, where and when is it to be located? There seem to be two main possibilities. (1) A case may be made for interpreting it as coming after the situation envisaged in 2:10 has arisen, with the people led off into exile. These verses would then refer to the return of the Jews from Babylon. There is, however, a difficulty with this, because in that case 2:12 and 2:13 would seem to be in the wrong order. If 2:13 is a picture of the people breaking out from the imprisonment of Babylon, it should surely come before the picture of security that is presented in 2:12? It is certainly improbable that Babylon itself would be presented in 2:12 as a pen and a pasture for the people of God during the exile. Indeed Babylon does not seem to have featured up to this point in Micah's message.

(2) There is much to be said for another interpretation which views 2:12-13 against the background of the threatened invasion with which chapter 1 had ended. That invasion would sweep through Judah, but though the Assyrians wreaked havoc and captured many important towns in the land, Jerusalem did not fall (2 Kgs. 18,19). Chapter 1 had ended with the land invaded, and Jerusalem with a noose around its neck. In this section Micah foretold to those who put their trust in the LORD that he would provide safety for them. Because that deliverance has many features in common with the other gracious acts of the LORD on behalf of his own, there are many parallels that may be traced.

The dominant note of 2:12 is that of certainty: no longer the certainty of the LORD's judgment, but of his deliverance. **I will surely gather. I will surely bring together** (*verse 12*). The promises of God are not vague aspirations, but settled and reliable. The situation is one where the people have been scattered, possibly in terror before the advancing enemy army, and the divine Shepherd is going to round up his dispersed flock. The theme of gathering is taken up again at 4:6-7.

I will bring them together like sheep in a pen, like a flock in its pasture. His care of them will be complete, extending to security in the pen and nourishment in the pasture. Jerusalem became this place of security in Sennacherib's invasion.

The three sections of the prophecy that focus on the hope that Micah brought to the people share the theme of the Shepherd. It is found again in the description of the LORD's deliverer in 5:4, 'He will stand and shepherd his flock in the strength of the LORD, in the majesty of the name of the LORD his God', and also in the prayer of 7:14, 'Shepherd your people with your staff, the flock of your inheritance.' The links that Micah himself introduces in chapter 5 between the shepherding and the Messiah make it natural to see in the deliverance the LORD provided for his people at that time a foreshadowing of the deliverance he provides through the Good Shepherd of the sheep (John 10:11).

There are two descriptions given of the people who are gathered — **all of you, O Jacob** and **the remnant of Israel**. These are alternative identifications of the same group, occurring in parallel lines of the text. 'Jacob' is a reference to the true covenant people. The principle Paul states of 'not all who are descended from Israel are Israel' (Rom. 9:6) applies here. It is not physical descent that counts but spiritual. The promise that the divine Shepherd will ensure that none of his flock is missing (John 10:27-29) refers to those who are loyal in heart to the LORD, and whose living evidences that loyalty. Those whose behaviour reveals their alienation in heart from God (2:1-11) are excluded.

'Remnant' is a two-sided word. In the first instance it speaks of disaster and loss ahead. Israel as a people will not emerge unscathed from the scrutiny and outpouring of divine judgment. But there is promise in it too. It will not be a total catastrophe, for there will be a divinely preserved remnant. It will consist of 'all', and the picture is of the vast number involved in that 'all'. **The place will throng with people**. The picture moves from sheep to people. The place (Jerusalem) will hum with noise because so many people will find protection within its walls.

There is another presentation of the LORD as his people's deliverer in 2:13 — not now as the Shepherd, but as the Breaker. We no longer hear the LORD himself speaking. The quotation marks of the NIV are misplaced, and should come at the end of 2:12, not 2:13. This is now the voice of the prophet, not relaying the LORD's words, but speaking about him and presenting for us another future scene he has been permitted to see. It is a different picture. The vision of the shepherd and the sheep had already faded by the end of 2:12.

Now we are presented with a view of the people hemmed in by their enemies in Jerusalem. But the day of liberation from their confinement has arrived. The **one who breaks open the way** (*verse 12*) has arrived. In this too we have a picture of Christ, though one that I don't think is found in these precise terms elsewhere. What he does is described by a word that could be used for breaking down the wall of a captured city (2 Kgs. 14:13). It was also used of divine anger breaking out against those who have offended God (Exod. 19:22). It can also mean to urge someone to a particular course of action (1 Sam. 28:23). It is a word which speaks of power that sweeps all obstacles before it, effectively undermining and demolishing all that would resist it. It is a presentation of the LORD as a warrior overthrowing his enemies (Isa. 42:13; Jer. 9:16-19).

But the picture is not that of a liberator who comes from outside to release those who are confined within some prison. The movement both of the liberator and the liberated in this verse is from within outwards. Not only is freedom provided for them by another, but it is by one who has been with them, who has identified with them, and who has shared in their lot (Heb. 2:14).

Mention is made of **the gate**, and this recalls the two previous occurrences of this word in 1:9 and more especially in 1:12, both referring to Jerusalem. We notice that **they will break through the gate and go out** because the breaker, the liberator, had done so first of all. Their deliverance is only possible because he **will go up before them** through the gap made in the encircling enemy lines and provide the path they follow. He is the captain of their salvation (the 'Pioneer of their salvation', Heb. 2:10, *Amplified Bible*; Heb. 6:20), and he is trailblazing the path his people have to follow. As Hosea had prophesied, the rescue extended to Judah did not depend on human effort, but came from the LORD himself (Hos. 1:7; Isa. 37:36).

The liberator, the one who breaks through the barriers and obstacles for them, is also **their king** who **will pass through before them**. We then see in the words **the LORD at their head** that merging which occurs also in Micah 5, where the one who will be ruler over Israel stands and shepherds his flock in the strength of the LORD. If it is not identification — and it may well be that — it certainly shows God's approval of him, something that the kings of Judah they had known had frequently lacked. Here is the king in whom the ideal of kingship would be realised, and of whom the LORD would so approve that he is prepared to identify with him and his actions. In that it is fitting to see a foreshadowing of Christ and his ministry.

Study questions: Micah 2:12-13
verse 12: Scripture frequently compares the relationship between God and his people to that between a shepherd and his flock. What do Ezekiel 34 and John 10:1-21 tell us about this relationship?
verse 13: In what ways does the salvation of God break through the hostile forces that surround his people? (Isa. 42:7,13; 59:16-21; 61:1-7; 1 Cor. 15:21-26; Heb. 2:9-15)

Micah 3:1-12: Exploitation Denounced
Micah 3-5 constitutes the second portion of the prophecy, marked as the others are by an initial summons to hear. This section follows the same general pattern as the first: exposure of evil, the LORD's condemnation of those involved, and then a message of hope and deliverance. But this time Micah alters the proportions of these themes, and says much more about the coming deliverance in chapters 4 and 5. Chapter 3, however, focuses on what was wrong in Judah in Micah's day.

Micah exposes the malpractice, motivated by greed, of three main groups in the land — rulers, prophets, priests — before going on to oppose their theology and overturn it. In 3:1-4 and also 3:9 he forthrightly presents his critique of the rulers for their perverse motivation (3:2,9), unsparing brutality (3:2-3,10), and greed (3:11). The focus is on the false prophets in 3:5,11. The inevitability of the LORD's judgment on all this is found in 3:12. In 3:8, in passing, Micah gives an impassioned statement of how it was that he came to act as a prophet.

The first section of the chapter covers 3:1-4. **Then I said** (*verse 1*) has caused considerable perplexity to commentators. Ordinarily it would form part of a conversation, but no background is given. Some have suggested it is to be understood as a continuation from 2:11. Micah is telling us what his preaching was in contrast to that of the false prophets. But it is not necessary to take 2:12-13 as intruding into an original block of material. The words may simply be resumptive, and could well indicate the major role that Micah himself played in producing the book that bears his name in the form we now have it.

Listen calls for attention. The summons is repeated, 'Hear this!' in 3:9. (The original words are the same on both occasions.) **You leaders of Jacob, you rulers of the house of Israel** both refer to the Southern Kingdom. Samaria had by this time been captured, and Micah uses the pair of names, Jacob and Israel, to address his hearers in Judah in their capacity as the surviving representatives of the people of God. Their nation was not just a political entity, but a people who derived their existence and constitution from the LORD himself. The description points to the basis of the following denunciation of their behaviour. They were not upholding the standards the LORD expected to be maintained by his covenant people.

The 'leaders' had originally been heads of households and tribes who sat in judgment in disputes, but by this time the reference is probably to the court officials in Jerusalem. The 'rulers' were literally the 'deciders' — a reference perhaps not only to the judiciary but also to the civil administration. The charge is put to them, **Should you not know justice?** That was what would be expected of the officials in the capital (Deut. 1:16-17; 16:18; 2 Chr. 19:7-8; Ps. 82). But the question implies they do not. It is not merely acquaintance with the law of the land that is lacking, as if they had not sufficiently studied the law codes they were administering. It is rather practical knowledge. As they claim to be rulers deriving their legitimacy from God's covenant, so their actions and decisions should reflect what is just and proper according to the norms the LORD had established for his people. These norms should have structured the way in which the civil affairs of the land were conducted. Justice, for the prophets, was never merely the product of man's ethical speculation. It was grounded in the revelation of God's will.

We then have a description of their perverse behaviour, for they are those who **hate good and love evil** (*verse 2*). Scripture frequently reminds us of the clear division between good and evil. All too often we, like the people of Micah's day, prefer to fudge issues and consider all grey. But there is no middle ground in the divine evaluation, and we must be forced to come to a decision about the rights and wrongs of our conduct. The rulers were not making abstract statements about hating good and loving evil. It was from their conduct rather than their profession that the judgment was made. 'A tree is recognised by its fruit' (Matt. 12:33).

The picture, then, in the rest of 3:2 and in 3:3 is a brutal one. It goes beyond comparisons made elsewhere of evil rulers to wild animals (Ezek. 22:27; Zeph. 3:3). Some have likened it to cannibalism. Certainly the language is that of butchering an animal whose skin is stripped from it, and the meat separated from the bones. **Who tear the skin from my people and the flesh from their bones** is a picture of callous indifference to human suffering. It is also a picture of exploitation. They **eat my people's flesh, strip off their skin and break their bones in pieces** (*verse 3*). 'Eating people' or 'eating their flesh' was used of the brutal oppression of the wicked (Pss. 14:4; 53:4; Hab. 3:14). Micah builds up the picture in even greater detail so that we may recoil from it with increased revulsion. They **chop them up like meat for the pan, like flesh for the pot**. Perhaps such a description would serve to stir the consciences even of those who were so cruelly exploiting their fellow citizens.

There is here again (see on 1:8-9) a note of the prophet's identification with those who are suffering. They are 'my people' (3:2-3). He identifies with them as they undergo suffering and harsh treatment. The intensity of his language is born out of his sympathy with those who are suffering.

And he envisages a situation of judgment arising. He says **then** (*verse 4*), and **at that time**, but does not specify when that will be. Possibly part of what was originally said has been omitted by Micah, and these other words made the reference clear. Perhaps it refers back to 2:3. We are certainly meant to understand that the day of retribution will not remain an indefinite threat to those whose behaviour does not conform to the norms of the covenant, but will at the time of God's determination surely overtake them.

They will cry out to the LORD refers to an appeal to a superior for help in time of trouble. Psalm 107 records the LORD's intervention in response to the cry of his repentant people (Ps. 107:6,13,19,28). **But he will not answer them**. This situation is different (Ps. 18:41; Prov. 28:9; Isa. 1:15; Zech. 7:13). Those who have despised their covenant obligations will not be able to avail themselves of their overlord's assistance in the day of calamity. Their sin separates them from their God (Isa. 59:2-3). **He will hide his face from them** indicates a terrible abandonment by God, when he does not extend his favour to relieve distress (Deut. 31:17-18; Ps. 13:1). **Because of the evil they have done** gives the reason for God's revulsion at their actions and his condemnation of them. It may perhaps go further and express the

measure of the divine sentence. It could be translated 'according to all
the evil they have done.' His requital is just and fits the crime. They
have not listened to those seeking justice when they cried out to them,
and so he turns from their entreaties as they suffer.

The second section of the chapter (3:5-8) concerns the prophets —
false and true. Micah here records, **This is what the LORD says** (*verse
5*), but it is not clear precisely where the divine speech begins. The NIV
starts it immediately **"As for the prophets who lead my people
astray"**, and this stresses the LORD's recognition of the bond between
himself and his people. An equally valid translation is 'about the
prophets who lead my people astray.' In that case we again have Micah
speaking out of his fellow feeling for those with whom he personally
identifies, and it is the words of judgment from God in 3:6 that are a
direct citation.

Now the problem was to recognise a false prophet when you
encountered one. These men were not obviously false. They were not
Baal prophets, but claimed to speak in the name of the LORD. They were
establishment figures, and seem to have been associated with the
temple. They were influential, and given a great deal of respect by the
rulers of the land. Perhaps these prophets reflect what happened when
the schools of the prophets no longer had an Elijah or an Elisha at their
head. History has certainly shown that no institutions can degenerate
so quickly as theological colleges. The false prophets were men
seeking to perpetuate a theological tradition. They would quote
Scripture, and seek to apply its truth to their own day. But they quoted
only half the message, and their applications fell short. They failed
utterly to see the distinctive experience that a true prophet like Micah
had had.

By describing their self-interested behaviour (Matt. 7:15; Rom.
16:18), the LORD exposes that these men have not been sent by him. **If
one feeds them**, provides them with money or reward, **then they
proclaim 'peace'**. That is, of course, more than just an absence of war.
'Peace' embraces a good relationship with God and all the blessings
of the prosperity he bestows. If you paid them enough, these prophets
would say, 'All will be well.' They sanctioned the conduct of those
who paid them, letting them hear what they wanted to hear. This was
not necessarily done in a blatant way. As 3:11 shows, the prophets
could and did provide a theological justification for their words of
blessing. But their primary motivation was not to expound the word of
God, but material self-interest. Anyone who did not support them with

goods or money became a target for them. **If he does not, they prepare to wage war against him**. It is 'sanctify war against him'. In the name of religion and God, using it to cover their real motives for opposing him, they would launch a crusade against him.

Therefore (*verse 6*) introduces the divine condemnation that inevitably ensues. It is a fourfold picture of the blackness and gloom of disaster (Isa. 8:22). **Night will come over you ... and darkness ... The sun will set for the prophets, and the day will go dark for them**. As Amos emphasised, the day of the LORD's intervention in judgment is 'pitch-dark, without a ray of brightness' (Amos 5:20) for those who are alienated from God. For these false prophets a further element is added to this extraordinary darkness in that it will be **without visions**. Night-time was usually associated with the receiving of visions, but in this situation the prophets will be unable to provide an explanation for what is going on. It will be **without divination**, which tried to obtain information about the future by examining omens. This was condemned in Israel, though common in surrounding nations. But no matter what method the prophets use to find out about the future, it will not work for them. In the darkness of divine visitation their methods will be shown up for what they are.

So in their failure **the seers will be ashamed and the diviners disgraced** (*verse 7*) leading to shocked despair. **They will all cover their faces** in a gesture of shame or grief (Lev. 13:45; Ezek. 24:17). There is nothing that they can relay to their patrons **because there is no answer from God**. Even their charlatanry fails them.

In the third section of the chapter Micah strongly dissociates himself from such prophets, **But as for me** (*verse 8*). He has not preserved for us any narrative about his call from the LORD, but here he shows us clearly the basis for his being a prophet. Like Paul (compare 2 Cor. 11:10-12; 12:11; Eph. 3:7-9), he does not do this to attract attention to himself, but to vindicate the message he is presenting from the LORD. **I am filled with power, with the Spirit of the LORD, and with justice and might.** The NIV translation fails to show that 'with the Spirit of the LORD' is not expressed in the same way as the other three endowments (compare the translations of the AV and NASB). It is the foundation of his being a prophet of the LORD — his Spirit has come and equipped him for the task. Micah has been given in full measure 'power' to persevere in presenting an unpopular message and opposing what was contrary to the LORD's will (2 Cor. 10:5). 'Justice' (compare 3:1) is that commitment to the standards of the LORD's covenant which was so lacking in Judah's rulers and prophets. That is how Micah knew what was right or wrong, rather than having his perception influenced by bribes (3:11). 'Might' refers to the courage a warrior displays when he goes out unflinchingly to meet the opposing army. The same boldness of speech was displayed by the early church (Acts 4:13,31; Eph. 6:19-20).

These gifts have been given to Micah **to declare to Jacob his transgression, to Israel his sin**. For the combination of 'Jacob' and 'Israel' see 2:12, and for 'sin' and 'transgression' see on 1:13. Micah did not choose his message to win popularity from the rich and newly influential of his day. His message was given him by God and was true to the requirements of the covenant. He addressed the spiritual needs of a community that had twisted aside from God's standards and forgotten his ways. His task was to confront them in the LORD's name with their shortcomings.

The mention of Jacob and Israel links in with the following address to the ruling classes in Jerusalem. **Hear this, you leaders of the house of Jacob, you rulers of the house of Israel** (*verse 9*). The description of 3:9 matches that of 3:1-2. In both places there is a surprising omission. There is no mention of the king, most likely Hezekiah. Perhaps Micah does not mention him out of respect for the reforms that he had instituted, though the reforms did not accomplish all that he wished. But he has no respect for those in the corridors of power because they **despise justice and distort all that is right**. 'Despise' is a strong word for expressing the utter contempt in which they hold God's law and twist to their own advantage standards of right and wrong (Prov. 17:15).

The administrators **build Zion with bloodshed, and Jerusalem with wickedness** (*verse 10*). This may well refer to the massive building programmes of Hezekiah's day. There had been a substantial influx of population from the North after the fall of Samaria. Archaeological data suggests that in the late eighth century Jerusalem grew to three or four times its previous size. Hezekiah also undertook a considerable number of public works in connection with his moves to defend the city against the Assyrians. Those who managed these schemes and supervised the forced labour involved are accused of acting without regard to life (presumably of the workers) or to the rights of those who owned land or materials. Later instances of similar behaviour are mentioned in Jeremiah 22:13-16 and Habakkuk 2:12.

Her leaders judge for a bribe, her priests teach for a price, and

her prophets tell fortunes for money (*verse 11*) spells out the venality that controlled the whole of the Jerusalem establishment. The justiciary was corrupt. Decisions went in favour of those who could pay the most. 'A bribe blinds the eyes of the wise and twists the words of the righteous' (Deut. 16:19). The priests had the task of teaching the law of God (Lev. 10:11; Mal. 2:7), but this they will do only if they are paid for it, over and above the ordinary payments made to support them. The prophets' perception of what was required of them was blurred by overwhelming greed. They had become mere fortune tellers.

Yet they lean upon the LORD. The physical act of putting one's weight on a staff or someone's arm for support is used as a metaphor for relying on someone and trusting them for guidance and assistance. The false prophets and the rest of the establishment of Judah did not appreciate how their behaviour had diverged from what the LORD required. 'They claim to know God, but by their actions they deny him' (Tit. 1:16). They continued to profess faith in him, and claimed the blessings of the covenant as theirs by right. **Is not the LORD among us? No disaster will come upon us**. They argued that the LORD had given an irrevocable commitment to be with his people and to preserve them. Such a view would have been reinforced by the deliverance of 701 BC, when Sennacherib had been divinely removed from the gates of Jerusalem (2 Kgs. 19:35-36). 'The LORD among us' was indeed a precious truth at the heart of Israel's covenant faith (Exod. 17:7; Ps. 46:7; Jer. 14:9), but the requirements of a holy God have to be met for this to be a comfortable truth to be lived with. God had made his blessing on his people dependent on their good conduct (Lev. 26; Deut. 28).

There again follows an announcement of judgment, preceded by **therefore** (*verse 12*) to link their behaviour with the penalty the LORD is imposing. **Because of you** indicates that as a direct result of the perverse reasoning and unjust behaviour displayed by the Jerusalem elite, they were going to experience the opposite of what they claimed would happen. Micah has not up to this point directly spoken of the destruction of the city of Jerusalem. Now, in words that came true with the fall of Jerusalem to the Babylonians in 586 BC, he says it will be a second Samaria (compare the description in 1:6). The very place they had felt secure will be conquered and devastated. **Zion**, which they had been so corruptly building, **will be ploughed like a field, Jerusalem will become a heap of rubble**. The verbs are passive. No agent is indicated. We are to understand it to be the work of the LORD. How true are the words of Solomon! 'Unless the LORD builds the house, its builders labour in vain' (Ps. 127:1).

The temple hill a mound overgrown with thickets does not just complete the picture of the physical destruction of the city. It indicates the fundamental cause of the disaster. Because of their sin, the LORD has departed from the midst of his people. Consequently the temple which was the symbol of his presence will also be taken away. God has left his people. It is a picture of total spiritual disaster, and one that clashed head on with the theology of the optimistic prophets. One is reminded that after denouncing the teachers of the law and the Pharisees in Matthew 23 for their misuse of their privileges, Jesus foretold the end of the temple that existed in their time (Matt. 24:2). Privilege is the measure of our responsibility, and there is ever the threat of God's chastisement if we do not live up to what we profess.

But there is one bright footnote to this prophecy. So often we wonder if all the prophets said fell on deaf ears. But we know that this prophecy was remembered by the elders of the land a century later and was used to secure Jeremiah's release (Jer. 26:18). This narrative incidentally shows us that in Jeremiah's time Micah was acknowledged as a true prophet of the LORD. Even more significantly, the elders' argument in Jeremiah 26:19 shows the impact of Micah's message in his own day. 'Did not Hezekiah fear the LORD and seek his favour? And did not the LORD relent, so that he did not bring the disaster he pronounced against them?' The LORD gave warning of his impending judgment so that there might be repentance among his people (Jer. 18:7-10). Unfortunately the people did not learn the lesson for long.

Study questions: Micah 3:1-12

verse 1: Those who speak on behalf of the Lord are directed to do so without consideration of the social or political status of those whom they address. What other instances can you find of fearless proclamation of what God wants to be known? (1 Kgs. 17:1; Matt. 14:4; Acts 4:13, 18-20, 31; Gal. 2:6,11)

verse 4: See Study Guide: Jonah, 1:6.

verse 8: There are many Old Testament passages which record God's Spirit coming upon individuals (for instance, Exod. 31:3; Num. 11:17; 27:18; Judg. 6:34; 1 Sam. 10:6; 1 Chr. 12:18; 28:12). What did this signify? Is it different from the way the Spirit is given in the New Testament? (Luke 24:49; Acts 1:8; 2:4; Eph. 3:16)

verse 11: What causes people to have a false sense of security as regards their future destiny? (Gen. 11:4; Isa. 28:14-19; 30:1-5; Rom. 2:3-4,17-27; Gal. 6:7-8; 1 Thess. 5:3)

Micah 4:1-8: Zion's Exaltation

Our notion of what was involved in being a prophet is very often oriented towards telling what lies in the future. But it is wrong to think of that as the essence of the role of an Old Testament prophet. His task was to be God's covenant messenger, telling the people of the LORD what he wanted them to know. Inevitably, as the LORD is the one who has all history under his control, the messages he gave his spokesmen to deliver could range over the past, the present and the future. But the information about the future was never given merely to satisfy our human craving to know what tomorrow will bring. It was a message controlled and shaped by the LORD's desire either to warn his people against the judgment that would follow if they persisted in their rebellious behaviour, or to encourage those who were loyal to him to remain so despite difficulties and catastrophes. By revealing the glory that yet awaited his people on the other side of the darkness, he strengthened them to endure steadfastly. It is this aspect of the prophetic message that Micah records for us in chapter 4.

There are two parts to the chapter, with a break after 4:8 where the time scale of Micah's vision is altered. In 4:1 he mentions 'the last days', and presumably referring to the same period, he talks in 4:6 of 'that day'. In the original, however, 4:9 begins with the word 'now', and the same word occurs at the start of 4:11, 'but now'. The third stanza of the poem continues in the next chapter and again, in the original, is introduced by 'now' (5:1), but not rendered so in the NIV translation. It would seem that these references to 'now' are about the more immediate future (see on 4:9), whereas in this first section Micah is granted a view further into the future.

In the last days (*verse 1*) points us forward to a time of whose date the prophet is uncertain. The phrase is literally 'at the back of the days', with the future being thought of as behind one, and therefore unable to be perceived. The prophet, however, has been given a view of the future by God. But even on these occasions when God gave such a vision, the precise timing of events was often left obscure (1 Pet. 1:10). Indeed the prophet's situation has often been likened to that of an observer looking at a landscape where there is a succession of ever higher hills. From one angle each peak may seem to lie immediately behind the one in front. But move round and look at them from a

different viewpoint, and there can often be disclosed hitherto unsus-
pected valleys — perhaps miles wide — between the successive
summits that had at first seemed so close. It may well be that Micah's
vision is from the first type of viewpoint. He is not permitted to see the
intervening valleys, and so his description merges features of various
periods when the LORD will decisively intervene in history. Certainly
this prophecy was not exhausted by the return of the Jews from
Babylon, though in such an event we can readily detect a partial
fulfilment of it.

There is another major interpretative problem that this prophecy
poses for us. The prophecy talks about the temple, Zion and Jerusalem.
Are we to understand these references as being to sites in Palestine, so
that we are being told about some restored Jewish state that will arise
before the consummation of all things? There are many problems with
such an approach, and it seems preferable to understand Micah as
having the future revealed to him in terms of realities that existed in his
own day. To make sense to us the future has to be described in terms
of what we are already familiar with, even though in retrospect such
a description is seen to be deficient in many ways. So for Micah, Israel
was the people of God, but that has now been extended and transferred
to the church (Gal. 6:16; 1 Pet. 2:9-10). The significance of Jerusalem
and the temple was that they were where God was pleased to reveal
himself in a special way. That role is now taken over by the Christian
church (1 Cor. 3:16; Heb. 12:22). The children of Abraham and
inheritors of the promises made to the patriarchs are now found
throughout the world, wherever the same faith as Abraham's exists
(Gal. 3:29). And yet, neither the return of the Jews from Babylon, nor
the expansion of the Christian church exhausts this prophecy. They
were occasions when the sovereignty and power of the LORD were no
longer obscured and acknowledged only by faith, and as such they
foreshadowed the ultimate revelation of glory which will be fully
realised when the Son of Man returns. It is then that this vision will
receive its complete fulfilment.

The picture of the future Micah has revealed to him is painted in
terms of features and institutions he already knew well. Incidentally,
the prophecy is also found in Isaiah 2:1-4, though we are unable to say
definitively with which prophet, if either, it originated. But it may well
have been with Micah in that there is an effective contrast between the
devastated temple mountain of 3:12 and the glorious mountain (same
word in the original) he now describes, **when the mountain of the**

LORD's temple will be established as chief among the mountains. The temple was the symbol of the LORD's dwelling with his people, and was where he especially revealed himself to them (1 Kgs. 8:10-11). It was built on mount Zion, which at 730 metres (2,400 feet) was not particularly high. The passive 'will be established' indicates the action that the LORD takes to ensure that all rivals to him will be seen in their true light. The religions of the ancient world frequently viewed mountains as homes of their gods, and so what is being stressed here is the incomparability of where the LORD has chosen to manifest his presence, and the incomparability of the LORD himself. **It will be raised above the hills** need not refer to a physical exaltation of Zion hill. The truth being conveyed by the imagery is spiritual: the supremacy of the LORD will be incontestably evident (Ps. 68:16).

The picture is not just of future prosperity for Israel. **Peoples will stream to it** envisages a universal recognition of the sovereign rights of the LORD. Israel's religion had always had this universal note. When the LORD called Abraham, he promised him 'all peoples on earth will be blessed through you' (Gen. 12:3), and this wider vision of God's saving purpose was always part of Israel's faith (Ps. 22:27; Isa. 66:20).

Three times a year all Israelite males had to present themselves to worship the LORD at the sanctuary (Deut. 16:16). The pilgrim festivals of Israel will be international in their scope. **Many nations will come and say, "Come, let us go up to the mountain of the LORD, to the house of the God of Jacob"** (*verse 2*). They are presented as doing this with enthusiasm, and also with right motives. (Compare Ps. 122:1.) **He will teach us his ways, so that we may walk in his paths.** It is not as tourists going sightseeing that the nations will come to Jerusalem. They are there as disciples who want to take full advantage of the teaching available in the temple. They are eager to learn how the LORD would have them live their lives in accordance with his will (compare Ps. 25:4).

In the second part of 4:2, Micah adds another dimension to this picture of Zion's exaltation. Not only will all nations converge on Jerusalem, but there will be a reverse movement whereby the standards of the LORD will be disseminated throughout the earth. **The law will go out from Zion, the word of the LORD from Jerusalem**. The word for 'law' is connected with that used for 'teach' in 'he will teach.' It is broader than the commandments of the Mosaic law, and includes all that God has revealed to Israel. That word spreads out in its transforming power as the gospel is proclaimed (Luke 24:47; Acts 1:8; Rom. 15:19).

There are then presented three aspects of what follows on from the international acknowledgment of Zion's God and acceptance of his revealed will.

(1) Nations will no longer have to go to war to settle disputes. This will be done by God. **He will judge between many peoples and will settle disputes for strong nations far and wide** (*verse 3*). A time is envisaged when all reasons for strife will be removed because of a common submission to the standards of the LORD and his enforcement of them (Pss. 96:13; 98:9; Isa. 11:3-5). How magnificent this prospect still seems, but even more so when viewed from Palestine. Over the centuries it has frequently been the battleground for the conflicts of neighbours to the north and south of her.

(2) In a picture that is the opposite of that found in Joel 3:10, national resources will be put to productive rather than military uses. **They will beat their swords into ploughshares and their spears into pruning hooks. Nation will not take up sword against nation, nor will they train for war any more.** International suspicion and tension result in the stockpiling of weapons, military manoeuvres, and training schools which use up a considerable proportion of a nation's assets. Disarmament releases these resources for better purposes. But we must not forget that the disarmament conference which has brought about these spectacular results has been between the nations and God. They have first to lay aside their hostility toward him, before there can be a true and lasting basis for them laying aside their hostility to one another.

(3) There follows a picture of idyllic satisfaction, again couched in Palestinian terms (Zech. 3:10). **Every man will sit under his own vine and under his own fig tree, and no one will make them afraid** (*verse 4*). Israel had already enjoyed this for a brief period during the reign of Solomon (1 Kgs. 4:25; 5:4), but it awaited a greater than Solomon to inaugurate it on an international scale. It is not a picture of great riches, but of domestic satisfaction. The ideal is that of contentment with the provision the LORD has made for each, and the opportunity to enjoy it without being harried by others. These arrangements have the best guarantee of all. **The LORD Almighty has spoken.** The LORD Almighty ('the LORD of hosts') is the one who has the powers of the universe under his control and so none will be able to overthrow the arrangements he has instituted.

This evokes the response of Micah's hearers. They profess their loyalty to the LORD despite the situation that surrounds them where **all**

the nations may walk in the name of their gods (*verse 5*). This is not
to ascribe any legitimacy to their conduct. It is just to recognise that
other nations do in fact rely upon and worship other gods. However,
the picture of what the LORD will establish strengthens the faith of his
people so that they do not fall in with the conduct of the nations that
surround them. They deliberately dissociate themselves from them.
'As for us' **we will walk in the name of the LORD our God.** 'Walk'
describes the whole conduct of their lives. They will live in faith and
obedience, and the phrase 'in the name' probably goes further and
brings out the aspect of conscious dependence on the strength of the
LORD. It will be **for ever and ever**. Faith sees no end to this loyalty as
it perceives no termination to the LORD's provision.

But the picture of future glory has not yet been related to the present
condition of the LORD's people. They have indeed voiced their anticipation of it, and now the prophet indicates how they are to get there.
"In that day," declares the LORD (*verse 6*) links back to 'in the last
days' of 4:1, and we are presented with the divine action, as God
graciously provides assistance to his stricken people. He does not give
them the promise of glory without also assuring them of his action to
bring them there.

I will gather the lame resumes the shepherd imagery of 2:12,
though the situation has now changed in two respects. It has been
located in the more distant future, and the people have experienced the
LORD's judgment in full. They are presented as exiles who have been
taken from their land in punishment. It is explicitly brought out that
they are **those I have brought to grief**. There is no disguising the
LORD's chastening hand upon his people because of their sin. But now
he acts to gather his afflicted flock. **I will assemble the exiles** is with
a view to their restoration (Isa. 35:3-10; Jer. 31:8; Ezek. 34:13). The
LORD is dealing with those who have faith and encouraging them even
in the experience of divine chastisement of their nation.

I will make the lame a remnant (*verse 7*). The 'lame' do not
automatically constitute a remnant, because the word 'remnant' is
used here to indicate more than just what has been left. To talk of a
remnant after judgment involves hope, because though only part come
through unscathed, yet they do in fact come through (2:12). The
remnant, though personally weak and incapacitated, are a monument
to divine grace. They **had been driven away** by God himself, but they
come back **a strong nation**. **The LORD will rule over them in Mount
Zion**. He will be their king in a city and temple restored to their proper

status (Ps. 48:1-3). The people of God are told about this to comfort and
encourage them to look forward to the eternal rule that will be
established **from that day and for ever**, even as John gives us the
description of the new Jerusalem (Rev. 21,22) so that we may eagerly
await the return of our Lord (Rom. 8:23).

As for you (*verse 8*) introduces a promise. Who is involved is
specified in two titles. **Watchtower of the flock** refers to Jerusalem as
the garrison round which the life of the nation revolved as their king
looked out and surveyed the affairs of his people. They are 'the flock'
of the LORD and Jerusalem will again afford them the security they
need. **O stronghold of the Daughter of Zion**. 'Stronghold' or 'hill'
(NIV, footnote) refers to Ophel, a fortified mound that had been a
feature of Jerusalem since Jebusite days, and which lay to the south of
the temple. Mentioning it here again emphasises the protective role
Jerusalem played at the centre of Israelite life. The descriptions
'Daughter of Zion' and 'Daughter of Jerusalem' do not refer to a group
that is part of, or other than, Zion and Jerusalem. This is rather a
Hebrew poetic mode of expression for the population of these places
as a whole (Isa. 1:8; Lam. 1:6; Zeph. 3:14). The fact that the Hebrew
word for 'city' is grammatically a feminine noun made it easy to
personify cities as women.

To Jerusalem **the former dominion will be restored; kingship
will come to the Daughter of Jerusalem**. The glorious future is seen
in terms of the outworking of the promises made to David, 'Your house
and your kingdom will endure for ever before me' (2 Sam. 7:16). A
king will once more rule in Jerusalem. This is indeed Messianic
prophecy in that the expected deliverance is being associated with the
figure of a king through whom the LORD will establish his rule over his
people.

Blessing will come, but it will only be enjoyed through obedience.
Promises given regarding Zion and Jerusalem will not come true
merely through human effort. They will come about despite the
disobedience of the people and of their king (Ps. 89:30-34), through
the restoring grace of God. Those who truly desired the establishment
of the LORD's rule are encouraged to look forward to the coming king
who would establish the blessing.

Study questions: Micah 4:1-8

verse 1: Future glory is revealed to encourage the faithful to persevere. What significance may prophecy of the future have for the unrepentant? (Ezek. 43:10-12)

How does the New Testament show the international aspect of this prophecy already becoming true? (Matt. 28; Acts 13:47; Rom.15:19; Rev. 5:9)

verse 2: How does Christ act as judge? (Isa. 9:7; 11:3-5; 42:1; Matt. 25:31-32; John 5:22-29; Acts 17:31)

verse 3: In what way should the absence of strife characterise the Christian church? (Isa. 32:16-17; Matt. 5:9; Rom. 14:19; 15:13; 1 Cor. 14:33; Eph. 4:3; Heb. 12:14)

verse 8: When did her king come to Zion? (Matt. 21:5; John 12:15; Rev. 17:14; 19:16)

Micah 4:9-13: The Road to Restoration

In the previous section Micah had moved on in 4:6 from describing the future glory of Zion to indicating that it would only be by divine intervention that this outcome would be achieved. It is this same theme that is continued in the rest of the chapter, but from a different temporal perspective. There are three stanzas (4:9-10; 4:11-13; 5:1-5), which are linked together by the use of the same initial word 'now' in the Hebrew. Each section focuses on a different aspect of the path from present distress to future glory.

'Now' is not just a formal device to structure the prophetic message. It also alerts us to the fact that the time scale is different from the earlier part of the chapter. There are two ways of understanding the word 'now'.

(1) It could point to the present situation at the time Micah spoke or wrote. In that case the historical occasion of these verses must be different from that of chapter 3, where calamity was prophesied on Jerusalem, but it had not yet arrived. The false prophets were still encouraging the people to believe that no disaster would come upon them. Here that disaster has undoubtedly engulfed the city. Also there is the mention in 4:10 of the command to leave the city, that is, Jerusalem, and that did not happen in Micah's day.

(2) The other, more probable, view is that, as in 3:12, Micah's vision stretches forward over a century to the time of the fall of Jerusalem. He is therefore not using 'now' of the historical circum-

stances of his own day, but as a way of vividly portraying what was going to happen in the future. Sometimes the prophets do use 'now' in this way, to describe the imminent activity of the LORD (Isa. 33:10; 43:19), or even activity which is still fairly far in the future (Isa. 29:22). Micah himself certainly uses 'now' in this way in 7:10. (See also the comments on 5:4.) He may well have adopted this use of 'now' in this passage to distinguish the time he is talking of from 'the last days' of 4:1 or 'that day' of 4:6. He knows he is viewing a future scene, but one which stands in some way before the ultimate realisation of Zion's glory.

Why do you now cry aloud? (*verse 9*) describes Zion in panic and distress. The descriptions of 4:10-11 indicate that the city has been surrounded and is under siege. The horrors of siege warfare were considerable as famine and plague reduced the inhabitants of the besieged town to walking skeletons unless they capitulated. So it is a cry of alarm and horror that Zion utters. But what note is to be detected in 'Why?': is it suddenness or sarcasm? The answer to that depends largely on how we understand the other question: **Have you no king?** It seems unlikely that the 'king' referred to is the LORD. There are contexts where the LORD is identified as the king who resides in Jerusalem, as when Jeremiah tells of the cry of the people in exile wondering what has happened to them, 'Is not the LORD in Zion? Is her King no longer there?' (Jer. 8:19). But the parallel expression 'your counsellor' is fairly certainly another way of looking at a human king, and to ask, **Has your counsellor perished?** would be an unusual way to refer to the LORD. It seems then that it is the human ruler of Jerusalem that is spoken about.

While the words might refer to the situation that prevailed in the exile, when Israel had no ruling monarch, the question is most probably sarcastic. The city is under siege. The king on whose wisdom and political manoeuvring they had been placing so much hope is unable to think of a way out of their difficulties (Hos. 10:3; 13:10-11). The prophet upbraids them for their previous attitude and questions them sarcastically. 'What has become of your king whose counsel you so much valued? Why are you afraid in your present circumstances, suddenly caught in distress as **pain seizes you like that of a woman in labour**?' It is a crisis to which they are unable to respond because they are overpowered by it. The comparison is one that is frequently found in the Old Testament for a commanding emotional response that leaves one unable to cope with a situation (Isa. 13:8; 21:3; 26:17; Jer.

22:23; 50:43). They are unable to alleviate or deflect their agony.

Then Micah tells Zion that that is how she should indeed act. **Writhe in agony, O Daughter of Zion, like a woman in labour** (*verse 10*). For 'Daughter of Zion', see on 4:8. The situation they will encounter will truly justify such a response, for they will be experiencing the LORD's judgment. **Now**, in the future situation envisaged, **you must leave the city to camp in the open field**. They had been relying on the false prophets' views of the future. They taught the people that Zion was inviolate, and that they should look back to how the LORD had delivered his people in the past. But Micah reminds them that an Exodus-style deliverance has to be from a foreign land.

You will go to Babylon. Babylon was a significant city in the Assyrian empire, but it was not its capital. This has led many to suspect that this passage is not from Micah's day when Assyria was the aggressor and the future resurgence of Babylon was as yet unanticipated. In view of the way this statement is integrated into its context, it is quite improbable that it was inserted at some later time. Rather we should question the assumptions made about the prevailing perception of Babylon. Babylonian envoys had already come to Hezekiah (Isa. 39), and it is very likely that mention of Babylon in this context of exile shows Micah's familiarity with the prophecy Isaiah had delivered to Hezekiah probably around 705 BC. 'The time will surely come when everything in your palace, and all that your fathers have stored up until this day, will be carried off to Babylon' (Isa. 39:6). Although he will later return to consider Assyria again, the vision granted Micah at this point enables him to relate the circumstances that will prevail at the time of the exile (586 BC). It would be some time before events would demonstrate the falsity of the majority teaching of his own day.

There is twice emphasised in 4:10 to show that it would not be Jerusalem, as was falsely supposed, that would be the scene of the LORD's intervention to deliver his people in the new Exodus. **You will be rescued. The LORD will redeem you out of the hand of your enemies**. 'Rescue' (Exod. 5:23; 18:9-10) and 'redeem' (Exod. 6:6; 15:13) would have taken the minds of the people of Judah back to the events of the Exodus, which formed the basic model for them to grasp what it meant to have God act as their Saviour. He intervenes to rescue his people when they are helpless. Redemption speaks of God's restoring what was once his to its rightful position. The enemies' power will not be a match for the LORD's. Although he will have used their enemies to chastise his people, judgment will not be his last word.

They will be restored, but in such a way as to ensure that all the glory accords to the LORD.

The second stanza of the poem (4:11-13) presents the same cycle of the LORD's people facing disaster and his subsequent intervention to overthrow the plans of those who plot against them. The situation resembles that described in Psalm 2, where the peoples plot in vain against the king of Israel and his God. They do not know that the Lord enthroned in heaven is looking with disdainful laughter at their puny efforts to overthrow the ruler he has established. Judah is being taught to look on her situation from the perspective of heaven.

But now (*verse 11*) brings us back again to the city under siege. It is no minor disaster that would engulf Judah because of the LORD's judgment against her. **Many nations are gathered against you.** The armies of the empires of the day included troops drawn from many different subject peoples. No doubt their various modes of dress marked out the composite nature of those who gathered against Jerusalem. This would serve to emphasise her isolation and seeming helplessness in political terms (Jer. 1:15).

The prophet quotes what would be on the lips of the invading troops. **They say, "Let her be defiled, let our eyes gloat over Zion!"** Their plan is not just to capture and loot her, but to defile her. Presumably this refers to the way they would treat the temple and its precincts. They come haughtily against the LORD's dwelling place, because they act as those who are in defiant rebellion against him. They yearn with malicious desire to gloat over Zion when they have humiliated her. What she experiences arises out of her relationship with the LORD, for the animosity of the enemy is not primarily directed against her but her God (John 15:20).

However, there is another dimension to the situation, one of which the enemy forces are ignorant. **But they do not know the thoughts of the LORD; they do not understand his plan** (*verse 12*). The LORD is using them. He has permitted them to gather against his people, but it is what he wills, and that alone, which will come to pass. In their proud self-confidence they are blind to what is really happening. In fact the LORD is the one **who gathers them like sheaves to the threshing floor**. Threshing floors were open areas of hard ground usually outside the city wall, where the sheaves were taken to be chopped up and the grain loosened by the threshing sledge. An army encamped in siege against a city would often occupy the site used for threshing in more peaceful times.

Then the LORD addresses his people, **O Daughter of Zion**, in the first part of 4:13. He commands them to **rise and thresh**. The threshing would usually be done by an ox pulling the sledge behind it (see on Hab. 2:12). But the picture seems to change from this. **I will give you horns of iron** conveys the power with which the LORD will endow his people for the task for which he commissions them. **I will give you hoofs of bronze and you will break to pieces many nations**. One is reminded of the victory assured to the Messiah (Ps. 2:8-9) because of what the LORD has given him.

The closing words of the verse seem to be those of the prophet himself as he describes the victory that will be granted to the LORD's people. **You will devote their ill-gotten gains to the LORD, their wealth to the Lord of all the earth**. He has seen the promised victory, and is sure of it. He talks rather of the allocation of the spoil. It will be done under the rules of sacred warfare. The enemy's loot will be presented to the LORD and for his service (Isa. 18:7; 60:6-10). It is his by right, for he is 'the Lord of all the earth.' 'Lord' here is Adon, 'master' (as in 1:2), not Yahweh, the covenant name for God. Its use may be a deliberate rejection of the unwarranted claims of some of the pagan rulers. Sennacherib certainly used for himself the title 'King of the world'. But he who truly is 'the King of kings and Lord of lords' (1 Tim. 6:15) is here presented with the booty his conquering people have captured.

Study questions: Micah 4:9-13

verse 9: What does Scripture teach us about relying on man? (Pss. 62:9; 118:8-9; 146:3; Isa. 2:22; 31:3; Jer. 17:5-6; John 2:24-25)

verse 10: What is the significance of 'redemption'? (Lev. 25:25-34; Ruth 3:9; 4:4,6; Acts 20:28; Gal. 3:13; 1 Pet. 1:10-11)

verse 12: What does Scripture teach about the plans of God? (Pss. 40:5; 77:19; Isa. 55:8-9; Matt. 11:25; Rom. 11:33-36)

Micah 5:1-6: The Ruler from Bethlehem

Although the NIV translation does not reproduce the word 'now', Micah uses it to begin 5:1 as he had in 4:9 and 4:11 earlier. For the third time he traces out the path by which Zion's fortunes will be transformed from the hopelessness of siege and exile by the wonder of the LORD's deliverance. But he does not simply repeat the message: each time he looks at matters from a different perspective. The first time he had shown how an Exodus style deliverance would require the people to be in a foreign land, exiled in Babylon. The second time he emphasised the LORD's control over what was happening even though those involved would not be aware of it. Now in the third, culminating description he is able to give a clear picture of the one through whom the LORD will restore the fortunes of his people. Perhaps this is the best known part of Micah's prophecy, when he tells of the Messiah, the kingly ruler, who would come from Bethlehem.

But before he introduces the Messiah, Micah again addresses Zion under siege. **Marshal your troops, O city of troops** (*verse 1*) may also be rendered as 'Strengthen your walls, O walled city' (as in the NIV footnote). The latter follows the Septuagint, the ancient Greek translation of the Old Testament, and involves a slight change in the Hebrew text. The city is clearly Zion. Literally, the address is 'daughter of troops', and is a development of the phrase 'daughter of Zion' (4:10; 4:13) in the previous two pictures, using a Hebrew idiom that means 'warlike city'. Micah has used the terminology of war to describe the crimes perpetrated in Jerusalem (2:8), and perhaps this usage here is ironically contrasting their willingness to engage in warlike activity against their own countrymen with the need to organise themselves to meet the enemy's assault on their city because **a siege is laid against us**. The prophet again identifies with the people, as he does also at the end of the section in 5:6 'our land' and 'our borders'. What happens to them is something that necessarily affects him also.

When did this occur? Some have suggested the reference is to the siege of Jerusalem in 701 BC by Sennacherib. More probably this is a continuation of the series looking forward to the downfall of Jerusalem more than a century later. **They will strike Israel's ruler on the cheek with a rod** points to the utter personal humiliation of the individual who is incapable of defending his face (Job 16:10; Ps. 3:7; Lam. 3:30). It seems to take place after the capture of the city, which did not happen in Hezekiah's day. The word 'ruler' is the same as that used for the judges of Israel after Joshua's time. But this ruler of God's people Israel (the reference is to Judah as the people of God) is unlike the judges of old — he cannot deliver the people. He is unable to rescue himself from personal abuse. The rod which should have functioned as the symbol of his royal authority (Ps. 2:9; Isa. 14:5) is, as it were, snatched from him and used to beat him.

Micah, however, turns from the depressing spectacle of Israel's humiliated king by citing a saying of the LORD which presents a startling contrast. **But you, Bethlehem Ephrathah** (*verse 2*) points away from the besieged city to a place whose very names Bethlehem, 'house of bread', and Ephrathah, 'fertile area', conjure up a vision of prosperity. Ephrathah was an older name for Bethlehem (Gen. 35:19; 48:7) and was also used for the surrounding area. **You are small among the clans of Judah**. The focus is not so much on its physical size, as on its political insignificance. In terms of the traditional subdivisions of the tribe of Judah it had not been very important.

But though as a place Bethlehem had not been particularly well known, it was the birthplace of David, who had been the king after God's own heart (1 Kgs. 9:4; 11:6). So in looking for a new ruler, the LORD says he will go back to the same outwardly unpromising beginning and **out of you will come ... one who will be ruler over Israel**. This is the Messiah, in whom the promises of the Davidic covenant are realised (2 Sam. 7:12-16), a king who will be the means of restoring and exercising the LORD's rule over his people. But the word 'king' is not used here, probably to emphasise the Messiah's acceptance of his subordinate role and his willingness to rule on behalf of the LORD and in his interests. **For me** is given special emphasis, and it, along with the notion of going back to Bethlehem, involves an implicit rejection of later kings who had made their own interests paramount.

Following upon this, we have the enigmatic words **whose origins are from of old, from ancient times**. The NIV translation conveys the truly royal ancestry of the Messiah. The LORD is not rejecting the house of David, but will establish as king one who is a legitimate descendant of that venerable line. But it is possible that the words indicate more than that. The phrase translated 'from ancient times' may be rendered 'from days of eternity', as in the NIV footnote, and could be understood as an ascription of eternal origins to this Ruler. However, 'whose origins' is literally 'his goings forth', picking up the similar word 'he shall go forth' earlier in the verse. It is more probable then that rather than directly indicating something of the personal, eternal origins of this Ruler, the word shows that his acts of going forth do not start with his future appearance, but have already been of old, even from days of eternity or of antiquity. It is in the latter sense that Micah uses the same phrase in 7:14. On either rendering, he expects a more than human figure. He will come in the future, yet his goings forth have also been in the remote past.

Therefore (*verse 3*) serves to bring out the implications of the way the LORD is going to deliver. The Messiah is going to come forth out of lowly circumstances at a time when the Davidic line will have receded into obscurity. In the meantime, however, **Israel will be abandoned** by God to devastation by her enemies and to exile, when her rightful kings will not reign over her. But it will be a limited abandonment. Two conditions are stated to establish its duration.

(1) It will be **until the time when she who is in labour gives birth**. In the light of the prophecy in Isaiah 7:14, which would have preceded Micah's by about thirty years, this may be a reference to Mary. But taken in the context of this threefold cycle of predictions, 'she who is in labour' may just as readily point back to a 'woman in labour' (4:9-10) which refers to Zion undergoing pain and agony until from within her there is born the Messiah (Rev. 12:2).

(2) The second condition is that the people will be abandoned until **the rest of his brothers return to join the Israelites**. Despite the hostility that had often existed between the Northern and Southern Kingdoms, Judah felt it deeply when her brothers in the North were deported. This condition reflects their desire for the people to be reunited. It is as they are brought together again into one that Israel's abandonment by God is brought to an end, and the LORD shows how completely he can reverse the effects of human sin. This was partially fulfilled in the return from the Exile, but supremely so in Christ in whom the whole building is joined together (Eph. 2:21). The Messiah's kingdom is not completely established until there is the unity and harmony of one fold and one Shepherd (Ezek. 37:22; John 10:16).

This thought is taken further in the following description of the Messiah. **He will stand** (*verse 4*) is probably a picture of regal majesty (Hab. 3:6). He **will shepherd his flock**. While the kings of the east frequently took the title of Shepherd, its use in the Old Testament recalls the way in which David was taken by God from being a literal shepherd to oversee his people (2 Sam. 5:2; 7:7-8; Ps. 78:70-72). The king who will come will shepherd the people with tenderness and consideration (Isa. 40:11; 49:10; Matt. 12:15-21). His success will stem from his recognition that the essential feature of a true king over the LORD's covenant people is that he does not act in his own strength, but **in the strength of the LORD**. He will draw from divine resources to provide for his people. **In the majesty of the name of the LORD his God** shows that his reign will be clothed in splendour because of the authority given him by the LORD (Pss. 93:1; 145:12) with whom he lives in especially close relationship so that he may be in a particular way called 'his God'.

Their king's true awareness of and responsiveness to the demands of the covenant bring blessing for his people. **They will live securely**, enjoying the benefits that having him for their king involves. **For then** (literally it is 'now', but obviously it refers to the future time of which the prophet is speaking) **his greatness will reach to the ends of the earth**. The dominion of the Messiah will be the actuality of what had always been dreamed of for the monarchs of Israel — a universal empire (Pss. 2:8; 22:27; 72:8; Zech. 9:10).

The way in which the text of 5:5 is printed in the NIV shows that it is easier to decide where this section of Micah's prophecy begins than where it ends. Many make a break in the middle of the verse so that the words **And he will be their peace** (*verse 5*) conclude the section by emphasising all that the Messiah will be to his people. 'Peace' here involves more than just cessation of warfare (Ps. 72:7; Isa. 9:6). It covers that total well-being before God which Paul has in mind when he says of Christ, 'He is our peace' (Eph. 2:14).

There are, however, good reasons to respect the way in which the Hebrew text treats the passage, with no break in 5:5. The two verses 5:5-6 then give a practical illustration of the way in which the Messiah destroys his people's enemies to ensure they can live securely. The introductory words 'He will be their peace' match the words towards the end of 5:6 'he will deliver us' and serve to bracket the verses together. Indeed the prophet's use of 'us' and 'our' at the end of 5:6 serves a similar function in bringing out the unity of this section, as this act of identification with the people and their interests picks up that which he had displayed in 5:1.

But there are problems in interpreting the passage. The references to Assyria seem to imply that Micah is talking again about the invasion that took place in 701 BC. It is just about possible to read 5:5b-6a as the vain boasting of the people that when the Assyrian comes, as they expected he shortly would, there would be a sufficiency of men capable of defeating him. 'Shepherds' and 'leaders of men' refer to those with the ability to rule and guide the forces of Judah. 'Seven... even eight' is an idiom that suggests multiplicity (Eccl. 11:2), as does 'six... even seven' (Job 5:19; Prov. 6:16). The people seem to say, 'We have an abundance of military skill and prowess. We will be so successful we will crush and rule the land of Assyria with the sword.' Against this boastful self-confidence, the prophet would then say, 'He will deliver us', directing the people to the God-given ruler who alone can deliver when the enemy threatens the people of God.

But a superior way of understanding these verses is to take Assyria, the enemy of God's people which Micah's contemporaries knew all about, as representative of all the enemies of God's people. Micah uses 'Assyria' in this typical fashion in 7:12 also, where the people when they are restored to the land are said to come from Assyria, the land of their enemies, even though that empire would have completely disappeared by then. (This is a theme that is taken up in great detail by Nahum, for example in Nah. 1:14.) Zechariah also uses 'Assyria' (and 'Egypt') in Zechariah 10:10 to represent the nations from whom the LORD will gather his people when he restores them. Such a typical usage is made more probable in this passage by the mention of 'the land of Nimrod' in 5:6, who is otherwise mentioned only in Genesis 10:8-12 and 1 Chronicles 1:10. The Genesis passage refers to Babylon as well as Nineveh (Assyria).

On this approach, the prophet represents himself as joining with those who have sworn allegiance to the Messiah as the one who secures the peace of his people. **When the Assyrian invades our land and marches through our fortresses** which he has taken, they confess that in this situation of their enemies' advance against them, they will be provided by their king with a wealth of talented leadership who will ensure their victory over their enemies. **We will raise against him seven shepherds, even eight leaders of men**, not as a display of merely human resources, but by divine gift. The people of God are still under attack, and have to be ready to fight, even though they 'do not wage war as the world does' (2 Cor. 10:3). Their enemies are 'the powers of this dark world' and 'the spiritual forces of evil in the heavenly realms' (Eph. 6:12). Nor are they left to fight relying on their own resources. The risen Christ who is the peace of his people gives his church those who will pastor and teach it so that it is ready for action (Eph. 4:11-12).

The action that is fought is not solely defensive. **They will rule the land of Assyria with the sword, the land of Nimrod with drawn sword** (*verse 6*). In their victory the leaders of the people crush the land of their enemies. Similarly today the spiritual battle involves more than resisting the inroads of the enemy. Paul tells the Corinthians, 'The weapons we fight with are not the weapons of the world. On the contrary, they have divine power to demolish strongholds. We demolish arguments and every pretension that sets itself up against the knowledge of God, and we take captive every thought to make it obedient to Christ' (2 Cor. 10:4-5).

The source of success is still the same. Those who act as under-shepherds to the Messianic King are not credited with the success of their endeavours. Rather, **he will deliver us from the Assyrian when he invades our land and marches into our borders**. The strength to obtain the victory comes from him. 'I can do everything through him who gives me strength' (Phil. 4:13).

Study questions: Micah 5:1-6
verse 2: What does Scripture teach regarding the pre-existence of the Messiah? (Isa. 9:6; John 1:1-2; 8:58; 17:5,24; Col. 1:15-19; Heb. 1:10)

verse 3: Show how important unity is as a feature of the Messianic kingdom. (Ps. 133:1; Isa. 11:12-13; Jer. 3:18; 32:39; 50:4; Ezek. 37:15-23; Hos. 1:11; Rom. 12:4-5; 1 Cor. 12:12-13; Eph. 2:14-18; 4:3-6)

verse 4: How significant a part of salvation is the security that is bestowed by Christ? (Lev. 26:5-6; Ps. 102:27-28; John 10:28; 17:12; 1 Pet. 1:5)

verse 5: How does peace come from Christ? (Isa. 9:6; Luke 2:14; John 14:27; Eph. 2:17)

Micah 5:7-15: The Victory of the Remnant
Micah brings the second main division of his prophecy to a conclusion by exploring further the role the people of God have to play in the victory that the Ruler from Bethlehem will gain. This has already been touched on in 5:5-6, but now it is spelled out in greater detail. First there are two contrasting pictures of the function assigned to the remnant of Jacob in connection with other nations. They both benefit many people ('the dew', 5:7), and overwhelm them ('the lion', 5:8-9). Then from 5:10 to the end of the chapter the spotlight falls on the condition of the LORD's people themselves. It is emphasised that it is only by way of purity and obedience that they will be able to participate in the LORD's universal victory (Eph. 5:3-5; Rev. 22:14-15). He works holiness in them, removing all that pollutes, so that they are fit for his service.

Micah uses two deftly drawn illustrations to describe the part which **the remnant of Jacob** (*verse 7*) will play. 'Remnant', as has been seen (2:12; 4:7), points beyond the calamities that would overtake the people in the LORD's judgment. It indicates that only some, not all, will come through the experience of the LORD's chastening hand upon the nation. Still some do come through, and the future verb **will be** points beyond the disaster to the restoration inaugurated by the Messiah. Then the remnant will function strategically in the furtherance of his kingdom.

On its own the phrase **in the midst of many peoples** might suggest that the remnant is once again found as a nation surrounded by others, but it is perhaps more in keeping with the comparisons that follow to view it as spread through the nations. It is going to influence the world **like dew from the LORD, like showers on the grass**. A similar description is also found of the benefits of the rule of the Messianic king (Ps. 72:6). In the dry climate of Palestine dew played a significant role in providing moisture for the growing crops, and could frequently be very heavy. The 'showers' were not light rain, but heavy, probably what came in the spring and permitted growth to start. Both the dew and the showers **do not wait for man or linger for mankind**. They are not under human control, but are part of God's provision for the natural good of the land. So the remnant that he preserves is going to be accorded a divine role in the destiny of the nations. Spread among them, it will exercise a spiritual ministry patterned after that of the Messiah. It will disseminate knowledge about God and call on the nations to turn to him. In this way it will fulfil what had been promised to Abraham: 'Through your offspring all nations on earth will be blessed' (Gen. 22:18).

The beginning of 5:8 is structured in a very similar way to the beginning of 5:7. **The remnant of Jacob will be among the nations, in the midst of many peoples** (*verse 8*). No longer, however, is the picture one of the beneficent influence of the people of God. The focus is now on a contrasting ministry. It will be **like a lion among the beasts of the forest, like a young lion among flocks of sheep, which mauls and mangles as it goes, and no one can rescue**. The lion was a figure that had been used of God's people in the past (Num. 23:24; 24:9), as those whose power would vanquish their foes. The remnant, even though its numbers are diminished, executes that role because it will be divinely empowered. When the LORD is with his people, there is no force that is able to resist and to oppose them effectively (Rom. 8:31-39).

But when does this take place? What is the realisation of this prophecy? Its position in this chapter places it after the appearance of the Messiah, and it is therefore a consequence of his rule. It may best be understood as the part that the church — both of Jewish and Gentile extraction — plays as the true children of Abraham (Gal. 3:29), taking on the mantle of God's people and bringing their role forward to its fulfilment. As the people of God are spread among the many nations of the earth (Acts 1:8; 1 Pet. 1:1), they are an irresistible force that affects for good or ill, all with whom they come in contact. As Paul writes, 'We are to God the aroma of Christ among those who are being saved and those who are perishing. To the one we are the smell of death; to the other, the fragrance of life' (2 Cor. 2:15-16).

The church's divinely assigned activity has triumphant consequences. **Your hand will be lifted up in triumph over your enemies, and all your foes will be destroyed** (*verse 9*). These words may also be translated as an exhortation, 'Lift up your hands in triumph over your enemies'. In the light of the task given her, the church is not to be passive but to go on and enter whole-heartedly into the role that the LORD has assigned her, because her victory is certain. The note is that of confidence in the victory the LORD will provide as in 4:13.

But there is a major condition that must be fulfilled before the people will be able to enter into the triumph presented here. There must be holiness prevalent among them (Zeph. 3:13). They must be the people of God in more than name. Their attitudes and behaviour will have to be such as to warrant that exalted title, and from 5:10 onwards God states that he will act to ensure that this condition is met.

'In that day,' declares the LORD (*verse 10*) does not seem to link directly back to the immediately preceding verses, as if only after the victory is won, will God act to ensure his people's holiness. Micah does not introduce this divine saying here because it is the temporal consequence of what has immediately preceded. It links back to 'that day' of 4:6-7, to the time when the LORD prepares the remnant so that they may be suitable and effective servants. By positioning the saying at this point in his prophecy, Micah is providing an effective application of the message of the coming Messianic reign to the situation of his own day. He has shown the glorious prospect that is in store for those who are loyal to the LORD, and now he points out to his hearers that the loyalty required is that of obedience. He is in effect saying to them that if you want to participate in the blessings God will provide, you must now reform your behaviour so that it coincides with what he expects of those who are in covenant with him. This is still the standard of behaviour that God demands (Gal. 5:19-21).

I will destroy uses the same verb that is translated 'cut off' in passages such as Leviticus 17:10; 20:3,5. It indicates the action that the LORD takes to remove from his people those who are themselves impure and so pollute the community of the LORD. In this way the LORD preserves for himself a people who can truly honour him. The thinking that lies behind this is expressed clearly in Leviticus 20:6-8: 'I will set my face against the person who turns to mediums and spiritists to prostitute himself by following them, and I will cut him off from his people. Consecrate yourselves and be holy, because I am the LORD your God. Keep my decrees and follow them. I am the LORD, who makes you holy.' This is the sanctifying work of God to render his people fit for his service. The fourfold repetition of 'I will destroy' along with the other words for removal bring out the extent to which the land has been polluted and the thoroughness with which the LORD purges his people.

He first says that he will destroy **your horses from among you and demolish your chariots**. This is not intended to leave his people defenceless, but to remove from them a source of false confidence, as was indicated in discussing 1:13. Scripture does not prohibit the use of legitimate means, but it has no place for putting confidence in false means. Cavalry and light war-chariots were the ultimate in military hardware in those days. God wishes his people to find their security in him and not in the equipment they provide for themselves. They must make David's sentiment their own: 'Some trust in chariots and some in horses, but we trust in the name of the LORD our God' (Ps. 20:7). In that way they will know how to stand firm in the day of testing (Ps. 33:16-22).

I will destroy the cities of your land and tear down all your strongholds (*verse 11*). This too looks at the military preparations in which they were placing their trust. A city was, of course, a fortified place, and the inhabitants were liable to find themselves looking to the strength of their walls for security rather than to the LORD. 'Strongholds' also refers to the cities of the land, as places that were designed to hold out against enemy invasion. Quite apart from their fortifications, they were often built on steeply sloping hills.

In 5:12 the LORD states that he will act to remove anything pertaining to the occult from his people. **I will destroy your witchcraft and you will no longer cast spells** (*verse 12*). The evidence of Isaiah 2:6 shows the extent to which Judah was permeated by these foreign influences in Micah's day. They represent attempts by man to gain knowledge of the future in ways which were forbidden to Israel, and must be removed to ensure that the people are blameless before God (Deut. 18:9-13). The people had to resist those who inveigle them

into such pagan practices. God's law and testimony should be their
only guide (Isa. 8:19-20).

**I will destroy your carved images and your sacred stones from
among you** (*verse 13*). God now focuses on the idolatry that was
prevalent in the land. This had been the root cause of Samaria's
downfall (1:7) and he is not going to permit any trace of it to remain
among his restored people. 'Carved images' were sculptured out of
wood, stone, or metal. Images of the LORD fell under the condemnation
of the Second Commandment (Exod. 20:4) lest the people fall into the
error of thinking that they could manipulate God through the image
they had made. But here it is more probable that the images purported
to be of other deities and this was prohibited by the requirements of the
First Commandment (Exod. 20:3). 'Sacred stones' were erected in
Canaanite sanctuaries as symbols of the male deity that was being
worshipped. **You will no longer bow down to the work of your
hands**. The prophets frequently presented scathing attacks on the
absurdity of people worshipping idols they had produced for themselves (Isa. 44:9-21; Jer. 10:3-10).

The first part of 5:14 continues with the removal of other aspects
of the customary equipment of Canaanite shrines. **I will uproot from
among you your Asherah poles** (*verse 14*). These wooden poles,
sometimes the trunks of trees, were symbols of Asherah, a goddess
who was widely worshipped in the East. As they were fixed in the
ground, the idea of their being 'uprooted' is an appropriate symbol of
their desecration. The continuation of 5:14 **and demolish your cities**
has presented a challenge to scholars, with no very satisfactory
solution being brought forward. The problem is that the phrase in the
second half of the verse does not seem to balance that in the first part,
as occurs in the other verses of this highly polished sequence. No one
knows what has happened. The text as it stands really reverts to the idea
of 5:11.

Then there is a final statement by the LORD. **I will take vengeance
in anger and wrath upon the nations that have not obeyed me**
(*verse 15*). Whereas in the previous verses we have the action of the
LORD to cleanse his people from all that was polluting them, we now
find the focus turns to his actions against the other nations who have
refused to obey him (Ps. 149:7). 'Vengeance' can easily mislead us
because we often think of it in terms of blood-feuds and vendettas that
cause untold misery. But this is the LORD asserting his rights as
sovereign ruler. It is the consequence of the title accorded him in 4:13

'the Lord of all the earth'. But the nations have not recognised his lordship by obeying his commands. The time will then come when he will vindicate his rule and his claims upon their obedience, by punishing their continued rebellion. They have mistaken the situation if they think that he has been viewing their rebellion with indifference. He has been treating them with long-suffering. But now they will experience his 'anger and wrath' at the way they have despised and set aside his claims on them (2 Thess. 2:8-10). 'Anger' is translated 'wrath' in Habakkuk 3:8, and wrath here renders a word expressing intense and passionate displeasure (Nah. 1:2, 6). When the LORD has prepared his people so that they are ready to serve him in holiness, he will also act to secure the punishment of those who have rejected his claims upon them and despised his authority.

Study questions: Micah 5:7-15

verse 7: What role is assigned to the people of God when they know his salvation? (Zech. 8:13; Matt. 5:14; Gal. 6:9-10; Phil. 2:15-16)

verse 8: How do we know that the people of God will enjoy victory over all opposition? (Isa. 25:8; Rom. 8:37-39; 1 John 4:4; 5:5; Jude 24; Rev. 7:9-10)

verses 9-14: In what ways are the LORD's people purified? (Rom. 6:6,11; 13:14; Col. 3:5)

verse 15: Is it right to punish the ignorant? (2 Thess. 1:8; Luke 12:47,48; John 15:22; Rom. 2:12-16; 3:9-18; 1 Tim. 1:13; Jas. 3:1)

Micah 6:1-8: The LORD's Indictment

As Micah begins the third part of his book, he turns back from unfolding the deliverance the LORD would provide for his people, to pressing home the reality of their present rebellion and estrangement from him. As before (compare 1:2; 3:1), Micah starts this major part of his book with a summons, **Listen to what the LORD says** (*verse 1*). What then follows takes the form of a legal indictment based on the covenant relationship the LORD had instituted between himself and his people at Sinai (Deut. 5:2).

Covenant is one of the major theological metaphors of Scripture. The LORD used it to teach Israel to think of the relationship between himself and them in terms of the relationships that existed in contemporary international treaties between emperors (suzerains) and their subject peoples (vassals). The emperors of the ancient world were no different from their later counterparts in viewing with disfavour any

behaviour that indicated a lessening of their subjects' loyalty to their
regime. Their treaties therefore strictly forbade behaviour that could
be construed as rebellious, or over-friendly to other powers. Consequently, 'treaty' or 'covenant' became a pervasive religious metaphor
in Israel alone among the peoples of the Ancient Near East, because
polytheistic beliefs did not give scope for an exclusive loyalty such as
characterised Israel in their unique engagement to serve only Yahweh,
their covenant LORD.

The use of analogies drawn from the sphere of international
relations is taken further in the ministry of the prophets. Just as a
suzerain would send a messenger to convey his orders to his vassals,
so too the covenant LORD sent his messengers the prophets (2 Chr.
36:15-16; Hag. 1:13) to remind his people of the provision he had
already made for them, and what he still intended to do for, and
through, them. The prophets also, as God's diplomatic messengers,
spelled out the obedience Israel should render in gratitude to their
covenant king.

When a country failed to please its overlord, it was often the case
that, rather than despatching troops to straighten things out, the
emperor would first of all send a messenger. His task was to charge the
people with their misdemeanours and see if threats of punishment
would recall them to loyalty and obedience. It is this pattern of
behaviour, often termed a 'covenant lawsuit' (compare Isa. 1:18; Jer.
2:9; Hos. 4:1), that is being used here to teach Judah how the LORD is
dealing with them. Yahweh, as Israel's king, is pressing charges
against his people for their infringement of the terms of the covenant
between them. If they accept the situation and repent, then they may
be restored to the king's favour. The object of the covenant lawsuit is
to recall them to loyalty, as can be seen in 6:8 which ends the section
on a note of pleading, rather than by threatening judgment.

One Scriptural example of a secular diplomat engaged on a similar
mission is to be found in the speech of the Rabshakeh ('field commander', NIV) as part of the campaign of the Assyrians against
Hezekiah in 701 BC (2 Kgs. 18:17-25; Isa. 36:1-10). Indeed, it is
possible that Micah first presented this message around that time,
saying in effect, 'You have heard the warnings of Sennacherib's
messenger. Now hear the far more serious warnings of Yahweh's
messenger.' The circumstances in Jerusalem would have given the
message an added force.

After the initial summons to get his hearers' attention, Micah continues by relating the commission the Lord had given him. (The quotation marks in the NIV should be closed at the end of 6:1.) **Stand up, plead your case**. These commands are singular and addressed to Micah, as can be seen in the AV translation, 'Arise, contend thou.' Micah has been delegated to act as the LORD's spokesman in legal proceedings. But what that case is, is not immediately revealed. Micah keeps his hearers in suspense by withholding the name or names of the persons involved.

The witnesses, however, are solemnly named, and this shows that what is in dispute is no light or trivial matter. Micah is told to initiate proceedings **before the mountains; let the hills hear what you have to say**. Mention of the mountains and the hills reflects another feature of ancient covenant making procedure. Witnesses were invoked at the making of the covenant, and in pagan cultures these were normally gods and goddesses. In Israel that was not an option, so heaven and earth are frequently called upon to play the same role (Deut. 4:26; 32:1; Isa. 1:2). If they could speak, they would testify to the undertakings given by both parties.

It is Micah who then speaks. He fulfils his commission as the LORD's prosecutor, and enjoins the witnesses to pay attention. **Hear, O mountains, the LORD's accusation; listen, you everlasting foundations of the earth** (*verse 2*). 'The everlasting foundations' (or, 'enduring foundations') refers to the mountains, looked upon as supporting the earth, with roots going deep into the soil (see Jonah 2:6). They have been in existence for a long time, and thus may bear testimony both to what the LORD had required in his covenant and how the people had in fact responded.

It is only in the second part of 6:2 that the parties to the dispute are clearly announced. It is the LORD versus his people. **The LORD has a case against his people**. He is putting into formal procedure his complaint against them — the ones who should be loyal to him, because he had saved them and claimed them as his own. **He is lodging a charge against Israel**. Israel is the covenant name of the people, even though it is only those in the Southern Kingdom who by this time are left to be cited to appear. It is not, however, a matter of an open-and-shut case. There is still the possibility of a rejoinder from the defence. The verb translated as 'to lodge a charge' is closely related to that translated 'let us reason together' in a similar context in Isaiah 1:18.

The Divine Accusation (6:3-5). Micah here directly quotes the LORD speaking to his people. In 6:3 and 6:5 the LORD calls them **My people**, and emphasises the bond that existed between them. Covenant was not just a formal legal procedure. It was intended to establish a friendly, loving relationship between the parties. It was not to be thought of on the lines of a contract between business partners, but more as a marriage bond between parties pledging themselves to each other. This form of address in itself constitutes a reminder and a rebuke.

The LORD's indictment is remarkable in what it does not do. It does not present a catalogue of Israel's misdemeanours. Rather than listing their transgressions, it focuses on what the LORD had done for them. The behaviour of the people should have reflected their relationship to him, and when their behaviour is wrong, it shows up a faulty understanding of where they were in relation to him. They did not appreciate all that he had done for them as a nation.

What have I done to you? (*verse 3*) asks if there was any charge they could levy against him that would justify their attitude towards him? A clue as to what Israel's attitude had been is found in the question, **How have I burdened you?** Israel felt their relationship with the LORD wearisome. They were tired out by the demands and restrictions they felt that he had placed on their living. They had no spiritual freshness or joy. They found the LORD, and by implication also the word that his prophet brought, unnecessarily tiresome and tedious.

But this was a travesty of reality. **Answer me**, or 'Testify against me', clearly implies that though this was the way they were thinking and speaking, it could not be backed up by evidence. It is a legal challenge to be specific and prove what they are alleging. It puts the people on the defensive.

God then reminds them of what he had done. **I brought you up out of Egypt** (*verse 4*). In Hebrew the words 'I burdened you' (6:3) and 'I brought you up' (6:4) are very similar in sound, and serve to bring out the contrast between the allegations made and the facts of the case. 'Far from pressing you down, I released you.' This looks back to the events of the Exodus, where the LORD had demonstrated his care for Israel. His action constituted his claim upon them, as the introduction to the Ten Commandments in Exodus 20:1 reminded them, 'I **redeemed you from the land of slavery**'. The Exodus is the basic Old Testament model for the salvation the LORD provides (4:10). God says, 'That is what I provided for you — freedom by paying the redemption price that was needed to achieve it.' We also see here, as in many other places in the Old Testament (for instance, Deut. 5:2-3; 29:14-15), the people of God viewed as a single entity over the centuries. Micah's contemporaries were the current representatives of the one covenant people of God. What had happened in the past was not to be written off as ancient history, but rather prized as the basis of their present privileges.

What the LORD had provided for his people had not been mere escape. **I sent Moses to lead you, also Aaron and Miriam**. No one doubted the standing of these great leaders of Israel in the past. They exemplified the quality of the LORD's provision for his people — and perhaps mentioning them was intended to stir up questions about why they were not still blessed with similarly outstanding leaders.

The LORD repeats his affectionate address, **My people** (*verse 5*). They are urged to **remember what Balak king of Moab counselled and what Balaam son of Beor answered.** The incidents referred to are recorded in Numbers 22-24, and remind them of the LORD's further provision when they were almost baulked at the entrance to the land. He protected them from their adversaries, and frustrated the schemes of their enemies to have them cursed so that they would be defeated.

Remember your journey from Shittim to Gilgal. This refers to the crossing of the Jordan when the Israelites came into the promised land. Shittim was the last place on the east bank of the Jordan where the people camped for a long time (Num. 33:49; Josh. 3:1), and Gilgal was the first encampment they had on the west bank (Josh. 4:19). The LORD had not intervened on their behalf only once, when they were passing through the Red Sea. He had continued to help them overcome obstacles, as Joshua reminded them. 'The LORD your God did to the Jordan just what he had done to the Red Sea when he dried it up before us until we had crossed over. He did this so that all the peoples of the earth might know that the hand of the LORD is powerful and so that you might always fear the LORD your God' (Josh. 4:23-24).

More could have been told, but the LORD breaks off the list of his actions on their behalf to emphasise that the same response is still required, **that you may know the righteous acts of the LORD.** The purpose of this historical recital was not mere intellectual knowledge. 'Know' conveys a wider meaning. It commanded them to acknowledge and respond appropriately to what their covenant overlord had done for them. The word 'righteous' can be used to refer to either secular or religious actions, but the 'righteous acts of the LORD' are what he has done in conformity with the covenant obligations which he had taken upon himself. They are the basic factor in the relationship between the LORD and his people, and what is required from them is a response which recognises all that he has freely bestowed on them. 'We love because he first loved us' (1 John 4:19).

The Bewildered Response (6:6-7). Micah then presents us with the sort of response a typical Israelite of his day would have made to such accusations. It is unlikely that we are meant to detect here any acknowledgement of guilt on the part of the people. If that had occurred, even though accompanied by considerable spiritual ignorance, it is improbable that the judgment speech of 6:10-16 would have followed. Rather the typical reaction is one of bewilderment. 'What more can I do than I already have done to express my loyalty to the LORD?'

If the LORD has been asking his people questions, perhaps the worshipper might now on their behalf ask the LORD some. His questions are like those traditionally asked by the people as they prepared to worship the LORD (Ps. 15:1), but they no longer embody the queries of those genuinely seeking the LORD. The questions are in fact a querulous protestation that they will go to any lengths to show their devotion to him, and so are being unjustly accused. However, even as they speak in such pious tones, they expose the self-justifying spirit that permeated their worship and the gross externality of their religion.

With what shall I come before the LORD? (*verse 6*) acknowledges that the worshipper is the servant of the God of the covenant, loyally seeking to worship him in the Temple. He claims it is the mark of true piety that he comes to **bow down before the exalted God**, literally the 'God of height', an unusual expression but clearly reflecting the transcendence of God (Isa. 33:5). The worshipper does not seek to blur the difference in status that exists between him and his God. Indeed he does not approach the LORD empty handed. **Shall I come before him with burnt offerings, with calves a year old?** In the burnt offering the animal was completely consumed by fire on the altar, unlike the fellowship offering where part was returned to the worshipper to eat. It is not just any type of sacrifice that is in view, but that which is the most costly that could be made. So too with the animals used. Calves could be sacrificed from seven days old, but obviously if they had been kept and fed for a year, what the offerer was presenting was worth very much more. The typical worshipper is then protesting his willingness to present to God sacrifices of the most costly type.

He goes on to make proposals that are far-fetched, as if to suggest the unreasonable nature of the demands that the LORD was making. It also reveals the worshipper's worldly spirit. He is not aware of any reason why *he* should modify *his* behaviour, but he will bargain with God to get *him* to change. He argues, 'If it is not just a matter of the quality of our sacrifices, we will make up for it with quantity.' **Will the LORD be pleased with thousands of rams?** (*verse 7*). Solomon had made such an offering (1 Kgs. 8:63), but it was extremely unusual. Fairly modest amounts of oil were incorporated into the grain offerings. **Ten thousand rivers of oil** is extravagant, hyperbolic language.

He even adds, **Shall I offer my firstborn for my transgression? the fruit of my body for the sin of my soul?** It is recognised that sacrifice was appointed for their 'transgression', rebellion against their covenant overlord, and for 'sin', those actions where they had missed the mark. But their theological perception was without any personal awareness of the dimensions of their wrong-doing. They felt their piety was more than adequate, and the question seems to refer not to the child sacrifices involved in the worship of the Canaanite god Molech (2 Kgs. 3:27; 16:3), but to Abraham, whose faith God tested by commanding him to sacrifice his son Isaac (Gen. 22). They were not offering to emulate the heathen, but rather claiming to be as willing as Abraham was to show their faith in God. They saw nothing wrong in their side of the relationship. Yes, God had done much for them, but they were ready and prepared to go to any lengths in their worship of him.

The Prophetic Rejoinder (6:8). 'Enough of these extravagant pretensions,' says Micah in measured tones that are in contrast with the far-fetched, almost hysterical language of the worshipper. **He has showed you** (*verse 8*). This is not necessarily a reference to God. The emphasis is not on who has done it, but on the fact that it has been done. All in the land had been informed about the terms of the covenant, so there was no need for such ludicrous speculations. **O man** serves to bring back a note of realism by pointing to man in his frailty, to cut him down to size, and to burst the bubble of his self-satisfaction, before the reality of God. **What is good** looks back to the covenant. 'Goodness' here is not something ethically abstract, nor a speculative exercise in moral philosophy. It is determined and expressed by the terms of God's covenant relationship.

What does the LORD require of you? It is the prerogative of the suzerain to make demands of his people, and so the verse is not to be understood as presenting an ethical standard in isolation from the saving work of the covenant LORD. In other words, it is not an expression of salvation by works, as if good outward behaviour on its own satisfied God and atoned for the past. Rather, it is a description of what is needed to preserve covenant fellowship. Their overlord's requirement is that those whom he has favoured with his salvation express their gratitude by living in the way he wants.

Three phrases are used to summarise the covenant requirements. The first two are essentially imitative in nature. The behaviour required is first known in, and so patterned after, what is seen in the LORD.

(1) **To act justly** goes beyond law courts that are fair. It includes that, but requires a total lifestyle that accords with the standards of what the LORD has shown is right and proper, particularly by his own words and actions. 'All his ways are just, a faithful God who does no wrong' (Deut. 32:4). So those who have known how the covenant LORD behaves are to model their own behaviour towards one another on him.

(2) Mercy, or covenant loyalty, is also to characterise the response of the vassal in covenant relationship with the LORD. His overlord is the compassionate and gracious God (Exod. 34:6) who delights to show mercy (7:20). As he has personally experienced that mercy, so he is to exhibit it towards others (1 John 4:11). The second phrase, **to love mercy**, adds to the first principally the idea of willingness and delight in acting towards one's fellows with the fidelity and consideration God requires. It is not an irksome performance of an imposed duty, but a glad and spontaneous action.

(3) The third expression relates to the heavenward attitude that is to permeate covenant living. **To walk humbly** is an expression of faith. The humility involved is not some ostentatious self-effacement, but a genuine recognition of the exaltation of the sovereign LORD. 'Walk' is a Hebrew idiom for the whole of one's life, viewed as a journey. It is a walk **with your God** with whom they willingly and lovingly should travel the journey of life. To do so, they must let him choose the path that they will take, living in conscious dependence on his gracious provision.

What was being condemned was not sacrifice as appointed by God, but sacrifices as a substitute for obedience. True worship is not a matter of outer attitudes, but the inner disposition of heart and spirit (John 4:24). Those who have experienced and responded to God's love will show that in conformity to his will (John 14:23). As they reflect on the magnitude of what God has done for them in love (1 John 4:10), their inner devotion will reveal itself both in a life of obedience and in worship that magnifies God.

Study questions: Micah 6:1-8

verse 1: Is 'covenant' a significant feature of New Testament teaching? (Matt. 26:28; Luke 1:72; 2 Cor. 3:6; Heb. 7:22; 8:6-13; 12:24; 13:20)

verse 5: The requirement 'to remember' is a key factor at all times. What should we be remembering now? (Matt. 16:9; 1 Cor. 11:24-25; Eph. 2:11; 1 Thess. 1:3; 2:9; 2 Tim. 2:8; Heb. 10:32; 13:3,7)

verse 6: What types of offering are required of the New Testament church? (Hos. 14:2; Rom. 6:19; 12:1; Heb. 13:15-16)

verse 8: What part should humility play in Christian conduct? (Matt. 11:29; Col. 2:18-23; 3:12; Jas. 4:10; 1 Pet. 5:5-6)

Micah 6:9-16: Curses of the Broken Covenant

In the previous section the LORD had called his people to account because of the emptiness of their religious practices, but still the covenant lawsuit had left the outcome of the situation open. There was scope for the people to admit the error of their ways and amend them. This section continues the theme of the LORD's dissatisfaction with his people, but now the focus is on the low public morality of the day (6:10-12), and the concluding note is the inevitability of their punishment because of their persistence in covenant breaking (6:13-16).

Listen! (*verse 9*) is a sudden cry, calling for attention. It is not the same word as is found at 6:1 to mark the beginning of the third major section of the prophecy. **The LORD is calling to the city.** 'The city' for Micah is always Jerusalem, and the LORD wants to ensure that it is listening to him. But before we are told what is said, Micah himself adds the words **and to fear your name is wisdom**. The 'fear of the LORD' indicates not an attitude of terror, but of reverent submission in awed obedience. It encapsulates the essence of the personal religious response that is enjoined in the Old Testament (Prov. 1:7). The 'name' of the LORD is not merely the sound of the word, but all that is revealed of God. Fearing his name is the response of a true follower of the LORD (Ps. 86:11). As Micah begins to tell Jerusalem what the LORD has said, he urges that they display true wisdom in their attitude to God and respond appropriately to the revelation he has given of himself and his purposes.

The message of the LORD then begins with the words: **Heed the rod and the one who has appointed it**. As the NIV footnote indicates, the meaning of the Hebrew for this line is uncertain, but 'the rod' is probably a reference to the Assyrians. When they invaded and devastated the land of Judah, they were acting as the instruments of God's righteous judgment. The same word is used in reference to them by Isaiah when God says that in their hand is the 'club of my wrath' (Isa. 10:5) and that they lifted up a 'club' against his people (Isa. 10:24). The people of Judah are called on to pay careful attention to the LORD's providential dealings with them, and to see God as the one who is really in control of the human agents he employs to carry out his purposes. In this way they will be able to interpret their experience as divine chastisement sent by the God who will not let his people go.

The LORD then specifies some of the offences that evidence their estrangement from him. Those who are satisfied with an empty religion are those whose departure from God will show itself in other areas. They thought they were placating God by their religiosity. The text of the question that is asked is also difficult to understand, but the NIV rendering **Am I still to forget?** (*verse 10*) implies they had mistaken the LORD's longsuffering for forgetfulness (Rom. 2:4). By affirming that God will certainly not forget, the rhetorical question challenges their self-contentment. He is ready to act against the **wicked house**. This unusual expression might be a distortion of the 'house of Judah' which was a way of referring to the whole nation (2 Sam. 2:4; Jer. 31:31; 33:14; Hos. 1:7).

Their **ill-gotten treasures** refers to what has been misappropriated (compare 2:2,8). One way this was done was by using **the short** (literally, 'lean' or 'scanty') **ephah**, which refers to the measuring basket for goods such as corn. It should have contained somewhat more than twenty litres (about five gallons). But there were no standard sizes, nor were there inspectors to assure the public that they were not being cheated by unscrupulous traders who used small measures when they weighed out goods in the market.

Such short measure was **accursed**. What God expected of his people went beyond worship in the sanctuary that outwardly conformed to his requirements. His covenant people should have ordered their lives totally in accordance with his wishes, and that extended to the every detail of their businesses and of their relationships.

The same thought is continued by another rhetorical question: **Shall I acquit a man with dishonest scales, with a bag of false**

weights? (*verse 11*). The expected answer is obviously 'No'. 'The dishonest scales' cheated because of the 'bag of false weights'. The weights used were stones, but their true weight would not correspond to what was marked on them: stones heavier than what was marked on them would be used to purchase commodities or weigh money, and others lighter than marked for sales or giving change. This was the all too prevalent commercial trickery of the day (Hos. 12:7; Amos 8:5). Its impact extended beyond the market place. Many would have paid rents in kind, and their value would have been underestimated if the weights used by their landlords were inaccurate. The use of such dishonest standards had been divinely proscribed (Lev. 19:35-36; Deut. 25:13-16), and it was recognised that honest scales and balances were from the LORD (Prov. 16:11; 20:23).

Her rich men (*verse 12*) refers to the royal household and the business community of Jerusalem (see on 2:1). They **are violent**, characterised by a grasping wickedness that had no respect for the rights of others (see on Jonah 3:8; Amos 5:11). They were prepared to break the law code regulating civil affairs if it was in the way of their ambitions. The implication is that this is how they had got on in the world, by treading on those they considered as obstacles. **Her people**, those who are resident in Jerusalem, **are liars and their tongues speak deceitfully**. The life of the capital had little or no respect for truth in business dealings or in ordinary living. The conduct required by the God of truth had been quite forgotten (Jer. 9:3-5).

Therefore (*verse 13*) translates a phrase which shows the LORD dissociating himself from those who behave in such a way. The action that he for his part will take will match up to what they have done. The NIV translation **I have begun to destroy you** points to the LORD's action in judgment as having already started. This involves changing the words slightly in the light of the evidence of ancient versions of Scripture. Literally, it reads 'I will make you sick, striking you', bringing you to ruin **because of your sins**.

The nature of this ruin is spelled out in 6:14-15. The curses listed remind one of passages such as Deuteronomy 28:15-68 and Leviticus 26:14-39, where the LORD details what will happen to his people if they fail to live up to his covenant standards. The curses share the characteristic of frustrating the expectations of those who have disobeyed the LORD by bringing about quite the opposite of what they had been hoping for. **You will eat but not be satisfied; your stomach will still be empty** (*verse 14*). Here again the precise meaning of the Hebrew is uncertain, but the overall thrust is clear. Famine will strike the land (Hos. 4:10; Hag. 1:6; 2:16), but it is not occasioned by natural disaster, rather by invading armies. **You will store up but save nothing, because what you save I will give to the sword.** It will be snatched from them by force.

The same theme of frustrated expectations is continued in **You will plant but not harvest; you will press olives but not use the oil on yourselves, you will crush grapes but not drink the wine** (*verse 15*). The people will not enjoy the yield of their hard work. They will be deprived of the opportunity to harvest the grain, to use the olive oil to soften their skin, or to drink the wine. Their enemies would take their produce for their own use, and the reward Israel had expected for all their hard work would elude them. They cannot expect to enjoy the fruits of the land of promise if they disobey the King who gave it to them by promise (Deut. 28:38-41; Zeph. 1:13).

They have been following the bad examples of the past and have not learned from past mistakes. **You have observed the statutes of Omri and all the practices of Ahab's house, and you have followed their traditions** (*verse 16*). This looks back to what had happened in the Northern Kingdom, where Omri (885-874 BC) had established a dynasty which had a period of success and entered into treaty relationship with the Phoenicians. Ahab (874-853 BC) was his better known son and heir. 'The statutes of Omri' and 'the practices of Ahab's house' are not direct references to the Baal worship that was then introduced in the North, and which subsequently infiltrated the South also. The emphasis is rather on the practical consequences of Baal worship. That religion had nothing corresponding to the ethical requirements of the covenant of the LORD but rather introduced an outlook on life which thought nothing of trampling on the rights of others. The attitude of Ahab and Jezebel towards Naboth's vineyard, where might grasps what it wants (1 Kgs. 21), had affected many in Judah who would have repudiated the idea that they were Baal worshippers. But their conduct was in practice moulded by that sort of thinking.

Therefore it follows as an inevitable consequence that just as the North was punished, so too the South. God cannot turn a blind eye to the misbehaviour of those who claim to be his own. **I will give you over to ruin.** This had also been an aspect of the covenant curses that the LORD had set before the people through Moses. In Deuteronomy 28:37 the word translated here as 'ruin' is rendered 'a thing of horror'.

So gruesome would be the devastation that the enemy would bring on them, that others would react with revulsion when they saw the state of their land. As in Deuteronomy, there is also mentioned the ridicule to which they will be subjected. **Your people to derision; you will bear the scorn of the nations.** For 'scorn, see 'insults' (Zeph. 2:8).

Religion needs to be practical and determine what we do in all aspects of ordinary life. Paul provides the key to achieving this, 'Serve whole-heartedly, as if you were serving the Lord, not men' (Eph. 6:7), because he is the Lord of all our living. Judah's behaviour in 6:10-12 shows what happens when religion is kept in a watertight compartment for certain situations and times, but not for business.

We are also reminded to avoid being subtly contaminated by the pressures and practices of the world around us. 'In the world', but 'not of the world' (John 17:11,14) is the pattern that the Lord sets out for his disciples. To achieve this requires constant vigilance to be sure that true righteousness and holiness determine the attitudes of our minds (Eph. 4:22-23) rather than the standards that we encounter in society.

Study questions: Micah 6:9-12

verse 9: Why should we always be ready to pay careful attention to God's rebuke? (Deut. 8:5; Job 5:17; Hag. 1:5-11; 1 Cor. 11:32; Rev. 3:19-20)

verse 11: False balances are forbidden both in the Old Testament and in the New Testament (Lev. 19:35-36; Prov. 11:1; Matt. 7:12; Phil. 4:8). To what other business practices may a similar ban be extended?

verse 12: Speech is a very important aspect of Christian conduct. What guidelines exist as to how we should speak? (Prov. 12:17,22; 21:6; 29:20; Isa. 59:4; Zech. 8:16-17; John 8:44; Eph. 4:15,25-27,29-31; Col. 3:9; 1 Tim. 1:10)

Micah 7:1-7: Micah's Lament

Micah now tells us what it was like to live in a land that had deserted the LORD and was under his sentence of judgment. But there is more to what he has to say than just an expression of misery and grief. He also tells us in 7:7 how he sustained himself in such conditions. Rather than becoming depressed by it all, he looked to God and that enabled him to win through. This prepares the way for the triumphant conclusion of the final two sections.

He begins **What misery is mine!** (*verse 1*). This is a heartfelt cry of grief and desolation over the circumstances he has to endure (compare the cry of Baruch, Jer. 45:3). Translations vary somewhat in the way they render the compressed language of what follows, but there can be no doubt about the main point of the comparison Micah makes. **I am like one who gathers summer fruit at the gleaning of the vineyard.** It was the God-appointed custom in Israel that gleanings were left for the poor at harvest (Lev. 19:9-10; Deut. 24:19-21). Micah pictures himself as one who comes to gather fruit at harvest time but the vineyard had been harvested and gleaned. **There is no cluster of grapes to eat. None of the early figs that I crave.** He had really been wanting a nice piece of fruit, but is frustrated that everything has been removed. Figs and vines were often grown together, as the picture in 4:4 shows.

But Micah goes on to explain that it was not fruit that he had really been looking for. The vineyard corresponds to the land of Judah, and the fruit he sought were those with whom he might have like-minded fellowship in the midst of general corruption. Micah's misery over the wrongs of his day was intensified by the isolation he felt. It is a natural response of the godly to strengthen one another by associating with those who are sympathetic and will engage in a ministry of mutual encouragement (Mal. 3:16; Heb. 10:25), but the land had so largely departed from the LORD that this was not an option for Micah.

The godly have been swept from the land; not one upright man remains (*verse 2*). The 'godly' person is the one who 'loves mercy' (6:8): the words are connected. Knowing God's goodness to themselves, they respond and live up to their obligations to him and their fellows. They are conscious of living before God, and this gives an extra dimension and quality to all that they do. 'Upright' describes those who live honestly and respect their neighbours' rights. But the standard of behaviour in the land had degenerated to such an extent that none could be found (Ps. 12:1; Isa. 57:1). Compare the situation outlined in Jeremiah 5.

The prophet then describes the conduct that was prevalent in his day. It is a picture of selfish exploitation prepared to go to any lengths to achieve its goal. **All men lie in wait to shed blood.** Perhaps it is not saying all are murderers in terms of the overt act, but their attitude is such that, if carried through to its conclusion, murder would result (Prov. 12:6; Isa. 59:7). Life is a battle, and the only way to succeed is by trampling on others. **Each hunts his brother with a net**. The picture is now that of the huntsman (Ps. 57:6; Jer. 5:26) rather than the soldier or highway robber. The covenant community, which should have been a source of mutual help and support, is set at odds, each trying to get the greatest advantage for himself.

The one thing everyone is good at is being bad. **Both hands are skilled in doing evil** (*verse 3*). It is not an occasional act of wrongdoing that is being talked about, but a situation where so much wrong has been perpetrated that they have all become adept at it. **The ruler demands gifts, the judge accepts bribes, the powerful dictate what they desire**. Micah traces the social ills of his day particularly to the behaviour of administrators (see on 3:9-11). The 'ruler' is a prince, someone who ranked next to the king and was his counsellor, responsible for administration of the affairs of the kingdom. Their advice was not given on the basis of what was just, or seemed best for the land, but on which individual or pressure group had sweetened them up sufficiently. The corruption spread from the inner circles round the king to affect the judges the king had appointed. Justice was not administered impartially. It was payment of money, not being in the right, that secured a verdict in your favour. 'The powerful', literally 'the great man', covers both social standing and economic influence. They have no trouble getting what they 'desire', and the word used generally implies what is not right or acceptable. There is top-level corruption in the land. **They all conspire together**. Those in power see to it that those who are in key positions get what they want. 'Conspire' is literally 'twist', or 'weave'. The intricate contortions of their actions form a complicated background to the social degeneracy of Judah.

The best of them is like a brier, the most upright worse than a thorn hedge (*verse 4*). Micah looks at the ruling classes of his day and tries to identify those who are the best of a bad bunch either in terms of benevolence towards others, or of maintaining an honest standard of conduct. But they did not amount to very much. 'Like brier' and 'worse than a thorn hedge' perhaps continue the theme of their twisted conspiracies. They are all entangled in the existing corruption. Some may not be as grasping as others, but they will not speak out against it and rather hinder those who would contend for justice. They are an obstacle in the way that is sharp and piercing. Because they are implicated in the general way of getting things done, their actions too are harmful to others.

Then in the middle of 7:4 Micah suddenly changes his approach, and sets in opposition to their conduct the reality of God's coming intervention. What God will then do is, of course, linked to the situation he will find, and the correspondence between them is brought out by the similarity in sound and spelling of the words for 'thorn-hedge' and 'confusion'.

The day of your watchmen has come. In ancient cities the watchman played an important role, not only in patrolling the streets at night to warn of crime or fire while others slept (Song of Songs 3:3; 5:7), but also in maintaining a lookout on the city walls by day and night to warn of enemy attack. There are a number of passages where the prophets are compared to watchmen (for instance, Hos. 9:8; Jer. 6:17; Ezek. 3:17; 33:7), and that seems to be the reference here. The prophets God had sent to warn the people had told them of the day when he would intervene in judgment. Micah now dramatically says it has come, perhaps in reference to the Assyrian armies surrounding Jerusalem. It could also be translated 'The day ... is coming', so confident is the prophet in anticipating the future.

The day God visits you is not the picture of a friendly gathering, but of a superior inspecting the affairs of a subordinate to ensure all is well, and to act appropriately if it is not (Zeph. 1:8). To show that he does not anticipate the people's conduct being approved by God, Micah adds **Now is the time of their confusion**, (or, understanding the reference as future, 'Then will be their confusion'). They will not know what to say when the LORD exposes and scrutinises their affairs (Isa. 10:3).

Micah next reverts to exposing the decadence of society in his day. He looks now not at the top, but at the basic building blocks of personal, and particularly family, relationships. **Do not trust a neighbour; put no confidence in a friend** (*verse 5*). It is not just in the world of business or public affairs that things have gone sadly wrong. People are so out for themselves that they cannot be relied on for assistance or keeping a matter confidential. The fabric of social relationships has reached breaking point.

Matters are even worse than that. **Even with her who lies in your embrace be careful of your words**. You cannot be certain of anyone when personal advantage is the criterion of every decision. This affects even the relationship between man and wife.

The tensions thus caused in the family circle are spelled out. **For a son dishonours his father, a daughter rises up against her mother, a daughter-in-law against her mother-in-law** (*verse 6*). 'Dishonours' is literally 'thinks of as a fool', or 'calls a fool'. 'Fool' is not just referring to lack of sense, but is a term of moral depravity and spiritual insensitivity (Ps. 74:18; Isa. 32:6). The respect for elders which was vital to the cohesion of family life in Israel had gone. There is tension: indeed, warfare. **A man's enemies are the members of his own household**. These words were used in the intertestamental period to describe the social anarchy that would characterise the period before the coming of the Messianic age. Jesus also takes them up and applies them to the situation that has arisen with his coming (Matt. 10:35-36; Luke 12:53).

In the Psalms, we often find an individual telling God of all that was disturbing him, and then from the midst of his woes, there comes a sudden switch to an affirmation of faith, for example at Psalms 13:5; 31:14; 55:16. When Micah begins **But as for me** (*verse 7*), he is acting in the same way. It is not just a literary technique that he has copied from the psalms. Rather in both it is the same psychology of faith that is exhibited. Faith is not concerned with constructing a logical path from present distress to the relief that is anticipated. Instead, it affirms the reality of God's control even over the dark circumstances that surround, and trusting in him, looks expectantly for his intervention (2 Cor. 1:10; 2 Tim. 4:18).

I watch in hope for the LORD. Micah, the watchman (it is the same word as in 7:4), knows there is more to come than the threatened judgment. It is with the LORD alone that the resolution of his people's destiny lies, and therefore it is for his intervention he waits. **I wait for God my Saviour.** Waiting is an expression of personal inability to bring about progress in the situation, and an expression of God's ability to hear and help (Pss. 38:15; 130:5). The salvation that is spoken of is not only personal rescue from sin but divine deliverance from any threatening situation.

My God will hear me acknowledges God's sovereignty over events in general, and also more particularly his identification with Micah as one who had committed himself to the LORD. It is out of his personal bond in covenant with the LORD that Micah is sure his prayer will be answered (John 16:26-27). Now that the situation has been put before him, Micah is not one characterised by apathy, but by intense eagerness waiting for God to respond (Ps. 130:5-8). There is no doubt that he will.

Study questions: Micah 7:1-7

verse 1: What role should mutual encouragement play in difficult circumstances? (1 Sam. 23:16; Mal. 3:16; 1 Thess. 5:11; Heb.3:13; 10:24-25) *verse 6*: What should characterise family relationships? (Prov. 6:20; Eph. 5:22-6:3; Col. 3:18-21; 1 Pet. 3:1-7)

verse 7: How should faith react to perplexing occurrences? (Job 13:15; 2 Chr. 20:12-15)

Micah 7:8-13: Zion's Confidence

In this section Micah moves forward from the degeneracy of the nation in his own day to a time when the LORD's chastisement has already fallen on the people and they are held by the enemy in captivity. At first (7:8-10) Zion, the covenant community, is heard challenging her enemies and expressing her confidence in the LORD's intervention to deliver her from her plight. To this confidence the prophet responds with a positive declaration of the community's restoration and return (7:11-13).

We are now presented with a much changed situation and a much changed people. The link between this section and the last is in terms of the attitude of faith. Previously it had been that of the prophet waiting for the LORD to act in times of social and religious degeneracy and apostasy. Now it is that of the repentant people waiting in faith till the LORD reverses the punishment they were undergoing. The reference in 7:10 to 'your God' has a feminine possessive in the original, and this probably resumes the feminines applied to Zion earlier (4:8). The city is viewed as representing the true people of God, and her enemies are personified in the same way in the address of 7:8.

Do not gloat over me, my enemy! (*verse 8*) shows that Micah is describing what he sees will happen when the curse of 6:16 has come into operation. The people have become the scorn and derision of the nations (4:11), but the situation is not one of total despair. They have also been brought to their senses, and now speak as those who have come to accept the prophet's warning and who realise how the LORD had been at work in their national existence. They have no quarrel with the LORD. He has acted justly. But they confidently expect that though his punishment is justified, he will reclaim his people. They are appropriating not only Micah's words of warning and condemnation, but also his message of a bright future beyond the catastrophe he had threatened. So they warn their enemies not to rejoice too soon over the downfall of the LORD's people. He has not given them up. He is using their enemies' success to teach them a lesson.

Though I have fallen, I will rise. The fall is the disaster that has overtaken the community. But just as certainly as that has occurred, so will the LORD restore a repentant Israel. **Though I sit in darkness, the LORD will be my light.** Light is associated with the felt presence of God (Pss. 27:1; 36:9). He is the one who will look favourably on his people. 'Sitting in darkness' is not a reference to death, which would rather be 'lying, or being in darkness', but rather to imprisonment (Ps. 107:10). The reference seems clearly to what Jerusalem was to suffer at the hands of the Babylonians. But the gloom will be relieved by the LORD's intervention. It is this note of confidence that pervades the closing sections of the prophecy. The LORD is the one who will intervene effectively and decisively on his people's behalf — and for this they wait in faith.

Their faith is accompanied by acknowledgement of their past failure. **Because I have sinned against him, I will bear the LORD's wrath** (*verse 9*). They are accepting that as a community they had departed from the LORD, and that consequently it was right they should 'bear the LORD's wrath', that is, the curse of the covenant they had broken. There is nothing they can say on their own behalf, but they do not anticipate that the punishment is to be without termination.

It is not the case that Zion expects to be able to do anything herself to rectify the situation that exists. She places the matter wholly in the LORD's hands, and expects the punishment to continue **until he pleads my case and establishes my right**. The case or law-suit does not seem to be a continuation of the one in chapter 6 between the LORD and his people. Now it is an action Zion is raising against her captors in that they have exceeded what God gave them permission to do when they came against her (Isa. 47:6). They had tried to destroy her, and now she seeks redress from the God of the covenant. As the oppressed party, she looks to him to advocate her cause and bring about justice for her. God as judge is a threat to those who are in the wrong, but he is the vindicator and deliverer of those who are wrongfully oppressed. Therefore Zion confidently states **He will bring me out** from the darkness of captivity and oppression **into the light** of salvation and enjoyment of his favour. **I will see his righteousness.** 'Righteousness' is used here in a way very similar to Isaiah (for example, Isa. 46:13; 51:6) and in some psalms (for example, Ps. 98:2). This is God's conduct in terms of the covenant norm he has set for himself in his dealings with his people. He has chosen them, and so he will not permit them to be badly treated but will provide them with deliverance and salvation.

Then my enemy will see it and will be covered with shame (*verse*

10). It is Zion, the LORD's people, who continue to speak. When Zion is vindicated, it will be her oppressors' turn to blush. The charge against them is specified in terms of their mocking of Israel in her plight — and especially their mocking of Israel's God. **She who said to me, "Where is the LORD your God?"** This is the voice of defiant irreligion taunting the people and denying the existence and effective loyalty of God. It is not dissimilar to the attitude described in 4:11. When the LORD vindicates his people, **my eyes will see her downfall**. The evil power that vaunted itself against the LORD's people will be no more. **Now** is again employed to show that the future is vividly before the eyes of the speaker. (We have seen this earlier in 5:4.) **She will be trampled underfoot like mire in the streets.** This will be indeed a just fate for her spiteful and uncaring attitude.

In the final verses of this section (7:11-13), the prophet relays the LORD's endorsement of the attitude of expectation by the repentant people. He assures them that the time will come when their fortunes will be restored. **The day for building your walls will come** (*verse 11*) may possibly refer to re-erecting the walls of Zion that were demolished when the city was captured. But it is not the usual word for a city-wall that is employed. It is rather that for a stone fence, and the reference is probably to the setting up again of stone walls throughout the rural community. It goes further. **It will be the day for extending your boundaries** from the smaller confines of the Judean kingdom back to the extensive territory held in David and Solomon's day, even the boundaries promised by the LORD (Gen. 15:18-21; 1 Kgs. 4:21).

When we read these words, we are inevitably led to ask if and when all this has been accomplished. To a certain extent we can see it coming true in the return from the captivity (Ezra 1:1-4). But Judah's fortunes were never restored to the extent that their original boundaries were regained. The prophecy awaits fulfilment on a grander scale, and this is associated with the rule of the Messianic king (Pss. 2:8; 72:8). At present the boundaries of his kingdom are being extended by his church as it fulfils the Commission he gave it (Matt. 28:19-20; Luke 24:47). The role of Zion has been taken over by the heavenly Jerusalem (Heb. 12:22), and this awaits the final consummation of the new Jerusalem (Rev. 21,22) in which all the promises of restoration given to God's people find their ultimate realisation in the presence of their King.

The picture of 7:12 continues to teach the people of Micah's day of the LORD's restoration in terms of images they would understand. **In that day** (*verse 12*) links the happenings of this verse to the revival of Zion's fortunes just described. It may imply that the restoration is to be accomplished by the return of the exiles from the places where they had been taken captive and where they had fled to seek safety. Alternatively, the description here may parallel that of 4:1-2, and **people will come to you** refers to those who have turned to the LORD from among the nations. **From Assyria and the cities of Egypt, even from Egypt to the Euphrates and from sea to sea and from mountain to mountain.** 'From sea to sea' is from the Mediterranean Sea through to the Persian Gulf, and 'from mountain to mountain', though a less common expression, seems to correspond to the area from the mountains in the north of Mesopotamia through to Sinai. But it is not the precise geographical area that matters. It is a picture of the extensive area covered by the realm of the LORD.

As well as the restoration of his people's fortunes, and the gathering of the nations to them, Micah presents a third element in the LORD's intervention on behalf of his own. He will judge those who remain apart from him and his loyal subjects. **The earth will become desolate because of its inhabitants, as the result of their deeds** (*verse 13*). The earth is here obviously with the exception of Israel's restored territory. Elsewhere in the day of the LORD's intervention on behalf of his own there will be experienced the destroying force of his anger. It is not capricious. What he does will be a warranted reaction to the misdeeds of the peoples of the earth (2 Thess. 1:9-10).

Study question: Micah 7:8-13
verse 9: When faith acknowledges the rightness of the LORD's chastisement, how does it react? (1 Sam. 3:18; Lam. 3:29; Heb. 12:11)

Micah 7:14-20: Grace and Truth
Micah ends his prophecy on a note of confident expectation based on the promised gracious deliverance of the LORD. With the exception of 7:15 where the LORD responds to the petitions of his believing people, Micah throughout this section gives voice to their prayers and praise. The day of deliverance has not in fact arrived, but the LORD in whom they trust has committed himself. Faith, confessing the character and power of the LORD, finds in his word a more than sufficient guarantee that his salvation will come.

7:14-15 are to be understood as a prayer of the people and the response of the LORD to their petition. The people ask on their own behalf, **Shepherd your people with your staff, the flock of your inheritance** (*verse 14*). The shepherd was the ruler and provider. In Micah's prophecy this way of viewing the LORD's activity provides a unifying theme, being found in the three sections of hope (see also 2:12; 5:4). The people are his 'flock' (Pss. 74:1; 80:1; 95:7; 100:3). They are pleading the promises of the covenant by which they had become 'your people' (Exod. 6:7) and 'your inheritance' (Deut. 4:20; 9:26,29), the people God had chosen for his own. Though now, as a consequence of their spiritual rebellion against their God, they are not enjoying the privileges which ought to be theirs, in repentance they plead not what they are in themselves, but what God had divinely constituted them to be. They look to their Shepherd to deal with them graciously.

It is difficult to be sure how the description the people give of themselves ought to be understood. **Which lives by itself in a forest, in fertile pasturelands** may well combine two elements of earlier prophecies. 'By itself' ('solitarily' AV) looks back to the ancient prophecy of Balaam about 'a people who live apart' (Num. 23:9), which was taken up again by Moses in his final blessing on Israel when he said they 'will live in safety alone' (Deut. 33:28). There is also reference to the bounty of the land that the LORD had provided for his people (Exod. 3:8; Deut. 6:10-11). If so, the people are anticipating a return to the ideal conditions they will enjoy as benefits of the divine shepherding.

But the word 'forest' is the same as that rendered 'thickets' in 3:12. That may point to the people speaking of a time when the conditions envisaged there have been realised, that is, the devastation of the LORD's judgment. Certainly, their words do seem intended to describe their circumstances as they speak. The ruined state of the Temple Mount, indeed of the whole land, has come as promised. 'In fertile pasturelands' is literally 'in the middle of a fruitful field'. The situation presented may be one where the much more fertile land lower down is under enemy control, and those of the people who are left in the land (for not all were taken into captivity) have been reduced to living in isolated circumstances in the less productive forest and mountain areas. It would then be on the basis of their present deprivation that they plead with God.

Let them feed in Bashan and Gilead as in days long ago. Bashan lay to the north and west of the Sea of Galilee, and was an area of considerable fertility. Gilead is a less well defined area on the west bank of the Jordan to the south of Bashan (see Map II). While more rugged, it was still a very productive area (Num. 32:1). These Transjordan territories had been occupied at the time of the Conquest, but lost since. This request looks back to the time of the settlement in the land, and probably also to the time of the Empire under David and Solomon, and asks in terms of the promise given of the former dominion being restored (4:8) that the people would enjoy what was promised in the covenant.

Micah then cites the words of the LORD's response to the prayer. The answer re-introduces the theme of the Exodus, already found at 4:10 and 6:4, and this continues to underlie the rest of the prophecy. **As in the days when you came out of Egypt, I will show them my wonders** (*verse 15*). The Exodus functioned in the thinking of the Old Testament church much the same way as the Cross does for the church now. It was the model by which they were taught about the LORD's saving intervention on behalf of his people. He now promises them that he will again intervene as dramatically and effectively on their behalf. His 'wonders' are his acts of power which bring about the redemption of his people (Exod. 3:20; Ps. 78:32). They are beyond human ability and cause astonishment when they occur.

In 7:16-17 we again hear the prophet present the response of the believing people. Encouraged by the reference to an Exodus-style display of God's power, they remember how the nations were then devastated before Israel (Ps. 136:10-22), and expect that those who were now oppressing them will be similarly treated. **Nations will see** (*verse 16*) what God has done for his people and **be ashamed**, referring back to 7:10. Completely **deprived of all their power** in the face of the might of God, **they will lay their hands on their mouths**. This was a traditional expression of surprised shock and wonder (Job 21:5; 29:9). **Their ears will become deaf** continues the picture of their consternation at the reversal of the fortunes of Israel. The news that reaches them is such that they will refuse to listen to it.

The enemies of the people of God will experience utter humiliation. **They will lick dust like a snake, like creatures that crawl on the ground** (*verse 17*). Licking the dust was often used to express abject defeat, and prostration before a superior (Ps. 72:9; Isa. 49:23). **They will come trembling out of their dens** so shaken will they be by what God has shown in his power. **They will turn in fear to the LORD our**

God, and will be afraid of you. The use of 'fear' here might indicate that the display of God's saving power has brought the nations to their senses and so they turn in reverence to the LORD. But probably the use of 'our God' rather than 'their God' indicates it is only the reaction of terror that is in view.

In 7:18-20 there is praise for the incomparable God. Micah's name means 'Who is like the LORD?' and there is obvious allusion to it here in **Who is a God like you?** *(verse 18)*. Such a question was a traditional device to indicate the supremacy and uniqueness of the one true God. It picks up the theme of the Exodus from 7:15 by echoing the question Moses asked in his victory song after the people had passed through the Red Sea, 'Who among the gods is like you, O LORD?' (Exod. 15:11).

But now in a very significant prophetic presentation of the spiritual significance of the Exodus, the emphasis turns from the liberation the LORD has granted his people from their enemies (7:15), to the even greater wonder of the liberation he grants them from the effects of their own sin. **Who pardons sin and forgives the transgression of the remnant of his inheritance** looks back to similar words in Exodus 34:6-7 where, after the incident of the Golden Calf, the people are restored because of the LORD's gracious pardon. The mention of 'the remnant' brings a shadow of judgment into the picture (2:12). His people have a history which is not all to their credit. But the focus is on the consummation of the promise to those who remain and are taken by the LORD as his own.

'Sin' (deviation from the right standard), 'transgression' (rebellion against a superior), and in 7:19 'iniquity' (missing the target) are three basic Old Testament words to describe the wrong that Israel had committed against her God. The occurrence of these three words intensifies the evil of their past conduct and throws into greater prominence the unmerited graciousness of God. The extent of his saving action is also brought out by the words that are employed to describe his mercy. He 'pardons' by lifting up the burden of their guilt that was crushing them, and carrying it away. He 'forgives' by overlooking their offences, and passing on to another matter.

You do not stay angry for ever but delight to show mercy. God's anger at his people's sin is justified, but his fatherly chastisement of them is not continued indefinitely (Ps. 103:9; Isa. 57:16). It gives him far greater satisfaction to extend 'mercy', which refers to what the LORD does over and above any claim that could be made upon him. It is his gracious pleasure to take back into his favour those who have wandered and strayed.

You will again have compassion on us (*verse 19*) speaks of the deep and tender love which the LORD displays towards his children (Ps. 103:13; 'mercy', Hab. 3:2). That had not changed. He had acted as a father to chastise his people when they wandered from him and refused to repent (Heb. 12:5-7). But now they look forward to entering into full and unrestricted enjoyment of the blessings of that love in recovered fellowship with him.

You will tread our sins underfoot. Their sin had been a hostile power acting against the LORD, but he will subdue it and render them subservient to his purposes. He is the Victor who crushes his people's sin and ensures that it is no longer their master (Rom. 6:17).

The people also describe the day when God will **hurl all our iniquities into the depths of the sea**. Micah here uses a vivid comparison drawn from the experience of the Exodus. Then the LORD had hurled Pharaoh's chariots and his army into the sea, and they had sunk to the depths like a stone and like lead in the mighty waters (Exod. 15:4,5,10). Now the enemy is the people's own wrongdoing, and in the renewal of the Exodus experience their sin will undergo the same fate at the LORD's hands. The Egyptians were prevented from catching up with the fleeing Israelites and reversing their deliverance. The freedom of the people of God will not be marred by some consequence of their past sin catching up with them to spoil their delight in the provision God has made for them. Just as not one of the entire army of Pharaoh that followed the Israelites into the Red Sea survived (Exod. 14:28), so too the consequences of 'all' their iniquities will be swept away by God.

Great though the Exodus had been in the history of God's people, there is an even greater wonder still to be found in God's gracious pardoning of his people and in the completeness with which the covenant God deals with sin and obliterates it from the lives and records of his people.

He does this because of his covenant commitment to them, or rather to their forefathers, to whom he had sworn in the past (Gen. 12:2-3; Ps. 105:9-10). **You will be true to Jacob, and show mercy to Abraham, as you pledged on oath to our fathers in days long ago** (*verse 20*). Truth and mercy are paired as descriptive of God's commitment to his covenant (Ps. 85:10, AV), and of what should characterise his people's response. Truth represents reliability. It is the consistency with which

God can be counted on to measure up completely to all that he has committed himself to. His 'mercy' or 'steadfast love' (7:18) reflects the extent to which he maintains all that is involved in the relationship with his people, no matter how forgetful they may have become. It is often translated by the word 'grace', reflected in the grace and truth that came through Jesus Christ (John 1:17). No matter how much time has passed since the pledge was given, his word and oath are 'two unchangeable things in which it is impossible for God to lie' (Heb. 6:18) and so faith is greatly encouraged. The affirmation of the divine promise is made sure in Christ (2 Cor. 1:20).

Study questions: Micah 7:14-20

verse 18: How should we praise God for his gracious intervention? (Deut. 33:26; 1 Kgs. 8:23; Pss. 35:10; 86:5; Dan. 9:9)

verse 19: What action does the LORD take with his people's sin? (Deut. 30:6; Ps. 103:12; Isa. 38:17; Jer. 50:20; Ezek. 11:19; 36:25; Hos. 14:4; Rom. 6:18; 8:2)

verse 20: What is true of the LORD's promises? (Luke 1:54-55, 72-74; Rom. 15:8-9; Heb. 6:18)

NAHUM

Overview

If a book of just forty-seven verses foretelling the destruction of an ancient city thousands of years ago is not to escape being quickly passed over, it must be shown to be relevant. That it is written in vigorous and dramatic language which equals anything in the rest of the Old Testament does not help much, because the descriptions are of war, death and crushing ruin. What have they to do with the revelation of God's grace? The emphasis on God's wrath and vengeance increases our unease. And the criticism frequently goes further. Nahum says nothing, it is alleged, about the faults of Judah. He rather gloats in a jingoistic fashion over what is to befall Assyria. Many have indeed gone so far as to exclaim that what we hear in Nahum is virtually the voice of the false prophets such as those who opposed Micah and Jeremiah — intensely nationalistic, down on their enemies, sure of their own future and blind to their own faults. That, however, is an inadequate and quite erroneous assessment of Nahum.

The relevance of Nahum begins to emerge when we consider the circumstances of the prophecy. In moving on from the book of Micah to that of Nahum, we have come forward by about fifty years, but the national and international scene is still dominated by the might of Assyria. The emphasis, however, has changed. In Micah, Assyria was the rod the LORD had appointed to chastise his wayward people (Mic. 6:9). Now, the stress is on the cruelty with which Assyria carried out this task, overstepping what God permitted, as Isaiah had prophesied she would (Isa. 10:5-7). This is a message directed at the agony of the people of God as they suffer at the hands of a barbarous regime. It claims our attention because of what it tells us about God and his attitude towards such behaviour. Just as much as in Micah's prophecy, we are being asked to exclaim 'Who is like the LORD?'

The world is still polluted with evil. Successive generations continue to provide examples of regimes that act with barbarous cruelty. Platitudes provide no remedy for those who are suffering in such situations, or for those who are compelled to look on helplessly. It is not easy to respond to the anguished query, 'How can there really be a God who allows all this to happen?' But faith's first step is to lay hold of the truth that God does rule over 'the world and all who live in it' (1:5).

The LORD is also implacably opposed to evil. 'I am against you' (2:13; 3:5). He will display his justice and power by bringing all that is opposed to him and his people to an end. The collapse of Nineveh is an outstanding example of how the empires of man may seem outwardly impregnable, and yet when the LORD decrees, their end comes swiftly.

We are also presented with the truth that the LORD's judgment on evil is linked with his purposes of grace (1:7-8; see also on 1:12-2:2). When he intervenes in judgment, there is inevitably a dual impact. To establish the righteous is to overthrow their enemies. 'Your kingdom come' is a two-edged prayer. The overthrow of Nineveh reveals the pattern common to every divine action against the kingdom of darkness, and so it foreshadows the final extirpation of evil from the LORD's domains when he brings his people into the heavenly kingdom in the consummation (Rev. 22:14-15). As Paul said, 'God is just: He will pay back trouble to those who trouble you and give relief to you who are troubled, and to us as well. This will happen when the Lord Jesus is revealed from heaven in blazing fire with his powerful angels. He will punish those who do not know God and do not obey the gospel of our Lord Jesus. They will be punished with everlasting destruction and shut out from the presence of the Lord and from the majesty of his power on the day he comes to be glorified in his holy people and to be marvelled at among all those who have believed' (2 Thess. 1:6-10).

Nahum 1:1: The Capital of the Empire

An oracle concerning Nineveh (*verse 1*). 'Oracle' indicates that this is a message given by God. But it has always been a problem to know just how to translate the word. Many would still prefer the translation 'burden', as in the AV. It is generally used of an ominous message, one of disaster and impending calamity (Isa. 13:1; 14:28; 21:1). It is the sort of message that would be like a weight tied round the neck of the place or country named, and would act as a load pulling it down to its doom. Certainly that is true of the message that Nahum here relays.

How we assess what the original impact of the title was depends very much on when we date the prophecy. Accepting it as a true prophecy, and not as something written up afterwards to look like a prediction, it must obviously have been written before Nineveh fell in 612 BC. Nahum also mentions the capture of Thebes in Upper Egypt as something that has already happened (3:8) — and that took place in 663 BC. Opinions differ as to precisely when in the interval Nahum delivered this prophecy. Some, wanting him to be little better than an

informed and astute political commentator, would date it only a short
time before 612. Others argue that, while Nahum was well informed
about the sack of Thebes, there is no indication that he is aware of its
recovery by the Egyptians in 654 BC, and so would place it before that.
Certainly, I think we must date the prophecy earlier than 635 BC when
the power of the Assyrians began to decline. 1:13 implies Judah was
still oppressed by the Assyrians, and that does not fit in with the reign
of King Josiah (640-609 BC) when the pressure of Assyria was
removed, but with the reign of Manasseh (686-642 BC), who paid
tribute to Assyria and was even deported for a time by the Assyrians
to Babylon (2 Chr. 33:11). Against that background Nahum's news
that he had a message of impending disaster for Nineveh would have
been a startling, almost unbelievable, revelation.

Nineveh was the capital of Assyria in Nahum's day, and was thus
at the centre of a vast empire, which was at the height of its power. It
was a city with a long history, being mentioned as early as Genesis 10.
It had been, however, only one of the many royal cities of Assyria till
Sennacherib (705-681 BC) made it his capital at the end of the 8th
century BC, i.e. around 700 BC. He spent most of his twenty-five year
reign enlarging and strengthening the old city. The former palace was
pulled down, and a vast new one built. Its remains have not yet been
fully excavated, but its large rooms and spacious halls are easily
traced. Sennacherib called it 'The Palace Without a Rival'. He provided the city with new temples, broad streets, and public parks. There
was also a massive aqueduct bringing water into it from the mountains
to the east. A double rampart encircled the city for the protection of its
perhaps 300,000 inhabitants, and an armoury covering 16 hectares (40
acres). Of the cities of the ancient world only Babylon would be larger.

What is more, Sennacherib was followed by two kings who also
enhanced the city, each building another grand palace: Esarhaddon
(681-669) and Ashurbanipal (669-626). Their empire stretched from
Egypt through Palestine and Syria, into much of Asia Minor, and down
through Mesopotamia to the Persian Gulf — and Nineveh was the
focus of its power and wealth. The Assyrian kings used much of the
tribute and booty that poured in from many nations to fortify and
enhance their capital.

Yet here is 'the burden of Nineveh': a message of impending doom.
How incredible to an empire at the height of its success! Yet with what
relief it would have been heard by those who were among its subject
nations. Judah had already lived through almost a century of Assyrian

terror and ruthlessness, and her circumstances were not exceptional. This was no benevolent regime. The Assyrians made no secret of the blood and torture by which they maintained control over their subjects. They used calculated cruelty as an instrument to repress opposition. The records they have left spanning two and a half centuries tell the same tale throughout. In terms of atrocities perpetrated, the Assyrian empire has to be ranked with the concentration camps of Nazi Germany, the Cambodia of the Khmer Rouge and Pol Pot and the Uganda of Idi Amin — once we start to list them, there are uncomfortably many. Assyria is but one instance of what happens when lust for power is combined with callous indifference to human suffering.

There is also a second part to the title. **The book of the vision of Nahum the Elkoshite**. Only here does 'book' occur in the title of a prophecy. We need not necessarily conclude that Nahum did not speak to the people of his day, but remembering that it was the reign of Manasseh the persecutor, his prophecy may well have been written down from the first. The book certainly shows that it was carefully composed.

It is also significant that it is called a 'vision'. Nahum recorded what would otherwise have been unknown, not because he was more gifted, or better informed than others in his day, but because God had permitted him to see what would happen. It is this revelation that he transmits, and in calling it a 'vision' he places himself in the ranks of the prophets, and claims divine authority for what he has to relate.

The name 'Nahum' is only found here in the Old Testament, though we know from archaeological remains that it was in fact fairly common. It probably means 'full of comfort', or is a short form of the name 'the LORD is full of comfort', and as such connected with the name Nehemiah.

He is not called a prophet, though 'burden' and 'vision' make that claim implicitly. 'The Elkoshite' identifies his home town as Elkosh, which might have been somewhere in Galilee, or more probably another site 32 kilometres south-west of Jerusalem, which would put him as coming from the same general area as Micah (see Map II). As we shall see, he shows considerable familiarity with the prophecies of Isaiah, citing them on a number of occasions, and it is speculative, but by no means impossible, that he was one of the disciples of Isaiah (Isa. 8:16).

Nahum 1:2-6: The LORD of the Covenant

Nahum lived in bleak times. Judah was under the heel of Assyria, and the king of Judah was Manasseh, of whom it is recorded that he led the people astray, 'so that they did more evil than the nations the LORD had destroyed before the Israelites' (2 Kgs. 21:9). In the face of national apostasy and persecution by the civil power, it would have been no wonder to those remaining loyal to the LORD that he had raised up Assyria to oppress the land. It was after all a just judgment for their national sins.

But there was more to it than national oppression as a result of national apostasy. The hideous cruelty of the oppressor far surpassed in enormity anything that had been perpetrated by Judah. Would this proud and cruel nation be allowed to get off with her atrocities? Her empire was vast; her power unchallenged; the nations were terrorised before her. How could she be stopped?

Nahum provides the response of faith. No matter how ominous the problem, faith resolutely refuses to view matters horizontally, looking only to man and what he can do to resolve the problem. Nahum does not talk about armed resistance, guerrilla fighting, or political intrigue. Instead he begins with a declaration of faith. He looks heavenward. He looks to God, and asserts in the perspective of what God is, what will happen to Nineveh.

But it is not the reality of God in general that Nahum focuses on. It is rather God as he has been pleased to enter into relationship with his people. By sheer repetition of the name, 'the LORD', Nahum emphasises his point. The NIV, in common with many English translations, uses 'LORD' with small capitals to represent the covenant name of God, Jehovah, or Yahweh, which is generally reckoned to be a more accurate pronunciation of it. It occurs three times in 1:2, and ten times in the first chapter. He is the one to focus on. He is the one who has to be taken into account in any final reckoning.

In contrast to the repetition of the name of the LORD, apart from 1:1, the name of Nineveh is not mentioned in chapter 1. It occurs only once in chapter 2 (2:8), and once in chapter 3 (3:7), and Assyria is named only in 3:18. If it were not for the title in 1:1, we would not at first be sure about the identity of the enemies Nahum talks about. The NIV does introduce the name of Nineveh quite often in underbrackets (for instance, in 1:8, 11, 14), but Nahum deliberately did not. He would not put her on a par with the LORD. In that perspective Nineveh is a nameless nobody. And, of course, Nahum was right. Who cares about Nineveh now?

But the truths Nahum expresses about the LORD are still valid — and alas (!) needed in a world where evil empires arise and men pitilessly butcher and terrorise one another. The strength of faith lies in being able to grasp that the seemingly unassailable Ninevehs of this world have to reckon with the reality of the LORD.

Nahum declares that **the LORD is a jealous and avenging God** (*verse 2*). The covenant LORD will deal decisively with all those who rise up to disrupt the bond he has created between himself and his people. We have, however, to be careful as to how we understand the idea of 'a jealous God'. Jealousy as expressed by sinful people is usually a corrupting, evil influence born of unjustified suspicion and personal insecurity. But in essence it is a vigilant commitment to maintain a relationship. The description of God as 'jealous' reflects the intensity of his love and of his determination to maintain the commitment between himself and his people. One implication of this is that his people must in turn devote themselves exclusively to him. He will permit no rival for their obedience and affections. 'Be careful not to forget the covenant of the LORD your God that he made with you; do not make for yourselves an idol in the form of anything the LORD your God has forbidden. For the LORD your God is a consuming fire, a jealous God' (Deut. 4:23-24).

Nahum also speaks of the LORD as being an 'avenging God', and goes on to say **the LORD takes vengeance and is filled with wrath. The LORD takes vengeance on his foes**. Three times he emphasises that the LORD is the one who takes vengeance (see on Mic. 5:15). Again that is easily misunderstood in terms of the blood feuds and petty malice that human squabbling often engenders. This vengeance, however, is not private retaliation, but the assertion of the sovereign rights of the LORD (Ps. 94:1). It is not vindictiveness, but vindication. The LORD clears his reputation for justice and righteousness over against those who would trample his requirements underfoot (Isa. 59:18). It is the exercise of due authority by one whose authority has been impugned. 'El', the word used here for God, emphasises his power, and so when he acts, those who oppose him will be unable to mount a successful response.

The LORD's vengeance is the corollary of his jealousy, for it not only requires his people to be single-minded in their devotion to him, it also means that he will not permit any third party to disrupt the relationship between himself and his people (Deut. 32:41-43). Notice how in the second part of 1:2 Nahum speaks of 'his' foes and 'his' enemies. They were Judah's enemies in the first place. This is an indication of the identification of interest between the LORD and his people.

He is also the LORD who is 'filled with wrath', that is, literally 'master or lord of wrath', possessing wrath. It is a word of intense and passionate feeling. God is not lukewarm about anyone or anything that mars the relationship he has created. Despite appearances, the Judge of all the earth has not shrugged off the infringements of his law as minor matters of little consequence. He has judicially determined to act against those who have pitted their puny might against him. He **maintains his wrath against his enemies**. It might appear that one act after another is perpetrated with impunity, but God is watching and he is waiting — and when he is ready, he will act.

Nahum then develops his argument against those who would say, 'Look at all that is happening. Why has God not acted sooner if he could?' In response to such an objection, Nahum points back to the covenant revelation of God. **The LORD is slow to anger and great in power; the LORD will not leave the guilty unpunished** (*verse 3*). Remember how he proclaimed his name and set out his character, 'The LORD, the LORD, the compassionate and gracious God, slow to anger, abounding in love and faithfulness, maintaining love to thousands, and forgiving wickedness, rebellion, and sin. Yet he does not leave the guilty unpunished; he punishes the children and their children for the sin of the fathers to the third and fourth generation' (Exod. 34:6-7).

God's justice is not impaired because of the apparent delay. It is because he is 'great in power' that he can let matters run on for so long, and they do not get out of his control. He does not act with the swift response of human anger, but with the deliberateness of the merciful and gracious God. Remember how he sent Jonah to that great city Nineveh with the call to repentance (Jonah 3:4-5).

In the second part of 1:3 and in 1:4-5, Nahum emphasises God's power. He uses graphic images, some of them generalised from the experience of God's people at the Exodus, and at the crossing of the river Jordan. His point is that if God can do this in the natural realm, can he not also act against the empires and united forces of man?

His way is in the whirlwind and the storm. The whirlwind and the storm are chosen to represent the suddenness of God's action (Ps. 18:7-15; Isa. 66:15; 1 Thess. 5:3) and the devastating effect of his power. **Clouds are the dust of his feet**. That does not seem to be a reference to a theophany as when God came to Mount Sinai enveloped in a cloud (Exod. 19:16). Clouds are often associated with the coming of deity to emphasise heavenly grandeur (Ps. 104:3; Rev. 1:7). But here the picture is developed from an army hurrying to battle, and kicking up dust with their boots. When God comes to act, so great is the power of his presence that clouds are what he stirs up.

The command of the Creator is sufficient to change the order of nature. **He rebukes the sea and dries it up; he makes all the rivers run dry** (*verse 4*). He is the one whose mere rebuke (Isa. 50:2) dries up the sea, which was viewed in the ancient world as a hostile deity. The language reminds one of descriptions of the Exodus (Isa. 51:10), and also of the crossing of the river Jordan (Ps. 114:3-5). **Bashan and Carmel wither and the blossoms of Lebanon fade**. Bashan, on the east of the Jordan (see on Mic. 7:14, and Map II), was noted for its rich pasture land and herds of cattle. Carmel was a fertile mountain on the Mediterranean coast of Lebanon to the north of Canaan. It was well-wooded and many vines and flowers grew there so that the fragrance of Lebanon was proverbial (Song 4:11). If the glory of nature shrivels up before the LORD, how much more the pride of man? Bashan and Carmel were not the sort of places liable to be affected by drought, but the LORD can reverse their condition. If that is so, who then can resist him? Who is not vulnerable?

The mountains quake before him and the hills melt away (*verse 5*) intensifies the argument. The LORD is the one who causes earthquakes and volcanic eruptions (Ps. 97:5; see on Mic. 1:4). What seemed most stable — the mountains — quake at him (Isa. 64:1). The LORD is in control of nature, and the forces of nature cause terror and devastation among the inhabitants of the world. **The earth trembles at his presence, the world and all who live in it**. Compare Isaiah 2:19,21.

The conclusion is drawn by means of two rhetorical questions. **Who can withstand his indignation? Who can endure his fierce anger?** (*verse 6*). The answer is clearly implied that this is not possible for anyone (Pss. 76:7; 130:3; Mal. 3:2; for 'indignation', see Hab. 3:12). **His wrath is poured out like fire; the rocks are shattered before him**. That is the reality that all those who are his adversaries, who are opposed to him, have to reckon with.

Scripture consistently asserts the reality of divine judgment on sin. The gospel message is twofold: there is the proclamation of the acceptability before God that is achieved through faith in him and his provision in Christ; and there is also the proclamation that his wrath 'is being revealed from heaven against all the ungodlessness and wickedness of men' (Rom. 1:17-18). To minimise the reality of God's righteous wrath against sin is to debase his holiness, to demean the significance of the cross, and to leave in frightful peril those who do not recognise the enormity of their conduct in the sight of God. Nahum's message here is an essential part of the statement of the whole revelation God has made of himself.

It is also the case that it is from the confession of God as creator and sustainer of the universe that Nahum argues to the impending judgment against the nations that make light of his requirements. Nations are without excuse because the eternal power and divine nature of God has been made plain to them (Rom. 1:18-20).

Study questions: Nahum 1:2-6
verse 2: Is the concept of 'jealousy' appropriate in describing God today? (Deut. 6:15; Josh.24:19; 1 Kgs. 14:22; Joel 2:18; Zech. 1:14; 8:2; Rom. 8:38-39; Heb. 13:5)

What is meant by God taking vengeance? (Ps. 94:1-11; Isa. 59:18; Rom. 12:19)

verse 3: Why can God not let the guilty go unpunished? (Isa. 2:12-17; 37:23,29; Dan. 5:22-24; Rom. 2:6; 2 Cor. 5:10; 2 Thess. 1:8)

Nahum 1:7-11: The Kindness and Sternness of the LORD
There is no stepping back from the reality of God's retributive justice, but Nahum now views it against a broader background. When the LORD vindicates his name, it is a two-sided operation. He pours out his furious wrath on those who have set themselves against him, but he also extends his protection and favour to those who are in covenant relationship with him (1:7-8). Nahum then proceeds to focus on how this sternness works itself out in the doom that awaits Assyria (1:9-11).

The kindness of God (1:7). Nahum frequently turns swiftly from one subject to another. No sooner has he ended 1:6 with 'His wrath is poured out like fire; the rocks are shattered before him' than he proceeds **The LORD is good** (*verse 7*). The jarring effect of the change emphasises the contrast that is being made. God's wrath is one aspect of his character that is almost too awesome to contemplate. Its implications for sinners are so overwhelming that we shrink from it. But there is another attribute of God that his people have to remember so as to have a full orbed appreciation of the God with whom they have to do.

Now 'goodness' may be ascribed to the LORD in various ways. For example, it may denote God as implacably opposed to what is morally wrong, and as himself the standard by which all goodness is determined. As such he stands apart from, and over against, his fallen creation, of whom 'there is no one righteous, not even one... there is no one who does good, not even one' (Rom. 3:10,12). It is this aspect of the LORD's goodness that we find in Psalm 25:8 where he is described as 'good and upright', and therefore the one who is supremely qualified to teach sinners the way.

God is also good in the sense that he is the source and provider of good things for all his creation. 'The LORD is good to all', as David reminds us (Ps. 145:9). But the benefit the LORD provides is supremely to be found in the realm of salvation. This provides the basis of the exhortation, 'Give thanks to the LORD, for he is good. His love endures for ever' (Ps. 136:1). This is his covenant love towards those he has chosen to be his people. It is seen not only in the forgiveness he extends (Ps. 86:5), but also in all his subsequent acts of covenant blessing towards those whose hope is in him and who seek him (Lam. 3:25).

This goodness is particularly encountered when his people find themselves in adverse circumstances of the most severe sort in life. He is **a refuge in times of trouble**. This is a general description, and is not confined to any one time in history. It applies whenever a person feels he is up against it — whatever 'it' may be. The word 'trouble' covers both intense turmoil in external circumstances, and inner distress. Then the LORD acts as a 'refuge' (Pss. 18:2; 62:7-8; 91:2), an impregnable mountain fortress which, since it cannot be taken by the enemy, provides security for the one who has felt himself about to go down in battle. 'God is faithful; he will not let you be tempted beyond what you can bear. But when you are tempted, he will also provide a way out so that you can stand up under it' (1 Cor. 10:13).

What is the basis for all this? **He cares for those who trust in him**. Literally, it is he 'knows' them, but it is not just with that knowledge which God has of everything, because he is omniscient. It refers to that covenant knowledge which said of Abraham, 'I know him' (Gen. 18:19, cf. AV); that knowledge which said of Israel 'You only have I known of all the families of the earth' (Amos 3:2, cf. AV); that knowledge of which the Good Shepherd speaks when he says 'I know my sheep' (John 10:14). It is the King of the covenant bestowing recognition upon those who are his. He has chosen them, and so is committed to providing for their needs (Ps. 23:1-2).

The recipients of this protection are 'those who trust in him'. The underlying picture is still that of the fortress. The LORD's people are described as those who 'take refuge' in him (Ps. 62:5-8). This is the recourse of the faithful when they are aware of their own frailty, and so commit their security to God (Ps. 61:2-3). It is not a one-off response that is described, but an ever-recurring characteristic of his people who have as their motto, 'God is our refuge and strength, an ever-present help in trouble' (Ps. 46:1).

The Sternness of God (1:8). But there are two sides to the LORD's action, as Paul brings out. 'Consider therefore the kindness and sternness of God: sternness to those who fell, but kindness to you, provided that you continue in his kindness' (Rom. 11:22). Nahum too recognises this as he says, **but with an overwhelming flood he will make an end of [Nineveh]** (*verse 8*).

Describing judgment in terms of a flood goes back to the days of Noah. Sometimes it conveys the idea of an invading army sweeping through a country (Isa. 8:7-8), and that may be what is foretold here. Though Nineveh is not named, it is clearly indicated (and hence the NIV supplement in brackets). When Nineveh fell, it was as a result of enemy invasion. But there is also the possibility that Nahum's reference here is to an actual flood. Later in 2:6 he distinctly mentions the flooding of the city as contributing to its capture.

He will pursue his foes into darkness. The LORD is himself light (Ps. 27:1; Isa. 10:17), and so brings light to those who enjoy the favour of his presence (Pss. 4:6; 36:9; 97:11). Darkness indicates the condition of those from whom his favour is withdrawn (Mic. 7:8). It is the darkness of defeat, and of terror, where God is not. As Job put it, 'There are those who rebel against the light, who do not know its ways or stay in its paths' (Job 24:13). Ultimately, it signifies the eternal doom of godless men 'for whom blackest darkness has been reserved for ever' (Jude 13).

Evil Plots Frustrated (1:9-11). This section poses a number of problems for translators, as can be seen by the variations in the different versions. The NIV translation represents a widely accepted way of understanding the passage, and we shall keep to it in the following comments.

Whatever they plot against the LORD he will bring to an end
(*verse 9*). This continues the theme of what happens to the LORD's foes.
They had not stumbled into sin against the LORD, but had deliberately
embarked on such a policy. All their scheming will, however, be of no
avail, for 'there is no wisdom, no insight, no plan, that can succeed
against the LORD' (Prov. 21:30). In words recalling the end awaiting
Nineveh (1:8), the LORD's action on behalf of his people 'will bring to
an end' all their intrigues (compare Ps. 2). Indeed, it goes a bit further
than a promise of what will happen in the future. It is implied that the
LORD is already acting to bring their schemes to an end for he is the one
who 'foils the plans of the nations' (Ps. 33:10).

Trouble will not come a second time. That looks back to 'the
times of trouble' mentioned in 1:7. When Nineveh is struck down by
the LORD, no more trouble shall arise from that source to vex the people
of God.

Nahum continues 'For', although this is not found at the beginning
of 1:10 in the NIV, because he wants to give the reason why there will
be no more trouble from Nineveh. Three terse descriptions that are
difficult to translate are presented.

(1) **They will be entangled among thorns** (*verse 10*). The thorns
are the prickly and useless bushes of the parched wilderness. Nothing
much else could be done with them, but to burn them where they lie (2
Sam. 23:7). To become entangled with them was to be presented with
an immediate problem that prevented attention being given to anything else. The Assyrians are going to be beset with many troubles.
They will have so much on their hands that they will not have time to
vex other peoples. That is one reason why there will be no more trouble
from that source.

(2) They will be **drunk from their wine**. Two thoughts seem to lie
behind this picture. The first is the ease and false sense of security that
will characterise the foes of the LORD even when disaster is already
threatening them. Zephaniah described Nineveh as the 'carefree city'
(Zeph. 2:15). There is also the idea of their helplessness when they are
engulfed by their fate (Isa. 19:14; 24:20). They have become so
stupefied by alcohol that they cannot take action to defend themselves
(see on 3:11).

(3) **They will be consumed like dry stubble**. The sun soon dried
out the stalks left in the ground after harvesting, and they were readily
combustible. The burning of stubble is found throughout the Old
Testament (Exod. 15:7; Mal. 4:1) as an illustration of the LORD's

judgment sweeping out of existence those who are the objects of his wrath. Here the completeness of their downfall is underlined in that they are likened to 'dry' stubble. There will be no difficulty in setting light to it, and once it is ablaze, there will be no putting it out.

In **From you, [O Nineveh,]** (*verse 11*) the form of 'you' in the Hebrew warrants the identification of the one addressed as Nineveh, which the NIV has made clear. **Has one come forth** refers to a specific individual, probably Sennacherib, who was the most powerful Assyrian aggressor against Judah. The *Annals of Sennacherib* relate how he captured Lachish and 47 fortified cities of Judah. He claimed he had carried away 200,150 people besides multitudes of animals. He also exacted heavy tribute from Hezekiah, and had planned to deport the people (2 Kgs. 18:14-16,32).

Sennacherib is instanced as an outstanding example of the behaviour described in 1:9. He **plots evil against the LORD**. His emissary to Jerusalem disparaged trust in the LORD (2 Kgs. 18:30,35). The Assyrian monarch had insulted and blasphemed against the LORD, heaping insults on him (2 Kgs. 19:22-23). He **counsels wickedness**. 'Wickedness' is 'belial', a term which indicated 'worthlessness, something done without moral principle.' In the intertestamental period it came to be used as an epithet for Satan. Such a usage is not established as early as Nahum's time, but it does indicate the background against which we are to view the policy of the Assyrian kings. Their conduct was unprincipled and directly antagonistic to the LORD and his people.

Study questions: Nahum 1:7-11
verse 7: How does God care for his people? (Pss. 25:4-6; 46:1; 59:16; Rom. 8:32; 2 Cor. 3:5; 12:9)

verse 9: What happens when human strategies conflict with God's plan? (Pss. 2:1; 21:11; Prov. 21:30; Isa. 8:10; Luke 12:16-21)

Nahum 1:12-2:2: On the Right Hand and on the Left
Nahum continues to develop the theme of 1:7-8, that the LORD's intervention to vindicate his name has two quite different results. The destinies of Nineveh and Judah are juxtaposed throughout this section, with abrupt, unsignalled changes of subject: Judah (1:12-13); Nineveh (1:14); Judah (1:15); Nineveh (2:1); Judah (2:2). The NIV softens the jarring effect of the original by introducing (in underbrackets) Judah in 1:12, and Nineveh in 1:14 and 2:1. But the succession of abrupt

moves is a deliberate feature of Nahum's style. It evokes the disturbed
and disjointed nature of the times when Nineveh would fall. More
significantly, it brings into effective contrast the twofold destinies of
the parties he is talking about. This is a theme that is found throughout
Scripture — the parting of the ways that the LORD effects in his
judgment, especially at the last day. 'He will put the sheep on his right
and the goats on his left' (Matt. 25:33).

Judah (1:12-13). In 1:12 Nahum for the first time presents the direct
speech of the LORD. He introduces it with the words, **This is what the
LORD says** (*verse 12*). Although this phrase occurs only here in his
book, it is frequently used by other prophets to indicate that they were
acting as the LORD's messengers, passing on what he had said to them
(Mic. 2:3; 3:5).

The LORD presents himself as the liberator of his people. His
intervention means the downfall of their enemies. **Although they
have allies and are numerous** indicates that it does not matter what
the power of the enemy is, or how many supporters they can call on to
provide them with reinforcements. Their strength will prove inadequate when the LORD moves against them. **They will be cut off** uses
a word that elsewhere refers to the shearing of sheep (Gen. 38:12) or
the mowing of a meadow (Ps. 72:6). It is a close cropping that awaits
Nineveh, which will also **pass away**. Often when cities were captured,
they were not totally destroyed, and many of their inhabitants would
remain in them as subjects of the conqueror. Here there is the first
intimation that Nineveh's fate is going to be different: not just capture,
but annihilation. After it was taken, it quickly fell into decay, and the
site was forgotten until 19th century archaeologists uncovered it.

Then the LORD brings out the significance of his action for Judah.
Although I have afflicted you indicates that there is no denying that
the LORD's fatherly chastisement of them because of their wilful
disobedience had resulted in their being brought low in suffering and
pain. 'No discipline seems pleasant at the time, but painful' (Heb.
12:11). The Assyrian armies had been the LORD's instrument to bring
his erring people to their senses. But now the time to show favour has
come (Ps. 102:13), and so he promises **I will afflict you no more**, that
is, on account of their past sins.

Now (*verse 13*) emphasises that though the promised change is still
future, it will not be long in coming. **I will break their yoke from
your neck and tear your shackles away**. A yoke was a shaped piece

of wood placed across the necks of two oxen, enabling them to work together in pulling a plough or cart. It was also used, as here, to refer to the rigours of political subjugation by a foreign power (Deut. 28:48; Isa. 47:6). Breaking off such a yoke gave freedom to those who were oppressed (Isa. 14:25). Similarly the shackles, probably of metal, that restrained their movement so that as prisoners and slaves they could not escape, would be done away with.

Nineveh (1:14). Nahum then switches his focus. Nineveh is addressed, or it may on this occasion be the king of Nineveh, representing the people, and the divine decree is announced. **The Lord has given a command concerning you, [Nineveh]** (*verse 14*). The matter is fixed (Isa. 14:24-27). The order has gone out to those who are to be the instruments for effecting the Lord's purpose. **You will have no descendants to bear your name.** This takes up the prediction of 1:12 that 'they will be cut off and pass away'. The defeat that is coming on them is of the most sweeping sort, involving national extermination. They will have no offspring to perpetuate their national identity (Ps. 109:13).

I will destroy the carved images and cast idols that are in the temple of your gods. The Assyrians worshipped many gods, Ishtar and Nabu in particular having outstanding shrines erected to them in Nineveh. Whenever the Assyrians captured another land, it was their custom to show the power of their own gods by pillaging the temples of those they had conquered, and bringing the booty to adorn the temples of Nineveh. Now it is their own temples that are to be desecrated. Their gods, of whom they had so many, would be shown to be powerless, just as God had exposed the worthlessness of the deities worshipped in Egypt (Exod. 12:12).

There is no future for Assyria. **I will prepare your grave.** This is a prophecy of national extinction. **For you are vile**, of little significance, no matter what they thought of themselves. Their deep rooted iniquity has led the Almighty to despise them, and regard them with utter contempt. 'Those who honour me I will honour, but those who despise me will be disdained' (1 Sam. 2:30).

Judah (1:15). Then Nahum cites words from Isaiah 52:7 to describe the joyful arrival in Judah of a messenger who proclaims deliverance. **Look, there on the mountains, the feet of one who brings good news, who proclaims peace!** (*verse 15*). The herald is seen as coming

over the mountains from a distant land. He is telling of the overthrow
of their oppressor: Nineveh is defeated. The people may now enjoy
restoration to all the privileges of dwelling in the land in tranquillity
and with divine blessing.

These words had earlier been used by Isaiah when he looked
forward to Israel's deliverance from Babylon. Paul later uses them of
the spread of the gospel message throughout the nations (Rom. 10:15).
This is an instance of where the prophets are led to see the general vista
of the divine deliverance from the captivity imposed by the enemies
of the LORD's people on them, and are more aware of the similarities
in God's way of working than of the precise time scale on which it is
worked out. See on Micah 4:1.

The response to this good news is to be expressed in worship,
because it is God who has been their deliverer and who should be
thanked (Ps. 107:8). **Celebrate your festivals, O Judah**. The removal
of the influence of foreign pagan rulers would permit the worship of
Judah to be reinstated in purity, while the religion of Assyria was
destroyed (1:14). **Fulfil your vows** refers no doubt to the many prayers
made for deliverance with solemn promises to honour the LORD when
he answered prayer. Therefore when the LORD's goodness has been
experienced, it is time to show that these pledges were not empty
gestures (Ps. 116:14,18).

No more will the wicked invade you resumes the theme of the end
of 1:9. The word for 'the wicked' is Belial, which is also found in 1:11
where it is translated 'wickedness'. Here Nineveh is being viewed as
an embodiment of the hostile power of evil. **They will be completely
destroyed**. In her ruination there is a foreshadowing of what will
happen to all the malignant powers of evil assembled against the
people of God.

Nineveh (2:1). Then Nahum goes back to telling what the future holds
in store for Nineveh, as he graphically portrays the vision he has had
of its overthrow. **An attacker advances against you, [Nineveh]**
(*verse 1*). The word 'attacker' presents the enemy as intent on
smashing Nineveh to pieces and scattering them on all sides (Ps. 68:1;
Isa. 24:1). Nahum hears a series of abrupt military commands being
given, as the Assyrians get ready to resist the invasion. **Guard the
fortress, watch the road, brace yourselves, marshal all your
strength!** But all their military watchfulness will be to no avail, as
Nahum will spell out in detail throughout the rest of his prophecy.

Judah (2:2). But before that, there is one further switch back to the LORD's people. The closer the hostile forces get to Nineveh, the nearer is the restitution of their fortunes. **The LORD will restore the splendour of Jacob, like the splendour of Israel** (*verse 2*). Jacob here refers to Judah, the southern kingdom, but the comparison with Israel is not so clear. It may be to the glories of the united kingdom back in the days of David and Solomon. Alternatively, this may pick up a theme that was common in the prophets (Mic. 5:3), as they looked forward to the time when the divided and scattered people of God would be found united once more, even **though destroyers have laid them waste and have ruined their vines**. Vines played an important role in the agriculture of Palestine, and indeed the vine was a symbol for Israel (Ps. 80:8-16). Despite the devastation they have suffered, the LORD is able to remedy their situation.

Nahum delivered this message to the people of God at a time when they were dejected and suffering from the ravages and oppression of the adversary. It was not intended to provide a warning to Nineveh, for the Assyrians no longer had ears to hear such a message. But those they oppressed were provided with hope through the message of divinely provided deliverance. There is a gleam here of the victory that the Messiah would bring to his people. Just as Nahum cites Isaiah 52:7 in 1:15a, so too would Paul in Romans 10:15, applying the words to the preaching of the gospel. The immediate deliverance of God's people, whether from Nineveh or Babylon, was but part of the total divine pledge of redemption from all thralldom by evil. This pledge is ultimately fulfilled in the deliverance that is effected by Christ (Heb. 2:15).

Study questions: Nahum 1:12-2:2

verse 15: What does the use of the same words here and in Isaiah 52:7 and Romans 10:15 tell us about the unity of Scripture and the ongoing purposes of God?

verse 2: How does the LORD restore his people's fortunes? (Isa. 44:26; Jer. 30:3; 33:10-11; Zeph. 3:20; Acts 3:21; 1 Pet. 5:10)

Nahum 2:3-13: "I Am Against You"

Nahum resumes his prophecy of the downfall of Nineveh, the capital of the Assyrian empire, from 2:1, where notice had been given of the approaching forces. Now they have arrived at the capital, and are vividly described (2:3-4). 2:5-6 tells of the fall of the city, and the next

section, 2:7-10, deals with the aftermath of its collapse. In 2:11-12
there is an extended comparison made between Nineveh and a lion,
which leads into the significant, interpretative pronouncement, " 'I am
against you,' declares the LORD Almighty" (2:13). It is his opposition
to the city that is being outworked in her capture by enemy forces.

The downfall of the Assyrian Empire began in the closing years of
Ashurbanipal's reign (669-626 BC). The details are obscure because
the Assyrian records for the period have not survived, but by 626
Babylon had successfully asserted its independence under
Nabopolassar. Events proved too much for Sin-shar-ishkun (623-612
BC) as other tributary states, including Judah, repudiated his control.
Various forces pressed into Assyrian territory capturing major centres,
including the former capital Asshur, which fell to the Medes in 614 BC.
In 612 the Medes, along with the Babylonians, and apparently also the
Scythians — a nomadic people from Central Asia who were making
their presence felt in Mesopotamia at this time, and who had at first
helped the Assyrians — surrounded Nineveh. Sieges of cities well-
fortified against attack could be protracted, but Nineveh fell in August
612 BC after only three months.

The vivid description enables us to envisage the scene around
Nineveh during this siege, because Nahum's prophecy was fulfilled in
detail. **The shields of his soldiers are red; the warriors are clad in
scarlet** (*verse 3*). 'His' refers back to the 'attacker' of 2:1. The shields
would have had a wooden frame with leather stretched over it, and
were probably coloured red, rather than being red because of blood
stains. 'Scarlet' seems to refer to the colour of the uniforms they wore.
The appearance of the troops outside the city wall was impressive and
designed to be intimidating.

Further details are given of the besieging army. **The metal on the
chariots flashes on the day they are made ready**. Chariots were the
most advanced weaponry of the time, and were particularly used for
fighting in open country. They had a light wooden frame, with wood,
leather, and metal fitments, which would flash in the sun. A chariot had
one axle for ease of movement, and was pulled by two horses. It could
have as many as four men in it: a driver, an archer, and two shield
bearers to protect them. **The spears of pine are brandished**, as the
waiting troops are drilled, and practise the manoeuvres they will
employ.

In the next verse Nahum continues his description of the activity of
the chariots. **The chariots storm through the streets, rushing back**

and forth through the squares (*verse 4*). Mention of 'streets' and 'squares' presents an interesting problem: is this before or after the fall of the city?

Nineveh was built on the east bank of the river Tigris and seems to have been surrounded by two defensive structures. One was an inner defensive wall between 11 and 13 kilometres (7-8 miles) in circumference and about 18-30 metres (60-100 feet) in height. This wall was so thick that three chariots could pass on its top. It had defence towers 60 metres (200 feet) tall and 15 gates by which entry could be made into the city. Outside it there was a moat 45 metres (150 feet) wide, filled with water diverted from two of the smaller rivers which flowed through the city. Apart from the western side of the city where the river Tigris provided a barrier, there was a further defensive structure which lay further out again. It consisted of a series of earthworks — ramparts and ditches — to prevent an enemy from coming close. Between the inner wall and the outer defences would be found the suburbs of the city, and it seems to be in this area that Nahum sees the chariots storming through the streets.

This would also fit in with what we know of the course of the siege of Nineveh. There seem to have been three decisive periods of fighting. The first, near the beginning, was won by the Assyrians, and left the enemy forces outside the outer defences. There are records which suggest that this victory led to a bout of drinking celebrations within the city. When this was reported by a deserter to the Medo-Babylonian forces, they suddenly attacked, and entered the area up to the inner wall. It is at this stage of the attack that 2:4 fits. The third stage of the fall of the city was when the inner defences were penetrated (2:6).

Nahum envisages the demoralising impact of seeing the chariots move impressively through the city suburbs before the final fall of the city. **They look like flaming torches; they dart about like lightning**.

Nahum then moves on to describe the final stage of the siege. **He summons his picked troops, yet they stumble on their way** (*verse 5*). At first this might suggests that 'he' is the Assyrian king, and even his finest men are unable to fight properly, and can only lurch into battle somewhat uncertainly. However, the verse continues, **They dash to the city wall; the protective shield is put in place**. 'The protective shield' was a covering used by those besieging a city to screen themselves from missiles hurled down at them as they approached the city walls. The troops at the end of the verse are definitely

those attacking Nineveh, and the whole verse probably refers to them.
The attacking commander summons his crack troops to try to breach
the inner wall. They rush up to it. Is it the ease of their advance that
causes them to stumble as they hurry forward at an unexpectedly quick
pace? Or, is it that they stumble over the rubble that has come from
ruined buildings near the wall? They move swiftly forwards and
protect themselves as they begin to use battering rams to breach the
inner walls.

We would then have expected a record of the success of their
manoeuvre. Instead another aspect of the situation is introduced. It
takes five words in the original to tell starkly of the overthrow of
Nineveh. **The river gates are thrown open and the palace collapses**
(*verse 6*). 'Collapses' is literally 'is dissolved', and pictures the mud
bricks, of which almost all structures in Mesopotamia were built,
washed away by the force of water.

Nineveh had fifteen gates in its inner wall, and all were near or on
one of the rivers of the city, but it does not seem as if 2:6 tells about
these. The unusual phrase 'the gates of the rivers' seems rather to refer
to dams and sluices that were used to control the flow of the two
tributaries of the Tigris that actually went through the city, and which
had caused flooding in the past. Perhaps the water supply had at first
been cut off, and then in the month Ab (July/August) when the rivers
attain their greatest height, the enemy opened the 'river gates'. At any
rate the river is recorded by a later Greek historian to have breached the
city walls and flattened them to let the invading armies in. Archaeologists have found flood debris at the highest ancient level of settlement
in Nineveh. With the ensuing destruction of the palace, all resistance
collapses and the city is taken.

The first word of 2:7 has caused considerable perplexity, but the
NIV rendering is as good as any: **It is decreed that [the city] be exiled
and carried away** (*verse 7*). Just as the Assyrians had done to many
others, so it would happen to their own capital. **Its slave girls moan
like doves and beat upon their breasts**. This is a picture of distress
and wailing over the catastrophe that has engulfed them.

Now after the city is taken, Nahum actually names Nineveh.
Nineveh is like a pool, and its water is draining away (*verse 8*).
'Pool' refers to part of an irrigation system (2 Kgs. 20:20; Eccl. 2:6).
When its wall is holed, it can no longer contain water. Opinions differ
as to whether the water flowing out of the pool represents the riches of
Nineveh, or its population, leaving the city. The NIV translation seems

to favour the latter. We hear officials shouting out to the fleeing people (and troops). **"Stop! Stop!" they cry, but no one turns back**. The city has been so devastated that they only think to escape from it. Perhaps this represented a reaction to an old superstition that the city would only fall when the river became its enemy, as was now the case.

We then hear another set of cries in the confusion of the fallen city. It is the voice of the invader shouting, **Plunder the silver! Plunder the gold! The supply is endless, the wealth from all its treasures!** (*verse 9*). Assyria had looted the lands it had defeated. Those who became tributary states were forced to pay heavy taxes, as Israel and Judah had often found out to their cost (2 Kgs. 17:3-4; 18:14-16). The wealth had flowed back to Assyria, and particularly to the capital, which became the richest city in the east. Now it has fallen, and is being subjected to the same treatment it had shown to others.

She is pillaged, plundered, stripped! (*verse 10*) renders a very effective play by Nahum on three similarly sounding words to reinforce the totality of the devastation of the city. Such features generally defy effective translation. 'Desolate, desolated, desolation' is a very poor attempt to convey the way he builds up this picture of ruin.

The inhabitants of the city are shattered and demoralised by what has happen to them. **Hearts melt, knees give way, bodies tremble, every face grows pale** lists the outward symptoms of their inward devastation. Fear and bewilderment grip all.

The prophet emphasises the helplessness of Nineveh by using a mocking analogy. **Where now is the lions' den, the place where they fed their young, where the lion and lioness went, and the cubs, with nothing to fear?** (*verse 11*). The lion is described in the Old Testament as 'mighty among beasts, who retreats before nothing' (Prov. 30:30). The violence of wicked men is often likened to the lion's savage attacks (Pss. 10:9; 17:12). The comparison also fitted the Assyrians because their kings compared themselves to lions in their terrible power. Lions featured prominently in the artwork on many Assyrian buildings. Once they had been able to behave like the lions, going about with no opposition. There had been no reason for them to fear, but now the situation has changed. Even their place of security has been destroyed.

The lion killed enough for his cubs and strangled the prey for his mate, filling his lairs with the kill and his dens with the prey (*verse 12*). The emphasis in this verse is on the killing of the prey by which the lion more than adequately provided for its own. In the art of the Ancient East lions are frequently represented strangling their prey. That was how Assyria too had behaved. It was not just a matter of gathering wealth into her capital, but doing so by violence and cruelty (see on 3:1).

This section then draws to a conclusion by looking beyond the human actors on the stage of history to the ultimate and controlling reality, the LORD and his opposition to Assyria's rapine and pillaging. **"I am against you," declares the LORD Almighty** (*verse 13*). There can be no greater threat uttered against the city than the LORD's opposition to it. 'The LORD Almighty' is the NIV rendering corresponding to 'the LORD of hosts' in the AV. It refers to God as the one who is in control of all the powers that are. He who has at his behest whatever forces exist in the universe has declared himself the enemy of Nineveh, and that is why this total destruction is going to ensue. No matter what power man may think he has, no matter what preparations he has gone to great trouble to make — if the LORD of hosts declares himself against him, it is all futile and doomed to collapse.

The two themes of the section, the invading army and the analogy to lions, are brought together in this verse. **I will burn up your chariots in smoke, and the sword will devour your young lions**. It is the LORD himself who is active in the affairs of man. A true understanding of history requires that we look beyond second causes to God himself, who causes their finest weaponry to be burned. The 'young lions' is a poetic designation for Nineveh's soldiers. **I will leave you no prey on the earth** continues the picture of 2:12. It implies no prey is left because the predator himself has been removed.

The voices of your messengers will no longer be heard. At one level this spells out the end of the empire. The heralds would have carried the royal proclamations to the most distant parts of the realm. Nineveh's commands would have been made known, and also the demands for tribute. But that is now all over. The rule of Assyria is broken.

There is also an implicit contrast with 1:15, where the messengers of Judah had brought her good news. This reminds us once more of the contrasting destinies of the people of God and of their adversaries.

Nineveh was a rich, powerful, and magnificent city, which arrogantly said, 'I am, and there is none besides me' (Zeph. 2:15). But her prosperity was not founded on righteousness. Therefore the LORD of hosts declares, 'I am against you', and divine justice makes it inevitable that disaster will come on those who have such a sentence pronounced against them. The sack of Nineveh represents the defeat of evil, as the LORD punishes Assyria, renowned for its cruelty, for the atrocities it had perpetrated.

Study question: Nahum 2:3-13

verse 13: In the fall of Nineveh we see the LORD's opposition to a city that was full of evil. Later the same would be true of Babylon. To what extent can we find here a foreshadowing of the fall of the final Babylon (Rev. 18)?

Nahum 3:1-7: The City of Blood

The third chapter of Nahum is a brilliant piece of poetry, which again tells of the overthrow of Nineveh. But it does not just go over ground that has already been covered. Each of the three sections of the chapter emphasises one particular lesson that has to be learned from the situation. The first section (3:1-7) shows that the city has brought her downfall on herself by her sin and her crimes against humanity. The God who controls all things has not set himself capriciously against Nineveh. In 3:5 he repeats his earlier declaration, 'I am against you.' God's sovereign rule over all nations is righteous. His retribution matches what comes on Nineveh to what she has done. 'Do not be deceived: God cannot be mocked. A man reaps what he sows' (Gal. 6:7).

Many features recorded in chapter 3 are also found in Babylonian and Greek sources recording the sack of Nineveh. There are those who deny the existence of truly predictive prophecy and account for these facts by supposing that Nahum was written up after the event as a hymn of praise to God for the overthrow of the capital of the evil empire. That, however, is to dismiss as fabricated the evident standpoint of the book, that Judah was still oppressed (1:9,12,13), and Nineveh's downfall awaited. Instead, these parallels are to be understood as evidence that the prophet did not speak from merely human knowledge, but was divinely inspired. Furthermore, when news about Nineveh did reach Judah, the many correspondences between the events in the news and the words of the prophet would have strengthened the faith of those who waited on the LORD for his deliverance.

There are five charges raised against Nineveh in this section: brutality, deceit, and pillaging in 3:1, and harlotry and sorcery in 3:3.

Woe! (*verse 1*) is normally used to bewail the dead, but is also employed by the prophets to introduce a dire warning, as if the one addressed were already as good as dead (see on Hab. 2:6). Nahum here addresses Nineveh as **the city of blood**, literally 'of bloods', the plural being used in Hebrew to signify blood shed by violence. War inevitably involves bloodshed, and can easily lead to atrocities. But the Assyrians gloried in violence, and made the committing of atrocities an instrument of their policy for subduing conquered peoples. With delight and pride the annals of the Assyrian kings describe the tortures that were used. Their wall pictures frequently show their victims with limbs torn off, or eyes gouged out, or treated as animals, or impaled, or flayed — spread out, pinned face down to the ground, and their skin systematically and completely removed from their living bodies. The Assyrian regime had for centuries deliberately employed such brutality to keep under their terror-stricken subjects.

The indictment continues with **full of lies**. This seems to deal with official statements made to secure the submission of weaker nations. Why fight them, if they will give in to false promises? We have a notable instance of this in the speech of the emissary of the Assyrian king to the besieged inhabitants of Jerusalem. 'This is what the king of Assyria says: Make peace with me and come out to me. Then everyone of you will eat from his own vine and fig tree and drink water from his own cistern, until I come and take you to a land like your own, a land of grain and new wine, a land of bread and vineyards, a land of olive trees and honey. Choose life and not death!' (2 Kgs. 18:31-32). This indifference towards truth may also be traced in the boasting records left by many of its kings, and ancient accounts of the business trickery of the merchants of the city.

The next item is **full of plunder, never without victims**. 'Victims' looks back to the description of the lions' prey in 2:12. The history of Assyrian imperial expansionism is one long record of pillaging and depredation, justifying the comparison with a ferocious animal snatching whatever it could. Assyria had grown rich at the expense of other nations.

It is not clear how we should understand 3:2-3. Many suggest that Nahum switches suddenly from the charges he is levying against Nineveh to a preview of its destruction. While such a switch would be in keeping with his style, it is just as probable that what we have here is a picture of the way in which the Assyrian forces bore down upon their hapless victims. **The crack of whips, the clatter of wheels, galloping horses and jolting chariots! Charging cavalry, flashing swords, and glittering spears! Many casualties, piles of dead,**

bodies without number, people stumbling over the corpses (*verses 2-3*). It is a picture of slaughter and carnage on all sides, and describes both the way the Assyrians had behaved towards others and what they were going to experience themselves.

What had been happening is to be explained in terms of the Assyrians' own behaviour. **All because of the wanton lust of a harlot** (*verse 4*). Frequently 'harlot' is used in the Old Testament to apply to Israel when she was unfaithful to the LORD and deserted him to engage in idol worship (Isa. 1:21; Jer. 3:1-3). The covenant bond was a solemn pledging of one party to the other, as in marriage. So when Israel broke her covenant commitments, she became an adulteress spiritually. What was more, in the debased rituals of pagan shrines she was practically involved in uncleanness (Jer. 2:20).

But this is Assyria. She had never made any covenant commitment to the LORD from which she could fall away. There was no bond between the LORD and Assyria to which she could be unfaithful, apart from the basic bond of all mankind to the Creator. The point of the comparison here seems rather to be to the harlot as one who gives her services out for hire. She was out for personal gain, and **alluring** brings out the devices she was prepared to use to draw others to her. There was the splendour of her wealth and power. What a one to have as an ally!

An instance of Assyrian willingness to sell their services is found in Judean history. When Rezin king of Syria and Pekah the son of Remaliah king of Israel made war against Judah, Ahaz sent messengers to Tiglath-Pileser, who then ruled Assyria, and became his ally and tributary (2 Kgs. 16:5- 9). But it was to prove a very one-sided bargain.

Nineveh is also described as **the mistress of sorceries**, one who understood and practised black arts. There have been recovered thousands of tablets which show the abysmal superstition that existed. Astrology flourished as a means of foretelling the future. Good luck charms made from many materials were worn to ward off evil spirits, who were thought to exist on every side waiting to plague their victims. Sorcerers would be involved both in trying to foretell the future and in trying to induce these demons to attack particular victims.

By her use of such means Nineveh **enslaved nations by her prostitution and peoples by her witchcraft**, selling her services wherever it would pay off and terrorising others by threats of demonic action. She 'sold' nations and their peoples into slavery. No action was beneath her if it would advance her purposes and contribute to her gain.

Here is the capital city of an empire characterised by ruthless oppression, depravity, and the advancement of her own power.

But **"I am against you," declares the LORD Almighty** (*verse 5*). This re-echoes 2:13. He is opposed to all behaviour which defies his authority and disregards the rights of others. Military might or economic power do not render a nation immune from the scrutiny of the LORD of hosts, to whom all he has created in heaven and earth are answerable. His condemnation of Nineveh means that she will receive a punishment that matches her crime of being a harlot. **I will lift your skirts over your face**. She had been ready to expose her nakedness in the course of her trade, but now it will be exposed to her shame (Jer. 13:26; Ezek. 16:35-39). She had enslaved nations, stripping her captives naked and exposing them to humiliation, but she herself will now be humiliated, as later Babylon would be also (Isa. 47:3). **I will show the nations your nakedness and the kingdoms your shame**. She will become an abject international spectacle to be viewed and derided by all the nations.

I will pelt you with filth (*verse 6*). God continues to effect his judgment through human agents. He will permit those he brings against Nineveh to throw at her any loathsome object on which they can lay hand. The word 'filth' is often used to describe idols and idol worship as 'detestable' in God's sight (2 Chr. 15:8; Ezek. 5:11). Here again Nineveh receives a fitting punishment. **I will treat you with contempt and make you a spectacle**. When Nineveh is exposed and displayed as a spectacle of God's derision, people will know that his verdict on her has been executed.

All who see you will flee from you (*verse 7*). They will look for a moment and then flee away in consternation at what has become of her. As they do so, they will say, **"Nineveh is in ruins — who will mourn for her?"** They express no regret at what has happened to her. They have no sympathy for her, and are sure no one else will be prepared even to pay last respects to her with decent funeral rites. God too recognises that all have been alienated from Nineveh, because the answer to the question he poses, **Where can I find anyone to comfort you?**, implies that there will be no one interested in giving even a word of encouragement to those left in Nineveh's ruins.

Study questions: Nahum 3:1-7

verse 1: By what standard does God judge human actions? (Isa. 3:11; 65:6; Ezek. 18:20; Matt. 16:27; 2 Cor. 5:10; Rev. 22:12) *verse 5*: Why are all nations accountable to God, even if they do not profess to be Christian? (Ps. 75:7-8; Prov. 8:15-16; Dan. 2:21; John 19:11; 1 Tim. 6:15; 1 Pet. 2:14)

Nahum 3:8-11: Learning from History

In the second section of chapter 3 (3:8-11) Nahum compares Nineveh to another great city of the ancient world. By using what happened to it he demonstrates that a similar fate can overtake Nineveh, and so he encourages the people of God to look forward to his intervention against their enemy.

The NIV margin tells us that the Hebrew name of the city Nahum uses as his example was No Amon: No represents the Egyptian word for 'city', and Amon (who was its principal god) the sun god. No Amon is better known to us as Thebes, one of the names the Greeks gave it.

Thebes was in upper (i.e. southern) Egypt, some 480 kilometres (300 miles) south of the modern city of Cairo (see Map I). It was the main city of upper Egypt, and its origins are lost in the mists of antiquity. The city grew to splendour around 2000 BC, and was the Egyptian capital for long periods. Homer speaks of its wealth, its one hundred gates, and its well-equipped chariots. It had been established on the east bank of the Nile, on a bend where the river sweeps furthest east and enters a broad and fruitful valley. The temples, obelisks, sphinxes, and palaces in the ruins at Karnak and Luxor are what remain there of the glory of greater Thebes.

Thebes spread across to the west bank of the Nile. Clustered along the foot of steep cliffs and slopes of the Nile valley were the great temples of many generations of pharaohs. Further west, penetrating into the cliffs is the Valley of Kings — where royal tombs of the New Kingdom (1500-1100 BC) are found. The picture many have of ancient Egypt is based on the impressive remains of this city.

The rhetorical question, **Are you better than Thebes?** (*verse 8*), was not asked to encourage comparison between the architectural heritage and splendour of Thebes and Nineveh. The focus is rather on the seeming invulnerability of Thebes as a great and well-defended city. **Situated on the Nile, with water around her**. Thebes was situated 'on the rivers', on branches of the Nile, which at that point is somewhat under a kilometre (about ½ mile) wide and divides into four channels. There was 'water around her' — not a reference to what happened when the Nile flooded, but to the channels of the river and to a moat filled with water from the river.

The river was her defence. The AV has here 'whose rampart was the sea', reflecting the Hebrew, but not allowing, as the NIV does, for the fact that the Hebrew word 'sea' can be used for any large body of water, and is here a term for the Nile itself. There is thus no geographical blunder, because Thebes was, of course, hundreds of miles upstream. **The waters her wall** probably refers to the fact that the river served Thebes in place of a rampart (a smaller, outer wall) before one reached the great city wall. The main wall of the city rose from the very edge of the Nile.

Thebes was not only situated in a very strong site. She also had considerable support from elsewhere. **Cush and Egypt were her boundless strength** (*verse 9*). 'Cush' refers to the territory south of Aswan, corresponding to the modern states of Sudan and Ethiopia. It was from there that the rulers of the Twenty-Fifth Dynasty of Egypt (730-656 BC) originated. 'Egypt' may perhaps be used in the restricted sense of northern Egypt. Thebes could thus draw on economic and military resources from north and south. It was 'boundless', says Nahum, deliberately using the same phrase that is translated 'endless' in 2:9, and so drawing a comparison between the resources available to the two cities.

Put and Libya were among her allies. Libya was, and is, to the west of Egypt, on the north African coast. Put has not been certainly identified. Many take it as a term for a region in much the same area as Libya, while others, supposing that Nahum is trying to say that Thebes could draw on resources from all points of the compass, argue that Put was a region on the Red Sea coast.

Yet she was taken captive and went into exile (*verse 10*). Despite the advantages conferred on her by her situation and by the allies she could call on to help her, Thebes fell. 'Are you better than her?' This question was rhetorically addressed to Nineveh at the beginning of 3:8. But the challenge is really to the people of God whom Nahum is addressing. They should not doubt his word. Nineveh appeared impregnable. The evil empire was at the height of its power. Nahum's prophecy seemed, if not impossible, then at any rate for the distant future. But he is teaching a lesson from history, and recent history at that. They all knew how disaster had suddenly engulfed Thebes. 'A week in politics is a long time.' Situations that seem impregnable can be turned round in a moment. Powers that seem entrenched for years to come can be overthrown very quickly, as even in recent times we have seen the Soviet Union disintegrate.

The sack of Thebes teaches another lesson. Early critics frequently maintained this was biblical fiction. The records for the period did not allow time for this to happen, and so they maintained Nahum had invented this disaster. But their conclusions were premature, and here, as in many other matters, the discoveries of the archaeologist have vindicated the truthfulness of the biblical narrative. We now have records for this troubled period in Egyptian history. Under the Ethiopian Twenty-Fifth Dynasty, Egypt constantly tried to stir up trouble for Assyria by inciting the smaller states of Palestine to revolt. In two separate campaigns Assyria decisively defeated Egypt. In the first Thebes surrendered (670 BC), but in the second (663) it was pillaged and razed.

The Assyrians carried out the task with their customary brutality. **Her infants were dashed to pieces at the head of every street**. They would not have survived the long march to slavery in Assyria, so they were exterminated on the spot. The common people were deported in groups, but **lots were cast for her nobles, and all her great men were put in chains**. Being better educated, they would have been more valuable slaves, and so were allocated to individual captors by lot.

The same fate awaits Nineveh. Thebes had all these great advantages, and what did they benefit her? Nineveh too enjoyed a similar situation and could call on the resources of a vast empire, but no matter how well Nineveh is defended, the same can, and will, happen to her. There is also the further note of the exact retribution that will befall Nineveh, for it was after all the Assyrians who had brought about the downfall of Thebes in so terrible a way. As they had done to others, so it would come upon them.

You too will become drunk (*verse 11*). The picture is of someone who has lost control of his faculties, and is unable to act with calm and deliberation (1:10). Thebes had reeled under the impact of the calamity that engulfed her, so too will Nineveh. **You will go into hiding and seek refuge from the enemy**. There was indeed a remarkable parallel with the Ethiopian Pharaoh, Tanut-amon, who was so unnerved by the approaching Assyrian forces that he abandoned Thebes to seek security further south in the Nile valley. When Nineveh itself fell, the ruling king died in the blaze, but his successor fled to Haran and held out there for a few years before that city too fell before the Babylonians.

Nahum was primarily speaking to the people of Judah in his own day and telling them that an impregnable city can be breached. Every age has to learn that it is easy to be deceived by current appearances. We put our trust in national prosperity and imagine our world and cities are different from those of old. They are not. They are part of the same world, ruled by the same God, who judges by the same standards. He does not condone sin. If we as a generation and civilization do not repent and conform to what God requires of us, it is the same destiny that awaits us also.

Thebes was powerful like Nineveh — and yet Thebes had not oppressed the people of God. Thebes typifies those who live for this life, abounding in wealth, ease and power, forgetful of God. Nineveh is more the image of the world oppressing God's people. If Thebes which did not actively oppose God's cause fell, what shall the end be for those who openly resist him?

Study questions: Nahum 3:8-11

verse 8: How may a false sense of security arise? (Pss. 20:7; 49:6, 13, 18; Prov. 14:12; 16:2; 30:12; Jer. 23:17; Luke 12:15-21, 33; Jas. 1:26)

verse 11: How does Scripture evaluate human expedients to find safety? (Pss. 20:7; 33:17; Prov. 21:31; Isa. 30:1-5; Obad. 3-4)

Nahum 3:12-19: The Final Collapse
In these concluding verses of his prophecy Nahum, as the LORD's spokesman, focuses on the internal weakness of Nineveh, and how it will contribute to her downfall. He uses a number of themes to make clear what is going to happen to her. She is the 'consumed', the 'eaten', city. The one word in Hebrew underlies 'the eater' of 3:12, 'has consumed' at the end of 3:13, and 'devour' and 'consume' (3:15). He also uses the illustration of a plague of locusts in four different ways (3:15-17). His message is not just that Nineveh will be overthrown by outside forces, but that the strong, cruel, harsh might of imperial Assyria is going to be the victim of its own internal depravity. Neither military might nor economic dominance will be able to avert the catastrophe.

As the enemy encircles them, the people of Nineveh will become demoralised. Not only will they be very frightened, but they will also have lost the moral fibre that is needed to halt corruption sapping their strength and will to resist.

Collapse of Military Might (3:12-15). **All your fortresses are like fig trees with their first ripe fruit** (*verse 12*). Nahum sees the situation that will prevail. Her military strongholds are going to collapse before the enemy. There would be no heroic resistance. The enemy would not need to invent some new weapon to overcome the Assyrians, or devise some tactical masterstroke. It will be like walking up to a fig tree with first ripe fruit and giving it a little shake. Down it comes, but not on to the ground. No, there is the turn given by Nahum to his description. **When they are shaken, the figs fall into the mouth of the eater**. It is a picture of easy success.

Nahum explains why there will be no resistance. **Look at your troops - they are all women!** (*verse 13*). Now that description is used in Scripture to denote weakness, or even cowardice (Isa. 19:16; Jer. 50:37; 51:30). But what Nahum is indicating here is probably something more than that: degeneracy, and effeminacy. That is how Greek history portrays Sin-shar-ishkun, the last king of Nineveh: a frightened, debased pervert. It seems that it was not mere cowardice that led to Nineveh's fall, but cowardice that sprang from moral corruption which had undermined the once strong and cruel race. The NIV does not translate a word that may be rendered 'in the middle of you'. It emphasises that this decay was very much a phenomenon of the capital, Nineveh, and affected those who were in positions of power there.

The gates of your land may refer either to the mountain passes at the borders of the Assyrian heartland, or to strategic fortifications on the route to the city. The troops have not defended them, and so they **are wide open to your enemies**. They have been taken and burned. **Fire has consumed their bars**. The bars were those placed behind the gates to keep them closed. They have been destroyed in the conflagration, and so the fortresses can no longer provide any defence.

In this situation where the way to Nineveh lies wide open, five taunting commands are addressed to the city. **Draw water for the siege!** (*verse 14*). The water supply within Nineveh was insufficient for the city. Most had to be brought in, and such external supplies would be the first thing an advancing army would cut off. Preparations would have to be made to withstand a siege by storing up vast quantities of water.

Strengthen your defences! Work the clay, tread the mortar, repair the brickwork! Stone was a scarce commodity in Mesopotamia, and most construction, including city walls, was made of clay bricks dried in the sun. The vast fortifications of Nineveh would have required huge quantities of bricks for the on-going maintenance of the city walls, quite apart from any additional defences that might have been hastily erected in view of the impending threat.

There (*verse 15*), in the very place where they had expended so much effort and resources, the inadequacy of all they can do will be harshly exposed. **The fire will devour you; the sword will cut you down**. Nahum sees the city ablaze and the people slaughtered by their enemies. Babylonian and Greek records confirm that Nineveh was set on fire.

The rest of 3:15 is rather difficult to understand. The NIV takes it to mean **the sword will cut you down and, like grasshoppers, consume you**. Grasshoppers are not renowned for their propensity to devour, nor would the sword be an effective weapon to use against them. Elsewhere (for example, Jer. 51:14,27) the NIV translates the same word as 'locusts', and that also seems to fit in better with what is required here. Hebrew has a varied selection of words for the locust, and this particular one seems to refer to it at an immature stage when it has no wings and moves about by jumping. The slaughter the enemy forces will inflict on the city will cause as much damage as locusts do when they sweep through a land.

Multiply like grasshoppers, multiply like locusts! 'Grasshoppers' is the same word as before and should be taken as 'locusts', while the word translated as 'locusts' refers to them as swarming insects which come in incredible numbers. If these words continued the earlier imagery of locusts as a source of damage, it is the enemy forces approaching Nineveh that would be bidden to come with a massive military presence and inflict as much damage as possible. Nahum, however, does not otherwise address those who besieged the city, and so it might be preferable to view a change in the use of the locust imagery in the middle of 3:15. Such a change is rendered more probable by the fact that other analogies using locusts are found in the following verses. These words are then spoken to Nineveh, as are those immediately before and after them. They continue the mocking commands to prepare for the onslaught, and the reference to locusts is just to their numbers. Nineveh is to gather as many troops as she possibly could, so that they resemble the locust swarms. But even so, the coming disaster will not be averted.

Collapse of Economic Power (3:16). **You have increased the number of your merchants till they are more than the stars of the sky** (*verse 16*) shows that trade followed Assyria's imperial conquests. Her traders were numerous. The number of the stars is often used to

describe the size Israel will grow to (Gen. 22:17). The shrewd
businessmen had readily taken advantage of the many opportunities
that were afforded for profit, as Assyria expanded its empire, but profit
was all they were interested in. **Like locusts they strip the land and
then fly away**. Once locusts have consumed the vegetation in an area,
they move on. The traders were acting only in self-interest, and once
there was no profit to be made from a place they left it. There may
perhaps here be a hint that Nineveh itself will become so devastated
that her trading community will leave her too. There will be no profits
for them in the rubble.

Bureaucratic Collapse (3:17). The imagery of the locust is then
applied in yet another way. **Your guards are like locusts, your
officials like swarms of locusts** (*verse 17*). But the comparison is not
only with the numbers of high-ranking officials that settled throughout
the empire as locusts **settle in the walls on a cold day**. It is the fact that
they are ever ready to move away when conditions are more favourable for them elsewhere. **When the sun appears they fly away, and
no one knows where**. The army and bureaucracy of Nineveh will act
in self-interest, just as they have done all along. When danger approaches the capital, they will find it suits them to move away. Many
of the administrators seem in fact to have moved to Haran in the
closing stages of the capture of Nineveh. The strength of the enemy
was not the only factor contributing to her downfall; the lack of
commitment in the army and bureaucracy was significant also.

Nahum turns to address the king of Assyria, and as he does so, he
traces even higher up in society the complacency and corruption that
had set in in Nineveh. **O king of Assyria, your shepherds slumber;
your nobles lie down to rest** (*verse 18*). 'Shepherd' was a term used
throughout the Ancient Near East to describe one who had the
responsibility for ruling and governing a nation. Nahum here deftly
ties together their previous easy-going attitudes ('the carefree city',
Zeph. 2:15), and the fate that came upon them in consequence. They
had whiled away their time in ease, neglectful of their duties, and so
their slumber and rest has turned into 'their last sleep' (Ps. 76:5), from
which they will not awaken (Jer. 51:39,57). These words seem to
envisage the situation after the capture of the city, and the king would
be Ashur-uballit who tried for a few years to keep the Assyrian empire
going in Haran.

As he looked around him, he would find that Nahum's words had come true. **Your people are scattered on the mountains with no one to gather them**. It would have been the duty of the nobility to give a lead in bringing the people together, but they have been killed, and the people dispersed without effective leadership to organise them.

Nothing can heal your wound; your injury is fatal (*verse 19*). The wound is that of the king, but it refers to the devastation that has come upon his land, and especially his capital. He has lost control, and the situation cannot be recovered. Nineveh lay in the dust, never to recover, its very location uncertain for centuries.

Everyone who hears the news about you claps his hands at your fall. No doubt, many of Assyria's subject people did gloat over their misfortune at the hands of the Babylonians (Zeph. 2:15). They had suffered so much from them that there would inevitably be rejoicing at their downfall. **Who has not felt your endless cruelty?**

But the rejoicing of the people of God will not be tainted by gloating. The focus of their joy is in the fact that the overthrow of evil vindicates the righteousness of God, and the removal of their enemies fulfils the promise of protection and deliverance he has given to them. Their faith in him has been justified (Rev. 19:1-3).

It is a warning also to others who resist him. He once sent Jonah to Nineveh, with the message, 'Forty more days and Nineveh will be overturned' (Jonah 3:4). Then they had turned from their evil ways and were spared. But now the injury is fatal. Matters can be left too late. The plea to return to God is addressed not only to individuals, but also to nations and civilisations. If it is unheeded, there is a day of reckoning coming which shall vindicate God and bring ruin to those who persist in rebellion against him.

Study question: Nahum 3:12-19

verse 19: How should we react when we hear of the downfall of those who have been enemies of the LORD?

HABAKKUK

Overview

The prophet in Old Testament times was God's spokesman to his people. But that was not the only role he had. In the prophecy of Habakkuk we do not find the prophet directly addressing the people and warning them of the consequences of their sin or pointing them to the realisation of God's promises if they were faithful and obedient to him. That is still the ultimate aim of the book, but it is achieved by the prophet allowing the people to overhear how he himself struggled to understand God's purposes. Habakkuk in the first place addresses God rather than the people. It is as his questions are answered that it becomes clear what he had to learn, and also what his contemporaries ought to understand about what was happening. These lessons are ones that we too should apply when we struggle with similar problems.

Habakkuk's problem was the difference between the world as he found it and what he believed regarding God. At first his difficulties arose in the domestic situation in Judah. Violence and corruption were rampant. Since God is just and holy and since he is the ruler of his people, how could he tolerate such behaviour (1:2-4)? Why had he not intervened so that those who despised the standards of God's covenant would not be able to continue dominating the land? God's answer is that he will intervene. Judgment will come upon the nation because of their wickedness, but it is going to come in an unexpected way. The Babylonians are going to overrun the land (1:5-11).

Later on, possibly when Judah was experiencing what it meant to have the Babylonians as their political masters, Habakkuk again comes to the LORD with much the same problem of the success of violence and oppression – but now on an international level. How can God be just and in control of the world, and yet let the Babylonians have a free hand to terrorise and dominate his people? How can he use such a nation as his instrument to punish his own people (1:12-17)? Habakkuk did not receive an immediate answer to this (2:1), but the LORD did reply. He assured Habakkuk that the wicked would be punished and that those who were the righteous remnant in the land would be saved (2:2-5). There then follows a poem in which the judgment that will engulf the wicked is graphically set out (2:6-20).

But the book of Habakkuk does not just consist of these two question and answer sessions. In chapter 3 we have Habakkuk's response to what he had learned. It consists of a prayer for divine intervention in mercy in the troubled times that the nation was to face

(3:2), a recital of how the LORD had acted powerfully and victoriously on behalf of his people in times past (3:3-15), and Habakkuk's resolve to remain steadfast and rejoicing in the knowledge that the LORD is working out his purposes in the history of his people. Present circumstances may cause problems and bewilderment, but the way out of the valley of perplexity is a confident trust in the LORD's wisdom and salvation (3:16-19).

Faith is never blind acceptance. To have questions and experience doubt is not the same as unbelief. There are many aspects of life – and particularly those connected with how God is working out his purposes in the course of human history – that raise honest queries for which we seek to find an answer. As we follow the course of the prophet's particular difficulties, the invitation to us is not only to bring our questions and doubts before God, but also to come to the same understanding of him and acceptance of his way of working as Habakkuk exemplifies for us. Evil will be judged when God deems it appropriate. In the meantime we are to wait expectantly (2:3-4), focusing on what we are sure of about God (1:12) and looking forward with joyful confidence to his intervention and deliverance (3:18-19).

Habakkuk 1:1: A Brief Introduction

The title given to this prophecy is terse in the extreme. **The oracle that Habakkuk the prophet received** (*verse 1*). It conveys three pieces of information.

(1) An 'oracle' is a divinely given message. Here it translates the same word 'burden' that Nahum had used to characterise his message of impending doom and calamity for Nineveh (Nah. 1:1). But now the word is appropriate to a message that concerns the future of the covenant people of Judah. Although the fate that awaits their conquerors is graphically set out (2:6-19), it is particularly the predicted time of oppression and hardship that is going to come on the people of Judah (1:6) that warrants the use of the word 'burden'. The prophecy is written against a background of foreboding as to the destiny of God's people.

This fits in with the situation that prevailed at the time of Habakkuk. Although no dates for this are given in Scripture – and indeed commentators have varied in their suggestions from 700 to 300 BC – mention of the emergence of the Babylonians in 1:6 is decisive in locating the prophecy in the closing years of the seventh century BC. 1:2-11 fits in with a time not long after the Babylonians had made an impact on the world scene – as they did when, along with the Medes, they overthrew Nineveh in 612 BC, but before they had invaded Judah, as they did after their victory at Carchemish in 605 BC. The later portions of the prophecy deal with the situation a few years afterwards when the cruelty of the Babylonians had been experienced in Judah, but probably before 597 BC, when Jerusalem was besieged and looted (2 Kgs. 24:10-16).

(2) The prophet's name is given, but there is no mention of his father or of his origins. This makes it very difficult to say anything about his background, but that did not stop the more inventive of the early scribes. In one of the apocryphal additions to Daniel known as 'Bel and the Dragon' Daniel has again been confined to the lions' den. Habakkuk, who had prepared stew and bread to take to reapers in the field, is miraculously taken by an angel from Judah to Babylon to feed Daniel.

The name Habakkuk, which only occurs in this verse and 3:1, has an unusual form for a Hebrew name. Some Jewish rabbis linked it to a Hebrew word for 'embrace', and Habakkuk was thought of as the one embraced by God, or the one who encouraged others. More recently it has been linked to a similar name found in Mesopotamia, *hambakuku*, which is derived from the name of a common garden plant. If that supposition is correct, it might well indicate that at the time of his birth, Judah was under strong Mesopotamian influence. This would fit in with the time of his birth being during the long dark reign of Manasseh (696-642 BC).

(3) He is called the prophet. In fact this is less usual than might be expected Only the two post-exilic prophets Haggai (Hag. 1:1) and Zechariah (Zech. 1:1) are called prophets in the titles of their books. Perhaps Habakkuk added this description here to make clear that although his book in many respects told of his personal spiritual pilgrimage, its message was one that he had been divinely authorised to relay for the instruction and encouragement of others.

This is reinforced by the word 'received', literally 'saw' (Mic. 1:1). The word is being used metaphorically to refer to the process by which the LORD made available to the inner eye of the prophet the information which he wished to make known to him (see on 2:1). It was not a matter of ordinary physical sight, but of what was divinely revealed to him. Habakkuk had become aware that he had been led by God even in the questions that he put to him, as well as in the answers he had received.

Habakkuk 1:2-4: The Perplexed Question

Habakkuk was not the first to ask 'How long, O LORD?' – nor will he be the last. It is part of the sin-warped condition of fallen humanity that time and again situations arise which seem to demand immediate divine intervention to rectify them. Those who violate the rights of others and perpetrate horrific atrocities act with impunity. Society plunges ever further away from the standards of God's word, and the witness of the church is ineffective to halt it. And God does not intervene. He does not answer the prayers of his people for revival. He does not punish wrong-doers nor deliver their victims. In such circumstances faith is acutely aware of the tension that exists between confessing that God is just and powerful, and witnessing the apparent triumph of wrong and cruelty. From this perplexity arises the cry of faith, **How long, O LORD, must I call for help, but you do not listen?** (*verse 2*). Why does God not respond to such entreaties for what is self-evidently in accordance with his will? Surely it is right to ask that the progress of evil be halted and the wicked called to account?

Now we must be careful not to understand these words as censuring God. In modern western society it is commonplace to demand that God, if he exists, justify his ways to man. The standard of judgment is human reason, and it is God who is required to vindicate his actions so that we may judge his conduct to be reasonable. But Habakkuk does not come as one who wants to reach a verdict on God's course of action. Rather he acknowledges the sovereignty of the LORD and the justice of what he does (1:13). Because he is sure of this, he is bewildered that he cannot work out what is happening, and why. This is faith seeking understanding, because faith is not a blind commitment. It trusts God whose ways are not arbitrary. They can be understood. God calls for an intelligent commitment to him, and that causes us problems when situations arise which we are unable to comprehend.

'How long?' emphasises that this is not a situation that has recently arisen, but is of long standing. It is not the detached inquiry of the philosopher, but the repeated and perplexed question of one who knows the anguish and suffering caused by the injustice he sees all around him. 'Call for help' is an intense word, which was also used by Jonah to describe his plea when he was hurled into the sea (Jonah 2:2). Why had the LORD not responded to the pleas for assistance from those who were suffering? Why had he not intervened and made clear his justice and power so that the prophet and the loyal remnant within the community who shared his commitment would be able to answer those who doubted if God existed or cared.

Or cry out to you, 'Violence!' but you do not save? The word 'violence' is *hamas*, a word with which we have more recently become familiar as the name of a Palestinian terrorist organisation. In Scripture it denotes situations of civil, as well as military, oppression. It describes malicious action intended to injure the person or property of another. Six times it occurs in this prophecy, and is a key word in it (1:3; 1:9; 2:8; 2:17, twice). One is reminded of the situation at the time of the flood, when society had disintegrated and the earth had become full of violence (Gen. 6:11, 13). That such conditions could be found recurring in pagan cities may not have been all that surprising (Jonah 3:8). So when it also occurs among those who are the covenant people (Mic. 6:12), it indicates that their relationship with God – and not just with one another – has gone sadly wrong.

The description of society in Judah in this and the following verse helps us narrow down the time of Habakkuk's prophecy. At the end of the seventh century BC there were two periods which fit. One is in the early years of Josiah's reign (640-609 BC) while he was still a minor and had not begun his reform movement, and the other is in the years after Josiah's death. Although some favour the former time period because they feel it does greater justice to the unexpected arrival of the Babylonians on the world scene (1:6), it is preferable to view Habakkuk as speaking of the disintegration that occurred in Judah after Josiah's untimely death. Unfortunately his reform movement had not taken deep root in the life of Judah. His preferred heir was his younger son Shallum (Jehoahaz), but he was taken captive to Egypt and his elder brother Jehoiakim (608-598 BC) was placed on the throne. His character was quite at variance with his father's, who had defended the cause of the poor and needy. Jehoiakim was only out to make a name for himself no matter what it cost in terms of the lives and poverty of others (Jer. 22:13-19). When the prophet Uriah withstood Jehoiakim and his policies, he had him put to death (Jer. 26:20-23). With such ruthless avarice and self-aggrandisement motivating the one on the throne, there was no check on similar behaviour throughout the ruling classes of the land (Jer. 23:10-11; see also Zeph. 3:4).

Why do you make me look at injustice? (*verse 3*). 'Why?' is the cry of bewilderment which also occurs in the psalms of lament (Pss. 10:1; 44:23-24; 74:1, 11; 80:12; 88:14). Repeatedly the prophet has seen standards of right and wrong flouted. This was a fact of life in his day. The emphasis is not so much on the pain that the prophet felt at having to witness flagrant wrong-doing, as on the fact that it seemed irreconcilable with the character of God that he should let it continue.

There were no statistics recorded in those days of criminal offences that had been committed. Indeed part of the problem would have been that they would not have been recorded, because society had become so decadent that those in authority saw nothing wrong with what was going on. Habakkuk uses six words in three pairs to describe the situation. The first pair is 'injustice' and 'wrong'. 'Injustice' translates a word that denotes an action intended to hurt others. It has overtones of deception and lying (in which sense it is also found in connection with idolatry, e.g. it is rendered 'idol' in Isa. 66:3), but it particularly focuses on the way in which those with power and influence abuse their positions to give a specious legality to actions that are intrinsically wrong. Micah had used this word to describe how the rich tried to increase their wealth by unjust means (Mic. 2:1). Isaiah talked of 'unjust laws' by which the ruling classes in society exploited those who were weaker (Isa. 10:1-2). Such corruption had again become prevalent in the land in Jehoiakim's reign.

Why do you tolerate wrong? This sentence may also be understood as expressing a very similar thought to what has gone before, and so may be translated, 'Why do you ... cause me to see trouble?' (NKJV). But the verb is elsewhere used of what one sees oneself rather than of what one makes another see (Jonah 2:4; 'watch' in 1:5; 'gaze' in 2:15; and 'tolerate' twice in 1:13). The thought therefore advances from what the prophet is aware of to the real problem – that God is aware of it also, and is doing nothing. It may be that Habakkuk's question is based on the words of Balaam, 'He has not observed iniquity in Jacob, nor has he seen wickedness in Israel' (Num. 23:21, NKJV: the NIV understands the verse differently), where the same verb is used and also the pair of nouns found here. There is a contrast between what the covenant people ought to be in view of their calling and what in fact they are, but especially there is the contrast between what the LORD as the God of the covenant now sees as actually happening and what he has stipulated ought to be the case. This intensifies the prophet's perplexity as to how the current state of affairs can be divinely tolerated.

'Wrong' comes from a root that denotes 'work' or 'labour'. Generally work is viewed positively in Scripture as part of man's privileged endowment from God (Gen. 2:15). But in an environment polluted by sin it now involves toil and drudgery (Gen. 3:17-19). It is these negative overtones which are emphasised in this word (Ps. 90:10; Eccl. 1:3; 2:11, 20-22). The word is then used to refer not only to the trouble and distress experienced by the one who toils, but also to trouble and vexation caused to others (Ps. 7:14). It is the misery and grievousness of the wrongs being perpetrated by the powerful that Habakkuk reflects on here.

In the following words the prophet describes the situation as he sees it around him. **Destruction and violence are before me.** 'Destruction and violence' are often found together (Amos 3:10; Jer. 6:7; 20:8; Ezek. 45:9), the former emphasising the physical havoc that results from a ferocious assault, while 'violence' (the same word as found in verse 2) focuses on the action itself. Society around Habakkuk was tearing itself apart. Rather than living in harmony by following the standards of God's revealed will, people were acting on the basis of their own ideas of what should prevail, and inevitably there were clashes as to what that should be. **There is strife, and conflict abounds.** 'Strife' denotes disputes between neighbours, such as would result in complaints being lodged before the courts. 'Conflict' too is a word that has legal associations, but both words are probably being used in a wider sense. 'Abounds' (literally 'lifts itself up') is an unusual expression, almost involving a personification of 'conflict'. Controversy and litigation had taken on such an existence of their own that they were an active force moulding the conduct of the land.

Therefore the law is paralysed (*verse 4*). The connection is not so much with strife and conflict as with the corruption and exploitation that existed in the land. They combined to render the law ineffective. 'Is paralysed' refers to what is faint or incapacitated, just as Jacob was 'stunned' on hearing the news about Joseph (Gen. 45:26). The law was the authoritative teaching of the LORD as the covenant king of Israel (Mic. 4:2). It clearly set out the way in which his people should live and work together. It was to be taught by the Levites (Lev. 10:11; Deut. 33:10; Mal. 2:7) and was to be the standard adopted by the king for his actions (Deut. 17:18-20). But it was the king and his officials who were the very ones who were corrupt. The impact of God's instruction and order on the land was therefore nullified.

And justice never prevails. 'Justice' is a broader concept than the giving of proper verdicts in the courts. It extends to include all the functions of government, and also the accepted basis on which the whole fabric of society depends (Mic. 3:1; 6:8). 'Judgment does not go out' (literally) relates to the authoritative promulgation of true standards. Micah had envisaged the law going out from Zion (Mic. 4:2). But in Judah God's standards were not being set out by those who had been entrusted with them, and so they were not permeating the life of the community at every level. Rather **the wicked hem in the righteous, so that justice is perverted**, that is 'goes out twisted'. The whole fabric of society is twisted because of the behaviour which continues unchecked. The courts were acting in such a way that their judgments did not check wrong-doing, but rather encouraged it. The 'wicked' were those who had broken the law and the 'righteous' those who had a legitimate claim to pursue for redress. But no matter how valid their case, their efforts to procure justice proved ineffective because they were blocked at every turn by the scheming of the wicked. There was no point in going to court to have matters straightened out because judicial decisions were not made on that basis. What a contrast all this is with the situation that should have prevailed among the covenant community, and in the land that the LORD had given to them (Ps. 85:9-13).

Habakkuk's prayers had not been answered, but he kept on coming to God because he knew that the answer to what was happening in his day could only come from him. It still remains the case that many aspects of the existence of evil in the universe have not been made clear to us. We do not yet fully understand how God is working. Even the saints in glory are presented as asking how long it will be until God acts in judgment (Rev. 6:10). But faith does not let go of the fact that God is in control and that he will intervene. There is therefore every reason to present to him our questions and queries as we wait for him to act when he sovereignly adjudges the time to be right.

Study questions: Habakkuk 1:2-4

verse 2: In what sorts of situations do the people of God ask 'Why?' and 'How long?' (Pss. 13:1-2; 35:17; 44:24; 74:10; 79:5; 80:4; 85:5; 89:46; Lam. 5:20).

Has the coming of Christ relieved the tension expressed in such questions? In what way ought we to approach God when we do not understand? (Rom. 9:20)

verse 3: Should we expect to understand all that God is doing? (Deut. 29:29; Job 11:7-9; Prov. 25:2; Isa. 45:15; Matt. 11:25-26; Rom. 11:33-34; 1 Tim. 6:16)

verse 4: How do rulers affect the standards that prevail in a nation? (Ps. 101:4-8; Prov. 25:5; 29:4, 12, 14; 1 Tim. 2:1-2; 1 Pet. 2:13-14)

Habakkuk 1:5-11: The Perplexing Answer

Habakkuk had complained that the LORD had not responded to him (1:2), but now that he receives a reply it is not what he had expected – or wanted – to hear. The LORD does not explain to him why he had not previously intervened in the turmoil and corruption that existed in Judah. He accepts the prophet's analysis of the situation, and asserts that as the one in sovereign control of affairs on earth he is going to intervene in the immediate future (verses 5 and 6a). However, these same verses show that the LORD's intervention is going to occur in such a way as to cause consternation to Habakkuk and those associated with him. The LORD is going to work through the agency of the ruthless and dreaded Babylonians, whose character and conduct are chillingly described (verses 6b-11).

There is obviously a change of speaker at the start of verse 5 although there are none of the usual markers in the text to identify that this has happened or who the new speaker is. We are overhearing a conversation, and this change of speaker and directness of address heighten the dramatic nature of what is recorded.

Although Habakkuk had approached the LORD as an individual, the response he gets uses plural commands. **Look at the nations and watch** *(verse 5)*. These plurals reflect Habakkuk's role as prophet. What the LORD says to him is to be passed on to others – either the whole nation, or those among them who shared the prophet's concern. They are directed to 'look' (the same verb as in verse 3) not within the borders of Judah but to the international scene, to the 'nations' (Mic. 4:2, 3, 7, 11; 5:8, 15; 7:16; Nah. 3:4). 'Watch' renders the same word as 'tolerate' in verse 3. The command directs them to scan closely the world of their day so that they will not miss anything of what is going to happen. They thought God was doing nothing, but if they paid attention they would learn how wrong they were.

And be utterly amazed shows that the answer given to Habakkuk's prayer is so far from being predictable as to cause utter astonishment. The verb is repeated in two related forms, 'be made amazed and be amazed', to emphasise the complete bewilderment that will fall on them. It will be like the amazement that struck Joseph's brothers when they were put in order of age at the table of the Egyptian official (Gen. 43:33), or like the astounded reaction of the heathen kings on surveying Zion (Ps. 48:5), or like the amazement of the inhabitants of Jerusalem described in Isaiah 29:9. Indeed later in that chapter we find a very similar statement regarding the LORD's method of working. 'Therefore once more I will astound these people with wonder upon wonder; the wisdom of the wise will perish, the intelligence of the intelligent will vanish' (Isa. 29:14). When the LORD acts, he marks what he does as his by not conforming to human expectations of what should happen next. The consensus of opinion in any society can be utterly and amazingly overturned by divine action.

For I am going to do something in your days that you would not believe, even if you were told. In fact 'I' is not expressed in the Hebrew and literally it might be 'one working will work'. But the 'I' can be readily understood from the following verse. While it might be the case that something has been dropped from the text, it is more likely that this is a device to heighten the dramatic effect of the statement through momentary suspense.

The word 'work' is used not only of ordinary human endeavour but frequently of God's wonderful deliverance of his people (Pss. 44:1; 64:9; 77:12; 92:4; 143:5). It refers to something that would happen 'in your days', within the lifetime of the generation that was then alive. That is significant as regards the dating of the prophecy. The divine action referred to might be the speed with which the Babylonians would become the dominant power of the day with their victory at Carchemish in 605 BC when they routed the Egyptians. More probably, however, it goes beyond that to include the havoc they were going to be permitted to bring on Judah and Jerusalem, culminating in the destruction of the city in 586 BC. That certainly ran quite contrary to the prevailing optimism of Habakkuk's day, an optimism which Jeremiah scathingly exposed. 'They have lied about the LORD; they said, "He will do nothing! No harm will come to us; we will never see sword or famine"' (Jer. 5:12; see also Jer. 6:14; 7:1-34; 8:11). So sure were the people that the LORD's blessing was guaranteed to them no matter how they thought and lived, that the sack of Jerusalem was utterly inconceivable even though prophetically announced to them. In Acts 13:41 Paul uses the words of this text (as found in the Greek translation, the Septuagint) to warn the Jews of his own day of what would come upon them if they too persisted in refusing to believe what was announced to them with divine authority, namely the Messianic status of Jesus, his resurrection from the dead, and the salvation that he alone can provide. Unfortunately history repeated itself. The solemn warnings were ignored and Jerusalem once more was devastated, this time by the Romans in 70 AD.

The next verse is introduced by another 'for' paralleling the one in the middle of verse 5. It gives greater detail regarding the events that would lead to the astonished reaction. **I am raising up the Babylonians** (*verse 6*) does not refer to their coming into existence, but rather their coming as enemies of the chosen people. This shows that the LORD's rule extends beyond the boundaries of Judah and determines the outcome of all events on earth (Amos 9:7). He who raised up individual judges and kings as deliverers of his people (Judg. 2:16; 2 Sam. 7:12) also raises up nations to chastise his people when they fail to live up to their covenant obligations. 'Because you did not serve the LORD your God joyfully and gladly in the time of prosperity, therefore in hunger and thirst, in nakedness and dire poverty, you will serve the enemies the LORD sends against you. ... The LORD will bring a nation against you from far away' (Deut. 28:47-49). He had already done so with the Assyrians, the club of his wrath (Isa. 10:5; see on Mic. 6:9), and now he is going to do the same with the Babylonians.

As the NIV footnote shows, Babylonians is used here for the people who are more strictly referred to as 'Chaldeans'. They were not the original inhabitants of Babylon, but a Semitic people who first appear in ancient records around 1000 BC when they occupied the marshlands south of Babylon. When the Assyrians, who came from the northern part of Mesopotamia, took control of Babylonia, the Chaldeans became the leaders of an anti-Assyrian movement. Not long before 700 BC, under the leadership of Merodach Baladan (Isa. 39:1), they captured Babylon from the Assyrians on two occasions and held it for a number of years. So troublesome did Babylon become to the Assyrians that Sennacherib devastated the city in 689 BC, after a nine months' siege. In 626 BC, when the Assyrian Empire was breaking up, a descendant of Merodach Baladan, Nabopolassar, became king in Babylon and founded the Neo-Babylonian Empire. From this time 'Chaldean' is virtually equivalent to 'Babylonian'. The forces of Babylon were instrumental in the overthrow of Nineveh, and after their defeat of the Egyptians at Carchemish in 605 BC, they extended their control over the whole of Syria and Palestine (2 Kgs. 24:7). The Neo-Babylonian Empire was at the height of its power under Nebuchadnezzar (605-562).

They are described here as **that ruthless and impetuous people, who sweep across the whole earth to seize dwelling-places not their** own. 'Ruthless' describes those who are 'bitter' or 'fierce' (Judg. 18:25; 2 Sam. 17:8). 'Impetuous' (rendered 'rash' in Isa. 32:4) presents them as in such a hurry to achieve their objectives that they dash on from one conquest to another. The implication is that they act without concern for the impact of what they are doing on others. There is no particular evidence to suggest that these had previously been characteristics of the Chaldeans. It took Nabopolassar some time to consolidate his position in Babylonia. He was a junior partner in a coalition with the Medes that captured Asshur, the old capital of Assyria in 614 BC and Nineveh two years later. It was over the following seven years that Babylonian supremacy was established, a process which culminated in their chasing Egypt, the other super-power of the day, out of Mesopotamia. They were set on a policy of unrestrained aggression and aggrandisement.

There is no direct reference here to the impact they would have on Judah, although the fact that they 'sweep across the whole earth' had obvious implications. However, their taking control of what was not their own might well have pointed to what Israel had once done in capturing Canaan (Deut. 6:10-11). Now Judah would be overthrown by others acting as instruments of divine justice. Since the behaviour of the people had descended to the level of the Canaanites, they would experience the same fate.

They are a feared and dreaded people (*verse 7*). 'Feared' also occurs in Song of Songs 6:4, 10 to describe the awe inspired by the sight of an army marching in full military regalia. A related word may be used to describe the reaction to the snorting of the warhorse (Job 39:20), or even the presence of God (Gen. 15:12; Deut. 32:25). 'Dreaded' describes the recoil from hazards to be faced (Deut. 1:19; 8:15) or hostile nations (Zeph. 2:11), or even a response to Yahweh's mighty deeds (Gen. 28:17; Exod. 34:10). Their military power spread terror among all they encountered. **They are a law to themselves and promote their own honour.** Literally, this clause reads 'from him (that is, the people) his judgment and his lifting up comes out'. They conduct themselves according to rules they have established for themselves, and consider themselves answerable to none. Their status and authority are what they have contrived for themselves. No more than the Assyrians before them (Isa. 10:13) did they see that the role they were to play had been laid down by God and was strictly within his control.

The following verses present the speed and violence of their advance. **Their horses are swifter than leopards, fiercer than wolves at dusk** (*verse 8*). Distance did not impede the progress of this army. The leopard moves quickly, and Jeremiah also uses it as an example of ferocity. 'A leopard will lie in wait near their towns to tear to pieces any who venture out' (Jer. 5:6). In the evening wolves which have not eaten all day are ferocious and ready to strike at their prey (Zeph. 3:3). This characteristic is here transferred from the riders to their horses. It is a picture of a nation eager for power, resolved on conquest and insensitive as to how they achieve it. **Their cavalry gallops headlong** involves a play on two words of similar sound which the NKJV brings out by 'their chargers charge ahead'. **Their horsemen come from afar.** 'From afar' certainly covers moving from Babylon into Palestine, but it may well go beyond that to horsemen of the distant steppes of Central Asia who had been pressed into the Chaldean army. These would constitute the crack troops, the most advanced military might of the day.

They fly like a vulture swooping to devour. This reflects the curse of the broken covenant threatened in Deuteronomy 28:49, 'The LORD will bring a nation against you from far away, from the ends of the earth, like an eagle swooping down, a nation whose language you will not understand.' A similar comparison is made in Jeremiah 4:13; 48:40; 49:22, Lamentations 4:19 and Hosea 8:1. Unlike modern perception which views the eagle as a noble bird in distinction from the vulture, Hebrew did not distinguish between them. Although the eagle hunts prey whereas the vulture is a scavenger, both have excellent vision which enables them to swoop down with accuracy on whatever they have spotted. Similarly the Chaldean armies could detect from a distance those lands that would provide them with rich pickings and they would swoop down on them to loot and ravage.

They all come bent on violence (*verse 9*). 'Violence' is again *hamas* (1:2). This had been the prophet's complaint regarding the conduct of the people in the land; now in the parity of divine justice they were going to be at the receiving end of such treatment. The Babylonian army had no inhibitions about using its power to grab whatever it wanted. They did not operate under any Geneva convention or with respect for the rights of those whose territory they overran.

Their hordes advance like a desert wind. As the NIV margin notes, 'hordes' is of uncertain translation, as the word does not occur elsewhere in the Old Testament, but a connection with a root meaning 'abundance' is not implausible. Literally the text would then read 'collection of their faces east/eastwards'. Since 'eastwards' is an improbable direction for a Babylonian advance in this connection, it is possible that 'east' should be taken as a reference to the east wind, which came in from the desert. It was a scorching wind which shrivelled up all before it (compare Jonah 4:8). **And gather prisoners like sand.** 'Like sand' is always a reminder of the covenantal promise of descendants to Abraham and the other patriarchs (Gen. 22:17; 32:12). Here it is used in the context not of blessing but of calamity. This too was one of the predicted curses if the covenant was broken (Deut. 28:41).

They deride kings and scoff at rulers (*verse 10*). The resistance the rulers of the lesser states in the area manage to muster is no match for the speed and might of Babylon. They are dismissed as being contemptible, hardly worthy of any effort needed to deal with them. This is the assessment of a militaristic culture with no qualms about its imperialist ventures. All is assessed in terms of military might and strategy. Why even Neco, pharaoh of Egypt, was unable to outmanoeuvre them!

They laugh at all fortified cities. A fortified city represented a more considerable obstacle to an invading army, but all of them together are just a joke to the might of the advancing Babylonian forces. In this they copied the attitude of the Assyrians before them. 'Where is the king of Hamath, the king of Arpad, the king of the city of Sepharvaim, or of Hena or Ivvah?' (Isa. 37:13). **They build earthen ramps and capture them.** The Babylonians were skilled at siege warfare. As well as using battering rams to cause city walls to collapse, they knew all about sapping to undermine them. The siege ramps mentioned here were gently sloping earth mounds slowly built forward to the height of the city walls, allowing entry to be made over the top of the walls. The Babylonians were so practised at this standard technique that it hardly stretched their resources at all.

Then they sweep past like the wind and go on (*verse 11*). Some cities posed a greater obstacle than others, but they too would eventually succumb leaving the aggressor free to move on to his next target. **Guilty men, whose own strength is their god.** Their guilt might look back to the preceding description of their unprovoked assaults on other nations, but it probably goes deeper than that by taking in what follows. What constituted the basis of their offence was that they were convinced might was right. As they had proved stronger than others, they thought that justified them in all that they did. They worshipped their own ability and resources. In doing this, of course, they denied any place in their thinking to God. They were showing their rebellion against him by putting at the centre of their policy and practice human might and wisdom.

The main lesson to be drawn from God's response to Habakkuk's prayer is the fact of divine control over what takes place throughout the cosmos. God's rule is not to be thought of as a series of powerful responses to events initiated by others. Events on earth occur 'according to the plan of him who works out everything in conformity with the purpose of his will' (Eph. 1:11). This is true not only in the broad sweep of history but also in the smallest details of the lives of individuals (Matt. 10:30). God's control is most evident at the Incarnation when he sent his Son 'when the time had fully come' (Gal. 4:4), that is, at just the right moment when he decided that all the varied strands of history had come together just as he had required.

In the present age God's purposes are determined by his plan to bring his people to holy perfection so that they will be capable of worshipping him eternally. Therefore, when we are baffled by what is happening, we are not to give way to despair, but to approach him, even in our bafflement, and ask that he sustain us. The forces that are ranged against God's people are working out his purposes. He is able to bring good out of evil, even though we may be blind as to how that can happen.

Study questions: Habakkuk 1:5-11

verse 5: Is prayer always answered as we expect? (Jer. 33:3; Matt. 20:21-23; 2 Cor. 12:8-9; Eph. 3:20)

How does Scripture show God's control over all events? (Gen. 45:5-8; 50:20; Pss. 75:6-7; 76:10; Acts 2:23; Rom. 8:28)

verse 11: What do people give priority to when they rebel against God? (Dan. 5:23; Rom. 1:22-32; Gal. 4:8-9; Col. 3:5; 1 Pet. 4:3)

In the light of the fact of God's purposeful control of all things, how should we respond to the challenges and difficulties we have to face? (Rom. 8:18-25; 2 Cor. 1:3-11; 4:7-18; 12:7-10; Heb. 11:26; 1 Pet. 5:6-10)

Habakkuk 1:12-17: Wrestling with Increased Difficulties

It seems that some time passed before Habakkuk came to the LORD with his second complaint. The Babylonians are no longer some distant power whose sudden arrival on the world stage is predicted as going to cause tremendous surprise. They have now arrived, and Judah is experiencing their aggression. Habakkuk is at a loss to know how this can be furthering God's purposes; that his people should be subjected to the tyranny of such an unscrupulous nation. Indeed, his problem goes deeper than that. How can God who is holy and righteous use such people as the Babylonians to punish his own people?

The prophet's approach to wrestling with problems of God's providence gives us an example of what we also ought to do. He does not let the problem undermine his faith in God. Rather than doubting God's existence, he begins by reiterating what he is sure about concerning God (verses 12 and 13a). With that as his foundation he then proceeds to set out his problem (verses 13b-17), so that what he is certain about may shed light on what he cannot comprehend, rather than difficulties being allowed to obscure and unsettle what is definitely true.

O LORD, are you not from everlasting? (*verse 12*). Again Habakkuk approaches God as the LORD, the covenant king of his people, the one whose very name is a reminder of his active involvement with his people's situation (Exod. 6:2-8). The question the prophet asks is not one of doubt, but is equivalent to a strong assertion, 'The LORD is from everlasting' (Deut. 33:27; Ps. 55:19). But how does this undoubted attribute of God fit in with the argument here? It is not dissimilar to part of the message the LORD sent to Hezekiah when his faith faltered. 'Have you not heard? Long ago I ordained it. In days of old I planned it; now I have brought it to pass' (2 Kgs. 19:25; Isa. 37:26). Nothing that is happening is a surprise to God, or too big for him to grapple with. He has known about it all along.

Equally the LORD has a long-standing commitment to his people (Mic. 7:20). What is happening will not be able to undermine that. The prophet is thus encouraged to the conclusion, **My God, my Holy One, we will not die**. In terms of the covenant relationship instituted by the LORD himself Habakkuk can claim on his own behalf (and on behalf of all those who are loyal to the LORD) that he is 'My God'. There is a personal bond between them which cannot be ruptured. God is also 'my Holy One' (1:12). Holiness here points to God's absolute purity and rectitude. He will not adopt a course of conduct that involves turning back on his commitment to his own. 'God is light; in him there is no darkness at all' (1 John 1:5). Therefore the thought that he will treat the righteous and the wicked alike must be rejected. 'Will not the Judge of all the earth do right?' (Gen. 18:25). So the prophet may be confident that the LORD who has promised life to his people will ensure that promise is realised no matter how dark circumstances become.

(The scribes who preserved the Hebrew text marked the words 'we shall not die' as a correction they supposed had been brought into the text by even earlier scribes. An original reading 'you shall not die', asserting the immortality of the LORD, was allegedly altered, perhaps because they felt it might have suggested the blasphemous possibility that the LORD could have died. Although this reading is accepted by some English versions, there is no manuscript evidence to support it, and it is not found in any of the early translations of the Old Testament. It is prudent to treat the information just as a piece of scribal lore and accept the text as it has been preserved in all manuscripts.)

O LORD, you have appointed them to execute judgment. What the LORD has decreed is the punishment of his people because of their covenant breaking. The justice of this is implicitly acknowledged. But the LORD will not step beyond what is just, and therefore there may be confidence for the future. 'To execute' is a supplement that effectively brings out the force of the Hebrew phrase which is simply 'for judgment'. On its own that would be ambiguous. It is not the Babylonian invaders who are in the first instance going to be judged (but see 2:6-20). They are rather the LORD's appointed means of chastising his people.

O Rock, you have ordained them to punish. 'Rock' is an ancient title applied to God, especially in Deuteronomy 32:4, 15, 18, 30-31, but evidence of earlier names shows it dates back even into Egypt (for instance, the name Pedahzur, mentioned in Num. 1:9, means 'the Rock has redeemed'). He is the certain and unchanging one on whom his people may rely. In the uncertainty which the prophet is experiencing, he clings to what he is sure about concerning God. It is the LORD who is in control. He has so set and positioned the Babylonians that they will assume the role he has allocated to them. Like the Assyrians before them (Isa. 10:5-7), the Babylonians would go too far (Isa. 47:6-7), but their divine assignment was to punish, not to destroy. 'Punish' translates a word usually employed in legal action. For instance, it occurs as 'settle disputes' in Micah 4:3 and 'lodge a charge' in Micah 6:2. In other passages it is used of the loving correction of the LORD who through it aims at bringing his people back to himself. 'The LORD *disciplines* those he loves' (Prov. 3:12), and 'Blessed is the man whom God *corrects*' (Job 5:17). The Babylonians were the LORD's means of bringing the discipline of the covenant on his erring people.

But surely the LORD has to be consistent. If he is punishing his people for their wrong-doing, how can he carry his purposes out by using a people who commit even greater wrongs? Again Habakkuk argues from what he is sure of. **Your eyes are too pure to look on evil** (*verse 13*). The purity of God was a lesson that was continually taught in Israel. Their camp had to be holy because of the LORD's presence in their midst (Deut. 23:14); no one who was in any way unclean was permitted to enter the LORD's sanctuary (2 Chr. 23:19; Isa. 52:11); and all sacrifices had to be pure and undefiled, for that alone was acceptable in the sight of the holy God. There was no doubt that 'the face of the LORD is against those who do evil' (Ps. 34:16), for he takes no pleasure in evil (Ps. 5:4). 'Look on' is not merely a matter of observation, but of approval and respect (Pss. 66:18; 138:6). Habakkuk is sure this is not true of God's attitude towards iniquity, for **you cannot tolerate wrong**. This repeats the phrase of 1:3.

But that is precisely what gives rise to Habakkuk's problem. **Why then do you tolerate the treacherous?** The 'treacherous' are those who are unfaithful in relationships, who do not honour agreements, who unscrupulously commit themselves but have no intention of being true to their promises (Zeph. 3:4). How is it that the holy God can seem to condone such behaviour, looking at it and not responding with immediate anger? Habakkuk would join with Asaph in asking, 'Why do you hold back your hand, your right hand? Take it from the folds of your garment and destroy them!' (Ps. 74:11).

Why are you silent while the wicked swallow up those more righteous than themselves? Problems have arisen over the identity of those who are called 'more righteous'. Some commentators have argued that they are the righteous remnant within Judah, who had been oppressed both by their own countrymen, and now also by the Babylonians. But the use of 'righteous' need not imply an absolute approbation of one party. In Jeremiah 3:11 the LORD records this verdict, 'Faithless Israel is more righteous than unfaithful Judah.' Neither Israel nor Judah were being unconditionally praised, but Israel's conduct had been more commendable. Here, therefore, there is no need to take the 'more righteous' as being just the pious remnant in the land. No claim is being made about the absolute correctness of Judah's conduct. It was just that in comparison with the Babylonians Judah was clearly less sinful. Yet God was silent while Judah was being swallowed up – a picture of the people being unable to resist as they are completely destroyed by their enemies (Lam. 2:5, 16; Hos.

8:8). But would not the LORD swallow up his enemies and the enemies of his people (Ps. 21:9)? Had this not happened to the Egyptians when they pursued Israel and were swallowed up in the Red Sea (Exod. 15:12), and to Dothan and Abiram in their rebellion (Num. 16:30-34; Ps. 106:17)? Why was it not happening again?

You have made men like fish in the sea, like sea creatures that have no ruler (*verse 14*). Habakkuk illustrates the situation by the analogy of a fisherman. Perhaps it was suggested by the fact, as we know from one relief, that major Babylonian deities were depicted holding a net in which conquered people were helplessly trapped. So Habakkuk sees the conquered peoples (and not only Israel) like fish gathered into a net by the Babylonians. Their victims are unable to do anything to help themselves because they lack effective leadership to organise their defence against predators. Of course, Israel did have a ruler who was committed to protecting them, but they had rebelled against him and no longer enjoyed his protection. They had descended to the level of the nations around them. 'Sea creatures' refers to the smaller animals, normally those which creep along the ground (Gen. 1:25), but also those found in the sea (Gen. 1:21; Ps. 104:25). Note that Habakkuk is clear that it is the LORD who has brought this situation into existence. The names of the oppressors have varied over the centuries, but the reality of their oppression has remained the same. How can the God of creation and order permit such inhumanity to be perpetrated? This was not the destiny for which God had created man; he was to rule over the fish not to be like them – helpless, vulnerable, without protector.

The wicked foe pulls all of them up with hooks, he catches them in his net, he gathers them up in his drag-net (*verse 15*). 'The wicked foe' is added by the NIV to indicate who is spoken about. It was the Assyrians who seem to have originated the custom of putting a hook through the lower lip of their captives to lead them off into slavery. The Babylonians continued this practice, as they did many other Assyrian ones. 'Net' refers to nets generally, including smaller hand nets used in both hunting and fishing, whereas 'drag-net' refers to a net which is weighted and sinks to the floor of the sea. Just as the fisherman catches in his nets all that he wants, so the great and powerful armies of the Babylonians sweep up all the nations before them. None are able to evade their advance. **And so he rejoices and is glad.** Their armies bring them success in which they rejoice. After all, that was what they were aiming for: not just military success, but the resources that accrue to the conqueror. There may even be a hint of fiendish gloating over those they have captured.

Therefore he sacrifices to his net and burns incense to his dragnet, for by his net he lives in luxury and enjoys the choicest food (*verse 16*). 'Therefore' translates the same phrase as 'and so' in the last clause of the previous verse. This is spelling out a chain of consequences – but not about fishermen. There is no evidence that fishermen in the ancient world worshipped their nets, but many military powers venerated their weapons. This is what Habakkuk had in mind. He is parodying the Babylonians attitude towards their weapons. They were out to succeed and enjoy the fruits of success. Both 'luxury' and 'choicest food' convey the idea of fatness and prosperity. They therefore worshipped the weapons by which they achieved their victories and amassed plunder.

Is he to keep on emptying his net, destroying nations without mercy? (*verse 17*). The picture of the fisherman merges with that of the hostile armies of Babylon. The question begins with 'Is it on account of this?' Will this process of catching nations to spoil them be permitted to continue indefinitely? How can God permit these atrocities to be perpetrated? It is not just the fate of Judah that weighs on the prophet's mind. His question involves the 'nations'. It is one of the most powerful pleas against senseless cruelty and slaughter in the Old Testament.

The questions raised have not gone away with the passing of the years. The suffering involved in God's providence still raises the question 'Why?' No explanation is given, but it is through suffering, even suffering that brought the cry of dereliction to one who was certainly more righteous than his oppressors, that God's way of salvation is to be worked out. Our problem is underestimation of the task undertaken in redeeming a fallen world, and our lack of awareness of the intensity of suffering on the part of the Son of God that was required to save it. This gives perspective to our view on the problem, but it still leaves us wrestling with what is ultimately incomprehensible.

We may not narrow this question of the existence of evil. Habakkuk here approaches the problem as it makes itself felt on the stage of world politics. Earlier he had considered it in the life of the nation. Every generation experiences similar problems as the realisation dawns that no matter how well intentioned human endeavours are to solve mankind's problems, they all contain within themselves the corrupting influence of human sinfulness that inevitably leads to their downfall. The existence of evil is ultimately a personal problem that leads to Paul's anguished cry. 'I see another law at work in the members of my body, waging war against the law of my mind and making me a prisoner of the law of sin at work within my members. What a wretched man I am! Who will rescue me from this body of death?' (Rom. 7:23-24).

Study questions: Habakkuk 1:12-17
verse 12: What is God's discipline designed to achieve? (Deut. 8:5; Job 34:31; Pss. 94:12; 119:71; 1 Cor. 11:32; Heb. 12:5-11; Rev. 3:19)

verse 16: The Babylonians abused their success. How should we react to success? (Deut. 6:10-12; 8:13-14; Prov. 27:2; 30:9; Matt. 23:5-7; 2 Cor. 10:18; 1 Thess. 2:6)

Habakkuk 2:1-5: Wait for it
One of the hardest lessons that faith has to learn is that waiting on the LORD is not some colourless religious metaphor used to describe those who are loyal to the LORD, but an intense and ever-present discipline that characterises all of life, particularly at times of tension and perplexity. In this section of his prophecy Habakkuk first recognises the need to wait for a reply to his question (2:1). But the response that comes from the LORD points to still further waiting as the way to find the resolution of the fundamental problem the prophet and his generation were grappling with (2:2-5).

On Sentry Duty (2:1) After Habakkuk set out his second perplexed complaint before the LORD, he realised that a reply might not be immediately forthcoming. So the prophet resolved upon the following course of action: **I will stand at my watch and station myself on the ramparts** (*verse 1*). The picture is that of a soldier on sentry duty, stationed at his 'watch' or 'post' (Isa. 21:8). The ramparts were situated on the top of the city walls as part of the defence precautions for a siege, and so also provided an ideal lookout point. We are not to suppose that the prophet actually went to some part of the walls round Jerusalem, or even to a pinnacle of the temple. The metaphor of the sentry or watchman was frequently used of the prophets carrying out their duties (see on Mic. 7:4). Here it denotes the unremitting and undistracted way in which Habakkuk was determined to wait for the LORD's response, just as a watchman had to be fully alert at all times (Isa. 21:6; 62:6-7).

Habakkuk's attitude was that of confidence. He has no doubt but that God will answer. His waiting is not an attempt to induce God to respond favourably. It is rather the policy of one determined not to make the mistake of those who pray and do not think they have got an answer because they forget the matter and do not recognise the reply when it is given. Habakkuk was determined to understand the LORD's way of working, and so he took measures to avoid that error (Ps. 5:3; Mic. 7:7). **I will look to see.** 'Look' continues the metaphor of the watchman (Mic. 7:4, 7). It involves the diligent on-going monitoring of a situation so as not to be taken unawares by any development – just what was expected of a sentry (2 Sam. 18:24-27; 2 Kgs. 9:17-18, 20).

What he will say to me is more general than the Hebrew warrants. The prophet wrote 'what he will say *in* me'. This relates to the inner way in which the LORD spoke to him, and shows that he was able to distinguish between his own thoughts and ideas presented directly to his inner consciousness by God. Such direct communication was a privilege extended to the prophets, but the LORD's answer can come in other ways also: it may come through the circumstances of providence (Jonah 2:1, 10), or through meditating on his word (Ps. 119:18).

And what answer I am to give to this complaint. These words have caused difficulties for interpreters. The alternative translation noted in the NIV footnote, 'and what to answer when I am rebuked', arises from the fact that the word translated 'complaint' can refer either to a formal statement of the grievance one has, one's argument (Job 13:6), or to the reprimand or rebuke given by whoever has heard a case (Ezek. 5:15). If it is used here in the latter sense, then Habakkuk is expecting a rebuff for his audacity in probing further how the LORD was at work in the affairs of his people. While some then take the answer he is pondering as one that he is preparing to give to the LORD so determined is he to get to the root of the matter, this seems a very bold and uncharacteristic response of a prophet in the face of a divine rebuke. Some early versions (and also modern translations) avoid the difficulty by changing 'I am to give' to 'he (that is, God) will give'. But that is avoiding rather than solving the problem.

It must be noted that the verb used here for 'answer' is literally 'bring back', and is employed in situations where there are three parties involved, with the answer being transmitted through the middle party (2 Sam. 24:13; 1 Kgs. 12:6, 9; Est. 4:13). Here then Habakkuk is considering how he will fulfil his function of being a prophetic intermediary and what answer he will relay to the people, particularly those who, like himself, were pondering God's ways of dealing with them. It is the same situation that is envisaged by the rendering of the NIV text. Habakkuk is not then considering that the LORD will rebuke him for approaching him with his complaint. As he waits to receive the LORD's answer, he anticipates that it will be difficult to grasp and wonders how he will be able to present it to his contemporaries.

The Divine Answer (2:2-5) We do not know how long Habakkuk had to wait for an answer, but when he did receive one, the LORD stressed that it was of special importance. **Then the LORD replied: 'Write down the revelation'** (*verse 2*). There was nothing new in the fact that it was to be written down. This had become standard prophetic practice after the ministries of Elijah and Elisha in the ninth century BC. It is the details which follow that mark the procedure as unusual. 'Revelation' is used here to translate the word 'vision' (Mic. 3:6; Nah. 1:1) because there is nothing in the immediate context to suggest that the prophet actually 'saw' anything, that is, had a pictorial image divinely presented to his mind.

And make it plain on tablets. 'Make it plain' is rendered 'write very clearly' in Deuteronomy 27:8 in reference to the letters to be used on the large whitewashed stones on which the law of the LORD was to be written. The message was so important that any possibility of misunderstanding or ignoring it had to be ruled out. For the same reason the message here was to be written on tablets, which may have been made from wood or clay. Clay tablets were the normal medium of writing in Mesopotamia, and were also used in Palestine. They were durable, and so would be preserved through the anticipated delay (2:3). **So that a herald may run with it** favours the idea of tablets that are easily portable. In relaying this message, a herald had not to be left to rely on his memory. He will have it written down, and so be able to report it far and near with more than ordinary exactitude.

However, the NIV margin suggests another rendering of the phrase, 'so that whoever reads it may run'. To 'run' is used of prophetic activity in Jeremiah 23:21, where the LORD says of the false prophets, 'I did not send these prophets, yet they have run with their message'. In that event the phrase would again indicate the spread of the prophetic message. All who read it can spread the prophetic word abroad. 'Run' is also used of obedience to God's word. The psalmist prays, 'I run in the path of your commands, for you have set my heart free' (Ps. 119:32; see also Isa. 40:31). The purpose of the clear writing would in that case be the ease with which the instruction given may be put into practice. But it is perhaps most likely that 'run' simply refers to carrying out an action quickly, as in our idiom of running one's eye over something. The writing was to be so clear that there would be no difficulty for anyone who tried to make it out. Perhaps it was written in larger than ordinary letters on wooden boards, rather than on the normally much smaller clay tablets.

But what precisely was the message that had to be written in this way? It is generally accepted that it included verses 4 and 5. But the use of 'tablets' may indicate that more was to be written than those two verses. The close links between 2:4-5 and what follows may mean that the message extended to the end of the chapter. Some interpreters have argued that the use of 'vision' may be more aptly understood of the imagery of 3:3-15, and would argue that the reference is to chapter 3, or that at any rate it was included in the material written down. In the absence of any clear indication as to what precisely constituted the revelation or vision, we cannot be certain.

The reason for the prophecy being written is then given. **For the revelation awaits an appointed time** (*verse 3*). God had set the time at which the predictions of the prophecy would come true. All history is under his control and unfolds precisely when it suits his purposes and precisely how he desires it to occur (Gen. 18:14; Pss. 75:2; 102:13).

It speaks of the end. 'Speaks' comes from a word whose basic meaning is to 'breathe' or 'pant'. There are possibly overtones of hurry and eagerness to reach the destination. But what is 'the end' that is spoken of? Presumably it refers to the same period as 'the appointed time' (which also has the definite article in the Hebrew text). Later, similar phraseology was used by Daniel to refer to the time of the coming of the Messiah, when judgment would finally fall on the powers of this world and the LORD's action against evil in all its manifestations would be made unmistakably clear (Dan. 8:19; 11:27, 35; 12:4). Does Habakkuk use the words in the same sense? Undoubtedly the immediate problem that perplexed him was the Babylonian oppression of Judah. The woes pronounced in 2:6-19 have the Babylonians as their primary target. But the problem posed by Babylon was only a particular instance of the wider and age-long problem of the existence of evil and how it will be dealt with by the God of righteousness and holiness. Judgment came on the Babylonians when the Persians under Cyrus captured their city at the end of October 539 BC. This brought relief to the exiled Judeans who were then permitted to return home and rebuild their city. However, like every other deliverance the LORD extends to his people throughout history, it is an anticipation of the final deliverance when the spiritual Babylon is ultimately overthrown (Rev. 18:2, 10). We must not suppose that Habakkuk was unaware of this. The expectation expressed in 2:14 shows that he too, albeit without the greater clarity that later revelation was to bring, was looking not only for an immediate resolution of the problem of evil, but for the ultimate solution also.

Habakkuk is assured that the revelation he has been given **will not prove false. Though it linger, wait for it; it will certainly come and will not delay.** There will be no need to think up elaborate explanations as to why the LORD's message has not been fulfilled. Though a delay ensues, the message will come true, and in the meantime the proper response is that of waiting. This word often relates to a confident expectation that the LORD will provide help and deliverance (Ps. 33:20; Isa. 8:17; 30:18; 64:4), which is here extended to the realisation of the prophecy (Dan. 12:12). 'Come' is applied to the fulfilment of prophecy in 1 Samuel 9:6 and Jeremiah 28:9. It is a call to wait with patience for God to act as he sees fit, and an assurance that there will be no disappointment to those who wait. Such a delay in divine action has often perplexed faith and given unbelievers occasion to scoff just as Peter warned, 'First of all, you must understand that in the last days scoffers will come, scoffing and following their own evil desires. They will say, "Where is this 'coming' he promised? Ever since our fathers died, everything goes on as it has since the beginning of creation"' (2 Pet. 3:4-5). But against this innate skepticism of fallen human nature there must be set the promise, 'And will not God bring about justice for his chosen ones, who cry out to him day and night? Will he keep putting them off? I tell you, he will see that they get justice, and quickly' (Luke 18:7-8).

Again, the NIV margin notes a variant translation, 'Though he linger, wait for him; he will certainly come and will not delay'. Such a personal understanding of the text dates back at any rate to the Septuagint, the early Greek translation, 'for one who comes will come'. It is this understanding that is brought out in the New Testament in Hebrews 10:37, 'He who is coming will come and will not delay'. Though this thought is not directly expressed by Habakkuk, his prophecy is ultimately realised only with the coming of the Messiah. He is God's answer to the existence of evil in this world – an answer that is both effective and gracious. It is after all easy to solve the problem of evil by annihilating all that has intruded into the perfect world God created. But that would be to let sin have the last word on God's creation, and there would be no possibility of hope for sinful humanity. It is in the tension of the historical process in which God is at work to redeem – not to exterminate – that the continued existence of evil in a warped world poses a problem until the final resolution when the risen Christ 'has destroyed all dominion, authority and power. For he must reign until he has put all his enemies under his feet' (1 Cor. 15:24-25).

Verses 4 and 5 contrast two attitudes towards God and his word. The one is that of the righteous, introduced almost parenthetically in verse 4b. The other is displayed by the arrogant oppressor. He is not directly identified, but the character traits described are evidently those of the Babylonians. **See, he is puffed up** (*verse 4*). Whoever falls within this description comes under the impending judgment of God. More traditional translations render this, 'His soul is puffed up'. Even though 'soul' is perhaps not the best translation of the word involved, it does convey the idea of the inward side to this self-exaltation. His view of himself is greatly inflated. 'Puffed up' is translated 'in their presumption' (Num. 14:44), and is related to the word for the tumours with which the Philistines were afflicted (1 Sam. 5:6, 9, 12). This cancerous swelling of pride and self-importance is the root of mankind's defiant rebellion against God.

His desires are not upright. Uprightness characterises conduct that is in accord with the requirements of God (Exod. 15:26; Deut. 13:18). But the phrase that is repeatedly found in the Psalms is 'upright in heart' (Pss. 7:10; 11:2; 32:11; 36:10; 64:10; 94:15; 97:11; 125:4). This emphasises that it is not mere outward conformity to God's requirements that meets the criterion of uprightness. The inner motivation must be right also. Those who are full of themselves give no thought outwardly or inwardly to what God requires in their lives.

The LORD then turns to consider the character of those who are upright and who display a proper attitude to him. **But the righteous will live by his faith** is not a consequence of what has just been stated. It stands as a contrasting and corrective thought to the attitude of the arrogant. Righteousness is conformity to a standard, and 'the righteous' are those who in heart and conduct are in true covenant relationship with God and what he requires. There is no thought that this has come about by any intrinsic merit or achievement of theirs. It is the result of divine intervention and renewal. 'I will put my Spirit in you and move you to follow my decrees and be careful to keep my laws' (Ezek. 37:27). He is 'a righteous God and a Saviour' (Isa. 45:21), that is, a God who is true to his covenant commitment and extends deliverance to his people. His righteousness is his salvation (Isa. 51:6, 8; see on Mic. 7:9), and seeking the LORD is equivalent to seeking righteousness (Isa. 51:1). It is in this divinely provided righteousness (right standing before God) that Zion is ultimately established (Isa. 54:14) and all the LORD's people are accounted righteous (Isa. 60:21). It is achieved through the work of the LORD's righteous servant who justifies (that is, procures righteousness for) many (Isa. 53:11). Having been brought into a right relationship with God, the righteous then serve him (Mal. 3:18).

The word translated 'faith' comes from a root denoting firmness and durability. As an attribute of God it designates him as the one whose word is utterly trustworthy and whose promises can be relied on (Deut. 32:4; Ps. 33:4; 89:34). It is also applied to man and his reliability, steadfastness or 'faithfulness', as the NIV margin renders it (cf. Jer. 7:28; 9:2; Ps. 37:3). As regards an individual's attitude towards the word and commitment of God, it indicates an attitude of total trust in them. In Nehemiah 9:8, Abraham is described as 'faithful' in heart because of the trust he showed in the LORD. This is set out in Genesis 15:6, 'Abram believed the LORD, and he credited it to him as righteousness', where 'righteousness' is from the same root as 'righteous' here, and 'believed' uses the same root as 'faith' or 'faithfulness' in the sense that Abraham made himself secure or firm in the LORD and what he had said to him.

The righteous exercise faith by putting their trust in God and his covenant promises. In contrast to the self-reliance of the arrogant, they are relying on God to solve the deepest problems of their lives, and not on any input of their own into the situation. In this way they 'live'. That includes being able to go on through the dark times when they are unable to see how God is at work in their lives. But 'live' refers to more than physical survival. Life in Scripture involves enjoying the full blessing of a covenant relationship with God (Deut. 8:1, 3; 16:20; 30:16, 19), 'life that is truly life' (1 Tim. 6:19). Faith in God's commitment to be their God gives them life in its highest sense no matter what their circumstances. It is of this that Habakkuk and the faithful remnant had to be reminded so that they would be able to persevere in the difficult times they were in.

Now Paul uses these words as the basis of the New Testament doctrine of justification of faith (Rom. 1:17; Gal. 3:11; see also Heb.

10:38). It has been argued that this is a distortion of Habakkuk's meaning in that Paul is primarily talking about how an individual acquires a right standing before God by his gift of salvation. 'This righteousness from God comes through faith in Jesus Christ to all who believe' (Rom. 3:22). Habakkuk, it is argued, is rather focusing on the human characteristic of on-going reliance on God's promise and emphasising that there is no answer that can be given to the problem of evil but the faith that waits for divine intervention and anticipates the final resolution of the tension that God will ultimately achieve. That is developed in the citation of this passage in Hebrews 10:38-39.

But the alleged discrepancy between faith and faithfulness is not as substantial as it may appear at first sight. Both look to the active intervention of God to restore what was lost by mankind in the Fall. Paul is not contradicting Habakkuk, but focusing on the presupposition that is integral to the trust to which he refers. Scripture does not know of a true faith that is without subsequent faithfulness, or of a true faithfulness that is not the product of genuine faith. Both look outwith mankind to God as the sole resolver of the human predicament, and both involve surrender to his requirements and his way from beginning to end. Faithfulness, that is, constancy throughout the varied circumstances of life, is inextricably linked with faith, that is, an on-going reliance on God and his provision.

After this brief, though highly significant parenthesis, the divine declaration reverts back to the behaviour of the arrogant described at the beginning of verse 4. **Indeed, wine betrays him** (*verse 5*). 'Indeed' is used to add another significant fact about the arrogant. They think themselves impervious to what threatens and upsets lesser mortals. But 'wine is treacherous'; the statement is proverbial, of general application. Those who indulge in wine think they are doing themselves good, but it leads not to strength and victory, but to defeat and death (Prov. 23:31-32). The fact that the Babylonians indulged in wine to excess is well known from ancient writers, and can be evidenced by the scene in Belshazzar's court on the night before the city was captured (Dan. 5). The betrayal that is specifically in view here is probably of the true character of the arrogant. Wine lets his inner rebellion against God come all the more into the open.

He is arrogant and never at rest. 'He is arrogant' is literally 'a man is arrogant' where the word for 'man' denotes man in his strength, with all his faculties fully developed. The word translated 'arrogant' occurs elsewhere in the Old Testament only in Proverbs 21:24, to denote the one who swaggers and boasts. He can never be satisfied with what he has got, and is always on the lookout for opportunities to get more. He cannot be content to remain within his allotted territory, but is always sizing up what he can grasp from others.

Because he is as greedy as the grave and like death is never satisfied. 'Is greedy' is literally 'makes wide his soul/desire'. His appetite knows no bounds, and his mouth gapes open to consume more. The 'grave' (Sheol, see on Jonah 2:2) is depicted as swallowing up every living thing and never having enough (Prov. 1:12; 27:20; 30:15-16). In the following words the description points more specifically to the Babylonians. **He gathers to himself all the nations and takes captive all the peoples.** In a similar way the Chaldean grasps to himself everything he can lay his hands on as he goes on his campaign of worldwide dominion.

The answer Habakkuk has been given assures him that God will act. He is not to ask *if* God will act or *when* he will act. It will happen at the appointed time. What the faithful are to do is to wait with confidence on their God. Avoiding the rebellious attitudes of the arrogant, they should rather humbly rely on God, 'being sure of what we hope for and certain of what we do not see' (Heb. 11:1). In this way they will already enjoy a life in communion and fellowship with God and will be sustained through the darkest hour.

Study questions: Habakkuk 2:1-5

verse 3: How should we balance waiting and action? (Mark 13:32-37; Luke 12:41-46; Gal. 6:9-10)

verse 4: How does one become righteous? (Isa. 51:5; 53:11; Rom. 3:21-24; Gal. 3:10-14)

What evidence can be cited that a person truly has faith? (Gal. 5:6, 22-23; 1 Thess. 1:2; Jas. 2:14-26; 1 Pet. 1:8)

verse 5: What attitudes should the Christian display rather than arrogance and greed? (Prov. 22:9; 25:21-22; Matt. 5:42; Phil. 2:3-11; 1 Tim. 6:6-11, 18; 1 Pet. 5:5-6; 1 John 3:17)

Habakkuk 2:6-20: The Five Woes

The prophets did not use the importance of their message as an excuse for presenting it poorly. On the contrary, its importance meant that it had to be communicated as effectively as possible. To accomplish this the prophets employed a variety of rhetorical techniques, including that of adapting forms of speech associated with other occasions to

capture the attention of their hearers and to ensure that their message
got across to them. In this section of Habakkuk, one such device is
employed five times. 'Woe!' or 'Alas!' was originally a cry associated
with a funeral, and was followed by the name of the one who had died.
It gave expression to the grief felt at the loss suffered (1 Kgs. 13:30;
Jer. 22:18 (four times); 34:5). The prophets instead linked the cry of
'Woe!' with a description of the behaviour of those who were still alive
(Mic. 2:1; Isa. 5:8, 11, 18, 20, 21, 22; Amos 6:1; Zeph. 3:1). It was a
very vivid way of pressing home how reprehensible their conduct was
in the sight of God. They were already as good as dead because God
had given his verdict against them.

When the cry of 'Woe!' was uttered regarding the covenant people,
it alerted them to the danger of their conduct and constituted in effect
a call for repentance. A similar pronouncement of woe could also be
made regarding foreign nations (Isa. 10:5; 18:1; Jer. 48:1; Nah. 3:1;
Zeph. 2:5). In such circumstances the aim of the prophecy was
primarily to assure the LORD's people that God's judgment was
impending for their enemies and to encourage them to remain loyal to
him despite their present difficulties. It is into this latter category that
the fivefold woe uttered here falls. It foretells the coming doom of the
Babylonians as a consequence of their cruel and unprincipled conduct.
They will be judged because of the plundering they have undertaken
(2:6-8), their use of force and scheming to achieve their ends (2:9-11),
their methods of building up their empire (2:12-14), the treatment they
dealt out to subjugated peoples (2:15-17), and their idolatry (2:18-20).
Babylon will have her due deserts and her downfall will be as extensive
as the proud empire she has managed to erect against God.

The five woes continue the portrayal of the arrogant oppressor of
2:4-5, and are directed at an unnamed individual. While this may be the
Babylonian king, there is no direct mention of Babylon. It is unlikely
that this was because of fears over potential repercussions since
Babylon had established political control over Judah. The use of
general descriptions probably invites us to go further than hearing
these denunciations as addressed only against Babylon, or a specific
individual. There were those within Judah who were unscrupulous and
corrupt, as Habakkuk himself had already complained (1:2-4). King
Jehoiakim himself is the subject of a woe-oracle of Jeremiah: 'Woe to
him who builds his palace by unrighteousness, his upper rooms by
injustice, making his countrymen work for nothing, not paying them
for their labour' (Jer. 22:13). These woes are a warning to all who are

like the Babylonians in their conduct – and that is a warning that is still
in effect. Rebellion against God is not just a matter of ancient history.
It still characterises the human race, and the consequences of it remain
what they have always been.

(1) *Woe to the plunderer! (2:6-8)* **'Will not all of them taunt him
with ridicule and scorn, saying?** (*verse 6*). The negative rhetorical
question constitutes an emphatic prediction. 'All of them' points back
to the peoples who have been conquered (2:5). A time is coming when
they will join together in mockery of their conqueror, that is, in the first
place, Babylon. Literally, they are said to 'take up a proverb and
ridicule, riddles with respect to him'. 'Proverb' is a word of wide
application in Hebrew. It is not only a pithy saying, but can also refer
to an extended parable (Ezek. 17:2-24) or an object lesson provided by
an individual or a group (1 Sam. 10:12; Ps. 44:14). It is that last use that
is relevant here. The nations will not just deride Babylon; they will do
so by specifically using Babylon as an example to which they can point
others for instruction in what happens to those who have no respect for
God or for their fellows (Mic. 2:4; Isa. 14:4). What a come-down for
the nation that was so full of itself!

'Ridicule' is associated with the action of those who delight in
mockery (Prov. 1:22), probably here referring to openly satirical
address. 'Riddles' on the other hand seem to point to less obvious
mockery. The word is used eight times in the story of Samson in Judges
14, but it is also employed of the 'hard questions' the queen of Sheba
asked Solomon (1 Kgs. 10:1; 2 Chr. 9:1), and also of 'hidden things'
(Ps. 78:2). This could well refer to the veiled allusions and oblique
sayings that will also be used to point at what has happened to Babylon.
All the nations, even those treated as of little significance by Babylon
(1:10), will join in this satirical parody of her come-uppance. 'Saying'
is literally 'and he will say', where one stands for the group as a whole.

**Woe to him who piles up stolen goods and makes himself
wealthy by extortion!** 'Woe!' or 'Alas!' is discussed in the introductory comments above. Here the ominous warning is directed against
two sorts of behaviour, both of which are expressed in Hebrew in a way
which indicates that it is the typical conduct of those being discussed
and not a one-off aberration. The warning is first of all directed against
'him who piles up stolen goods', literally 'the one making many [what
is] not his'. 'Not his' constitutes a word play in Hebrew, the two words

being virtually identical in sound. Whereas 'stolen' may suggest an
ordinary thief, the phrase used easily covers the pillaging of the
Babylonians armies as they looted conquered territories and seized
whatever they wanted to send back to Mesopotamia.

The conduct condemned also covers one who 'makes himself
wealthy by extortion', literally, 'the one making heavy on himself
pledges'. 'Make heavy' can be used of 'making rich' (compare Gen.
13:2), but the word 'pledge' can be heard as two words, suggesting 'a
cloud (or mass) of dust' (or dirt; 'mire' in Mic. 7:10; hence the AV
'thick clay'). These woes have been described as riddles, and so such
word-play and oblique references are to be expected. The implication
is that their wealth is polluted and a burden to them. What is more, a
pledge was given by the debtor to the creditor as a token that his loan
would be repaid (Deut. 24:10-13). So the wealth the Babylonians have
gathered is not really theirs. It is a heap of goods taken on pledge, and
the day will come when they will be reclaimed by their rightful owners.

Between these two descriptions in the Hebrew are the words the
NIV puts last: **How long must this go on?** They constitute a sigh at all
the trouble that has already been caused by the Babylonians, and echo
the prophet's own complaint (1:2).

Will not your debtors suddenly arise? (*verse 7*) continues the use
of the language of commerce, but it is better to take it as a different
metaphor. The nations are now viewed as 'creditors' (NIV margin),
having been forced to give the Babylonians loans which they are going
to demand be repaid. The Hebrew word for 'to lend on interest' is 'to
bite'. When a sum of, say, 10 shekels was borrowed in the ancient
world, the usual practice was for the lender to hand over only 9 shekels,
'biting off' one shekel as the interest. This double meaning is employed to continue the enigmatic character of this taunt. Like snakes
(Gen. 49:17; Prov. 23:32; Jer. 8:17), the nations will arise against
Babylon and reverse the situation: no longer forced loans, but immediate repayment of the whole loan, both what had been advanced and
the interest due. The word-play brings out the unpleasantness of the
experience for Babylon.

It is also going to happen 'suddenly'. The false security of the self-
deceived is subject to unexpected and complete reversal (Prov. 6:15;
29:1). That is how God will answer the sighs of those who ask, 'How
long?'

**Will they not wake up and make you tremble? Then you will
become their victim.** When a loan could not be repaid, then the

borrower could be enslaved. Babylon would be unable to compensate the nations when they demanded a reckoning, and she would in her turn be completely overrun. 'Victim' is a plural word 'spoils, booties', intensifying the idea of how completely Babylon will be plundered. This was the judgment that would be later executed on them by the Medes and Persians.

Because you have plundered many nations, the peoples who are left will plunder you (*verse 8*). The justice of their retribution is emphasised by the repetition of 'plunder'. 'The peoples who are left' or 'the remnant of the peoples' represents those who are left after the Babylonians have acted so unsparingly towards them. The empire that has established itself by brute force will be overthrown by the very means that had been used to set it up.

For you have shed man's blood; you have destroyed lands and cities and everyone in them. Literally, 'because of blood of mankind and violence (*hamas*, see on 1:2) of earth, city and all dwelling in it.' This is repeated in verse 17. In their militaristic aggression the Babylonians held life cheap, but God takes a different view. 'Whoever sheds the blood of man, by man shall his blood be shed; for in the image of God has God made man' (Gen. 9:6; see also Num. 35:33).

The idea of reciprocity of punishment is often felt to be part of the negative image of the Old Testament that is now done away with, but note Matthew 18:21-35 and 2 Thessalonians 1:6. The God of all the earth will justly punish those who have done wrong. It is not possible to ravage his creation with impunity.

(2) *Woe to the empire builder! (2:9-11)* The second woe develops the thought of the first, but focuses more on what the Babylonians were doing with the plunder they had taken from others. **Woe to him who builds his realm by unjust gain** (*verse 9*). 'Realm' is literally 'house', but the word is frequently used in the sense of dynasty (2 Sam. 7: 11, 16; 23:5). Although it refers primarily to the dynastic ambitions of the Babylonians, it is readily generalised to the conduct of other kings, officials, or even quite ordinary folk. Who does not have a house? 'Gain' may be used in a neutral sense (Gen. 37:26; Job 22:3; Ps. 30:9), but more often it is presented negatively just because it can so easily grab hold of the human heart (Prov. 1:19; Jer. 6:13; 8:10; Mic. 4:13). It is here explicitly characterised as 'evil', obtained in an unscrupulous and wicked fashion.

The aim was **to set his nest on high, to escape the clutches of ruin!**

To set one's nest on high was a figure of speech for securing one's self and property from any attack. The eagle builds its nest in a rocky eminence and so escapes being plundered by others (Job 39:27). This was the strategy followed by the Kenites (Num. 24:21) and by the Edomites (Obad. 4; Jer. 49:16) when they built mountain strongholds. It was obviously not literally possible in the flat plains of Babylon. But the same haughty spirit of self-confidence animated the rebuilding of Babylon. This reached its peak in the massive building programme of Nebuchadnezzar, who congratulated himself, 'Is not this the great Babylon I have built as the royal residence, by mighty power and for the glory of my majesty?' (Dan. 4:30). 'Ruin' or 'evil' is represented as ready to grasp him, but he thinks he can place himself out of its reach. The Babylonians knew they had made many enemies for themselves, but were confident that they had made adequate preparations to deal with any rebellion.

You have plotted the ruin of many peoples (*verse 10*). This was the strategy that the Babylonians had adopted in their aggressive expansionism. Their aim had been to bring to an end the national identity of other peoples. They continued the Assyrian device of deportation by which conquered nations were uprooted from their home territory and lost their sense of national identity, becoming part of a dispossessed workforce scattered throughout the empire. Babylon's rulers were unaware that in fact they were **shaming your own house and forfeiting your life.** To make the thought clearer the NIV has altered the order of the original text: 'You have plotted shame for your house, the end of many peoples, sinning [against] your soul.' They have brought inevitable retribution on themselves by their actions. 'Sinning' emphasises that they are continuing to be at fault and are still incurring guilt which condemns them. 'These men lie in wait for their own blood; they waylay only themselves! Such is the end of all who go after ill-gotten gain; it takes away the lives of those who get it' (Prov. 1:18-19).

The stones of the wall will cry out, and the beams of the woodwork will echo it (*verse 11*). This verse begins 'for' (not translated in the NIV) and advances the reason for the previous verdict. It can be understood in two ways. In the previous verses 'house' has been used twice to refer to the empire built by the Babylonians. If that sense is continued here, then the parts of the house are images for parts of the empire. Just as a shoddily built house creaks and groans until it collapses in the storm, or even through its own weakness, so an empire

built on injustice and cruelty is not secure. It too will creak and groan
till it falls down. 'Righteousness exalts a nation, but sin is a disgrace
to any people' (Prov. 14:34). The way Babylon has gone about
extending her power had built an empire doomed to collapse.

Alternatively, the thought may be of actual buildings in Babylon
with their imposing outside walls and huge pieces of timber which
were needed to bind the whole structure together. As they looked at
them, the Babylonians viewed them as a monument to their skill and
prestige. But just as when Cain slew Abel, his shed blood cried out to
the LORD from the ground as testimony against Cain (Gen. 4:10), so
this timber and these stones, inanimate though they are, will testify not
to the prowess of the builder but to his wickedness and rapacity. They
had been plundered from other nations. When an enterprise has an
improper foundation, no matter what success it achieves, it is inevitably flawed and those flaws will not remain hidden.

(3) *Woe to the slave driver! (2:12-14)* A major building project in the
ancient world required a huge workforce, often obtained by conscript-
ing forced labour (Exod. 1:11-14; 1 Kgs. 5:13; 9:15-22). Conditions
were harsh, and little concern was shown for the welfare and safety of
those involved (Mic. 3:10; Jer. 22:13). The lives of those transported
to Babylon to help realise Nebuchadnezzar's grandiose building plans
were treated as of no significance, but a day of reckoning would come.
**Woe to him who builds a city with bloodshed and establishes a town
by crime!** (*verse 12*). The description emphasises that this was
recognised policy, not merely a one-off event. 'With bloodshed'
(literally, 'bloods' the usual Hebrew idiom for murder) might also take
in the loss of life in battle as well as the unsafe conditions on the
building sites. The 'crime' referred to is violation of international
rights. The word refers to any deviation from the standards of right
conduct, 'wickedness' (Mic. 3:10) or 'wrong' (Zeph. 3:5, 13).

Scripture shows that cities developed as an expression of human
civilisation moving forward on the basis of its own strength and
determination (Gen. 4:17; 10:8-12; 11:4). While the coordination of
human effort achieved in the integrated life of the city may be used to
God's glory – is not Jerusalem 'the city of the Great King' (Ps. 48:2)
and the 'Holy City, the new Jerusalem' (Rev. 21:2) the goal of the
redeemed? – if a city is not founded on morally and spiritually correct
principles, it readily degenerates into what is a parody of true life.

The third woe now presents the oppressor's behaviour in terms of the purposes and control of God. **Has not the LORD Almighty determined?** (*verse 13*) is literally, '[Is it] not, behold, from the LORD of hosts?' The negative interrogative question combined with "Behold!" (not translated in the NIV) serves to mark this as something of considerable importance that is now being presented. For the title of God that is used, see comments on Micah 4:4 and Nahum 2:13. In his control of events on earth, he has structured human history in a way that works out his purpose.

That the people's labour is only fuel for the fire presents the idea that the labour of the peoples (plural, not singular as the NIV punctuation would suggest) in the projects they carried out for their Babylonian overlords is divinely ordained to be futile. The word 'labour' conveys the thought that they had had to work to the point of exhaustion. But in the rise and fall that is characteristic of the flow of history, there will come along another superpower that will capture Babylon and set fire to its grand buildings. God does not allow any empire to remain, and so it inevitably is the case **that the nations exhaust themselves for nothing** as they have used their time, resources and effort in Babylon's interests. However grand the immediate outcome, it is an empty achievement. Jeremiah quotes and expands this thought in reference to Babylon: 'This is what the Lord Almighty says: "Babylon's thick wall will be levelled and her high gates set on fire; the peoples exhaust themselves for nothing, the nations' labour is only fuel for the flames"' (Jer. 51:58).

Human empires glorify man, and in the divine purpose it is intolerable that there be any who challenge him. He will not yield his glory to another (Isa. 48:11), but works instead to accomplish his purposes in history. **For the earth will be filled with the knowledge of the glory of the LORD, as the waters cover the sea** (*verse 14*). This verse is close to Isaiah 11:9 which concludes a description of the anticipated reign of the Messiah with the words, 'They will neither harm nor destroy on all my holy mountain, for the earth will be full of the knowledge of the LORD as the waters cover the sea' (Isa. 11:9). The verb form is slightly different here, 'be filled' rather than 'be full', in accordance with the emphasis of the present passage that this outcome will only be achieved when evil and perpetrators of evil are overthrown. The knowledge referred to in Isaiah involves the acknowledgment of the LORD's rightful place and submission to him (cf. Jer. 31:34). Here there is the added thought of 'the knowledge of *the glory* of the LORD'

His 'glory' is the visible manifestation of what God is in himself. His divine attributes are not directly accessible to human scrutiny. 'You cannot see my face, for no one may see me and live' (Exod. 33:20). But that does not mean that God is unknown. 'The heavens declare the glory of God' (Ps. 19:1) as they bear testimony to his wisdom and power as revealed in the created realm, so that 'the whole earth is full of his glory' (Isa. 6:3).

But creation is not the ultimate revelation of God's glory. The presence of God in the glory cloud in the tabernacle and Temple (Exod. 40:34; 1 Kgs. 8:11) manifested something more of his inner being, namely his grace and love as reflected in his redemptive presence in the midst of his people. That Old Testament presentation of the character of God has in turn been eclipsed by the revelation in his Son who is 'the radiance of God's glory and the exact representation of his being' (Heb. 1:3). Not only did the disciples see 'his glory, the glory of the One and Only, who came from the Father, full of grace and truth' (John 1:14), but this is also the privilege of all those into whose hearts God has made his light shine 'to give us the light of the knowledge of the glory of God in the face of Christ' (2 Cor. 4:6). Our vision here is often obscured, but there is still the eternal glory to come in which enjoyment of all that God is will not be clouded over or marred in any way (Ps. 73:24; 2 Tim. 2:10; 1 Pet. 5:10; Rev. 21:23).

In the light of the all encompassing purpose of God, Habakkuk – and we with him – may find comfort and courage to face the difficulties around us. God's determination to exhibit his glory ensures that all that is contrary to him will be judged and banished from his eternal kingdom. The fall of tyrants in the past encourages us to await the final overthrow of all that Babylon represents (Rev. 18:2).

(4) *Woe to the debaucher!* *(2:15-17)* The theme of the fourth woe is the debasing treatment that the Babylonians inflicted on the peoples they conquered. **Woe to him who gives drink to his neighbours** (*verse 15*). This description is figurative. It was certainly not the case that the Babylonians ordered free drinks for the peoples they captured. But their behaviour was like that of someone who deliberately gets his neighbour drunk so that he can take advantage of him (Jer. 51:7).

Pouring it from the wineskin till they are drunk is literally 'one joining (or, pouring out) your wrath and also making drunk.' 'Wrath' conveys the basic idea of 'heat', but in this sense is always associated in the Old Testament with divine anger in judgment (Ps. 79:6; Jer. 10:25). Sometimes, however, the word has the meaning 'poison' (Deut. 32:24, 33; Ps. 58:4), and that is a distinct possibility here, as in the NASB 'who mix in your venom even to make them drunk'. It is a poisonous as well as an intoxicating draught that is employed. The NIV understands the word 'wrath' as a form of a rare word for 'wineskin' along with an alternative derivation of the verb to give the meaning 'pour out'. The debilitating effect is then achieved by the copiousness of the provision made. It may well be that Habakkuk here uses another word-play, some of whose overtones escape us.

So that he can gaze on their naked bodies, literally 'their nakednesses'. The Hebrew here switches to a plural reference 'their' (the NIV has used the plural earlier to make for a smoother translation). Being exposed naked involves shame and humiliation (see on Nah. 3:5; Lam. 4:21). It is the ignominy of a drunk man that he cannot preserve his own modesty (Gen. 9:20-23). Although the figure of a drunk man is used of the overthrow of a nation (Nah. 3:11), in the comparison here the drunkenness is the result of the action of the individual seeking to demean his neighbour and to gloat over him. The comparison is not with the open aggression of the Babylonians, but with the psychological techniques they employed to keep conquered peoples cowed and submissive by subjecting them to indignities and stripping them of self-respect. In this way they were able to maintain their empire, while debasing their subjects.

You will be filled with shame instead of glory (*verse 16*). But again their actions boomerang against themselves. 'Fill' refers to that state of satisfaction in which no more is desired. That had been true of the conquests of Babylon and the extension of her empire. She had acquired for herself earthly prestige and renown. But the tables are going to be turned. She will experience 'shame' instead, that is, she will experience the disgrace and insults that result from being brought down from lording it over all to experiencing defeat herself.

Now it is your turn! Drink and be exposed! In the Hebrew this reads, 'Drink, you also, and show yourself uncircumcised.' Various early translations attempted to tone down the starkness of the picture by transposing two consonants in the text and so reading 'stagger' rather than 'be exposed'. Perhaps the closeness of sound was intentionally used as part of the satire of the woe (2:6). 'Be exposed', however, fits the retributive nature of the penalty inflicted on them: just as they had caused others to be naked, so they too would suffer the same fate. 'Uncircumcised' also hints at what will be developed more fully in the last section: the condemnation to come on them was the consequence of their alienation from the one true God.

The cup from the LORD's right hand is coming round to you. The cup of the LORD indicates the portion he allots to an individual or nation. It may be 'the cup of salvation' (Ps. 116:13; see also Pss. 16:5; 23:5), but most of the references are to 'the cup of his wrath' (Isa. 51:17; Rev. 14:10), which is also described as the 'cup filled with the wine of my wrath' (Jer. 25:15; Rev. 16:19). Drinking of this cup causes the nations to 'stagger' (Isa. 51:22; Jer. 25:16) under God's chastisement. Ultimately it is because Christ has drunk 'the cup the Father has given' him (John 18:11), which is the cup of his wrath against sin, that his people are exempt from the punishment which would otherwise be inflicted on them. The 'LORD's right hand' is associated with his power and ability to shatter his enemies (Exod. 15:6) as well as to save his own (Pss. 20:6; 98:1; Isa. 62:8). Here it ensures that when the cup is presented there is no option but to drink it (Jer. 25:26). There is no escaping the execution of the LORD's sentence.

Disgrace will cover your glory. The cup which the Babylonians had given to others was now going to be replaced by one given them by the LORD. A similar prediction is also found in Isaiah 51:21-23. The word translated 'disgrace' comes from a root conveying the idea of being of little account. The word is found only here, and is probably used because it can also be heard as two words, meaning 'vomiting of shame'. That fits the allusive language frequently used throughout the woes, and echoes the scene in which the impending punishment is viewed in terms of drunkenness (Jer. 25:26-27). Though the Babylonians had been used as the instrument of divine judgment (Jer. 51:7), that did not exempt them from being answerable to the LORD.

The violence you have done to Lebanon will overwhelm you (*verse 17*). 'Violence' is the same word as occurred earlier (1:3, 9). But why is Lebanon singled out for mention? Some have argued that Lebanon stands here for Palestine as a whole, because it was part of the territory allocated to Israel (Deut. 1:7-8; Josh. 1:4). However, it is preferable to take the reference as being to the territory itself. It was renowned for cedars and pines (1 Kgs. 5:8; Ps. 104:16; Isa. 2:13; 37:24; Zech. 11:1-2). Because so much timber from there was used in building Jehoiakim's palace, it was known as 'Lebanon' (Jer. 22:23), doubtless to remind his subjects of Solomon's Palace of the Forest of Lebanon (1 Kgs. 7:2; 10:21). Like the Assyrians before them (2 Kgs.

19:23), the Babylonians made ruthless use of Lebanon's timber resources, to construct siege works against cities that withstood them, and also to export back home for use in their own massive building programmes. They cut down timber without regard to the regeneration of the forests (Isa. 14:8). Perhaps they also set fire to the forests just so that no one else would have access to their resources. But their action in this respect also will return to haunt them. Others in turn will do the same with Babylon.

Your destruction of animals will terrify you. 'Animals' refers to domesticated animals rather than wild animals which lost their natural habitat with the destruction of the forests. Lebanon was also known for its herds of animals that could be used in sacrifice. 'Lebanon is not sufficient for altar fires, nor its animals enough for burnt offerings' (Isa. 40:16). These choice animals were driven off as spoil by the Babylonians. The Hebrew is literally 'destruction of animals will terrify them'. The NIV treats this as an instance of a change of person, which, while possible in Hebrew, is awkward and intolerable in English. 'Terrify' usually denotes a devastating and demoralising reaction, but perhaps here it is used in the sense of bring a terrifying calamity on you.

The devastation wrought by the Babylonians extended beyond the environment and wildlife to people. The conclusion of the first woe is repeated. **For you have shed man's blood; you have destroyed lands and cities and everyone in them.** Their attitude was to exploit and destroy without regard to anyone or anything, and it would not go unpunished.

(5) *Woe to the idolater! (2:18-20)* The fifth woe has a different structure from those preceding in that it does not begin with 'Woe!' but rather with the grounds on which the threatening is made. This is the fundamental reason why what Babylon was doing was irretrievably misguided and wrong. They refused to accept the LORD as their ruler and God.

Of what value is an idol, since a man has carved it? (*verse 18*). The thought and expressions used here are typical of the many denunciations of idolatry in the Old Testament (Ps. 115:4-7; Isa. 40:18-20; 41:7; 44:9-20; 46:6-7; Jer. 2:27; 10:3-5, 14-15). An 'idol' is an image carved out of wood or stone (2 Kgs. 21:7; Isa. 45:20). It is manmade and therefore any hope of deliverance for the Babylonians from that quarter will prove illusory. It cannot withstand or avert the imposition of the will of the LORD in judgment. It never has been of any value, and it never will bring any profit to its worshippers.

Or an image that teaches lies? An 'image' refers to what has been cast in metal (Exod. 32:4, 8; Lev. 19:4; Isa. 40:19). In Micah 3:11 the teacher of lies was the priest or prophet of the idol, but here it is the idol itself. It sustains the delusion that it is a divine power to be reckoned with.

For he who makes it trusts in his own creation. 'Trust' as a means of acquiring security is critically dependent on whoever or whatever is relied upon. 'His own creation' is what he has carved or moulded for himself, and therefore his confidence has no more secure basis than his own craftsmanship and ability. Quite the contrary is the outcome for those who have obeyed the injunction, 'Trust in the LORD for ever, for the LORD, the LORD, is the Rock eternal' (Isa. 26:4). Their trust has a more than adequate basis which will not prove illusory, as the Psalmists repeatedly celebrate (Pss. 21:7; 22:4-5; 33:21; 125:1).

He makes idols that cannot speak. 'Idols' here is a word formed by a play on the ordinary word for God, with a meaning something like 'godlets' (Pss. 96:5; 97:7; Jer. 14:14; Zech. 11:17). They are dumb (a word that echoes the sound of 'godlets'), and cannot provide guidance for their worshippers (Ps. 135:15-17).

Woe to him who says to wood, 'Come to life!' Or to lifeless stone, 'Wake up!' (*verse 19*). 'Wood' is a block of wood shaped into an idol. The cry 'Come to life!' or 'Awake!' probably has the idea of 'Help me!' understood (Pss. 35:23; 44:24; 69:6; Isa. 51:9). Wood may have been a pagan symbol of life and stone of permanence.

Can it give guidance? The silent stone is in contrast to the words of the living God, written indeed in stone, but a record of what was spoken by the living God. 'Give guidance' is 'teach', and from the same root came the word for the law of the LORD, which was his instruction and guidance to his people. The psalmists repeatedly prayed the LORD to guide them by the way set out in his law (Pss. 25:4; 27:11; 86:11; 119:12, 33, 64, 108), but there was no possibility of such help coming from idols. They were lifeless. **It is covered with gold and silver; there is no breath in it.** How futile to worship what is quite without life (Jer. 10:14)!

Over against the folly of idolatry there is set the reality of the true God. It is difficult to tell whether this is part of the fifth woe, or a concluding verse that completes the response begun at 2:4. It fulfils both roles.

But the LORD is in his holy temple (*verse 20*). The 'holy temple' is probably a reference not to the Temple in Jerusalem, but to God's heavenly dwelling, of which the Temple in Jerusalem was just a representation. 'The LORD is in his holy temple; the LORD is on his heavenly throne' (Ps. 11:4; see also Ps. 2:4; Isa. 66:1; Mic. 1:2). From there he is able to survey all that goes on upon earth. 'He observes the sons of men; his eyes examine them' (Ps. 11:4). From there he scoffs at all who defy him on earth, and the time will come when he will act in wrath against those who oppose him and his Anointed One (Ps. 2:4-6).

Because of this, the injunction goes forth, **Let all the earth be silent before him.** They should wait submissively for the divine ruler to declare his will and judgment on the matters that are under dispute (Zeph. 1:7; 2:13). 'Be silent' is a call for reverential awe before him. All the earth, and not just Judah, is brought within the scope of this declaration (Ps. 22:27; Isa. 2:2-3). If the whole earth has to wait in this way, what then can the fate of the Babylonians be when he judges them? Perhaps also there is a personal word to Habakkuk in this. If all the earth should be silent before their Sovereign ruler and judge, should not the prophet also recognise his greatness, wisdom and power, and wait in silence for the LORD to act to resolve the perplexities that so worried the prophet?

Even though this series of woes was first directed against Babylon, it contains vital information about present living. We are not to get so drawn down to an earthly perspective that we forget about God's control of history. Whatever people put in their lives in place of God, will ultimately be shown to be futile. He is in control, and the command that goes out to his people in the midst of the wars and tumults that arise on earth is ever the same: 'Be still, and know that I am God; I will be exalted among the nations, I will be exalted in the earth' (Ps. 46:10).

This is guaranteed because of the LORD's sovereign control over affairs on earth. 'He brings one down, he exalts another' (Ps. 75:7). 'A man's steps are directed by the LORD' (Prov. 20:24), no matter who he is. 'The king's heart is in the hand of the LORD; he directs it like a watercourse wherever he pleases' (Prov. 21:1). Even through the violence and pride of Babylon and her kings, the LORD was working out his purposes, and when it pleased him he called them to account.

But we are also reminded that though the hand of the LORD can be seen throughout history, it is to the finale of history that we must look for the ultimate revelation of his power and disclosure of his purposes with the return of Christ (Mark 13:34-37; 1 Cor. 1:7; 1 Thess. 1:10; Jas. 5:7). Realising this we have to heed the injunction of Peter: 'You ought to live holy and godly lives as you look forward to the day of God and speed its coming' (2 Pet. 3:11-12).

Study questions: Habakkuk 2:6-20

verse 6: In what ways are woes pronounced in the New Testament? (Matt. 23:2, 13-36, 37-39; Luke 6:24-26; 17:1; 22:22; 1 Cor. 9:16; Jude 11)

These pictures reach their consummation in Revelation where Babylon epitomises the wickedness of the nations. Trace the ways in which what was said of Babylon in Old Testament times is applied to 'Babylon' in Revelation 17 and 18?

verse 12: What guidelines can be established from Scripture about the way workers ought to be treated? (Lev. 19:13; Deut. 24:14-15; Luke 10:7; 1 Cor. 9:9-10; Col. 4:1; Jas. 5:4)

verse 14: What part should thinking about future glory play in our present living? (Rom. 8:23-25; 2 Cor. 4:18; Heb. 11:14-16)

verses 18-19: Is idolatry something we no longer have to worry about? (Rom. 1:25; 1 Cor. 10:7; Eph. 5:5; Col. 3:5; 1 John 5:21)

verse 20: How may we practise being silent before God? (Job 1:21; Ps. 76:8; 1 Thess. 5:18; Heb. 12:28; Jas. 4:7)

Habakkuk 3:1-2: The Prophet's Prayer

Habakkuk's problems began with what he saw happening around him in his own nation (1:2-4) and on the international scene (1:12-17). How could God permit the violent and corrupt to prosper? How could God use the arrogant and evil Babylonians as the instruments through whom he would chastise his people? The answer he was given assured him of God's intention to intervene, but counselled him that the outworking of the divine purposes would occur on God's timetable, which might seem to involve delay (2:3). What the faithful have to do in the meantime is to continue to trust in God (2:4), confident that in accordance with his promise he will bring judgment on the wicked (2:5-19). Now Habakkuk responds to that revelation as one whose eyes have been lifted up from earth to heaven (2:20). His faith is no longer perplexed by looking at problems from below – from the standpoint of human understanding. The triumph of faith is to look at difficulties from above, from the perspective of heaven. Confident of the LORD's saving intervention, Habakkuk engages in worship and prays for the realisation of God's promises (3:2). He also makes provision that the community of faith can join with him in his confident praise.

Title (3:1) **A prayer of Habakkuk the prophet. On** *shigionoth* (*verse 1*). We are left in no doubt that the prophet was engaged in worship. He sets out what he has to say in the style of one of the psalms. On this basis some have supposed that he was in fact a prophet in the Temple, who took part in the worship there (1 Chr. 25:1-3). While it is remarkable that it is only here outside the Book of Psalms that there is such information as occurs in verses 1 and 19, it is too much to conclude from this that Habakkuk was employed in the Temple. The Psalms were part of the heritage of all Israel, and the prophets who so readily adapted forms of speech from other life situations did not hesitate to draw on the resources that were to hand in the Psalms. What Habakkuk has to say here fits into the whole message of his book: perplexity resolving itself into prayer and praise. This argues conclusively against the view that chapter 3, which is clearly labelled as coming from Habakkuk, has in fact a different origin from the rest of the prophecy.

The title 'prayer' is found in the superscriptions of Psalms 17, 86, 90, 102, 142 (see also Psalms 4:1; 6:9; 55:2; 61:1; 72:20). In many of these psalms the psalmist complains about injustice and oppression and asks God to rectify the situation. The description 'prayer' is particularly appropriate here in view of the character of verse 2 where in the light of all that he had learned Habakkuk asks God to carry out his plans speedily.

Habakkuk is given his official title 'prophet'. What he has experienced and the response he is about to utter are not to be taken as pertaining to an individual in isolation. The prophet was a channel of divine communication, and that also applies to his approaches to God. Intercessory prayer was one of the duties and privileges of God's prophets (Gen. 20:7; Exod. 32:31-32; Ezra 9:5-15; Isa. 63:15-64:12; Jer. 14:7-9, 19-22; Dan. 9:3-19). Habakkuk here expresses the response that is appropriate for all those who wait on God through times of darkness and confusion.

'On *shigionoth*' is described in the NIV footnote as 'probably a literary or musical term'. A similar term *shiggaion* is found in the superscription to Psalm 7. Both words come from a root that means 'to err' and then 'to reel to and fro'. In combination here with the word 'on' the most plausible suggestion regarding its meaning is that it should be sung to a tune that conveys great excitement, or perhaps rapid changes of emotion. In setting such a title to his psalm (note also the concluding subscription in verse 19) Habakkuk was not just using the psalms as a model for expressing his thought. He was composing a psalm for Israel to use in her worship.

Introduction (3:2) The introductory verse sets out the theme of the whole psalm. There are two parts. Firstly Habakkuk looks back to the way in which the LORD had in the past intervened powerfully on behalf of his people. Then, on that basis, he prays that the LORD intervene again on behalf of his people. This basic structure of prayer pervades the entreaties of Psalms such as 42, 44, 68, 74, 78, 80, 83, 89, 105, 106, 135, 136. There is the movement from remembrance of what the LORD has done – 'We have heard with our ears, O God; our fathers have told us what you did in their days, in days long ago' (Ps. 44:1) – to entreaty for action now – 'Awake, O Lord! Why do you sleep? Rouse yourself! Do not reject us for ever. Why do you hide your face and forget our misery and oppression?' (Ps. 44:23-24). Such a progression of thought in prayer is not confined to the Old Testament. However, it now looks back not to the Exodus but to the cross and resurrection as the definitive unveiling of God's power to save. 'May the God of peace, who through the blood of the eternal covenant brought back from the dead our Lord Jesus, that great Shepherd of the sheep, equip you with everything good for doing his will' (Heb. 13:20-21).

LORD, I have heard of your fame (*verse 2*). 'Fame' is that which is generated by hearing news relayed by another. The word is used about the news of Nineveh's downfall (Nah. 3:19), and also of the Queen of Sheba hearing of the fame of Solomon through the reports that were brought to her (1 Kgs. 10:1). Job used the word to set up the contrast between how he had previously known God and how he had come to know him through his personal encounter with him: 'My ears had heard of you (literally, With report of ear I heard of you) but now my eyes have seen you' (Job 42:5). The point here is that Habakkuk is not basing his prayer on something that was a private experience of his, or had been specially revealed to him as a prophet. Rather he is talking about the common heritage of Israel, 'things from of old – what we have heard and known, what our fathers have told us' (Ps. 78:3-4). From the foundation of faith in the LORD, the God of the covenant, the people are invited to join in singing this psalm of prayer and to make their own what is said in it.

I stand in awe of your deeds, O LORD. 'LORD' is repeated to emphasise that the prophet is continuing to think of what the covenant

God has done in relation to his people. 'Deeds' (literally, 'deed' or 'work') is the same word as is used in 1:5 (rendered 'something' in the NIV) to point to what the LORD was going to do in raising up the Babylonians. Despite that, it is used here in its general sense to refer to the way in which the LORD has been at work in the history of his people (Pss. 44:1; 77:12; 95:9). When he calls to mind the whole sweep of what the LORD has done in the past, the prophet can only say, 'I stand in awe'. The word is literally 'fear' which covers both the reaction of fright and terror (Jonah 1:5; Mic. 7:17) and also that of respect and reverence (Jonah 1:16). This was no momentary and passing attitude on the part of Habakkuk, but is the affirmation of a faith that focuses on the all-knowing and all-powerful God of the whole earth, whose abhorrence of sin is total, but who repeatedly and wonderfully displays his grace to sinners (Heb. 12:28-29). As he recalls the mercy God has shown to his people in the past, Habakkuk no longer questions that the LORD will work. He has no doubts about the wisdom of what the LORD will do. The prophet simply prays that it be not delayed.

Twice the prophet pleads with the LORD to act 'in midst of years'. The NIV varies its translation of this phrase, rendering it first as 'in our day' and then by 'in our time'. These words have been understood in a variety of ways. Undoubtedly they refer to Habakkuk's own time, but why does he describe it in this way?

One way of looking at matters is that the prophet considers himself to live between the time when the LORD intervened on behalf of his people at the Exodus (he is going to describe that in 3:3-7) and the time of the LORD's final intervention. The 'middle of years' then refers to the prophet's own time, which was neither the beginning nor the end of the LORD's dealings with his people, but which was still a time when his relief from distress was required.

Such an understanding cannot be totally rejected, because the prophet's vision is directed forward in 2:14 to the time when the earth will completely know the deliverance and glory of the LORD. But we are not sure how clearly even the LORD's prophets understood how God was going to intervene in the future (1 Pet. 1:10-11). Certainly in Old Testament times the fact that Christ would come twice had not been revealed, and there does not seem to have been sufficient definite information given for them to distinguish before the event between the next intervention of God in their history and the ultimate Messianic intervention. There is much then in favour of relating Habakkuk's phrase to a much less broad time perspective.

What was facing Habakkuk was the reality of Babylonian power being exercised in Judah. The LORD had already directed him to look forward to an appointed time, which though it was certain to come, might linger and not come as quickly as desired (2:3). At that time the predicted woe and judgment of Babylon would surely be realised. Habakkuk is speaking as one in the middle between the coming of the LORD's hand in chastisement on his people in the form of the Babylonians and the LORD's intervention to overthrow these oppressors. Aware of his people's present anguish, he pleads that God act now on their behalf. He may have been looking for some token of divine favour to alleviate their misery and bolster their faith. Or it may be a plea that the LORD hasten his work and act now at the middle of what seems to be a long-delayed relief, as if to say, 'Do not wait for the end; act now even though it is just the middle of the years.' (A similar thought, though expressed negatively, is to be found in Ps. 102:24.)

Renew them in our day. 'Renew' may refer to keeping alive what is threatened with death (Exod. 1:7; Ps. 71:20) or to bring back to life what is dead (Deut. 32:39; 1 Sam. 2:6). Because it has employed a plural 'deeds' in the previous clause, the NIV uses 'them' instead of a singular 'him/it' as in the Hebrew. Other translations combine 'your deeds' or 'your work' with 'renew' to yield, '[as for] your work, renew him/it' but the NIV rendering is to be preferred. What, however, does 'him/it' refer to? It is improbable that a personal reference to the nation as God's work is intended, though the verb can be understood as 'revive' (Pss. 80:18; 85:6). 'Work' or 'deeds' is the nearest antecedent. So severe has the Babylonian oppression become, Habakkuk is viewing the LORD's work on behalf of people either dead or on the point of extinction. In either event, he is pleading that the LORD again act to save and deliver.

In our time make them known. 'Them' is a supplement, but one that is easily supplied from the context. It is not merely the knowledge that this will happen that the prophet prays for, but the actual experience of it.

As one of the curiosities of Biblical interpretation, it might be noted that the Septuagint understood these two phrases in an entirely different light and translated them as 'in the middle of two living creatures (probably referring to the cherubim) you will be known.' In English translation they seem far apart, but the Hebrew is much closer together. The early church further blended into this interpretation the ox and the ass from Isaiah 1:3 as the living creatures, and this seems to be the origin of the traditional picture of animals surrounding the manger in Bethlehem.

In wrath remember mercy. This is the essence of the prophet's plea. It does not focus on any merit of his own or of the people. The reference to 'wrath' can only be to that which the LORD is exhibiting towards his people. His attitude is described using a rare word which denotes quaking or shaking through strong emotion (see also 3:7). A related word is used by Isaiah to describe how the LORD is *roused* to carry out his unfamiliar and unwanted task of acting in judgment against his people. 'The LORD will rise up as he did at Mount Perazim, he will rouse himself as in the Valley of Gibeon – to do his work, his strange work, and perform his task, his alien task' (Isa. 28:21). The prophet implicitly acknowledges that this wrath is justified, but that does not stop him from presenting along with it the LORD's known attribute of 'mercy' as the basis of his plea for assistance. Asking for mercy is an admission of guilt (Ps. 51:1).

'Mercy' refers to deeply felt love and compassion (Mic. 7:19). It is a sovereign attribute of God. 'I will have mercy on whom I will have mercy, and I will have compassion on whom I will have compassion' (Exod. 33:19). But in calling Israel into covenant relationship with himself, the LORD has created a bond that elicits a merciful response towards his own. 'For the LORD your God is a merciful God; he will not abandon or destroy you or forget the covenant with your forefathers, which he confirmed to them by oath' (Deut. 4:31). It cannot be that his anger, however justified, will block out his compassion (Ps. 77:9). 'For a brief moment I abandoned you, but with deep compassion I will bring you back' (Isa. 54:7). When the prophet asked that the LORD remember mercy, he was seeking that it be exercised. When God remembered Noah in the ark, it was not just an act of mental recall but the beginning of action on his behalf (Gen. 8:1; see also Exod. 2:24 and Lev. 26:44-45). The action the prophet had in mind might have been an alleviation of the people's sufferings or it might have been an immediate intervention to overthrow the power of Babylon.

The present era is still one in which God chastens and purifies his own by judgment (1 Pet. 4:17). The church continues to experience times of spiritual coldness rather than vitality. Habakkuk's prayer provides an appropriate model for approaching God, confessing our sin and pleading for his mercy. In our weakness and helplessness we know our need for immediate help both to sustain us through times of difficulty and to restore the church to what it ought to be – alive and

ever striving to establish God's kingdom on earth as it waits for the
return of its king.

Study questions: Habakkuk 3:1-2

verse 1: Habakkuk intended that his prayer be used in the worship
of the Temple. What role should be given to corporate, as distinct from,
individual prayer? (Matt. 18:19-20; Acts 12:5, 12; 2 Cor. 1:11; Eph. 6:18)

verse 2: How is God's mercy made known to us? (Eph. 2:4-7; 1
Tim. 1:13; Tit. 3:4-7)

What part does revival play in the life of the church? (Acts 2:41;
8:6; 9:35; 11:21; Rev. 3:19-20)

Habakkuk 3:3-7: The Splendour of the LORD

The introduction to Habakkuk's prayer had mentioned the past (3:2a)
and his own day (3:2b). The same division is reflected in the structure
of the main part of the prayer. What is to occur in the prophet's own
time (3:2b) is taken up in the second section of the prayer (3:16-19),
while before that Habakkuk sets out in greater detail his meditation on
God's past intervention in power on behalf of his people (3:3-15). This
section is itself in two parts: in the first, Habakkuk speaks about God's
past actions (3:3-7); in the second, he addresses the LORD (3:8-15).

Habakkuk's portrayal of what the LORD did is of unsurpassed
intensity and grandeur. His description alludes to many earlier portions of Scripture, particularly Exodus 15, Deuteronomy 33 and
Psalms 18, 68 and 77 to build up a picture of the splendour and majesty
with which the LORD revealed his power. His language is on occasion
archaic, perhaps reflecting on the earlier sources from which he drew,
but probably also constituting an attempt to evoke the greatness and
certainties of past days at a time of turmoil and confusion.

When we read a passage like this one, we become more than
ordinarily sensitive to the distance between our age and that of the
prophet. We can readily sympathise with Habakkuk as he struggles
with the question 'Why?', but when he speaks of God coming from
Teman (3:3) or trampling the sea with his horses (3:15), we are acutely
aware that we do not usually talk or think in that way. Our difficulties
may in part arise from our unfamiliarity with the references that are
made, but probably of greater significance is our modern tendency to
ask the wrong sort of questions about an ancient poem. Once we have
understood the allusions made, we are to stand back from the detail and
appreciate the impact of the whole presentation of the splendour and

power of the presence of the LORD.

God came from Teman (*verse 3*). It is not the usual word for 'God' that is found here, but an older, related form that is especially common in the book of Job. It first occurs in Deuteronomy 32:15 where it is used of God as the creator of Israel. Here it denotes God as the creator and governor of the world, the one to whom all must show respect, and the one by whom all are controlled.

God 'came' is expressed in such a way as to suggest that the description of ancient events had come alive for Habakkuk. It may be that he had not had to rely just on the records of the past, but that God permitted the prophet to see these events unfolding before his inner eye (see also on 3:7). What is described is known as a theophany, that is, a way in which God makes his presence known on earth by external phenomena. The particular events that Habakkuk describes are those associated with the LORD's appearance to his people at Sinai (Exod. 19:16-19).

Teman was the name of a district, and its main city, in the south of Edom (Jer. 49:7; Obad. 9), called after a grandson of Esau (Gen. 36:11). As Edom lay south and east of the Dead Sea (see Map I), Teman was about half-way between the Dead Sea and the Gulf of Aqaba.

The Holy One from Mount Paran. The desert, or wilderness, of Paran was a large, ill-defined area to the west of Edom and stretching from there down to Egypt. Israel moved into it immediately after leaving Sinai (Num. 10:12). Mount Paran was located within this territory. The only other place it is mentioned in Scripture is in Deuteronomy 33:2, 'The LORD came from Sinai and dawned over them from Seir; he shone forth from Mount Paran. He came with myriads of holy ones from the south, from his mountain slopes.' Here, however, Habakkuk does not explicitly mention Sinai, but he gives sufficient details to evoke for his hearers the descriptions of ancient events that they had heard so often. This was the glorious way in which God had made his appearance, coming over the northern hills to Sinai.

It was particularly as 'the Holy One' (1:12) that he came. This fits in with the majesty of his appearance ('majestic in holiness' Exod. 15:11), and also its awe-inspiring nature. He is personally pure, separate from all that taints and is impure, and requires that his people gathered round to serve him reflect this holiness (Lev. 11:44-45). His holy presence causes wonder, awe and reverence (Isa. 6:2-3; Rev. 15:4). Those who are aware of their own sin shrink back before such a revelation (Isa. 6:5; Luke 5:8).

Selah. This word is not part of the subject-matter of the prayer. It is a word found 71 times in the book of Psalms and three times here (3:3, 9, 13). It probably indicated the way in which the psalm should be sung or accompanied, perhaps that there should be a musical interlude. The suggestion sometimes made that the accompanying music should be played more loudly would certainly fit the present theme of the majestic coming of God.

The prophet then describes the universal impact of this display of the LORD's glory (see on 2:14). **His glory covered the heavens** so that wherever one looked the grandeur of his appearance was reflected (Pss. 8:1; 19:1-4; 68:34; 148:13). 'Glory' is associated with the status and dignity of a ruler ('authority' Num. 27:20; 'splendour' 1 Chr. 29:25; Ps. 45:3; 'majesty' Zech. 6:13). This is the resplendence of the Creator reflected throughout his realm. **And his praise filled the earth** does not seem to envisage that the inhabitants of earth sing to him in praise. It is rather that the revelation of his majestic glory is such that he ought to be praised (Ps. 18:3).

Habakkuk then brings out the intense radiance of the display of divine splendour. The NIV interprets this picture in terms of the glory of dawn. **His splendour was like the sunrise** (*verse 4*). However, 'splendour' is used of the brightness of a shining light whatever its source: the glow of a fire at night (Isa. 4:5), the stars (Joel 2:10; 3:15), the burning of a lamp (Ps. 18:28), or of the sun ('brightness' 2 Sam. 23:4; 'first gleam' Prov. 4:18). Also, 'sunrise' is simply 'light', though it can be used more particularly of 'dawn' (Judg. 16:2; 1 Sam. 14:36). Later in the chapter (3:11) these two words are translated 'flash' and 'glint' respectively in the context of a thunder storm. The NIV interpretation may be correct in bringing out the grandeur of the theophany, but other Scripture passages depict it in terms of awesome fire. 'To the Israelites the glory of the LORD looked like a consuming fire on top of the mountain' (Exod. 24:17; see also Deut. 5:4, 22-25). Associated with this there were thunder and lightning (Exod. 19:16; 20:18).

Rays flashed from his hand. This part of the description is consistent with either sunrise or a lightning storm. Hebrew uses the word 'horns' to describe 'rays'. When Moses had been in the presence of God, his face was radiant, literally 'was horned' (Exod. 34:29-30). So here it may describe the radiance of the theophany in terms of the rays coming from either side of the rising sun. **Where his power was hidden** refers to the fact that for all that there was a glorious manifestation, far more was concealed than revealed of the attributes of God. The brilliance of his appearance also acted like a veil, to emphasise how much of God cannot be seen (Exod. 33:20-23; Ezek. 1:27; 1 Tim. 6:16; Heb. 1:1-3). His power particularly refers to his control over the created realm, through which he acts on behalf of his people (Exod. 15:13; Pss. 68:34-35; 74:13; 77:14).

Plague went before him; pestilence followed his steps (*verse 5*). Plague and pestilence (literally, fever, burning heat) are personified as part of the retinue of the LORD as he comes in judgment. This reminds us that these hostile forces are made subservient by God to the outworking of his purposes. In Ezekiel 14:21 he lists sword, famine, wild beasts and plague as 'my four dreadful judgments' (see also Jer. 14:12; Zech. 14:12; Rev. 6:8). 'Plague' refers in general terms to a variety of infections that could strike suddenly and mysteriously, and with high mortality (Ps. 91:3-6). When Israel was disobedient, one of the ways the LORD chastised them was to strike them with plague and pestilence (Deut. 28:21-22; 32:24). Here, however, the plagues in view are undoubtedly those that fell on the Egyptians (Exod. 7-11). The word found here as 'plague' is also used in Exodus 9:3, 15 (see also Ps. 78:50) as part of the LORD's judgment on the oppressors of his people.

The next two verses describe the impact of the LORD's coming on the physical structure of the earth and on the peoples of the world. **He stood, and shook the earth** (*verse 6*). 'Stood' describes the majestic presence of the sovereign LORD as he surveys his domain (Mic. 5:4). Under his gaze even the inanimate realm shudders. The verb translated 'shook' may also be derived from a root meaning 'to measure'. 'He measured the earth' too fits the context as a picture not of the LORD establishing its dimensions but of him evaluating it to see if it matches up to his requirements.

He looked, and made the nations tremble. This is the look of the judge of all the earth. 'He observes the sons of men; his eyes examine them' (Ps. 11:4). Under this scrutiny the nations react with terror. Job used this verb to describe his emotional turmoil when his heart 'leaped out' of its place (Job 37:1). So the self-confidence of those who opposed the LORD and his people utterly collapsed. This happened both in Egypt (Exod. 12:33; Ps. 105:38) and among the people of Canaan, of whom Rahab reported that they were melting in fear, and the hearts had sunk and their courage failed (Josh. 2:9, 11; see also Exod. 15:14-16; Num. 22:3).

The ancient mountains crumbled and the age-old hills collapsed. This picks up the first clause of the verse. There are similar descriptions in Micah 1:4 and Nahum 1:5. The ancient mountains are the firmest and most durable parts of the earth, formed at the creation (Ps. 90:2; Job 15:7; Prov. 8:25). They symbolise permanence and solidity, but the impact of the LORD's presence was such that Sinai trembled violently (Exod. 19:18; Pss. 68:8; 77:18; 114:4).

His ways are eternal. 'Eternal' is the same word as has just been translated 'age-old' in relation to the hills. True permanence cannot be ascribed even to what seems most durable in creation, but it can be applied to God's ways, his goings, because ultimately he alone is 'age-old', 'the Eternal God' (Gen. 21:33; Jer. 10:10; Rom. 16:26; 1 Tim. 1:17). 'Ways' does not refer here to the conduct he expects from his people, but to his own actions and behaviour. They can be relied on, and so this description has a promise within it. God has come before in the history of his people and he can be confidently expected to do so again. After all, is he not the LORD of the covenant who has promised, 'I will walk among you and be your God, and you will be my people' (Lev. 26:12)?

Habakkuk now gives further details of the reaction of the nations. **I saw the tents of Cushan in distress** (*verse 7*). 'I saw' relates to the prophetic vision granted him by the LORD through which the records of the past had come vividly alive for him. In form 'Cushan' seems to be lengthened from 'Cush', the Old Testament name for the peoples of the Upper Nile or Ethiopians. But such a reference is improbable here. Further, though Cushan is found as an element of the name of the Mesopotamian king, Cushan-Rishathaim, who oppressed Israel in the days of the judges (Judg. 3:8), that seems too far to the north to fit into this description of the time of the Exodus. The view that Cushan is a tribe of Midian, or another term for Midian, fits this context, and also provides a solution to the conundrum of how Moses' wife could be identified as both Midianite (Exod. 2:15-21; 18:1-5) and Cushite (Num. 12:1) – the other explanation being that Moses was married twice. Their tents (standing for the people as a whole) are 'in distress', a phrase which usually would be translated 'because of iniquity' or 'because of injustice' – which is how the word is translated in 1:3. It does, however, also have an extended meaning referring to misery and suffering, which are so frequently the consequences of injustice. Proverbs 12:21, 'No harm befalls the righteous', uses the word in that sense. There is no thought here of their distress being caused by injustice.

The dwellings of Midian in anguish repeats the same thought. The Midianites inhabited the territory on the opposite, or Arabian, side of the Red Sea, south of Edom (see Map I). Their 'dwellings' is literally 'tent-curtains', a reference to their nomadic lifestyle. 'Anguish' comes from the same root as lies behind 'wrath' in 3:2, and denotes an intense quivering (see also 3:16). The picture may be that of the impact of the LORD's theophany in Sinai. The shock-waves spread throughout the surrounding territories and their intensity caused panic. Indeed the clause might be translated, 'The tent-coverings of Midian shook violently'. Alternatively, this may refer to what was to happen later in Israel's wilderness journey. The Midianites were associated with the plotting of Balak, king of Moab, against Israel (Num. 22:4, 7). They tricked Israel and were subsequently defeated by them (Num. 25; 31:1-9). The 'anguish' they endured would then be that which Israel inflicted on them at the LORD's command. That this is a consequence of the LORD's appearance at Sinai fits the description given in these verses better than a reference to later events.

The mention of Cushan and Midian parallels that of the Teman and Paran in 3:3. This is highlighted by the fact that they all end in *-an*. This repetition serves to indicate that this section of the psalm has been brought to an end.

Biblical religion is historical in its orientation. Memory of the past plays a vital role in the on-going life of the church (Mic. 6:4-5; 1 Cor. 11:25). This is not just because God's past goodness provides reasons for continuing thankfulness. Since God is unchanging in his covenant commitment, what he has done in the past is a promise of what he will do again. The constancy of his power, control and committed love underwrites the certainty of what faith waits for. 'Look, he is coming with the clouds, and every eye will see him, even those who pierced him; and all the peoples of the earth will mourn because of him. So shall it be! Amen' (Rev. 1:7; see also Rev. 19:11-18).

Study questions: Habakkuk 3:3-7

List the attributes of God that are referred to in this passage. Work out how they are also evident in the first and second comings of Christ, e.g. for glory compare John 1:14 and 2 Peter 1:17 with Matthew 24:30 and 2 Thessalonians 1:10.

Habakkuk 3:8-15: The Victorious Warrior

The prophet now approaches matters from a different angle. This is indicated by a change in his presentation, from a description of the LORD's coming to Sinai to directly addressing the LORD, so as to bring out the purpose that lay behind the divine presence. The LORD had come as the divine warrior, demonstrating his control over everything and everyone that threatened to disrupt his realm. He therefore displayed his anger and wrath at the forces opposed to his people, and also acted to secure their salvation and deliverance. These two themes are set in contrast in 3:12-13, which form the centre of this section of the psalm.

God the Warrior (3:8-11) **Were you angry with the rivers, O LORD? Was your wrath against the streams?** (*verse 8*). 'With the rivers' and 'against the streams' represent virtually identical phrases, and the double question may be considered as a single thought which is not completed at its first utterance, but is partially repeated to bring out the vehemence of its expression. 'Was it against rivers, O LORD – was it against the rivers that your wrath was kindled?' It is a rhetorical question to which no answer was expected, and emphasises the greatness of the judicial wrath of God. 'Angry' refers to what is stirred up to burn (Jonah 4:1, 4, 9). 'Wrath' is the most common term for divine anger that is aroused by human sin.

What rivers are referred to? The Nile (Exod. 7:14-25) and the Jordan (Josh. 3:13-17) figure in the deliverance from Egypt and the entry into Canaan. But 'rivers' can also apply to the currents of the sea (Jonah 2:3), and that may well be what is intended here.

Did you rage against the sea when you rode with your horses and your victorious chariots? 'Rage' is related to a verb meaning 'pass over' or 'overflow', and denotes the wrath which passes through or breaks through every barrier ('wrath' Zeph. 1:15, 18). God is presented as the one 'who rides on the heavens' (Deut. 33:26; Ps. 68:4, 33) and who 'makes the clouds his chariot and rides on the wings of the wind' (Ps. 104:3). He is in control of all the forces of nature, which do his bidding. On the night when Israel passed through the Red Sea, 'the LORD drove the sea back with a strong east wind and turned it into dry land' (Exod. 14:21). Moses described the same event more poetically as 'by the blast of your nostrils the waters piled up. The surging waters stood firm like a wall; the deep waters congealed in the

heart of the sea' (Exod. 15:8; see also Ps. 77:16-19). That was how the
LORD displayed his power and control over the sea and its mighty
currents.

But in an important sense the answer to these questions is 'No'. The
LORD was not angry with the sea, though he displayed his power
against it. His anger was against those who had enslaved his people and
the sinister powers that controlled them. 'I will bring judgment on all
the gods of Egypt' (Exod. 12:12). The 'victorious chariots' are
therefore 'chariots of salvation'. God's power was extended to deliver
his people from the political and religious oppression of Egypt and to
free them to serve him.

You uncovered your bow (*verse 9*) extends the picture of God
riding to battle on a chariot. Like ancient charioteers he is equipped
with bow and arrows, which were the most convenient weapons to
fight with from a chariot. The covering that was used to protect them
has been removed, and all is ready for action. There can be no doubt
about the determination of the divine warrior to engage in battle, and
to pursue his foes until he has defeated them.

You called for many arrows. This is a very obscure statement
which might be represented as 'rods being sworn by word'. It has been
given many diverse interpretations. Though 'rod' ordinarily denotes
an instrument for punishment (Mic. 6:9), it may here be used for the
shaft of weapons such as lances, spears or arrows, the context favour-
ing arrows. 'Many' renders a word that could mean 'being sworn', or
'groups of seven'. It may be possible to detect in the former rendering
a reference to the arrows as being a sworn covenant commitment
('word') on the part of the LORD to take vengeance on his enemies and
avenge the blood of his servants (Deut. 32:40-42). On the other hand,
'groups of seven' might suggest a sevenfold volley of arrows, and
'word' could refer to calling for them. The NIV gives as reasonable a
translation as any. For **Selah**, see on 3:3.

You split the earth with rivers. 'Split' is used of the division of
the waters of the Red Sea (Exod. 14:16, 21), but here it is the impact
of God's presence on the land that seems to be described. It caused an
earthquake, which opened up new fissures down which streams could
flow (Mic. 1:4). These two elements of earthquake and downpour are
found in many descriptions of this theophany. 'The earth shook, the
heavens poured down rain' (Ps. 68:8; see also Judges 5:4-5 and Ps.
77:16-17). **The mountains saw you and writhed** (*verse 10*) resumes
the picture of the earthquake found in 3:6. 'Writhe' (Mic. 1:12; 4:10)

is to turn and twist in fright ('be in anguish', Deut. 2:25) or pain (Isa. 26:18). **Torrents of water swept by** refers to flooding caused by heavy rain ('storm', Isa. 4:6; 25:4; 'downpour', Isa. 28:2).

The picture of the convulsions caused in the created realm by the divine appearance is extended by referring to the sea. **The deep roared and lifted its waves on high,** literally, 'lifted his hands', perhaps with overtones of helpless terror before its Maker's power which is greater than its own (Job 38:8-11). 'The deep' is not just the sea, but the very depths of it (Ps. 77:16; see also Gen. 7:11). The scope of this appearance was cosmic in its implications. **Sun and moon stood still in the heavens** (*verse 11*). Even the symbols of the permanence of the created order (Pss. 72:5, 7; 89:36-37) withdraw from their usual course. They enter 'heaven', an infrequent word usually reserved for the exalted dwelling place of God (1 Kgs. 8:13; Isa. 63:15; 2 Chr. 6:2). When the sun and moon stood still while Joshua fought the Amorites (Josh. 10:12-14), it meant that the day was prolonged. It may be that the sun and moon are also graphically portrayed here as awestruck by the brilliance of the divine glory so that they are frozen in their place, and time stopped. However, the picture may also be one of refusal to compete. They withdrew into their dwelling as in an eclipse and did not give any light at all. In this way the brilliance of the theophany would have been intensified.

At the glint of your flying arrows, at the lightning of your flashing spear. For 'glint' and 'flashing' see 'sunrise' and 'splendour' in 3:4. The LORD's lightning 'lit up the world' (Ps. 77:18; see also Exod. 19:16; Pss. 18:14; 144:6). The weapons of God the warrior flashed menacingly as he appeared in awesome glory, and revealed his power and dominion so that nothing in the created realm was able to compete with him.

The Victory Won (3:12-15) The display of divine power was not just to terrify the world, but to deliver his people as the following verses bring out clearly. He comes as the Warrior Lord to do battle on behalf of his own, and this provides the answer to the questions of verse 8. His anger is not ultimately directed at things, but at people who have rebelled against his sovereign rule.

In wrath you strode through the earth (*verse 12*). 'Stride' is used of marching (Judg. 5:4; Ps. 68:7) – the picture is still military. 'Wrath' refers to an indignant anger that gives rise to denunciation (Nah. 1:6;

Zeph. 3:8). 'His lips are full of wrath' (Isa. 30:27) and he 'expresses his wrath' (Ps. 7:11) both employ this root. **And in anger you threshed the nations.** 'Anger' is the same word as 'wrath' in 3:8. Threshing grain separated the seed from the chaff. Isaiah speaks of a 'threshing-sledge, new and sharp, with many teeth' (Isa. 41:15). It would have consisted of a wooden board, with pieces of stone or wood fixed underneath, which would be drawn over the wheat spread out on the threshing-floor. The process was used as a metaphor for a thorough and painful defeat (2 Kgs. 13:7; Mic. 4:13).

But the LORD's mission was not simply one of punishment and defeat for his enemies. There was another side to it also. **You came out to deliver your people** (*verse 13*). This is God coming out to fight for his people. The verb is found along with that for 'to stride' in Judges 5:4 (see also 2 Sam. 5:24; 'march out', Isa. 42:13). 'To deliver' is from the same root as 'victorious' (3:8), which is also the origin of the name Joshua, or Jesus, 'the Lord saves' (Matt. 1:21). **To save your anointed one** represents the same word as 'to deliver', and this repetition links the two actions together. The 'anointed one', or messiah, refers to the divinely installed leader of the nation. It came to be associated exclusively with David and his successors (2 Sam. 23:1; Pss. 18:50; 89:38, 51), culminating in the Messiah or Christ (Dan. 9:25-26; John 1:41; 4:25; see on Mic. 5:2-5). However, Hannah had used the term earlier to refer to the expected king (1 Sam. 2:1), and Habakkuk seems to stretch it back to refer to Moses, who is himself represented as a king (Deut. 33:5). This reminds us that Habakkuk is not just looking at past history. He is seeing there a divinely established pattern that links the fortunes of the people of God with those of their leader. 'The LORD is the strength of his people, a fortress of salvation for his anointed one' (Ps. 28:8). He expects that pattern to be repeated, and it is ultimately realised in the Messianic deliverance achieved by Christ.

You crushed the leader of the land of wickedness, literally, 'the head from the wicked house.' There need be no doubt that this is a reference to Pharaoh. 'To crush the head' is a figure of speech for a devastating military defeat (Pss. 68:21; 110:6; Num. 24:17), such as the one suffered by Egypt at the Exodus (Exod. 14:28; 15:4-5). Once more, however, Habakkuk is seeing the pattern of the past as the promise for the future, and Babylon would not have been far from his thoughts as he uttered these words particularly as the word 'house' alludes both to Egypt as 'house of slaves' (Exod. 13:3; 20:2, literally) and Babylon (2:10). But neither Egypt nor Babylon of old exhausts all that is depicted here. Those struggles of the Warrior Lord on behalf of his own culminate in the Cross, when he triumphed over all the demonic powers that were against him (Col. 2:15).

You stripped him from head to foot is literally 'laying bare foundation as far as neck'. It is unclear whether the picture is of a person stripped naked or of a building which has been gutted. The former picture would reflect the language of 2:16, probably now in the context of the victor stripping the armour off the vanquished (1 Sam. 31:8). However, the word 'foot' (or 'foundation') refers to a building, but the 'neck' of a building is not a straightforward concept. It could possibly refer to the upper part of the walls on which the roof rests. In either event, the victory won by the LORD is complete and devastating. For **Selah**, see on 3:3.

With his own spear you pierced his head (*verse 14*) or 'the head of his warriors', reading 'warriors' with this clause and not the next. Both alternatives present a picture of self-imposed confusion and disaster in which their weapons are turned against themselves. It may well refer to the confusion that struck the Egyptian army in the Red Sea (Exod. 14:24-25). **When his warriors stormed out to scatter us.** Literally it is 'to destroy me', with the prophet including himself among the nation. Possibly 'me' is to be understood as coming from some source Habakkuk is quoting. 'Storm' compares the movement of the Egyptian armies to that of a tempest (Jonah 1:11, 13), and the figure behind 'scatter' is that of the wind dispersing dust or chaff (Isa. 41:16; Jer. 13:24; 18:17; Zeph. 3:10). **Gloating as though about to devour the wretched who were in hiding.** They were so sure of their success that they were already rubbing their hands in anticipation like bandits waiting for the unsuspecting traveller, waiting to 'swallow the poor in secret.' To 'devour' is to take violent possession of his life and all that he has (1:8; Ps. 10:8-10; Prov. 30:14). The 'wretched' often refers to those who are suffering oppression and hardship (Ps. 10:2, 9; Isa. 14:32; 54:11; Zeph. 3:12). This fiendish attitude seems to have characterised the Egyptians as they pursued the Israelites. 'The enemy boasted, "I will pursue, I will overtake them. I will divide the spoils; I will gorge myself on them. I will draw my sword and my hand will destroy them" ' (Exod. 15:9).

Habakkuk completes the picture in the same way as the Song of Moses had. 'But you blew with your breath, and the sea covered them. They sank like lead in the mighty waters' (Exod. 15:10). **You trampled the sea with your horses, churning the great waters** (*verse 15*). This resumes the picture of 3:8, and so indicates that this section is coming to an end. The power of the LORD's armies is irresistible. He 'tramples' or 'treads' (Mic. 1:3; 5:5, 6; also in 3:19 here) as the victor who has totally overthrown his enemies, who are powerless to resist him.

When the great day of the wrath of God and of the Lamb comes, the question will inevitably be asked, 'Who can stand?' (Rev. 6:17). There is no possibility of any successfully resisting the unrestrained power of God, who crushes kings on the day of his wrath (Ps. 110:5). He has given his Anointed One the nations as his inheritance and the authority to break them with an iron sceptre (Ps. 2:8-9). By looking back to the display of God's power at the Exodus, Habakkuk was encouraged as to what divine intervention would mean in his own day and circumstances. By looking back now to the further display of God's power in the death and resurrection of Christ, we are encouraged to await the renewed display of that power at his second coming when every opposing power is put under his feet (1 Cor. 15:24-25). 'Gird your sword upon your side, O mighty one; clothe yourself with splendour and majesty. In your majesty ride forth victoriously on behalf of truth, humility and righteousness; let your right hand display awesome deeds. Let your sharp arrows pierce the hearts of the king's enemies; let the nations fall beneath your feet. Your throne, O God, will last for ever and ever; a sceptre of justice will be the sceptre of your kingdom' (Ps. 45:3-6).

Study questions: Habakkuk 3:8-15
verse 13: What links exist between Christ and his people? (John 10:14-15; Eph. 2:6-7; 4:15-16; Col. 1:13; 2:10; 3:1-4)
verse 14: How often do we see the wicked caught in their own devices? (Judg. 9:19-20; Est. 7:10; 2 Chr. 20:24; Dan. 6:24; Zech. 14:13)

Habakkuk 3:16-19: Living by Faith
In the final section of his psalm of prayer, Habakkuk again expresses his own thoughts and feelings as he had done at the start (3:2). In describing the events of the past, he had often used archaic language, perhaps drawing on ancient sources, but now in the language of his own time he sets out how he reacted to what was happening around him. He is no longer wrestling with 'great matters or things too wonderful' (Ps. 131:1), but frankly relates his anxiety at all that is going to occur, and yet he resolves to take the advice he has been given

to 'wait' (2:3) and to 'be silent' before the LORD (2:20). His is not an
attitude of mere resignation, nor yet is it an attempt to cocoon himself
from what is happening around him. He does not try to summon up
from within himself the moral or psychological resources needed to
cope with the situation. Rather Habakkuk displays a faith by which he
can say 'I have stilled and quieted my soul' (Ps. 131:2), because he
focuses his being on the LORD, on what he has already done, and on
what he has committed himself yet to do.

I heard (*verse 16*) recalls the start of the psalm by using the same
word as in 3:2. What, however, is it that Habakkuk tells us he has
heard? From what follows it is clear that there were two matters that
affected him. He has just related his experience in vision of the reality
of what is involved in the LORD's intervention in power. Receiving
divine revelation was such an intense experience as to leave one
physically and emotionally drained (Ezek. 1:28; Dan. 8:27; 10:8, 15-
17; Rev. 1:17), and especially so when the message being conveyed
was one of impending disaster (Jer. 4:19). Habakkuk has experienced
such a vivid anticipation of what is going to befall the enemies of God
and his people that it leaves him distraught. Verse 17, however, also
indicates that his reaction is not just to what awaits the Babylonians,
but also to the suffering to be endured by his own people in the
meantime. Certainly the LORD had intervened in power at the Exodus,
but before he did so again, would there be as many years of oppression
as there had been in Egypt?

And my heart pounded. Literally it is his 'belly' or lower
abdomen, which was where the Hebrews metaphorically located the
seat of their emotions (Prov. 18:8; 20:27; 22:18; Hos. 12:3). The word
'pounded' is repeated later in the verse where it is translated 'trembled'. It was used earlier in 3:7 (see also 3:2) to denote an intense
quivering. Habakkuk could not hide his agitation within himself. **My
lips quivered at the sound.** It would seem that the prophet not only
had a vision of the LORD's intervention, but also experienced full sound
effects as the foe was overwhelmed. **Decay crept into my bones.**
'Bones' are often referred to in Hebrew as being affected by emotions
(Pss. 38:3; 42:10; Jer. 20:9; 23:9), and 'decay' or 'rottenness' in one's
bones denotes a feeling of weakness or paralysis, the inability to act
and cope with a situation (Prov. 12:4; 14:30). **And my legs trembled,**
or 'and under me I trembled'. He was ready to collapse when the full
impact of what had been revealed to him hit home. For 'tremble', see
'pounded' earlier in the verse and also 3:7.

Yet I will wait patiently. The precise force of the word rendered 'yet' is uncertain. It might introduce the reason why Habakkuk felt this way. He was overwhelmed because there was nothing for it but to wait until the enemy was overthrown. Alternatively, one might understand it, as does the NIV, as his resolution despite his feeling of helplessness – particularly since he does not know how long it will be until matters are resolved. 'Wait patiently' is the same word as is found in 'It is good to wait quietly for the salvation of the LORD' (Lam. 3:26).

But here it is **for the day of calamity to come on the nation invading us** that the prophet waits. This seems a better rendering of the phrase than 'for the day of calamity, for the coming up of the nation invading us'. The prophet's focus has changed, and he is looking for the appointed relief of his people when a day of calamity comes on their oppressors. This does not refer to the great eschatological day of the LORD, though it is in a real sense an anticipation of it. Babylon's day of calamity finally came when it fell to the Medes and Persians in 539 BC. For 'calamity', see on 'distress' (Zeph. 1:15).

The prophet then describes the disasters that had already struck the nation because of the inroads of the Babylonians. **Though the fig-tree does not bud and there are no grapes on the vines, though the olive crop fails and the fields produce no food, though there are no sheep in the pen and no cattle in the stalls** (*verse 17*). These were all key elements in the rural, agricultural economy of Palestine. Fig trees and vines are frequently mentioned as most important crops in the land (Joel 1:7; Hos. 2:14; Mic. 4:4). Increase in the produce of the land and in the offspring of their livestock were blessings the LORD bestowed on them for covenant obedience (Lev. 26:3-5; Deut. 28:2-14; Ps. 144:13-15). But disobedience was rewarded by a loss of such blessing (Lev. 26:20, 22, 26; Deut. 28:49-51). When an invasion took place the land was ravaged and cattle driven away. This is a picture of economic and social devastation.

Though the prophet is well aware of the difficulties that the land has been plunged into, he recognises another, more significant perspective on the matter. **Yet I will rejoice in the LORD, I will be joyful in God my Saviour** (*verse 18*). As often in the Psalms, there is a turning point introduced by, 'But as for me' (Pss. 5:8; 13:6; 31:15). God is an inexhaustible source of joy, because he is the God of salvation, bringing judgment on the nations and deliverance for his people (3:13). (For 'rejoice' see on Zeph. 3:14, and for 'be joyful' see on 'rejoice' in Zeph. 3:17.) Despite the bleak circumstances that surround

him, the prophet's faith has been strengthened so that he can affirm his
jubilant confidence in the God of his salvation (3:8, 13; Pss. 18:2, 46;
25:5; Mic. 7:7). This is all the more remarkable an expression of faith
in that it is set against such a gloomy background. It is good and fitting
in times of prosperity and abundance to bless the LORD for the blessings
he has bestowed, and how much more so when faith has to struggle
against outward appearances and lay hold of what is not yet seen (Job
1:21; Pss. 27:1-6; 73:23-26; 2 Cor. 4:16-18; Heb. 11:13). Here is a faith
that is surely attached to God himself, and not merely to the gifts that
he gives.

But Habakkuk has more to express than the confidence of faith.
The Sovereign LORD is my strength (*verse 19*). Habakkuk has no
doubts left that the LORD, the covenant God of Israel, rules over the
nations and all that they do (Mic. 1:2; Zeph. 1:7). Events as they unfold
on earth are controlled by him, and he is therefore able to provide for
his people. A variety of words is used in the Old Testament to convey
the thought that God is the source of his people's strength (Pss. 18:1;
27:1; 46:1). Many of these are metaphors drawing primarily on the
concept of physical strength. Habakkuk here, however, uses for
'strength' a word that conveys not only 'power' or 'might', but also
'wealth' (Mic. 4:13; Zeph. 1:13). There may be physical and economic
devastation in the land, but God provided him with resources of
whatever sort were required.

**He makes my feet like the feet of a deer, he enables me to go on
the heights.** Habakkuk's language is drawn from Ps. 18:32-33, where
the same word for 'strength' also occurs. 'It is God who arms me with
strength and makes my way perfect. He makes my feet like the feet of
a deer; he enables me to stand on the heights.' In the last phrase,
Habakkuk uses the language of Deuteronomy 33:29, to 'go' or
'trample on my heights'. Originally this was a picture of the successful
conquest of Palestine (Deut. 32:13), and here indicates the triumph
that Habakkuk enjoys. He has all the inheritance that God wishes to
give him; how then could he want more? Having the swiftness
associated with the feet of the deer was one of the qualifications of a
soldier (2 Sam. 1:23; 1 Chr. 12:8), so that he could attack the enemy
suddenly and pursue him effectively. Here it is fresh and joyful
strength acquired in the LORD (Isa. 40:29-31), which the people of God
possess no matter what they have to face. All else can be taken away,
but no power in heaven or earth is able to disrupt this (Rom. 8:38-39).
For the director of music. On my stringed instruments. These

are technical terms, similar to those found at 3:1, added at the close of the psalm. The 'director of music' is also mentioned in 55 psalm headings, including Psalms 4, 6, 54, 55, 67, 76. He was the person in charge of the Temple music, and this psalm was intended to be used in the public worship of God in the sanctuary to the accompaniment of musical instruments. The 'stringed instrument' (Pss. 4:1; 6:1; 54:1; 55:1; 67:1; 76:1) was possibly a harp (1 Sam. 16:16-23), but 'my' probably does not indicate that Habakkuk was a member of one of the Levitical families involved in the music of the Temple. 'On my stringed instruments' is also used in Isaiah 38:20 of Hezekiah (the NIV has simply 'stringed instruments'), and he was certainly not a Levitical temple musician! The full significance of the phrase is now lost.

Even though the immediate prospect was one of hardship, Habakkuk has such a relationship with God and such a trust in his provision that he is able to rise above his fearfulness. Like Paul he can say: 'I have learned the secret of being content in any and every situation, whether well fed or hungry, whether living in plenty or in want. I can do everything through him who gives me strength' (Phil. 4:12-13). Knowing God and relying on him provided the secret of his strength. The challenge that faces each of us is to grow in faith so that we too will share Habakkuk's joy and strength as we await the final deliverance of God.

Study questions: Habakkuk 3:16-19
verse 16: What attitude should we have towards our enemies when they encounter adverse circumstances? (Ps. 35:13-14; Matt. 5:44-48; Luke 19:41; Rom. 12:14-21)

verse 17: What are the modern equivalents of the disasters mentioned in this verse?

verse 19: How may we acquire the strength that Habakkuk had? (Pss. 73:26; 121:1-2; Rom. 8:35-37; 2 Cor. 3:5; 4:8-9; Phil. 4:19)

What are the sources of true contentment? (Prov. 30:8; Eccl. 2:24-25; Gal. 5:26; 1 Tim. 6:6-11; Heb. 13:5)

ZEPHANIAH

Overview

The prophet Zephaniah has been largely neglected. Perhaps this is accounted for by the fact that his prophecy does not introduce any new themes. In his commentary on Zephaniah written in 1528 the reformer Martin Bucer wrote: 'If anyone wishes all the secret oracles of the prophets to be given in a brief compendium, let him read through this brief Zephaniah.'

The three sections of the prophecy deal with main prophetic themes.

(1) *Impending Judgment on Judah* (1:2-18). Zephaniah warns of God's coming day of judgment on the wicked, particularly those in Judah and Jerusalem whose lives are lived at variance with his requirements. This includes the famous description of the dire nature of the day of the LORD (1:14-18).

(2) *Judgment on the Nations* (2:1-3:8). This section begins with transitional verses (2:1-3) in which the possibility of repentance is set before the nation. They are further motivated to act by the descriptions of God's judgment on other nations (2:4-15; 3:6, 8) and on the leaders in Jerusalem who refused to amend their ways (3:1-5, 7). But the prophet's message is not only one of doom.

It is balanced by (3) *Transformation and Joy in the LORD's Restoration* (3:9-20). His judgment will be followed by a process of purification of all peoples (3:9-10), which will particularly involve the renewal of Jerusalem. Zephaniah envisages a time when Zion's fortunes will be restored by the LORD, and she and her King will delight in each other.

These staple themes of the prophets would have had even greater impact in Zephaniah's day because he was breaking the prophetic silence of the dark days of Manasseh and Amon. Nahum had probably prophesied earlier, but his message had been about the doom of the Assyrian oppressors. Zephaniah focused inwards on the corruption and apostasy within the nation, and his no-nonsense approach sounded a note that had long been lacking in her national life. His ministry helped prepare the ground for the reformation of the nation that took place under Josiah, and would have had an even greater impact if he spoke as one with inside knowledge of what was going on in the highest circles of the land (see on 1:1).

Zephaniah 1:1: A Royal Connection?

Zephaniah's prophecy begins in traditional fashion with a statement of its divine origin, a note of the prophet's identity, and an indication of when he prophesied. **The word of the LORD that came to** (*verse 1*) is the same introductory formula as is found at the beginning of Hosea, Joel and Micah (see also Jer. 1:2; Ezek. 1:3; Jonah 1:1). What Zephaniah has to say is no merely human message, but one that has been given directly to him by the LORD alone.

The name Zephaniah means 'the one whom the LORD hides (or shelters)'. It may have been given to him by a pious father during the religious persecution that existed throughout most of the reign of Manasseh. Zephaniah is not an uncommon name. We know it was shared with three other Old Testament characters (a priest mentioned in Jer. 21:1; 29:25, 29; 37:3; 52:24; 2 Kgs. 25:18; a descendant of Kohath, 1 Chr. 6:36; and in a genealogy in Zech. 6:10, 14).

We have no personal information about the prophet apart from what may be inferred from his book and from the unusually long genealogy with which it begins. **Zephaniah son of Cushi, the son of Gedaliah, the son of Amariah, the son of Hezekiah** stretches back four generations to end with Hezekiah. The obvious reason for doing so was to include the name of the famous king and show that Zephaniah was of royal descent. Hezekiah was not a common name in the Old Testament. It occurs in the lists of returning exiles (Neh. 10:17), and there are two similar names, Hizkiah (1 Chr. 3:23) and Jehizkiah (2 Chr. 28:12). If then, as seems most probable, Zephaniah was a member of the extended royal family, then his critique of the ruling classes in Jerusalem is that of an insider. The princes and the king's sons (1:8) were people whom he knew personally. The description given of various parts of Jerusalem (1:10-11) shows Zephaniah's familiarity with the city and makes it probable that he in fact lived there.

There are two other features of his genealogy that should be mentioned. The name 'Cushi' is a word that is normally translated 'Ethiopian' or 'Nubian' referring to someone from Cush, the region of the Upper Nile (Nah. 3:9). But it does also occur as a proper name in another genealogy (Jer. 36:14 – also a long one) and may have no great significance. Another background for the name may be that discussed in Habakkuk 3:7 in reference to Cushan.

There is also the fact that Zephaniah's genealogy is one generation longer than that of Josiah, the king during whose reign he prophesied. Josiah's full genealogy would have been 'Josiah son of Amon son of

Manasseh son of Hezekiah'. While this can be explained by the fact
that Manasseh was aged 67 when he died, and his son Amon was born
when he was 45, it does make it probable that Zephaniah was
comparatively young at the start of his ministry.

The period when Zephaniah was given his message is described as
being **during the reign of Josiah son of Amon king of Judah**. That,
however, covers a 31 year period from 640 to 609 BC (2 Kgs. 22:1), and
so the question arises as to whether it was early or late in Josiah's reign
that Zephaniah's ministry fell. His prophecy of the destruction of the
Assyrian Empire and its capital Nineveh (2:13-15) must have occurred
before that city fell in 612 BC, and so it was in the earlier part of Josiah's
reign that he was active.

There are two key events within that period: the twelfth year of
Josiah's reign (628 BC) when he began to purge Judah and Jerusalem
of idolatry (2 Chr. 34:3) and the eighteenth year (622 BC) when the
Book of the Law was found in the course of renovation work on the
Temple and gave the impetus for further major reforms (2 Chr. 34:8-
33). The description Zephaniah gives of conditions in Jerusalem
points to a time before Josiah's reforming activities of 622, and may
well predate his earlier reforms of 628. Since it is recorded that when
Josiah was sixteen he 'began to seek the God of his father David' (2
Chr. 34:3), it is possible to view Zephaniah's ministry as influencing
the course of Josiah's activity. At the latest Zephaniah had begun his
ministry by the time Jeremiah was called to the prophetic office in the
thirteenth year of Josiah's reign (Jer. 1:2).

That means that Zephaniah was active before Habakkuk even
though Habakkuk's prophecy precedes his in the Old Testament. The
factors which influenced the ancient scribes in their arrangement of the
twelve minor prophets are not totally clear. Chronology played some
part. Hosea and Amos are generally agreed to be among the oldest of
the Twelve and they are placed at the beginning, just as the post-exilic
prophets, Haggai, Zechariah and Malachi, are placed at the end. But
Amos prophesied before Hosea though the book of Hosea comes first
in the canonical order. Perhaps the fact that Hosea was longer was
viewed as significant. Here I think Zephaniah is placed after Habakkuk
for thematic reasons. Zephaniah's concluding vision of God in the
midst of his people was deliberately placed before Haggai's prophecy
which deals with the rebuilding of the Temple, the first stage in the
realisation of Zephaniah's prophecy.

Zephaniah 1:2-3: Sweeping Judgment on the Earth ...

There can be no doubt that judgment to come is to be a major theme of Zephaniah's prophecy. He places it right at the start of the record of his ministry. That was because his task was to challenge the consensus viewpoint of his day. It was a time when commitment to the LORD had been largely blotted out from the national consciousness by years of state-sponsored paganism. The thinking of a generation had been warped by exposure to, and promotion of, all sorts of perversion and idolatry. Zephaniah was trying to counteract the thinking of people who were unconcerned about religion (1:6) and who no longer had a true conception of God (1:12). They had devoted themselves to idolatry and religious compromise (1:4-5), and as a result the land was morally bankrupt (3:1-4). Zephaniah challenges their world view with an uncompromising statement of divine judgment. As we shall see, it was not the only message he presented to turn the people back to the LORD. He also presented a picture of what it would mean to enjoy the LORD's favour (3:9-20). But that's not where he begins. He must first try to make the people realise how far they had strayed from what was right and how horrendous the consequences of their conduct would be.

The situation facing Zephaniah was one that had arisen as a result of the long reign of Manasseh. At the age of twelve, he had become co-ruler with his father Hezekiah in 696 BC, and on his father's death in 686 he had become sole ruler. The next forty years marked the height of Assyrian power – even Egypt could not stand before them (see on Nah. 3:8-11). Throughout this period Manasseh was subject to Assyria. He turned his back on his father's promotion of true religion, and officially sponsored pagan practices of every sort throughout the land, even in the Temple at Jerusalem (2 Kgs. 21:2-9). Persecution was also a feature of his reign. 'Manasseh also shed so much innocent blood that he filled Jerusalem from end to end' (2 Kgs. 21:16). We do know that later in his life Manasseh saw the error of his ways (2 Chr. 33:12) and instituted certain reforms (2 Chr. 33:15-17). But the damage had been done. Those who had grown up during his reign had lost sight of the truth. They no longer had any commitment to the LORD. On his death his son Amon reverted to his father's former ways (2 Kgs. 21:20-22; 2 Chr. 33:22- 23) and the land remained alienated from God.

It is against that background that Zephaniah begins with an oracle of universal judgment. God will not compromise with evil. He has the right to judge, and the power to execute his judgment. From this none will be exempt.

'**I will sweep away everything from the face of the earth,**' **declares the LORD** (*verse 2*). The verb is intensified to indicate the thoroughness of the divine action, 'I will utterly sweep away everything'. 'Sweep' indicates bringing to an end, often in the context of judgment, such as when the wicked are 'completely swept away by terrors' (Ps. 73:19), the harvest is divinely taken away from unrepentant Judah (Jer. 8:13), or the mansions of Samaria are demolished (Amos 3:15). 'Declares the LORD' is a phrase frequently found in the prophets in the middle or at the end of a divine saying to emphasise that it has come from God himself. The authoritative nature of the assertion is more adequately brought out by 'declares' than by 'says'. Zephaniah uses this phrase five times (1:2, 3, 10; 2:9; 3:8).

The word translated 'earth' refers originally to the 'ground', but it came to be employed both of the world (Gen. 12:3; Isa. 23:17; Amos 9:8) and of the land of promise (Gen. 28:15; Exod. 20:12). Some translations (e.g. NKJV) employ 'land' here, but the whole context favours a message of universal scope that is then localised to Judah (1:4-13). This is particularly brought out by the use of the phrase 'from the face of the earth'. This would have evoked in the minds of Zephaniah's hearers the stories that even they would have heard when they were young about the earlier occasion when the LORD had intervened in the judgment of the Flood. 'I will wipe mankind, whom I have created, from the face of the earth – men and animals, and creatures that move along the ground, and birds of the air' (Gen. 6:7; see also Gen. 7:4). There had been no escape then, and there would be no escape now.

I will sweep away both men and animals; I will sweep away the birds of the air and the fish of the sea (*verse 3*). This gives greater detail regarding 'all' in verse 2, with the categories in the same order as Genesis 6:7, extending downwards from mankind. However, the scope of the judgment is even more extensive than at the Flood because now fish are also to be involved (Hos. 4:3). The sin of mankind affects the whole of the created realm (Gen. 3:17-19; Jer. 4:23-26; 12:4). Since Adam and Eve were made rulers over God's creation (Gen. 1:26, 28), their fall affected the destiny of all that was under their sway, and human sin continues to impact the whole world (Rom. 8:20-21).

Zephaniah takes up 'I will sweep away' from verse 1 and repeats it twice to convey repeated and thorough action. After the Flood, God had promised Noah that he would never again destroy all living creatures as he had done – a promise that applied 'as long as the earth endures' (Gen. 8:21-22). This universal description shows that Zephaniah is beginning by presenting the reality of final judgment, and the fact that all will have to answer before 'the Judge of all the earth' (Gen. 18:25).

The wicked will have only heaps of rubble. As the NIV footnote indicates it is difficult to translate this line. Literally it is just 'heaps of rubble (or, ruins) with the wicked'. 'Heaps of rubble' is used elsewhere in the context of the social disintegration of Judah and Jerusalem because of the people's rebellion and sin (Isa. 3:6). It is perhaps easier then to take the phrase as continuing the list of what the LORD will sweep away. He will also sweep away the ruinous society that has come into existence on earth along with the wicked. Mention of the wicked shows that the LORD's action is fully justified. This is the harvest that sin brings.

'When I cut off man from the face of the earth,' declares the LORD. There is here the same word-play on 'man', 'mankind' and 'ground' as is found in the Creation narrative, where man is *'Adam'* from the 'ground', *'adamah'*, groundling from the ground (Gen. 2:7). 'Cut off' is a strong term indicating utter removal (Lev. 26:22; 1 Kgs. 9:7; Ezek. 14:13; Mic. 5:10). It may even be used of the infliction of the death penalty (Exod. 31:14; Lev. 20:3-6). This is the judicial sentence that will be imposed on mankind because of sin and rebellion. The repeated 'declares the LORD' solemnly affirms the certainty of the realisation of these predictions. It is the LORD who has spoken and what he has determined shall surely come to pass.

It is never easy to know where to begin in challenging an age that no longer has any respect for God. Zephaniah begins with the impending reality of divine judgment on sin. This is not just an Old Testament approach. Jesus never avoided speaking about the reality of the day of judgment (Matt. 12:36; 13:30, 37-43; 22:13), and judgment to come was part of the apostolic presentation of the gospel (Acts 10:42; 17:31; 24:25). Even in pagan contexts where knowledge of God has been suppressed and corrupted, the testimony of conscience to our responsibility remains (Rom. 2:14-15), and this provides a point of contact for urging the need for a right relationship with God.

Study questions: Zephaniah 1:2-3

What part should divine judgment and condemnation have in our presentation of the gospel? Is it right to mention them on their own? (See passages cited in the paragraph above.)

Zephaniah 1:4-9 ... and on Jerusalem

It is possible to live comfortably with the thought of the universal judgment of God. Somehow it does not seem to involve us. Zephaniah is concerned that the people of Judah and Jerusalem are not ensnared by a false sense of security because they view the universal judgment of God as something from which they have been granted exemption. So, to bring home their involvement, he presents the LORD's intention as regards those aspects of their behaviour which he finds so abhorrent (1:4-9) before going on to reveal how judgment will come on the city (1:10-13), and how awesome and inescapable the day of the LORD will in fact be (1:14-18).

I will stretch out my hand against Judah and against all who live in Jerusalem (*verse 4*). 'Stretching out the hand' or arm denotes taking action. When it is God who is said to do so, there is the added note of the power and irresistibility of such action. Such expressions had characterised God's deliverance of his people from Egypt 'with a mighty hand and an outstretched arm' (Deut. 5:15), but there is also another side to God's action. It can be directed in judgment against those who have opposed him (Exod. 7:5; Jer. 6:12; Ezek. 6:14), and that is the way it is used here. When the judgment of the LORD is experienced throughout the world, the favoured tribe of Judah (Gen. 49:8) and the city of Jerusalem which they thought were secure for ever (1 Kgs. 11:13, 36; 2 Kgs. 20:6) are not going to be exempt. Covenant privilege demands covenant responsibility, and the scrutiny of God falls first and especially on those to whom he has given most (Jer. 25:29; Luke 12:47-48; 1 Pet. 4:17).

I will cut off links this back to God's general judgment in 1:3. **From this place** refers not just to the city of Jerusalem but more particularly to the Temple. God had instructed Israel 'to seek the place the LORD your God will choose from among all your tribes to put his Name there for his dwelling' (Deut. 12:5; see also 1 Kgs. 8:29). So when the Temple was polluted with pagan abominations, it was an act of brazen defiance, committed in the very presence of God. From the sanctuary and the capital such influences permeated the whole land. Five objects on which divine wrath will fall are listed, and they present a sorry catalogue of how far Judah had fallen away from the LORD.

(1) In **every remnant of Baal**, 'every' is added from the context to bring out how completely the LORD will act. 'Baal' was originally a common noun meaning 'master' or 'lord', but it became the title of the Canaanite god Hadad. Baal worship here no doubt stands for all

idolatrous worship. As Assyria had recently dominated the land, it is possible that the reference is in part at least to their deity Bel who was taken to be equivalent to Baal. Mention of the 'remnant of Baal' might suggest that only traces of Baal worship were left in the land, and so God would cut off the few remaining devotees. In that case, this would be evidence that Josiah's reforms of 628 BC had already had an impact (2 Chr. 34:3-5). But there is nothing here to suggest that the LORD is acting only against a residual problem. Rather the phrase points to the totality of the LORD's action – not even a remnant would be left. The word 'remnant' is connected with that used in Micah 2:12 regarding Israel (see also Zeph. 2:7, 9; 3:13). It was a characteristic of the LORD's covenant chastisement of his people that he did not totally exterminate them, but left a 'remnant'. Had it not been for this, their fate would have been no different from that of Sodom and Gomorrah. 'Unless the LORD Almighty had left us some survivors [literally, a small remnant], we would have become like Sodom, we would have been like Gomorrah' (Isa. 1:9; see also Isa. 10:21-22; 11:11). For those who worship Baal there will be no remnant spared. All will be cut off.

(2) It is not clear who precisely constituted the two groups referred to in **the names of the pagan and the idolatrous priests**. The first word is rare, occurring in only two other places. In the Kings narrative of Josiah's reforms it is used of 'the pagan priests appointed by the kings of Judah to burn incense on the high places' (2 Kgs. 23:5), and Hosea also mentions them in connection with the worship of the calf-idol at Bethel (Hos. 10:5). Such priests would also have been royal appointees, and not Levitical priests (1 Kgs. 12:31). The root of the word may mean 'to be black', suggesting that they were dressed in black rather than the white linen of the tunics the Levitical priests wore (Exod. 28:40), or it may mean 'to be excited', suggesting perhaps that they engaged in dervish activity (1 Kgs. 18:26-28). The second word is the ordinary word for 'priest' used of Levitical and pagan priests alike. Perhaps here these priests were those of Levitical descent who rather than condemning the syncretistic practices that were imposed by Manasseh in the Temple took part in them (as well as engaging in other perversions, see on 3:4). Both groups are going to experience the judgment of the LORD. 'To cut off the name' involves more than their death (2 Kgs. 23:20). They will have no descendants to perpetuate their line, and they will just become a memory from the past (Deut. 7:24; 9:14; Ruth 4:10; Ps. 109:13; Isa. 56:5).

(3) But the LORD's anger will not be limited just to those who are

the officials of the debased or pagan cults. It will extend to all who have indulged in idolatry. **Those who bow down on the roofs to worship the starry host** (*verse 5*) reflects practices that were both Canaanite and Mesopotamian. In Canaan the sun, moon and stars were worshipped as bearers of the powers of nature associated with Baal and the other gods. This was part of the worship of Canaan with which Israel had been sternly warned to have no truck (Deut. 4:19; 17:3-7). In Assyria and Babylon the stars were viewed as the originators of all change in life and the regulators of all that happened on earth – such ancient paganism being revived in modern astrology. This had appealed to the northern kingdom of Israel and contributed to its downfall (2 Kgs. 17:16). It also took a firm hold of Judah in the reign of Manasseh (2 Kgs. 21:3, 5), and though Josiah acted against it (2 Kgs. 23:5), it continued even after the fall of Jerusalem (Jer. 44:15-19, 25).

Rooftops were flat and we know the kings of Judah had erected altars on them (2 Kgs. 23:12), but rooftop shrines were not just a matter of royal activity. Jeremiah talks about 'all the houses where they burned incense on the roofs to all the starry hosts and poured out drink offerings to other gods' (Jer. 19:13; 32:29). Pagan influences had penetrated the family piety of the land (Jer. 7:18; 44:19).

(4) There is also mention made of another type of religious degeneracy: **those who bow down and swear by the LORD and who also swear by Molech**. This is a group who are trying to combine two types of worship (compare 'How long will you waver between two opinions?' 1 Kgs. 18:21). 'Bow down' refers to prostration in worship. Indeed the same word is translated 'bow down ... to worship' in the earlier part of the verse. Here the worship takes the particular form of an oath of allegiance. They 'swear to the LORD' as happened in the revival under Asa (2 Chr. 15:14), in the envisaged conversion of Egypt (Isa. 19:18), and in the universal oath of those from the ends of the earth (Isa. 45:23). But while they claim to be loyal followers of the LORD, they are also prepared to 'swear by Molech'. This is a reference to the god of the Ammonites, whose worship was characterised by child sacrifice (Lev. 18:21; 20:2-5). It was Solomon who in order to please his foreign wives had built a high place (shrine) east of Jerusalem dedicated to Molech (1 Kgs. 11:7). Here swearing by Molech is calling upon him to witness to the truthfulness of an oath, and so acknowledging his existence and authority. They had made a public profession of faith in the LORD, but had no hesitation in conforming to the current religious – or rather irreligious – practices of their day. Their religious

commitment was at best superficial, and they displayed their lack of heart loyalty by adopting whatever usage was prevalent so as not to give offence, but thinking nothing of the offence they gave to the LORD by disobeying his command (Deut. 6:13; 10:20).

(5) **Those who turn back from following the LORD and neither seek the LORD nor enquire of him** (*verse 6*) does not describe two groups but one. They are the religiously indifferent, who made no pretence of following the LORD at all. 'Turn back' often has negative overtones. It is used of the friends of Zechariah who deserted him (Jer. 38:22), the retreating armies of Egypt (Jer. 46:5), and the disloyal in Israel (Ps. 78:57). Rather than taking their place after the LORD, they went off on ways that suited them. They did not 'seek' the LORD, that is, make every endeavour to find him, enter into a living relationship with him, and serve him (2:3). It was a basic expression of Israel's covenant faith that they seek God (Pss. 24:6; 27:4). Often that would overlap with 'enquire of him', which was more directed at using the means he had appointed to ascertain his will (Gen. 25:22; Exod. 18:15; Deut. 17:9; Ps. 119:45).

In this catalogue of religious malpractice there is a broad movement from the gross and outward forms of idolatry to its root in the inner disaffection of the people from the LORD. But no matter how sophisticated the veneer with which rebellion against the LORD is disguised, it offends him, and he shall certainly expose and punish it.

Verse 7 is one of the many places where it is difficult to tell if it is the prophet speaking directly, or if he continues to relay what God has said to him. On balance it seems as if this verse is the prophet's own advice on the basis of what has been revealed to him. He warns the spiritually indifferent and the apostate alike: **Be silent before the Sovereign LORD** (*verse 7*). This calls for the same attitude of reverence and awe as described by Habakkuk (Hab. 2:20; Rom. 3:19). The Sovereign LORD (Mic. 1:2; Hab. 3:19) points to God as the omnipotent ruler and supreme God (Deut. 10:17; Josh. 3:13). Those who are gathered in his presence should await him in silence and hear his pronouncements with due respect. What is more, urgency is required in obeying this command **for the day of the LORD is near**.

The term 'the day of the LORD' occurs throughout the prophets as the time when the LORD will intervene in the affairs of earth so as to reveal his character and vindicate his purposes (for further discussion see on 1:14). There will then be displayed 'the dread of the LORD and the splendour of his majesty' (Isa. 2:10, 19, 21) so that all the proud and haughty will be brought low. 'The Lord alone will be exalted in that day' (Isa. 2:11, 17).   As the time of his intervention cannot be predicted, it is always 'near' (Isa. 13:6; Ezek. 30:3; Joel 1:15) and 'close at hand' (Joel 2:1). In the light of this it is wise to humble oneself before him now and submit obediently to his rule.

Zephaniah gives an unusual description of the day of the Lord as a time of sacrifice, followed by a banquet to which guests have been invited. **The Lord has prepared a sacrifice**. The sacrificial victims have been chosen – they will not be animals, but those who have offended him. The process of slaughtering a sacrifice involved lots of blood, and so readily suggested the carnage of a time of war.   A comparison between judgment and sacrifice had been made by Isaiah (Isa. 34:6; see also Jer. 46:10 and Ezek. 39:17).

He has consecrated those he has invited. Those who are invited or called to the sacrificial celebration are not the people of Judah but the nations whom the Lord has set apart to be the instruments of his judgment upon them. Appropriate preparations were required for participating in a sacrifice. 'Consecrate yourselves and come to the sacrifice with me' (1 Sam. 16:5). There is no reason to understand the nations as possessing any particular holiness. The root meaning of the word 'consecrate' is to 'set apart'. The nations have been specially designated by God as the guests at this banquet to feed on Judah. A similar use of 'consecrate' or 'sanctify' is to be found in Isaiah 13:3 ('holy ones' referring to the Babylonians) and in Jeremiah 22:7 where 'I will send destroyers' is literally 'I will set apart, or consecrate, destroyers'. It is a divinely appointed mission that they have. This may also be compared with the summons to the birds and wild animals in Ezekiel 39:17-20, which is alluded to in the summons to all birds flying in the air to the great supper of God to eat the flesh of kings and mighty men (Rev. 19:17-18).

On the day of the Lord's sacrifice I will punish the princes and the king's sons (*verse 8*). 'Punish' refers to the action of a superior in appointing, inspecting or appropriately rewarding an inferior (1:9, 12; 3:7; Mic. 7:4). Here it shows that judgment will begin with the leaders of the nation from whom corrupting influences had spread through the land (Mic. 3:1). The groups the Lord identifies as being those on whom he will bring punishment do not include the king himself. Josiah was recognised as one who 'did what was right in the eyes of the Lord and walked in all the ways of his father David, not turning aside to the right or to the left' (2 Kgs. 22:2). When Zephaniah's contempo-

rary, Jeremiah, condemns the conduct of Josiah's successors, he does
not include him in the list of those criticised. Indeed, he makes
favourable mention of him as one who 'did what was right and just'
(Jer. 22:15-16).

But though the king had set his heart on following the LORD, the
court and the officials of the land were still those who had served under
Manasseh and Amon. Their attitudes and conduct had not changed.
Indeed there is the possibility that with the decreasing influence of
Assyria at this time the scope for the native administrators to engage
in malpractice and extortion might have increased. Josiah's minority
may have been a time of weak control over what they were up to.
'Princes' does not necessarily refer to those with a blood link to the
ruling family, but to highly placed courtiers and those who were
influential leaders of the nation ('rulers' Mic. 7:3). The second group
to be punished, 'the king's sons', may also not refer to Josiah's own
sons, who were probably still quite young at the time of this prophecy.
In 622 Josiah's two oldest sons, Jehoahaz and Jehoiakim, were twelve
and ten years old (2 Kgs. 23:31, 36). The reference is rather to
members of the extended royal family. (Zephaniah himself may have
been among their number! See on 1:1.) However, it was not their
position that would bring about their downfall, but the example that
they set in the land.

And all those clad in foreign clothes probably refers to the
courtiers, royal family and all who copied their example. It is unlikely
to refer to dress that would mark them out as worshippers of foreign
gods. It was rather the zeal they displayed to copy the fashions of the
great empires of the day, Assyria or Egypt, doubtless imported at great
cost. Their inclinations as regards clothing reflected their total cast of
mind. It was not just a matter of fashion, but of where their true desires
lay. They modelled themselves on these foreigners because they
wanted to be like them, and had lost sight of what God desired to see
in his people.

**On that day I will punish all who avoid stepping on the
threshold** (*verse 9*) has perplexed many. In 1 Samuel 5:5 it is recorded
that the priests and worshippers of Dagon at Ashdod do not step on the
threshold of the temple there. The NIV translation and footnote favour
this as the background to the reference here. It is then a picture of those
who have adopted pagan religious practices along with their moral
code. They are those **who fill the temple of their gods with violence
and deceit**. 'Violence' is used for what is obtained by oppression and

force (Hab. 1:2), and 'deceit' ('false' Mic. 6:11) for what has been procured by fraudulent means. They have no hesitation in bringing such ill-gotten gains as gifts to the pagan gods they worship.

But doubts arise as to how likely it was that an obscure Philistine custom should have been adopted in Jerusalem at a much later date, and why it was singled out for particular condemnation when there were many other more significant aberrations prevalent at the time. There is no evidence to suggest that what happened in Ashdod was anything other than a local custom. Indeed 1 Samuel 5 is explaining why it was specific to that temple. Furthermore, 'avoid stepping' is literally 'leap', and the phrase 'the temple of their gods' can be equally properly translated 'the house of their lords'. (But notice that the singular 'house' is awkward if 'lords' refers to a number of human masters.) The picture would then be of those who are so eager to get into premises that they jump through the door. They are there to get what they can by violence or by trickery. Their masters would be the influential figures mentioned in the previous verse. They use their henchmen to carry out raids for them on the poor and unfortunate.

The behaviour of the upper classes in Jerusalem showed how completely they had abandoned the standards of God's covenant. The morality of a nation can only be established when it is based on a living relationship with God and a genuine desire to live in a way that pleases him. When the leaders of a country lack such a commitment then there is inevitably a pernicious effect on the life of a nation as a whole. But God is not indifferent to such behaviour, and there is a solemn warning given that his judgment will come on those who despise him and his law.

Study questions: Zephaniah 1:4-9

verse 5: What problems arise when our loyalties are divided? (Matt. 6:24; Rom. 6:16-22; 2 Tim. 4:10; Jas. 1:8; 4:4-5)

verse 6: What means are to be used to seek God and find out his will?

verse 8: Zephaniah refers to the 'day of the LORD's sacrifice'. In how many ways does the New Testament refer to the coming day? What may we learn from the variety of expressions used? (Matt. 10:15; John 11:24; Acts 2:20; 1 Cor. 1:8; 2 Cor. 1:14; Phil. 1:6, 10; 2 Pet. 3:12, 18; Jude 6; Rev. 6:17; 16:14)

Does it matter how we dress? (Lev. 19:19; Deut. 22:11; Matt. 6:28-29; John 7:24; 1 Tim. 2:9-10; 1 Pet. 3:3-4; Jas. 2:1-4)

Zephaniah 1:10-13: Searching in Corners

Judgment will come on the city at the hands of invading forces. None will be spared. Zephaniah describes the cry of hopeless despair that will arise from every part of the city as the LORD thoroughly scrutinises all that was going on, and his judgment falls on those who think they are secure.

'On that day,' declares the LORD, 'a cry will go up from the Fish Gate' (*verse 10*). 'That day' continues the description of the day of the LORD (1:7). 'A cry' is literally 'a voice, or sound, of a shout' of anguish or for help, such as those uttered by the Israelites in Egypt (Exod. 3:7, 9), by those bewailing the destruction and havoc caused by enemy forces (Jer. 48:3, 5), by the poor and needy in their distress (Job 34:28; Ps. 9:12), or by those oppressed by their fellow countrymen (Neh. 5:1; Isa. 5:7). The precise cause of their anguish is not immediately made clear.

Details of the topography of pre-exilic Jerusalem are still uncertain. The description of Manasseh's building activity late in his reign suggests the Fish Gate was in the eastern wall of the city (2 Chr. 33:14). However, in post-exilic times it was definitely located in the northern wall of the city to the west of the Temple Mount (Neh. 3:3; 12:39). Probably the name arose from the fact that fish from the Mediterranean or the Sea of Galilee were sold here.

Wailing refers to mourning over the dead. It seems, however, to be particularly associated with the grief of a community experiencing an extraordinary catastrophe (Isa. 14:31; Jer. 25:34) rather than with the funeral rites for an individual. It would arise from the New Quarter, the second district of the city (2 Kgs. 22:14; 2 Chr. 34:22). This seems to have been located to the west of the Old City, on the other side of the Central Valley, which would later be known as the Tyropoean Valley.

And a loud crash from the hills. The loud crash is that caused by the city being torn apart and demolished – in the event by enemy forces. The hills may be those on which Jerusalem stood, and the scene is one of destruction throughout the city. Alternatively, the reference may be to the hills surrounding Jerusalem, and it is the sound of destruction echoing back into the devastated city.

Wail (*verse 11*) repeats the word of the previous verse, indicating the reaction of a community struck by disaster. They are described as you who live in the market district, or the Mortar (as in the margin). A mortar is a bowl in which a substance is pounded (Prov. 27:22), and the term was applied to a hollow place in a rock in Judges 15:19. 'The market district' assumes on the basis of the rest of the verse that 'mortar' here refers to the area where this implement would be used. If so, we do not know the location of the market district. The description 'the Mortar' may, however, point to the shape of the area, in which case it probably refers to the valley that separated the eastern from the western city. It is much less likely that the name was coined to describe the city surrounded by hills and ready to be beaten to powder.

All your merchants will be wiped out. 'All your merchants' is literally 'all the people of Canaan', but the word is used in a more general sense to refer to the Canaanites or Phoenicians as well-known traders, and so is used here to refer to the merchants, of whatever racial origin, in this part of Jerusalem. They are going to come to a violent end. **All who trade with**, or 'in' (NIV margin), **silver will be ruined**, or 'cut off' (1:4). 'Trade *in* silver' would indicate particularly bankers and moneylenders. But 'trade *with* silver' is more likely. Most bargains involved barter, but if that was not possible, silver was the usual medium of exchange. The traders are described as those 'laden down' with silver, or those who weigh silver. They too are going to perish in the catastrophe that will engulf the community.

Zephaniah then goes behind the description of the disaster to show why it will occur. This is the fate of those who lived heedless of the divine warnings, carrying on as they pleased. **At that time I will search Jerusalem with lamps** (*verse 12*) describes a painstaking and thorough examination. To keep the interior of Eastern houses cool, there were generally few openings for air or light, and the interior was consequently dim even in the middle of the day. That was why the woman in Jesus' parable who had lost one of her coins lit a lamp before she searched her house for it (Luke 15:8). It was not because it was night time, but because she did not want to miss it in one of the many dark corners of her home. The LORD too is going to conduct a search – not a cursory glance for the obvious, but a close inspection from which even the smallest item cannot be successfully concealed. The lamps that were used were small clay vessels holding olive oil with a strip of linen cloth acting as a wick. The light they emitted would not be very strong, and so here 'lamps' are used to show that nothing will escape God's scrutiny. There will be no escape from the lamps God uses (compare Pss. 44:21; 139:7-12; Amos 9:2-4). This divinely instigated search for those who had despised his way and warnings would of course be conducted by the enemy troops as they searched the city they had captured.

And punish those who are complacent, who are like wine left on its dregs. 'Punish' (1:8) refers to the divine King's scrutiny of those who are his subjects. He will not permit those who despise his covenant to escape unscathed. They are described by a simile drawn from wine-making. Literally, it is 'I will punish the men who have settled down on their dregs', but the NIV expands this to bring out the sense.

The dregs were the sediment that gathered at the bottom of the vat during fermentation. Wine was often left 'on its dregs' to improve its strength and flavour. Hence at the LORD's banquet the provision is of wine 'on the lees' which has been 'well-strained' to remove the sediment (Isa. 25:6, literally: NIV 'aged' and 'the finest'). However, this process had to be monitored. If left too long on its lees, the wine would become thick and unpalatable. To prevent such deterioration it was moved from vat to vat. That has not happened in the case of the inhabitants of Jerusalem. They had been left undisturbed, and so their behaviour had gone from bad to worse (compare Jer. 48:11-12). They have settled down into 'complacency' as if a secure and prosperous life was their right, no matter how badly they behaved.

Who think, 'The LORD will do nothing, either good or bad.' In their affluence they do not deny the existence of God, but his effectiveness. They had become practical atheists, for whom God, if he existed, did not matter. All this talk of covenant obedience being rewarded and covenant disobedience being punished seemed to them as idle tales. They were quite justified in carrying on as they were. They effectively downgraded the LORD to the level of the idols, which really were incapable of acting in any way at all (Isa. 41:23; Jer. 10:5).

To those who thought in this sceptical fashion there would come a total reversal of their fortunes. **Their wealth will be plundered, their houses demolished** (*verse 13*). 'Wealth' refers to all the resources at their disposal (Hab. 3:19). God will show who is really in charge and will exercise his prerogative as the ruler of all by having the false objects of their security – their goods and property – taken away by others. He had earlier warned his people not to attribute their wealth to their own endeavours by saying to themselves, 'My power and the strength of my hands have produced this wealth for me.' Rather they were to 'remember the LORD your God, for it is he who gives you the ability to produce wealth, and so confirms his covenant, which he swore to your forefathers, as it is today' (Deut. 8:17-18). For 'demolished', see on 'left in ruins' (2:4).

Zephaniah does not use the term 'covenant', but the demands of the covenant permeate his message. He here refers to the frustration that will be experienced by those who set themselves against the LORD and disobey his covenant demands. His curse on their plans and objectives will completely reverse what they anticipate. **They will build houses but not live in them; they will plant vineyards but not drink the wine**. This is the covenant curse on disobedience. 'You will build a house, but you will not live in it. You will plant a vineyard, but you will not even begin to enjoy its fruit' (Deut. 28:30; see also Amos 5:11 and Mic. 6:15). Frustration is characteristic of the lot of those who set themselves against the LORD (Gen. 3:19).

Study questions: Zephaniah 1:10-13

verse 12: Will God let anything escape his scrutiny on the day of judgment? (Ps. 44:21; Prov. 20:27; Eccl. 12:14; Matt. 12:36; Rom. 2:16; 1 Cor. 4:5; 2 Cor. 5:10; Heb. 4:12-13)

Consider the dangers that arise from spiritual complacency. (Ps. 92:6; Isa. 64:7; Amos 6:1; Matt. 22:1-6; 24:12; Luke 12:42-47; Rom. 3:11; Rev. 3:1-6)

verse 13: What does Scripture have to say about the frustration of those who oppose God? (Gen. 3:19; Neh. 4:15; Job 5:12-13; Ps. 33:10; Isa. 8:10; 59:18; Jer. 5:17)

Zephaniah 1:14-18: The Great Day of the LORD

The description that Zephaniah gives in this section is the classic prophetic presentation of the sombre and dire aspect of the day of the LORD. He is seeking to impress the indifferent of his day with the reality that all have to face: that God is in control of the world he has made and that he will intervene in human history to judge those who disregard him and his sovereign rights.

The origin of the expression 'the day of the LORD' has led to much scholarly speculation. While many have associated it with the religious festivals of Israel, it more probably has a military background. 'The day of Midian's defeat' (Isa. 9:4) points to a time when the LORD secured the overthrow of those who were oppressing his people (Isa. 10:26; Judg. 6:1-6; 7:19-25). There were two aspects to that situation. First of all, Gideon's victory was achieved in such a way as to make it evident that it was not human numbers that counted, but the part the

LORD played. The day of the LORD then denotes any time at which he decisively intervenes in the affairs of earth to achieve his purposes and vindicate his name.

But, secondly, judging Israel's enemies meant deliverance for Israel. This led the people into thinking that any divine intervention would be a time of rejoicing for them. Amos (and subsequent prophets) had to battle against such a misconception. The people were expecting the day of the LORD to be a time of light and prosperity, but it would be darkness and gloom because of their rebellion against God (Amos 5:18-20). The day of the LORD is 'a day of reckoning' (Isa. 10:3) when God demands that mankind answer for their actions.

This led to the day of the LORD being seen not only as a particular intervention in history such as against Midian (Isa. 9:4), against Babylon (Isa. 13:6-22), or, as here, against Judah and Jerusalem. Each intervention in time was increasingly recognised as an anticipation of the LORD's final intervention (Mal. 4:5). It is not always clear if an Old Testament prophet is describing the next, or the final, intervention of the LORD. This is linked with the fact that when God revealed to the prophets information about the future he frequently did not give them specific details about the time when prophecies would come true. This left the prophets 'trying to find out the time' (1 Pet. 1:11). They knew that God had given them a preview of the reality of his intervention in judgment, but they could not always clearly tell what related to the immediate future and what to the more distant future. So too here Zephaniah speaks both of what Jerusalem would experience at the hands of the Babylonians, culminating in the sack of the city in 586 BC, and also of a universal judgment (1:18). None are exempt from divine scrutiny and judgment (Rom. 3:23; 2 Cor. 5:10).

Because the whole world is 'accountable to God' (Rom. 3:19) and because he has the right to demand an account whenever he sees fit, it is true that **the great day of the LORD is near** *(verse 14)* at any time. It is 'great' in that it is incomparable in its revelation of divine majesty and in its impact on humanity (Jer. 30:7; Joel 2:11). Being reminded of how close it might be constitutes a demand that all turn with repentance to God (Joel 1:13-15). **Near and coming quickly** reminded them that Israel had always been warned that abandoning God's ways would lead to their quickly perishing from the land (Deut. 4:26; 7:4; 11:17; 28:20). They had no reason to presume on a stay of execution of God's sentence against them.

Listen! dramatically marks the suddenness of its arrival. It inter-

rupts what is being said like an abrupt shout. The NIV actually
translates the word twice, rendering it 'cry' at the beginning of the next
clause – **the cry on the day of the LORD will be bitter, the shouting
of the warrior there**. The strong soldier will cry out in distress
because the enemy is too strong and overpowers him. He is unable to
save himself. 'There' seems to refer to the field of battle where the
conflict takes place. This fits in with the LORD's intervention being
accomplished by means of enemy forces who invade and conquer the
land. For 'warrior' see on 3:17.

There then follows a list of characteristics of that day to emphasise
the terrible nature of that time. By its very repetitiveness it builds up
a solemn and ominous picture. **That day will be a day of wrath** (*verse
15*). 'Wrath' refers to the overflowing displeasure of God ('rage' Hab.
3:8). The effect of this is that for mankind it becomes **a day of distress
and anguish** in terms of its impact on them. 'Distress' refers to intense
emotional disturbance, 'the troubles of my heart' (Ps. 25:17), when an
individual feels pressed in on every side ('distress' Jonah 2:2; 'trouble'
Nah. 1:7, 9; 'calamity' Hab. 3:16). 'Anguish' is a word of very similar
meaning. Indeed in Psalm 107 the NIV translates it four times as
'distress' (Ps. 107: 6, 13, 19, 28). It is also **a day of trouble and ruin**.
In Hebrew these two words are similar in sound, and this reinforces the
impact of the language. Both words emphasise the physical devastation of the day (compare Nah. 2:10). They occur together in a
description of the wilderness as 'desolate wasteland' (Job 30:3;
38:27). When the calamity has struck, there is just wilderness, nothing
left to sustain or comfort in the wreck and ruin. What is more, it is **a
day of darkness and gloom, a day of clouds and blackness** (Joel
2:2). 'Black clouds and deep darkness' were associated with the
theophany at Sinai (Deut. 4:11), and so the language suggests here
divine involvement in what is occurring. However, the fourfold image
of darkness primarily indicates intense, unremitting disaster. This is
what Amos had predicted would be the impact of the day of the LORD
if the people persisted in their rebellion: 'darkness', 'pitch-black'
(Amos 5:18-20).

A more particular description of the day as a time of conflict is
given in the following words, **a day of trumpet and battle cry against
the fortified cities and against the corner towers** (*verse 16*). This too
has resemblances with Joel's description (Joel 2:1). The 'trumpet' was
a ram's horn, which was used to summon men to fight and to give
signals in battle (Josh. 6:3-5; Judg. 3:27; 7:15-20; Jer. 4:19; 6:1). In a

military context the word rendered 'battle cry' refers not to the general noise of fighting but to an organised shout to intimidate the enemy or to rally one's own forces (Josh. 6:5; 'war cries' Amos 1:14). 'Fortified cities' were those with protection against invaders. The city walls would not be built in straight lines, but followed the contours of the land. There might even be curves and angles introduced into them to expose the rear of a besieging army as it advanced right up against certain sections of wall. The 'corner towers' were built at the angles in the walls to capitalise on this defensive feature (2 Chr. 26:15). The description is definitely that of a siege, such as Jerusalem underwent in 597 BC (2 Kgs. 24:10), and again disastrously in 586 BC (2 Kgs. 25:1). This was one aspect of the predicted curses on covenant breakers (Deut. 28:52).

Although the NIV began verse 14 with quotation marks, it is only here that we can definitely identify divine speech as beginning. **I will bring distress on the people** (*verse 17*), literally 'man' or 'mankind'. 'Bring distress' is the verb from which the noun 'distress' (1:15) is formed, and is also used to denote pressing in on a city in siege (Deut. 28:52). **And they will walk like blind men** is a reference to the covenant curse, 'At midday you will grope about like a blind man in the dark' (Deut. 28:29). Their efforts to find a way out of their difficulties will prove futile and unavailing. That was certainly true of the attempts to plot against Babylon and to find help from Egypt in the decade before Jerusalem fell (Jer. 27:1-6; 37:5-7).

There can be no doubt as to why this has come on them. The change of person in this expression suggests that the explanation has been added by the prophet himself. They would be overwhelmed by the catastrophe **because they have sinned against the LORD**. The heinousness of their conduct derives from the fact that they had strayed from the way that their covenant king had directed them to go in, and so had corrupted their relationship with him. That was the reason why these horrors had engulfed them. They had indulged in idolatry; they had treated God as ineffectual and written him off; they had ignored his covenant requirements for their living. Their punishment and distress was therefore inevitable.

Their fate is gruesome and horrendous. **Their blood will be poured out like dust and their entrails like filth**. The comparison with dust here is not to emphasise the quantity (as in Gen. 13:16) but the worthlessness of it (2 Kgs. 13:7; Isa. 41:2; 49:23; Zech. 9:3). Just as dust is trodden under foot without a moment's notice or thought, so their blood would be (compare 1 Kgs. 14:10; Jer. 9:21). The word rendered 'entrails' is found also in Job 20:23, but neither passage is conclusive as to its meaning. The picture is that of the inner organs poured out on the ground like dung.

Neither their silver nor their gold will be able to save them on the day of the LORD's wrath (*verse 18*). The rich will not be able to escape on that day because of their wealth of which they thought so much. 'Wealth is worthless in the day of wrath' (Prov. 11:4). They may have been able to get their own way by corrupting human courts, but God cannot be bought and his justice cannot be corrupted by bribery. Furthermore, nothing they can pay to the enemy will make them want to stop their attack; they will be unable to avoid the horrors of a city under siege (Ezek. 7:19). The invading army will get all they want once the city is fallen (Ezek. 7:21). The LORD is pouring out his fury through their adversaries, and his purposes will not be thwarted.

It is not immediately clear how the final sentence of the chapter should be translated because the same Hebrew word can stand for 'land' (NKJV) and for 'earth' or 'world' (NIV). Is the prophecy that of judgment against Judah, or is it universal? The preceding context has focused on Judah, and this, along with the mention of 'jealousy', favours the reference being to the whole land. However, it is probable that Zephaniah has already referred to universal judgment by recalling the flood (1:2-3, but note NKJV there translates a different word as 'land' and not 'earth'). Reverting at the end of a section to words or a theme found at its beginning was a recognised technique of indicating that a section was being brought to a close. Furthermore, in 3:8 the whole expression is repeated in a context where the translation must be translated 'the whole world' ('all the earth' NKJV), and so on balance the NIV translation is to be preferred.

In the fire of his jealousy the whole world will be consumed. Divine jealousy is not to be misunderstood in terms of the sinful reaction of mankind (Prov. 6:34; 27:4). It is a measure of the intensity of God's love for his people that he will allow nothing to interfere with the bond that exists between him and them. They were not to make idols and bow down and worship them because that imperilled their relationship with him (Exod. 20:3-5). 'Do not worship any other god, for the LORD, whose name is Jealous, is a jealous God' (Exod. 34:14). Those who contravened this requirement would experience his anger (Deut. 29:20; Ezek. 16:38). This then would be a prophecy of Judah's downfall, and the 'fire' as the heat of his jealousy would point forward to the fire with which Jerusalem was consumed (Lam. 1:13; 2:3-4; 4:11).

However, as has been indicated, there are grounds for thinking that what is asserted here is God's jealousy for his rights as Sovereign Lord, the Most High who 'gave the nations their inheritance' (Deut. 32:8), just as much as he had given Israel her land. It is looking beyond the fate of Jerusalem to the time when the LORD's unrestrained judgment and wrath will come on the creation that has forgotten him. **For he will make a sudden end of all who live in the earth**. The language is emphatic and final. Literally it is 'an end, assuredly a terrifyingly-sudden one, he will make'. 'End' refers to a finishing stroke (Nah. 1:8), and it is one whose suddenness will frighten and alarm. No doubts should be entertained about the outcome.

This description of the day of the LORD was designed to counter the view that God was inactive, a view that was prevalent throughout society in Zephaniah's day. It is a message that still needs to be heard. God will surely execute his threat to make a complete and final end of all who live in antagonism to him and his ways (Matt. 3:7; 1 Thess. 1:10; Rev. 11:18; 14:10; 16:9; 19:15). But we must also remember that there was originally a bright side to the day of the LORD. It was to be a time when he would deliver his own from their enemies that oppressed them. Though the people of God should not thoughtlessly presume that God will overlook carelessness or disobedience, the other impact of divine intervention still holds. Indeed it has become more evident in New Testament times in that the wrath of God against sin has been poured out on Christ as the sin-bearer. The threat of that day has been evidently removed for all who are in Christ, and so there is joy in looking forward.

Study questions: Zephaniah 1:14-18

verse 14: How are we to think now about the nearness of the day of judgment? (Matt. 24:32-33; Rom. 13:11; Phil. 4:5; Rev. 1:3; 22:10)

verse 16: Blindness was used to indicate the spiritual condition of those determined on rebellion against God. What spiritual significance is given to the restoration of vision? (Isa. 61:1; Luke 4:18; Matt. 11:5; 20:30; 22:14)

verse 18: What is the ultimate evaluation Scripture gives of wealth and material possessions? (Ps. 49:6-9; Prov. 11:4; Matt. 6:19-20; 19:23-26; Luke 12:13-21; 1 Tim. 6:17; Jas. 5:1-3)

Zephaniah 2:1-3: Seek Humility

In this transitional section Zephaniah applies the message of the impending day of the LORD to the situation of his countrymen. The revelation of coming judgment had not been given just to inform them about the future, but primarily to spur them to appropriate action in the present. However, no matter what they do, Zephaniah can see no way of averting the disaster that is to come on the nation. He accepted the verdict of the LORD that the fate of Jerusalem and Judah had been sealed by the impact of the reign of Manasseh (2 Kgs. 21:6-14). However, all was not lost. It was possible that some would recognise the peril of their situation and find shelter for themselves in the looming catastrophe. The key lay in abandoning their self-confidence and abasing themselves before the LORD. It is for the humble alone that Zephaniah sees a possible ray of light in the darkness of the day of the LORD.

Gather together, gather together (*verse 1*) repeats two forms of the same verb in a way reminiscent of 1:2, and Zephaniah may well have done this to indicate the start of the next section of his prophecy. He summons Judah to act, but the precise significance of what they are to do has eluded commentators. The verb that is used comes from the word for 'straw' or 'stubble' and it was used of gathering straw (Exod. 5:7, 12) and firewood (Num. 15: 32-33; 1 Kgs. 17:10). A number of views have been taken as to why it is employed here, of which three may be mentioned.

(1) The verb may indicate no more than 'gather oneself together', the idea being parallel to that of Joel 2:15-17 where the people are gathered in a solemn assembly to plead for mercy in view of the coming day of the LORD. But while that is an appropriate thought, it involves reading a lot into this passage and does not explain the occurrence of such an unusual verb for 'gather'.

(2) It is possible that the verb picked up the thought of the type of action involved in gathering stubble from the ground, and so the meaning is 'Stoop together, join in stooping'. Such an emphasis on humility fits the message of 2:3. The nation as a whole would then be called on here to abase themselves before God, rejecting their former self-assurance and pretentiousness.

(3) Another approach is that the idea of stubble should be retained, 'Make yourselves as stubble and gather stubble'. This too conveys the need for self-abasement, and the mention of 'stubble' would then be picked up by 'chaff' (2:2). That 'fire' is mentioned in 1:18 suggests the thought is similar to Malachi 4:1: 'Surely the day is coming; it will

burn like a furnace. All the arrogant and every evildoer will be stubble, and that day that is coming will set them on fire.' To avoid being treated as stubble then, they should now humble themselves before the LORD, repenting of their arrogance and abandoning all their evil ways.

O shameful nation has from earliest times presented translators with difficulties which are still not totally resolved. 'Shameful' renders two words, a negative and one from a root meaning to 'desire' or 'long for' in the other passages in which it occurs (Gen. 31:30; Job 14:15; Pss. 17:12; 84:2). That would suggest a meaning of 'not desired' (AV) or 'undesirable' (NKJV). However, post-Biblical Hebrew uses the word in the sense of 'growing pale', usually as a result of shame. This association of ideas is evidenced in Isaiah 29:22 where 'be ashamed' is connected in the following line with 'their faces grow pale'. In that case, the description here is of the people as those whose faces do not grow pale, that is, they are shameless and do not recognise how disgraceful their attitudes and conduct are.

That they are described as a 'nation' may also be of significance. 'Nation' may be applied to Israel in a positive fashion (2:9; Exod. 19:6; Deut. 4:6; Isa. 1:4; 9:3; 10:6), but it is generally used of the heathen nations as distinct from the people of God. It may therefore be used negatively. A pejorative sense here would emphasise that their conduct was not such as to qualify them to be the people of God. They were living as the heathen would, not feeling shame despite their atrocious conduct.

What is being said to them is a matter of urgency. Three times 'before' is repeated to emphasise the need for immediate activity. Indeed, on the second and third occasions an intensifying particle is added. They should act **before the appointed time arrives** (*verse 2*). Literally, this is 'before a decree gives birth', which seems to be an idiomatic way of saying before the divine decree comes into effect. It has already been determined, but there is an interval – who can say for how long? – when alleviating action can still be taken. **And that day sweeps on like chaff**. 'Chaff' refers to the husks of the grain which would be blown away from a threshing floor by even a slight breeze (Isa. 29:5). This is not a picture of the character or impact of the day when it comes, but of how effortlessly and speedily it may come, traversing the intervening period of time and arriving quite unexpectedly.

Before the fierce anger of the LORD comes upon you. 'Fierce anger' is literally, 'heat of the anger', where the word for 'heat', which occurs 34 times in the Old Testament, is used only of divine anger (cf. Jonah 3:9; Nah. 1:6). **Before the day of the LORD's wrath comes upon you.** 'Wrath' repeats the word 'anger' found in the previous clause. Indeed the original clauses are identical except for the replacement of 'heat' by 'day'. Such deliberate repetition emphasised the certainty of the calamity that would engulf them.

Against this threefold background of the imminence of the LORD's wrath, the prophet issues a threefold injunction to 'seek'. The society that was so self-satisfied and thought it had all that it needed is warned that they have not made adequate preparation for the coming eventuality. Fundamentally what was missing from their lives was a living relationship with God, and so Zephaniah urges them, **Seek the LORD** (*verse 3*). This is what they had neglected to do because of their complacency (1:6). The only way to avert the consequences of the soon-to-arrive day of the LORD is to seek the LORD himself now whole-heartedly and unremittingly. It is not spelled out that this involves repentance, but seeking had always required a total inner commitment. To be successful it had to be undertaken 'with all your heart and with all your soul' (Deut. 4:29). That required a complete change of heart on the part of those who had written God off (1:12; see also Isa. 55:6-7).

All you humble of the land need not refer to a closed group, and so there may be an element of entreaty that an arrogant generation humble themselves, for it is only to the humble that the prophet can extend a measure of hope in what is to befall the nation. 'Humble' is closely associated with 'afflicted' (Pss. 9:12, 18; 34:2), from which it developed into a description of those who recognised their subordinate position before God (Num. 12:3) and their dependence on him for help (Pss. 76:9; 147:6; 149:4). (See on 'meek' 3:12). Their possession of the land (a much more appropriate rendering here than 'world', NKJV) is a grant from the LORD (Ps. 44:3), and so they live acknowledging him and receiving guidance from him (Ps. 25:9). They are thus **you who do what he commands**. Whatever the LORD announces as right, they willingly do. They are living in conformity with the norms of their covenant king.

Seek righteousness, seek humility do not offer a different course of conduct, but expand on what has already been said. 'Righteousness' is conformity to what God's law requires, and 'humility' is not asserting themselves and their own desires over against what he requires (Deut. 16:20; Isa. 51:1, 7; Mic. 6:8). It is a characteristic displayed by David (2 Sam. 7:18, 19) and by Christ himself (Matt. 11:28-30).

If they persevere in this course of conduct, then **perhaps you will be sheltered on the day of the LORD's anger**. Being 'sheltered' or 'hidden' is equivalent to being saved from the disaster that will engulf their nation (Pss. 17:8; 27:5). They will know the LORD's protection (Isa. 26:20). 'Perhaps' is used not to imply doubt as to the effectiveness of the shelter provided, but to emphasise that there can be no presumption in the matter. It is not human action or merit that saves, but the sovereign grace and power of the LORD. Even the most pious are still among those who have broken God's law. As addressed to the nominal people of God as a whole, it indicates their privilege. They have a warning not given to others, but they should not suppose that salvation is easily achieved (1 Pet. 4:18).

The rebellion of mankind started with the desire to decide for oneself what was good and what was evil rather than accepting God's standards on the matter. Humility involves accepting that such rebellion is wrong, and also that God alone can provide a remedy to overcome the estrangement that now exists between God and mankind. Those who accept God's remedy and acknowledge his authority then proceed to live as he requires. Such humility is not a matter of weakness because God gives strength and wisdom to his people for every situation they have to encounter.

Study questions: Zephaniah 2:1-3

verse 3: What do the following passages teach about what is involved in repentance? (Ps. 78:34; Prov. 28:13; Isa. 22:12; Ezek. 18:30-31; Dan. 4:27; Hos. 14:2; Jonah 3:5)

What reward does Scripture promise to the humble? (Prov. 22:4; Isa. 57:15; Matt. 18:4; Luke 14:10-11, 18:14; Jas. 4:10)

'Perhaps' qualifies certain statements in Scripture in an important way. What is its significance in the following passages? (Exod. 32:30; Jer. 36:3, 7; Ezek. 12:3; Amos 5:15; Acts 8:22, 17:27; 1 Cor. 16:6; Phil. 15)

Zephaniah 2:4-15: The LORD's Universal Rule

Zephaniah now records what has been revealed to him regarding the judgment to come on a representative selection of foreign nations. Presumably the nations are chosen from the four corners of the earth to symbolise the universal rule of God: the Philistines (2:4-7) from the west of Judah; the Moabites and Ammonites (2:8-11) from the east; the Cushites (2:12) from the south; and Assyria (2:13-15) from the north.

'Prophecies against the nations' are a frequent feature of prophetic writings (Isa. 13:1-23:18; Jer. 46:1-51:64; Ezek. 25:1-32:32; Amos 1:3-2:16; Obadiah). Usually they functioned as a message to God's chosen people that despite the hostility their enemies showed towards them they should not fear that they would ultimately triumph. The LORD would justly punish those who set themselves against his people. This was also a feature of what Zephaniah prophesied (2:8, 10), but when he gathered these prophecies together here, he had a more particular purpose in mind. Verse 4 begins with a word not translated in the NIV and usually rendered 'for'. There are passages where it serves to provide emphasis (for instance, the second 'surely' in verse 9). Here, however, it links the prophecies to what has preceded them. Looking back to 1:18, it expands on the thought of the universal judgment of God by working it out in particular cases. Also, developing the appeal for humility (2:1-3), it emphasises that since other nations who lived in rebellion against the LORD will be duly punished, Judah has no grounds for presuming she will be exempt from a similar fate if she persists in her rebellious ways (3:1-8).

The prophecies are not, however, all gloom and doom. The LORD's purpose is to cleanse and reclaim. There are two vistas of a brighter future. (1) 2:3 had already suggested that the humble would be sheltered in the coming catastrophe. In these prophecies further details are given of the LORD's provision for the remnant within the nation (2:7, 9). (2) But not only Judah will experience a time of renewal. It will extend to 'the nations on every shore' who will come to acknowledge the LORD (2:11).

Against the Philistines (2:4-7). **Gaza will be abandoned and Ashkelon left in ruins. At midday Ashdod will be emptied and Ekron uprooted** (*verse 4*). The four places named were four of the five main cities of the Philistines (Josh. 13:3; 1 Sam. 6:17), and they represent the people as a whole. The fifth, Gath, is not mentioned here or in a similar saying in Amos 1:6-8 (also Zech. 9:5-7). It is generally supposed that it never recovered from its destruction by Uzziah (2 Chr. 26:6) and remained uninhabited. The southernmost city of Gaza is mentioned first, then moving northwards Ashkelon and Ashdod, while Ekron which lies somewhat inland is mentioned last (see Map II). There is an alliterative play on the names of two of the cities in that their fate is described by a word of similar sound to their name (compare Mic. 1:10-12): Gaza (*'azzah*) will be abandoned (*'azubah*) – its site no longer built on – and Ekron (*'eqrôn*) uprooted (*te'aqer*) like a plant ripped out of the soil and tossed aside.

Ashkelon is 'left in ruins', a 'desolation', a word used to refer to a great disaster that makes a place like a desert (Joel 2:3) without inhabitants (Jer. 32:43). (It is similar in origin to 'ruin', Mic. 6:16). That Ashdod's fate is associated with the middle of the day may indicate that the city fell easily. The attack that would begin in the morning would not last even a whole day before the city would 'be emptied' (literally 'they will drive her out'; Mic. 2:9). The inhabitants will be forcibly removed from their homes, presumably taken off into slavery. Alternatively, 'at midday' people generally rested from the heat (2 Sam. 4:5), and so an attack at midday might catch them unawares (Jer. 6:4; 15:8). The thought would then be that Ashdod would be overwhelmed by a sudden and unexpected calamity.

Zephaniah then dramatises the situation by addressing the Philistines whose fate he has just described. **Woe to you who live by the sea, O Kerethite people** (*verse 5*). 'Woe!' (Hab. 2:6) alerts them to the deadly blow that was to come upon them. They are described as residing in the 'land (or portion) of the sea'. 'Portion' originally designated a part marked off by a surveyor's line. The territory they occupied was the southwestern coastal strip along the Mediterranean on the way to Egypt. This area had been allocated to the tribe of Judah (Josh. 15:45-47), but they seem to have been unable to take it because of the iron chariots used by its people (Judges 1:18-19, see footnote to verse 18).

They are called the 'Kerethite people', or rather 'nation', although there was no single ruler of the Philistines, but rather an alliance between the lords of their five cities (Josh. 13:3; 1 Sam. 7:7; 1 Chr. 12:19). The Kerethites were a Philistine clan, presumably originating in Crete, with which their name is linked (Jer. 47:4; Amos 9:7). The Philistines themselves were part of the Sea Peoples who moved from Asia Minor to occupy various sites around the Mediterranean coast. They seem to have come at first in small groups around the time of Abraham (Gen. 20:1; 21:22-34; 26:1), establishing control over the area and becoming the ruling class in it. However, they adopted the customs and religion of the Canaanite peoples they conquered. David's personal bodyguard was drawn from the Kerethites and Pelethites (2 Sam. 8:18).

The prophet warns them of the reason for the doom that is about to come on them: **the word of the LORD is against you, O Canaan, land of the Philistines**. The LORD has uttered this pronouncement, and so it will certainly come to pass (Amos 3:1). It is 'against (or upon) you', hanging over and threatening them. The use of Canaan to refer to the land of the Philistines is unusual, though Palestine is in fact derived from Philistine. But generally Canaan refers to the territory occupied by the Canaanites before Israel or the Philistines overran them. It may be used here to associate the Philistines with the fate of extermination the LORD had ordained for the Canaanites on account of their great wickedness (Deut. 7:1-5). Their destiny is expressed in the actual words of the divine pronouncement: **'I will destroy you, and none will be left.'** 'Destroy' uses a verb with the same three consonants in its root as the name Kerethites used earlier. (The same word-play is also found in Ezek. 25:16.) The sentence imposed on them is a fitting one.

The land by the sea, where the Kerethites dwell, will be a place for shepherds and sheep pens (*verse 6*). This sense of the verse is clear: the land, which had formerly been densely inhabited, is going to be depopulated. The word 'portion' or 'tract' found at the beginning of verse 5 is repeated in the phrase 'the land by the sea'. 'Where the Kerethites dwell' renders two words, but the reference to the Kerethites is uncertain. Instead the word may be related to a root meaning 'to dig', and the verse would mean 'the land by the sea will become dwellings that shepherds dig and pens for sheep.' Alternatively, there might be a threefold description 'pastures, diggings of shepherds, and pens for sheep.' The practice of making hollows in the ground to provide protection for animals in open ground is attested. As shepherds would pasture their flocks away from populated areas, the idea conveyed is that of an area which has been devastated (Isa. 5:17).

There is now added a surprising dimension to the overthrow of the Philistines. Although Judah is not going to remain unscathed in the impending time of trouble and calamity, she is in fact going to be the ultimate beneficiary. **It will belong to the remnant of the house of Judah; there they will find pasture** (*verse 7*). 'It' stands for the word 'portion' or 'tract' repeated for a third time. Now it is going to be allotted to the people of the LORD. It had already been such, but only in the times of David and Solomon had there been effective control over the area (1 Chr. 18:1). The Philistines never became a major power again, but they were always ready to cause trouble (2 Kgs. 18:8; 2 Chr. 17:11; 21:16-17; 26:6-7; 28:18). In the time to come, however, that threat will be over for ever.

Yet the picture does contain a sombre note for the people of God. It is 'the remnant of the house of Judah' who are going to enter into possession of this territory. That means the people of Judah will themselves have experienced calamity and judgment. But the difference is that they have not been totally overwhelmed. The LORD will preserve from them a remnant who would be faithful to him, and so there were some grounds for hope (see on 1:4; Mic. 2:12; 5:7-8). As a result of this they would enjoy the blessings he provided. **In the evening they will lie down in the houses of Ashkelon**. 'In the evening' indicates a time of rest and security. They will enter into the possessions of their enemies. 'Lie down' has overtones of safety and being satisfied (Gen. 29:2; Isa. 11:6-9; Ezek. 34:14). They can enjoy the LORD's covenant provision without being threatened by man or wild beast.

The reason they can do this is then stated. 'For' (as in verse 4) is not translated in the NIV, but the fact that it recurs here was probably a deliberate indication that this section against the Philistines was being concluded. **The LORD their God will care for them**. 'Care for' is the word 'visit' in its old sense of the action of a superior towards an inferior (1:8, 9, 12; 2:7). Often when God visited his people it was to take note of their delinquencies and transgression, but here his action towards the remnant is to their advantage (Exod. 4:31). He bestows on them his blessing. **He will restore their fortunes**. This phrase was traditionally understood as 'He will bring back their captives' (see NIV margin), but the more general translation is required by some passages of Scripture (see on 3:20; Job 42:10; Pss. 85:1; 126:1; Ezek. 16:53), and seems preferable here as Zephaniah has not explicitly said that the LORD's judgment would come on the people in terms of deportation by their enemies. But in reference to the remnant of Judah the two renderings amount to the same thing. They were taken into captivity, and so their fortunes were restored by the return from the Exile. Here this is viewed as not just to the territory they had occupied, but to the whole land the LORD had originally allotted them.

Against Moab and Ammon (2:8-11). The focus of the message now switches from west to east. The Moabites inhabited the land to the east of the Dead Sea, while the territory of Ammon lay just to the north of that, stretching as far as Gilead (see Map II). Both nations were descended from Lot (Gen. 12:4-5; 19:30-38), and had a history of hostility towards Israel (Moab: Num. 22-24; Judg. 3:12-30; 1 Sam. 12:9; 2 Kgs. 3:5-27; 13:20; Ammon: Judg. 10:6-11:33; 2 Sam. 10:1-11:1; Neh. 2:10, 19; 4:3, 7). It is only here that they are considered together in the prophets, though there is a joint conflict described in

Judges 3:13, and 2 Chronicles 24:26 does mention a conspiracy involving a Moabite and an Ammonite.

It is the LORD himself who speaks out against them and says, **'I have heard the insults of Moab and the taunts of the Ammonites, who insulted my people and made threats against their land'** (*verse 8*). What has happened has not escaped divine attention, especially as it concerned the welfare of 'my people' to whom the LORD had bound himself in covenant relationship (Mic. 6:3). Opposition to them concerned the LORD. Moabite and Ammonite hostility showed itself especially when the people of God were in trouble and distress (Amos 1:13-2:3; Jer. 48:26-27). It was particularly evident at the time of the capture of Jerusalem (Jer. 40:14). With 'insults' they scorned the people, and their 'taunts' were intended to cut and wound. 'Made threats' is literally 'did great things', presumably threatening the land (literally, 'border', Mic. 5:6) of Judah. Such an interpretation fits Ezekiel 35:13 where 'you boasted against me' is literally 'with your mouth you magnified yourselves against me'. But it may have gone beyond words. The response of hiding in Psalm 55:12 where a foe raises himself ('magnifies himself') suggests the possibility of physical assault. Quite possibly marauding raids against Judah's territory are indicated (Jer. 49:1-2).

Therefore (*verse 9*) points out that the certain consequence of this behaviour is punishment, to which the LORD commits himself in solemn oath: **'As surely as I live,' declares the LORD Almighty, the God of Israel, 'surely Moab will become like Sodom, the Ammonites like Gomorrah.'** The seriousness of their affront to the LORD and to those who are his covenant partners is emphasised not only by the oath formula, 'As I live' (Isa. 49:18; Jer. 22:24; 46:18), but also by the array of titles given to God. He is the LORD of hosts (see on Mic. 4:4), and by his covenant pledge he has made himself particularly the God of Israel.

Sodom and Gomorrah had been located at what is now the southern end of the Dead Sea, to the east of which lay the territory of Moab. They had been completely destroyed because of their fearful sin (Gen. 19:24-26), and their overthrow became a proverbial standard for devastating judgment against a rebellious and immoral community (Deut. 29:23; Isa. 1:9; 13:19; Jer. 49:18; 50:40; Amos 4:11; Matt. 10:15; 2 Pet. 2:6). It is not the particular form of catastrophe ('burning sulphur') that is the focus of the comparison, but its sweeping nature, with no inhabitants left. Besides their geographical closeness to

Sodom and Gomorrah, added point is given to the comparison here by
the fact that the ancestors of the Moabites and Ammonites had been
incestuously conceived when Lot had fled from Sodom and Gomorrah
(Gen. 19:30-38).

The area of Sodom and Gomorrah had been transformed from
being 'well watered, like the garden of the LORD, like the land of Egypt'
(Gen. 13:10). A similar change is going to overtake Moab and
Ammon, which will become **a place of weeds and salt pits, a
wasteland for ever**. A 'place' is a 'breeding ground' or 'possessed'.
It is quite overgrown by weeds or nettles, land that is untended and
uncultivated (Job 30:7; Prov. 24:31). There were many salt pits along
the southern coast of the Dead Sea (Deut. 29:23). What a transformation will come on the 'orchards and fields of Moab' (Jer. 48:33) and
the fruitful valleys of Ammon (Jer. 49:4)! It will be just a devastated
'wasteland' ('left in ruins' 2:4).

**The remnant of my people will plunder them; the survivors of
my nation will inherit their land**. Again the solemn shadow is cast
over the future of the LORD's people (2:7). All of them will not
participate in this time of expansion and prosperity, but only those who
are preserved through the judgment looming over the nation. However, 'my people' and 'my nation' mark the LORD's continuing care of
them. They are going to dominate those who had treated them so badly
(Jer. 49:2).

The grounds of the judgment imposed on them are clearly stated.
This is what they will get in return for their pride (*verse 10*). The
prophets Isaiah and Jeremiah had heaped up terms such as overween-
ing pride, conceit, insolence, arrogance and haughtiness of heart to
describe the attitude of Moab (Isa. 16:6; Jer. 48:29-30). Ammon too
was given to boasting and reliance on the success of her economy (Jer.
49:4). This was particularly shown in their attitude towards God's
people, **for insulting and mocking the people of the LORD Almighty**.
'Insulting' translates the same word as 'taunts' (2:8), and 'mocking'
corresponds to 'made threats'. The precise phrase 'the people of the
LORD Almighty' does not occur elsewhere. It reveals the source of their
strength and the enormity of their enemies' conceit in speaking and
acting against them.

The next verse treats Moab and Ammon's downfall against a wider
background. Their sin was rooted in their idolatry. **The LORD will be
awesome to them when he destroys all the gods of the land** (*verse
11*). The LORD will cause fear and terror when his judgment is revealed

(Exod. 34:10; Pss. 47:2; 66:5; 89:7). He will no longer tolerate the worship of Molech (or Milcom), the god of Ammon (1:5), or that of Chemosh, the god of the Moabites (Num. 21:29; Jer. 48:46). 'Destroys' comes from a root meaning 'become lean' or 'waste away' (Isa. 17:4; see also Mic. 6:10). This is a mocking reference to the pagan gods dying from malnutrition as their devotees no longer have the means to offer them sacrifice, or are not left alive to do so. 'Land' involves the same problem as before (1:18; 2:3), with 'earth' (NKJV) probably to be preferred here. 'The land' does not fit the joint reference to Moab and Ammon, which, although treated together, were not a single entity, and also the second part of the verse supports the more general rendering. What is to happen in these two nations will be part of a universal process when the vanity of all false worship is conclusively demonstrated (Isa. 2:20). The fulfilment of these prophecies is therefore to be located not at any particular time in history, but at the consummation of the ages when God brings all that opposes him under his sway. Events such as Moab and Ammon being overrun by the Babylonians, or their territory coming under Jewish control for a time during the intertestamental period, are at best merely precursors of the total fulfilment of what is said here.

The prophet sees this future era not only as a time when idolatry is done away with, but also as one characterised by universal acknowledgment of the sovereignty of the LORD. **The nations on every shore will worship him, every one in its own land**. 'The shores of the nations' was used to refer to those lands which travellers from Palestine would usually access by sea, particularly countries surrounding the Mediterranean. As the false gods of idol worship are exposed for what they are, distant nations will turn to worship the true God. 'In its own land (or, place)' is literally 'from its own place', and this is an advance on what was revealed to Micah. He saw the peoples streaming to the Temple mountain and there learning the ways of the LORD (Mic. 4:1-5; Zech. 14:16). Here, however, true worship is seen spread throughout the earth, 'from the rising to the setting of the sun' (Mal. 1:11). This is partially achieved as the gospel spreads throughout the world, but its full realisation awaits the final day.

Against the Cushites (2:12). There is then a brief prophecy which looks to the south, not indeed to a country that immediately adjoined Judah, but to Cush which was located in the southern Nile valley (Nah. 3:9; Hab. 3:7). In the recent past the pharaohs of the Twenty-Fifth Dynasty had come from this area. It might thus be a sarcastic reference to Egypt, with which Cush was still allied (Jer. 46:9; Ezek. 30:4). If so, the prophesy might find its fulfilment in Nebuchadnezzar's invasion of Egypt in 586 BC (Ezek. 30:25). Alternatively, Cush represents as distant a land as could be thought of, and the inclusion of this oracle reinforces the point that none will escape the LORD's judgment. The brevity of what is said could then be explained by its not being an area that Judah had direct contact with.

'You too, O Cushites, will be slain by my sword' (verse 12). Again the words of the LORD are directly cited, though the Hebrew text has a sudden change of person in the middle: 'You too, O Cushites, they [will be] slain ones of my sword.' Perhaps the change brings out the idea that the sword will come on them so swiftly that they cannot continue to be addressed as they are already dead. 'Too' implies that they share the devastation to come on Moab and Ammon. They will be slain by the LORD with the sword of his justice (Deut. 32:40-42; Isa. 34:5-6; 66:16).

Against Assyria (2:13-15). Finally, the prophecy turns north and reaches a climax by describing the LORD's action against the dominant superpower of the day – Assyria. The fall of that empire was to be a remarkable reversal of worldly power, and quite contrary to all 'reasonable' expectations when it was first announced by the LORD (Nah. 1:1). **He will stretch out his hand against the north and destroy Assyria** (verse 13). For 'stretch out his hand' see on 1:4. 'North' is a general reference in that Assyria and its capital Nineveh were strictly speaking to the north-east, but travel there from Judah would go first north and then east. For Nineveh itself see on Jonah 1:2, and for its fall see on Nah. 3:19. **Leaving Nineveh utterly desolate and dry as the desert**. For 'utterly desert' see 'left in ruins' (2:4). In view of the famous irrigation system this was a remarkable prediction. This passage also helps to date Zephaniah's prophecy before 612 BC when Nineveh fell.

Flocks and herds will lie down there, creatures of every kind (verse 14). The word translated 'flocks and herds' usually refers to sheep, though it may be used of groups of various animals (Gen. 32:16, 19). The picture may thus be one of the ruined city becoming only fit for grazing flocks (Isa. 17:2; 32:14; compare 2:6 above). But associated with the picture of dryness at the end of the preceding verse, what is foretold here may go even further. It may be only wild animals of all types that will forage here. **The desert owl and the screech owl will roost on her columns**. This is an eerie picture of a ruined city, no longer inhabited or cared for. The exact identity of the animals is uncertain, but they are associated with desolation (Isa. 14:23; 34:11), and would not have been ordinarily found in cities. The first is certainly a bird as it is included in lists of unclean birds (Lev. 11:18; Deut. 14:17), though some argue that it might be a cormorant or pelican. To take 'the screech owl' as a reference to a hedgehog implies that the columns, the stone pillars that supported the roof of the buildings, have been toppled and are lying on the ground. **Their calls will echo through the windows, rubble will be in the doorways, the beams of cedar will be exposed**. 'Their' is an addition. It is just 'voice' or 'sound', which may be that of the animals, or even of wind blowing through the ruins. 'Beams of cedar' were costly building materials used in walls and ceilings. The final clause may be translated 'for he will expose the beams of cedar' and taken not as an indefinite reference to someone who will do this (and so equivalent to the passive used in the NIV), but as an oblique reference to what God will do. The elaborate construction projects of his enemies will become ruins before his wrath.

There is then an epitaph pronounced over the ruins of Nineveh. **This is the carefree city that lived in safety. She said to herself, 'I am, and there is none besides me'** (*verse 15*). 'Carefree' applies to a joyful tumult, a picture of a carnival and revelry (Isa. 22:2; 23:7; 24:8; 32:13). Isaiah described Babylon in similar terms: 'You said, "I will continue for ever – the eternal queen!" But you did not consider these things or reflect on what might happen. Now then, listen, you wanton creature, lounging in your security and saying to yourself, "I am, and there is none besides me. I will never be a widow or suffer the loss of children." Both of these will overtake you in a moment, on a single day: loss of children and widowhood. ... Your wisdom and knowledge mislead you when you say to yourself, "I am, and there is none besides me." Disaster will come upon you, ... a catastrophe you cannot foresee will suddenly come upon you' (Isa. 47:7-11).

Nineveh too considered herself able to ward off all hostile advances and to deal effectively with anything that might undermine her security. Her claims defy God. He alone can say 'I am' (Exod. 3:14). His claim, 'I am the LORD, and there is no other' (Isa. 45:5, 6, 18, 21), cannot be gainsaid. Recognition of the uniqueness and incomparability of the LORD was fundamental to what Israel had been taught by God about himself (Exod. 15:11; 20:3; Deut. 4:35).

How her state has changed! **What a ruin she has become, a lair for**

wild beasts! All who pass by her scoff and shake their fists. 'Ruin'
(Mic. 6:16) is devastation so great that it causes those who see it to
shudder. 'To scoff' is literally 'to hiss', a common way of expressing
scorn and derision (Mic. 6:16; Jer. 19:8; Lam. 2:15-16; Ezek. 27:36).
'Shake their fists' seems to have been a gesture of dismissal and
reproach, rather than one of aggression – the time for that had passed.
'Fists' is literally 'hand' and again this sort of repetition (note 'hand'
in verse 13) indicates the conclusion of the section. When Xenophon
passed the site of Nineveh in 401 BC there was no trace of it.

The messages regarding the nations emphasise the universality of
the LORD's rule. He is in control of what is happening on earth.
Although he will bring judgment on those who live in rebellion against
him, the future is not totally bleak. Glimpses are given of the restoration of Judah (2:7) and of worldwide blessing (2:11). But the main
lesson is that if God so treats these other nations, then Judah should not
suppose she has immunity despite her sins. Zephaniah brings this out
clearly in the following section.

Study question: Zephaniah 2:4-15

verse 11: The conversion of the nations to the LORD is not just taught
in the New Testament. What do the following passages tell us about
this time of blessing? (Gen. 12:3; Pss. 22:27; 72:8-11; 86:9; Isa. 42:1;
49:6; 60:3; 66:19-21; Mal. 1:11; Eph. 2:14-19; 3:6)

Zephaniah 3:1-5: In the Midst of the City

Zephaniah is still trying to bring Judah and Jerusalem to see the error
of their ways. Inasmuch as the capital was the focus of life in the
kingdom, and what went on there set the tone for the rest of the nation,
the prophet describes what is going on in its midst as God sees it (3:1-
4), so that they may be ashamed of themselves and repent. He also
reminds them that it is not only the leaders of the nation that are to be
found in the midst of Jerusalem. The nation's ultimate leader is there
too (3:5), and he is the one who will have the final say. It is only by
repenting that his wrath may be averted, and the inhabitants of
Jerusalem join in the time of universal salvation which is envisaged.

Woe to the city of oppressors, rebellious and defiled! (*verse 1*).
It is not immediately obvious which city is being referred to. Following on as it does from the portrayal of the fate of Nineveh, it might at
first appear to continue that description. Indeed, in many respects
Zephaniah here adopts the technique of Amos, who after pronouncing

the LORD's judgment on surrounding nations focuses in on Judah and Israel. They were no different from the others and would have to answer for their sin (Amos 1:3-2:16). So as it becomes clear that it is Jerusalem that is being described – though it is never named outright – it gives added edge to the prophet's analysis of her situation. Zephaniah uses this device to carry the people over from their agreement about the justice of Nineveh's condemnation into seeing that their own behaviour is no better.

Jerusalem is such that the prophet has to utter a lament over it as if it were already dead (2:5; Hab. 2:6). The order of the description in Hebrew begins with 'rebellious and defiled', which emphasises that this is the core of the indictment against her. Though some English versions prefer the translation 'filthy' (AV, REB, NRSV), it is better to take the first word as a variant spelling of the word for 'rebellious'. This indicates not just unwillingness to submit to God's general rule over the world he created, but is more particularly defined as covenant rebellion in verse 2 (Jer. 4:17; 5:23; Hos. 14:1). This had been Israel's problem from the beginning. Even those who had seen God's saving power displayed at the Exodus proved to be 'a stubborn and rebellious generation, whose hearts were not loyal to God, whose spirits were not faithful to him' (Ps. 78:8). That spirit of rebellion continued to be a problem throughout their history (Jer. 4:17; Ezek. 20:13, 21; Hos. 13:16). 'Defiled' denotes stained with sins and evil doing (Isa. 59:3; 63:3; Lam. 4:14) They are no longer fit for the distinctive role God had in mind for them as his covenant people.

Their attitude towards God and his covenant requirements worked itself out in their national life to such an extent that Jerusalem could appropriately be called 'the oppressing city'. It was not a matter of conquering other nations and disregarding their rights as the Assyrians did, but of disregarding the rights and welfare of those living in her own midst. There is a similar description of her unfaithfulness in Isaiah 1:21. Oppression was specifically taking advantage of those in a weaker position ('ill-treat', Exod. 22:21; Lev. 19:33; Deut. 23:16). Jeremiah includes it in his list of what he expected to be banned in the life of the nation. 'Do no wrong (do not oppress) ... to the alien, the fatherless or the widow, and do not shed innocent blood in this place' (Jer. 22:3; see also Ezek. 22:7, 29). Those who had no place for the LORD in their lives had no scruples about furthering their own selfish ends by exploiting the unfortunate and disadvantaged in their own community. The feeling of brotherhood that should have existed in the covenant had been lost (Lev. 19:18; Deut. 15:2, 11; 25:3).

Four facts are advanced to substantiate the description given. The problems of civic morality had arisen because of Jerusalem's spiritual condition and her disregard of the LORD's dealings with her. **She obeys no one** (*verse 2*). This is not just a matter of a self-willed spirit that goes its own way regardless. 'No one' is literally 'not a voice', and that may be taken either generally or absolutely as the voice of the LORD giving instruction. It was the unique privilege of Israel to hear 'the voice of God' (Deut. 4:32-36), but repeatedly the nation failed to translate hearing into obeying (Num. 14:22; Deut. 28:45, 62). The LORD's demands were not to be thought of as just for the past, of relevance only at Sinai. 'The voice of the LORD their God and the message of the prophet' continued to present God's demands to them, as occurred through the prophet Haggai (Hag. 1:12).

She accepts no correction. 'Correction' or 'discipline' applies to the LORD's dealings with his people. This was exercised in love 'as a father [disciplines] the son he delights in' (Prov. 3:11-12; Deut. 8:5), seeking to educate Israel into obedience not only by the message revealed to them, but also by his providential dealings with them (Deut. 8:2-5). The discipline of the LORD is seen in 'his majesty, his mighty hand, his outstretched arm; the signs he performed' (Deut. 11:2-3). Throughout their history God continued to send circumstances (natural disasters like drought and famine, or foreign aggression) to alert his people to the fact that they had broken the covenant and bring them to their senses. But they ignored what they were being taught. 'In vain I punished your people; they did not respond to correction. Your sword has devoured your prophets like a ravening lion' (Jer. 2:30; 5:3; 7:28). The horrors of the reign of Manasseh and the brutality of Assyrian overlordship had not been sufficient to turn them back to the LORD.

Jerusalem no longer had a correct disposition towards God, in whom alone true security and prosperity can be found (see on Hab. 2:18). **She does not trust in the LORD**. Instead she turned to all the substitutes people put in God's place when they rebel against him – wealth (Ps. 52:7), extortion (Ps. 62:10), princes, mortal men (Pss. 146:3; 118:8-9), the idols of the nations (Pss. 135:18; 115:8). She had no interest in, or attachment to, the covenant promises of the LORD, because she had no interest in, or attachment to, the one who had made them.

She does not draw near to her God. Though she has turned away

from him, Jerusalem cannot escape the fact that he remains 'her God'.
'Draw near' or 'come near' is a verb which basically indicates coming
physically closer and is found in many contexts. It is used of approaching God (Exod. 3:5; Deut. 4:11; 5:23, 27; Isa. 48:16; 'enquire' 1 Sam.
14:36), and in a related expression is frequently used of 'bringing near'
a sacrifice to present it to God. Here it indicates that whatever outward
acts of worship were engaged in, there was no true reverence for God
or fellowship with him. He was 'near in their mouth but far from their
heart' (Jer. 12:2, literally).

Then in a description reminiscent of Micah 3, Zephaniah picks out
four influential groups in the city to show how widespread the malaise
had become in Jerusalem society. **Her officials are roaring lions**
(*verse 3*) looks at those in positions of political influence ('ruler' Mic.
7:3). These were the men who surrounded the king and helped him to
administer the affairs of the land. Their conduct illustrated the truth
of the proverb, 'Like a roaring lion or a charging bear is a wicked man
ruling over a helpless people' (Prov. 28:15). They had no hesitation
about snatching from others whatever they wanted (1:9). The NIV
unfortunately does not translate one word – 'within her' or 'in her
midst' – which forms a recurring theme throughout this chapter (see
on 3:5). 'Her officials in her midst' form a contrast with her divine king
in her midst.

Her rulers are evening wolves seems to describe a different
group, which is also associated with the officials in Micah 7:3. The
term used to describe them was traditionally rendered 'judges', and
here it seems to be employed with that narrower reference to those who
administer justice. They are insatiable in their desire for gain. The
evening wolf is hungry after lying low all day (Ezek. 22:27) and
becomes desperate to find food (Isa. 11:6; Jer. 5:6; Hab. 1:8). **Who
leave nothing for the morning** is literally, 'they do not gnaw bones
for the morning'. This describes the way in which they gnaw
everything they can find, and there is nothing left come daybreak.
'Morning' was the time associated with the administration of justice
(verse 5; 2 Sam. 15:2; Ps. 101:8; Jer. 21:12).

The religious leaders of the community were as corrupt as the civil
leaders. **Her prophets are arrogant; they are treacherous men**
(*verse 4*). This refers to the false prophets, who have had no call from
the LORD (Mic. 2:11; 3:5, 11). 'Arrogant' or 'reckless' (Judges 9:4)
refers to the way in which they disregard the consequences of their
actions, here presumably their claim to be speaking in the name of the

LORD. Such presumption and rebellion was liable to the death sentence (Deut. 13:5; 18:20). They were 'treacherous' (Hab. 1:13) because they were speaking from their own minds and not by divine revelation. Therefore they prove to be deceitful not just in the way in which they conduct business with others, but particularly in the way in which they deceive those who come to them seeking divine guidance. However outwardly impressive their words seem, they only promote rebellion and apostasy against God and deceive those who accept what they say as being genuine. The divine evaluation of such conduct was scathing. 'They ... lead my people astray with their reckless lies, yet I did not send or appoint them. They do not benefit these people in the least' (Jer. 23:32).

The priests were no different. **Her priests profane the sanctuary**. The priests who had custody of the holy place were evading their responsibilities for maintaining the standards of the law. 'To profane' is 'to desecrate', to treat what was holy and dedicated to the service of the LORD in an improper and unbecoming way. This had not been just a matter of technical infringements of the details of the Mosaic law, but of going along with blatant introduction of pagan practices into the Temple under Manasseh and Amon. Josiah ordered that there be removed from the Temple 'all the articles made for Baal and Asherah and all the starry hosts', 'the Asherah pole', 'the quarters of the male shrine-prostitutes', 'the horses ... dedicated to the sun', and the pagan altars (2 Kgs. 23:4-12). Such abominations had not been there without the connivance of a compromised priesthood.

One aspect of the duties of the priests was to teach God's law to the people (Lev. 10:10-11; Deut. 33:10). This too was neglected. Indeed it was worse than that. They **do violence to the law**. The priests too had become greedy for gain and prepared to practise deceit (Jer. 6:13). They were therefore quite prepared to overlook the requirements of the law if there was something in it for them. 'Violence' refers to the breakdown of law enforcement in the community (Hab. 1:2). God's appointed guardians of his law were leading the way in undermining it! 'Her priests do violence to my law and profane my holy things; they do not distinguish between the holy and the common; they teach that there is no difference between the unclean and the clean; and they shut their eyes to the keeping of my Sabbaths, so that I am profaned among them' (Ezek. 22:26).

But that is not all that can be said about Jerusalem. She is 'the city of the Great King' (Ps. 48:2) and his Temple was his royal residence in their midst. **The LORD within her** (*verse 5*) was the reality she had to reckon with. 'Within her' or 'in her midst' is a key phrase that recurs throughout this chapter. In 3:3 it is 'her officials in her midst' which points to the corrupt public standards that prevailed in the city. But it was not only a human administration that was to be found within Jerusalem. The LORD too had his seat of earthly government there, and he stood opposed to the prevailing venality and oppression. Later on it is brought out how he will deal with it by removing 'from this city' (literally 'from within you' or 'from your midst') those who pride themselves in their own cleverness (3:11), but he will leave 'within you' (or 'in your midst') those who trust in him (3:12). This will enable the LORD's presence 'with you' ('in your midst', 3:15, 17) to become the tremendous source of blessing that it ought to have been (Pss. 46:5-7; 48:3; Isa. 12:6; Jer. 14:9; Zeph. 3:17). When the privilege of his presence was misunderstood and abused (see on Mic. 3:11), it became a source of false optimism that undermined the integrity of the nation.

Zephaniah sets out the character of their covenant king. He **is righteous** (Deut. 32:4; Pss. 99:4; 145:17). His character should have been their example, but now it stands as a threat because of their misconduct. **He does no wrong** (Deut. 32:4). There is no deviation from uprightness in his conduct ('crime' Hab. 2:12). Instead **morning by morning he dispenses his justice**. 'Morning by morning' is associated with the regularity of sacrifice in Israel (Exod. 30:7; Lev. 6:12; 2 Chr. 13:11; Ezek. 46:13-15) and of the provision of manna (Exod. 16:21). Here it is a matter of the administration of justice. The judges of the land normally met in the morning (verse 3), but they were corrupt. The morning was when the king heard cases as the final court of appeal in the land (Jer. 21:12), but Josiah was the exception among Judah's kings of this time in that he sought the LORD and promoted justice (Jer. 22:15-16). **And every new day** (literally, 'to the light' of the day) **he does not fail**. He can be utterly relied upon in the matter (2 Sam. 17:22; Isa. 40:26). Surely his people would trust such a God.

But the sad verdict is **yet the unrighteous know no shame**. The translation suggests the contrast is between the righteous God and the unrighteous. In fact the word used for 'unrighteous' is related to that for 'wrong' in 'he does no wrong'. Those who were acting in a wicked and criminal fashion in Jerusalem could see nothing wrong with what they were doing. That was how to make one's way in the realities of this world, and they therefore felt no embarrassment or guilt about their conduct. They no longer had any real awareness of God, their consciences were seared (1 Tim. 4:2), and they had forgotten how to blush (Jer. 6:15; 8:12).

God's presence with his people is no longer localised in a temple at Jerusalem. The church of God wherever it is found is the temple of God which he indwells by the presence of the Holy Spirit (1 Cor. 3:16). It is in the light of this that the believer should see what standards of behaviour ought to prevail in the corporate affairs of the church. Indeed, it is not just the church which is a temple of God. So too is the body of the individual believer, and this ought to determine our conduct. 'Do you not know that your body is a temple of the Holy Spirit, who is in you, whom you have received from God? You are not your own; you were bought at a price. Therefore honour God with your body' (1 Cor. 6:19-20).

Study questions: Zephaniah 3:1-5

verse 5: How was God present with his people in Old Testament times? (Gen. 28:15; Exod. 23:20-21; 29:45; 33:14; 40:34-38; Deut. 31:6; Isa. 41:10; 43:2)

How is God present with his people now? (Matt. 18:20; 28:20; Rom. 8:28; 1 Cor. 5:4; 10:13; 2 Thess. 3:3; Heb. 13:5-6)

How will God be present with his people in the age to come? (John 14:3; 17:24; 2 Cor. 5:8; Phil. 1:23; 1 John 3:2; Rev. 21:3; 22:3-4)

Zephaniah 3:6-8: Arguments that did not Persuade

The middle section of the prophecy (2:1-3:8) is brought to an end with a direct plea from the LORD which reinforces the message that Zephaniah has been presenting. The LORD's judgment on the nations should have given Judah sufficient reason to review her conduct (3:6 as compared with 2:4-15). The warning messages he sent through the prophets should also have led them to amend their ways (3:7). As nothing has availed, the people will have to take their place among the nations and wait for the LORD's judgment. The last two lines of verse 8 repeat the thought of 1:18 and mark the end of this section.

The LORD sets out how he had reacted to the conduct of nations which had offended him in the past. **I have cut off nations** (*verse 6*). 'Cut off' points to major destruction, if not annihilation (1:3-4; Mic. 5:9). The reference to 'nations' is general, but that this had already happened to others means that the prophecies of chapter 2 ought not to be lightly dismissed. The LORD's judgment had already fallen on others, and there was every reason to suppose he would act in the same

way again. **Their strongholds are demolished**. 'Strongholds' renders
the same word as 'corner towers' (1:16) and stands for all their
defensive works by which they sought to protect themselves. Their
ruins testify to the ineffectiveness of human devices when the LORD
decides to act. **I have left their streets deserted, with no one passing
through**. All signs of life in the cities and towns are taken away.
'Passing through' may refer either to strangers travelling through the
land or simply to the ordinary movement of citizens. **Their cities are
destroyed; no one will be left – no one at all**. The verb rendered
'destroyed' occurs only here, but the context makes its meaning clear.
It is emphatically declared that nothing remains and all the inhabitants
have been utterly taken away. It is not clear why the NIV has added
the supplement 'will be' rather than simply 'is', which is more
appropriate to the preceding description of the devastation as already
existing.

This had not been capricious conduct on the LORD's part, but fully
warranted by the sin of the nations (Gen. 13:13; 18:20; Lev. 18:25-27;
Deut. 9:4; 1 Sam. 15:2-3). He had not acted a moment sooner than was
proper; for instance, he waited because the sin of the Amorites had not
yet reached full measure (Gen. 15:16). If such solemn judgments have
befallen others, should not Jerusalem have learned that she too would
be called to account for her conduct?

What was more the LORD had not left the people to work out for
themselves the significance of what was happening. **I said to the city,
'Surely you will fear me and accept correction!'** (*verse 7*). 'I said'
presumably relates to the messages sent through the prophets. 'To the
city' is a supplement to make clear who is addressed, and is justified
by the form of the following verbs in Hebrew. 'Fear' (see 'stand in
awe' Hab. 3:1) denotes a proper attitude of respect and awe before the
LORD, mingled here with fright at what he had done to others. 'Accept
correction' repeats the words of 3:2, but this was precisely what Judah
was not prepared to do. 'Though I taught them again and again, they
would not listen or respond to discipline' (Jer. 32:33). If they had
listened, **then her dwelling would not be cut off, nor all my
punishments come upon her**. A timely and appropriate response to
the divine warnings would have averted disaster. 'Her dwelling' refers
to the city itself, and 'cut off' was the punishment the LORD inflicted
on the heathen (3:6). The relationship of the words translated 'all my
punishments come upon her' (literally, 'all that I visited upon her') to
what precedes is unclear. This punishment (see 'visit', 1:8) is the

action of Jerusalem's overlord who is scrutinising and rewarding her actions. It does not fit the context to think of the punishments as being in the past, because up to this time, though Jerusalem had experienced times of difficulty, it had not been 'cut off'. That indeed was what gave rise to the popular opinion that she was secure, come what may. The past reference here seems rather to be a Hebrew idiom for emphasising the future certainty of what the LORD has decided to do. It is as certain as what has already taken place.

But despite the LORD's entreaties the people had a mind of their own (Ps. 81:8-14; Isa. 1:4). **But they were still eager to act corruptly in all they did.** 'Eager' is literally 'rose early to do' reflecting that how easy it is to rise in the morning to do what one wants. Their attitude contrasts with the way Jeremiah portrays the LORD as rising early to warn them (Jer. 7:13; 26:5). 'Act corruptly' corresponds to the behaviour of the generation before the Flood (Gen. 6:12). The people of Jerusalem showed the same propensity in every aspect of their living.

As a consequence of their failure to learn from the downfall of others and from the prophetic warnings given them from the LORD, there must inevitably come divine intervention. **'Therefore wait for me,' declares the LORD** (*verse 8*). 'Wait' usually describes the attitude of faith (Hab. 2:3), and this raises the question of who it is that is addressed here. Is it all the people of the city or the believing remnant? While the remnant would be the only ones likely to respond positively to this entreaty, there is nothing in the context to suggest that they are being directly addressed. This is the attitude that should be adopted by all the people of Jerusalem.

In Hebrew **for the day I will stand up to testify** is 'for the day I will rise up to plunder' (NIV margin). The thought of the victorious LORD receiving the resources of the nations back into his service as the outcome of his final intervention is not impossible (compare Mic. 4:13). However, early translations and comments on this verse read the same Hebrew consonants with different vowels to give the meaning 'witness'. This idea is also found elsewhere in the Old Testament (Jer. 29:23; Mic. 1:2; Mal. 3:5). When the LORD sits in judgment, he is the only competent witness who can be called. There will be none able to question the accuracy of his testimony, and it will provide abundant grounds for the conviction of those before him. The pattern of the divine tribunal is not that of a modern courtroom, but of a hearing before an absolute monarch, whose own prerogatives have been infringed.

I have decided to assemble the nations, to gather the kingdoms.
'I have decided' refers to judicial action. This is the LORD summoning
all nations before him (Ps. 96:13; Eccl. 3:17). 'To gather' is more
precisely 'that I may gather'. It takes place completely under his
control and is not like the hostile gathering described in Psalm 2:1-2.
It is so that the LORD may carry out his decision **to pour out my wrath
on them – all my fierce anger**. 'Pour out' denotes the impossibility
of resisting all that engulfs them (Isa. 42:25). For 'wrath' see on
Habakkuk 3:12, and for 'fierce anger' see on 2:2. **The whole world
will be consumed by the fire of my jealous anger**. The Hebrew is
identical to the corresponding words in 1:18, and is repeated here to
conclude this section.

The problem still remains of those who have cogent testimony
given to them of the inevitable outcome of their behaviour, but who
refuse to accept it. 'The god of this age has blinded the minds of
unbelievers' (2 Cor. 4:4), and as a result they will not respond to the
gospel. Their continuing refusal does not give the church valid
grounds for giving up on them and not presenting the message of God.
It does, however, show that success in spreading the gospel does not
come from a mere human eloquence or superior wisdom, but by the
power of the Spirit (1 Cor. 2:1-5; 1 Thess. 1:5). He alone is able to
prepare the heart for accepting the word of life.

Study questions: Zephaniah 3:6-8
How do problems arise in understanding God's providence? (Ps.
77:19; Ecc. 11:5; Luke 13:1-5; Rom. 11:33)

Why do people not respond as they should to the warnings and
invitations of the gospel? (Mark 4:1-20; Luke 14:16-24; John 8:44;
9:41; Rom. 1:18-25; 2 Thess. 2:10-12; 1 Tim. 4:2; Rev. 3:17)

Zephaniah 3:9-13: Jerusalem Restored
After the outpouring of the LORD's fierce anger described in the
previous verse (3:8), it does not seem possible that there can be
anything more to say. But God's judgment is not just retributive,
giving the wicked the punishment that is their due. It is also restorative.
The God of creation will not let his universe be wrested from his grasp
by the rebellion of mankind. The God of salvation will not let his claim
upon his covenant people be abrogated even by their folly. In his grace
he works to reclaim even through judgment. Though there had been
destruction as devastating as that of the Flood (1:2-3), yet even then

there had been a Noah (Gen. 6:8). Though the threat of judgment because of covenant disobedience had been clearly set before Israel, yet there was a future beyond the curse of the broken covenant (Deut. 4:29-31; 30:1-10; 1 Kgs. 8:46-51). When the day of the LORD destroys the heavens by fire and the earth is laid bare, it is the prelude to 'a new heaven and a new earth, the home of righteousness', that is, where everything and everyone is just as God would have them (2 Pet. 3:10-13). It is that time that Zephaniah describes here in Old Testament language.

Babel reversed (3:9). 'For' begins 3:9 to connect it back to the injunction 'wait for me' (3:8). The day of the LORD brings judgment, but it also brings restoration and vindication. **Then will I purify the lips of the peoples** (*verse 9*). The change affects 'peoples'. There is no limitation implied: it goes beyond Judah and Jerusalem (Pss. 22:27; 102:22; Isa. 56:6-7; Mic. 4:1-3). The LORD says, 'I will turn to peoples a pure lip' (literally). 'Turn' is a verb of wide scope (see 'overturn' Jonah 3:4), but there can be no doubt that it indicates a radical change. The verb associated with 'pure' is used to describe the removal of those who have revolted and rebelled against God (Ezek. 20:38) and also of the condition of the redeemed (Dan. 11:35; 12:10). 'Lip' denotes the speech or language of the peoples, which had been defiled by their words of rebellion against God, particularly in worshipping idols. Indeed, confusion of language was the divine sentence on the third great early rebellion of mankind at the Tower of Babel (Gen. 11:1-9). Before that there had been 'one lip' ('one language' Gen. 11:1, NIV). The suppression of language barriers at Pentecost (Acts 2:4-12) inaugurates the age to come, and anticipates the unison of heavenly praise (Rev. 5:9-14). So here the LORD acts to ensure that those 'from every nation, tribe, people and language, standing before the throne' (Rev. 7:9) are able to co-operate harmoniously in the worship of heaven. Such outward purity is, of course, the result of an inner heart change (Isa. 6:5-7; Matt. 15:18).

That all of them may call on the name of the LORD uses an early idiom for worship (Gen. 4:26; Ps. 105:1; Isa. 12:4). Calling on the LORD's *name* involves an acknowledgment of what the LORD has revealed himself to be by his name (Exod. 34:5-7; Lev. 22:2; Deut. 28:58), while *calling* on God implies a sense of need (Pss. 4:1; 28:1; 34:6; 120:1). Together the terms point to a worship that is humble and reverential. This is associated with salvation on the day of the LORD (Joel 2:32; Acts 2:21), whereas those who do not call on his name will

have wrath poured out on them (Ps. 79:6). 'All of them' again marks
the unity that characterises heaven, which is further emphasised in **and
serve him shoulder to shoulder**. This is literally '[with] one shoulder', and is an expression for unanimity, presumably derived from
men or animals carrying a burden with the load equally shared between
them. (Similar phrases occur with different parts of the body, such as
'one mouth' 1 Kgs. 22:13; Jer. 32:39.) This service is the obedience
and praise of those who are the loyal subjects of the heavenly king
(Deut. 10:12; Ps. 2:11).

God's gathered people (3:10). When the LORD finally intervenes in
the flow of earthly history, he will ensure that the cause of his church
is vindicated and that all who are his are gathered to him. This is
presented here in terms of the removal of the greatest curse that came
on the Old Testament church for its disobedience, namely deportation
from the land of God's presence and dispersal among the nations. That
had already happened to the northern kingdom of Israel (2 Kgs. 17:22-
23), and would soon befall Judah. In the day of the LORD, however,
**from beyond the rivers of Cush my worshippers, my scattered
people, will bring me offerings** (*verse 10*). Cush (2:12) is mentioned
as representative of distant lands. The rivers referred to would be the
Nile and its tributaries, the Blue and White Nile (Isa. 18:1). From
beyond them, that is, from all the earth, no matter how remote a part
you may care to think of, the LORD will restore his people (Isa. 11:11;
27:13).

'My worshippers' is a rare expression, indicating those who 'pray
to me' or 'supplicate me' (used of the prayers or cries in Gen. 25:21;
Exod. 8:30; Job 33:26; 1 Chr. 5:20). They are also referred to as 'my
scattered people', literally 'the daughter of my dispersed ones'. This
views them not as so many individuals, but as a group which remained
the congregation of the people of the LORD even in their dispersion to
all the lands. This term is developed in the New Testament into one that
applies to all the people of God whatever their origin (John 11:52;
James 1:1). 'Offerings' is literally 'my offering', where the singular
perhaps reflects the unity of the scene. 'Offering' is also the word that
most frequently is used of the cereal offering. Though it can be used
of blood offerings (1 Sam. 2:17, 29; 26:19), its use here is appropriate
for the time after the one great final offering for sin (Heb. 9:26-28).

Called to a holy life (3:11-13). The restored people of God are
described as those whose character has had all blemishes removed and
who enjoy all the benefits God bestows on them untroubled by sin. **On**

that day you will not be put to shame for all the wrongs you have done to me (*verse 11*). 'You' in Hebrew is feminine singular, resuming the style of address to Jerusalem in 3:7 and perhaps also the mention of 'the daughter of my dispersed ones' (3:10), and anticipating the use of 'daughter of Zion' (3:14). In the day of the LORD those whom he recognises as truly his people will not have to answer for their rebellious acts. This lack of shame is not the brazenness of the unrepentant (3:5) but arises from their confidence in the LORD's ability to rescue and redeem them.

They are a purged community **because I will remove from this city those who rejoice in their pride**. The phrase 'rejoice in their pride' can be used in a positive sense (Isa. 13:3), but here it refers to the attitudes of those groups in the city who had been arrogant and defiant in their sin (3:3-4). As regards the holy city of God 'nothing impure will ever enter it, nor will anyone who does what is shameful or deceitful' (Rev. 21:27; 22:15). The restored community will not be a mixed community of saints and sinners, but one totally dedicated to him and not causing embarrassment to one another by disobedience. 'From this city' is literally 'from within you' or 'from your midst', picking up the theme of what was at the centre of Jerusalem (3:5). Her king in her midst could not tolerate those who were acting contrary to his will being with him in the midst of the city.

Never again will you be haughty on my holy hill. The English word 'haughty' has the same connotation of 'highness' as the Hebrew word it translates. It describes those who exalt themselves and think highly of their talents or power. Such superior attitudes are utterly condemned in Scripture. 'The LORD detests all the proud of heart. Be sure of this: They will not go unpunished. ... Pride goes before destruction, a haughty spirit before a fall' (Prov. 16:5, 18). How much more certain is the downfall of those who vaunt themselves 'on my holy hill', that is Zion (Ps. 2:6; Joel 2:1; 3:17). All who professed to be part of the LORD's people and gathered to worship him, but who harboured hearts of pride and rebellion against him, will be disowned by him and removed from the assembly of his people as having no true part in it (Matt. 13:40-43; 2 Tim. 2:19).

But I will leave within you the meek and humble, who trust in the name of the LORD (*verse 12*). 'Leave' is closely related to the word for 'remnant' (3:13). They are not left by some accidental omission, but are deliberately preserved by the LORD to honour him. 'Within you' or 'in your midst' picks up the phrase 'from your midst' in the

previous verse. This is the character of those whom God delights to
have surround his palace and throne. They are not those who have 'a
haughty spirit' but those who are 'lowly in spirit' (Prov. 16:18-19), and
as such are welcome in God's presence. They are described in three
ways, the first two of which are also found together in Isaiah 26:6 and
Job 34:28.

(1) 'Meek' comes from a root meaning 'afflicted' or 'oppressed'
(Ps. 72:2, 4). The idea of suffering became associated with an attitude
of acceptance and of trust in God, recognising one's own inability to
remedy the situation and seeking divine assistance (Isa. 49:13). The
word is translated 'gentle' when applied to the Messiah (Zech. 9:9) and
'humble' in Psalm 18:27 where the contrast is with 'those whose eyes
are haughty'. If it is possible to discriminate between this word and that
translated 'humble' in 2:3, it is that the word used here looks more to
their circumstances and personal history, whereas in 2:3 it describes
their character. However, it seems that the words did come closer in
meaning over time. Here those who have turned from self-assertive-
ness and relied on the LORD for deliverance are found suitably
rewarded.

(2) 'Humble' is often translated 'weak' or 'poor', a term which
refers to a lack of possessions. In a spiritual sense it denotes those who
are aware of their own lack of resources, and seek divine provision.

(3) They put their trust in all that the LORD has revealed himself to
be (see on 'name' 3:9). For 'trust' see on Nahum 1:7. They have sought
refuge in all that the LORD has declared to them and in that way they
have found the blessing he provides (Ps. 2:12). 'The name of the LORD
is a strong tower; the righteous run to it and are safe' (Prov. 18:10).

The remnant of Israel will do no wrong (*verse 13*). For 'remnant'
see on 1:4 and 2:7. The 'remnant of Israel' does not refer to those who
return from the ten northern tribes. Israel is here used for all those who
are loyal to the LORD's covenant. They are divinely transformed into
his likeness (1 John 3:2). 'He does no wrong' (3:5) and in the age to
come neither will they. At present there is still much that blurs his
image in them, but then it will be clearly seen (Col. 3:10; Eph. 4:24).
They will speak no lies, that is falsehood. Again this is in the pattern
of the God who does not lie (Num. 23:19; Ps. 89:35; Tit. 1:2). Not only
is God the standard of truth, he is also the standard with respect to
observing the rights of truth. **Nor will deceit be found in their
mouths**. 'Deceit' is literally 'tongue of deceitfulness' referring back
to the description of 2:9. 'Deceit' refers to conduct and words that

cheat and mislead (Gen. 27:35; Mic. 6:12). A related word is found in the description of the servant of the LORD in whose mouth there was no deceit (Isa. 53:9).

They will enjoy the fulness of the blessing that the LORD has promised. **They will eat and lie down and no one will make them afraid.** 'Eat' is literally 'graze' and compares the remnant of Israel to a flock (Mic. 7:14; Zech. 11:7). 'Lie down' or 'rest' (Ps. 23:2) is part of the same picture. This freedom from fear is part of the redemption the LORD extends to his people (Lev. 26:6; Jer. 30:10; 46:27; Ezek. 34:28; 39:26; Mic. 4:4; Nah. 2:11).

The bliss of what God will provide for his people has an allure which appeals to those who have experienced the bitterness of life and to those who are sensitive to their own failings. But the description of the inhabitants of the restored Jerusalem also serves notice of how great a change is needed before an individual is fit to join them. It requires nothing less than being born again (John 3:3). There is thus added to the motivation to repent based on avoiding the threat of God's wrath, a desire to repent based on the need to know the purifying and sanctifying work of his Spirit so as to be in a position to enjoy the provision and security of the people God recognises as his own.

Study questions: Zephaniah 3:9-13

verse 9: How do the lips and speech act as an index of the inner workings of the heart? (Jer. 17:9; Matt. 12:33-37; Mark 7:15, 21-23; Jas. 1:26; 3:3-12)

verses 12-13: Trace the ways in which the character and conduct of the transformed inhabitants of Jerusalem differ from the description Zephaniah gives earlier in his prophecy of the people of his own day.

Zephaniah 3:14-20: The Rejoicing of the LORD and his People

The climax of the prophecy is a paean of joy and praise as the LORD and his people rejoice and sing over all that has been accomplished. The section may be divided into prophetic description (3:14-17) and divine speech (3:18- 20), but much more significant is the threefold portrayal of the LORD as King (3:15), Warrior (3:17a) and Bridegroom (3:17b) with a corresponding threefold description of his people in terms that reflect this: no longer undergoing punishment (3:18), rescued and victorious (3:19), and brought home as his bride (3:20).

Sing, O Daughter of Zion; shout aloud, O Israel! Be glad and rejoice with all your heart, O Daughter of Jerusalem! (*verse 14*).

292 pv29 peppinti>

The prophet calls on the reassembled remnant of Israel, that is, the
LORD's covenant people, to rejoice whole-heartedly at the salvation
the LORD has given them. The exuberance of the occasion is brought
out by the multiplication of words to indicate their joy. 'Sing' is often
translated 'sing for joy' as an outpouring of emotion at the realisation
of all God is and has done (Pss. 92:4; 96:12; 145:7; Isa. 12:6). It is also
translated 'shout' even in contexts of joy at the LORD's deliverance
(Isa. 24:14; 52:8; Zech. 2:10). We are probably not to think in terms
of choral singing but of an acclamation of victory. That is even more
obvious of 'shout aloud' which can refer to a signal blast on a trumpet
(Num. 10:7, 9), but it also covers 'make a joyful noise' (Pss. 95:1; 98:6)
and 'extol' (Ps. 95:2). Perhaps we can grasp something of what is
involved by noting that the word is found as 'shout' in Zechariah 9:9
which is reflected in the cries of acclamation at Christ's entrance into
Jerusalem (Matt. 21:5-9; John 12:12-15). 'Be glad' refers to the
emotion of joy as experienced in all sorts of situations, and it could also
refer to the holy rejoicing at the stated festivals (Num. 10:10).
'Rejoice' captures the exultant jubilation of the faithful (Pss. 68:4;
149:5). It is used of God in the sense of triumphant (Ps. 60:6), though
the jubilation of the wicked degenerates into mere gloating (Ps. 94:3).
True praise of God can never be less than an exercise of the whole
person (Ps. 103:1).

There are also three terms in this verse for God's people. For the
use of the term 'daughter' see on 3:10 and Micah 4:8. Zion, Israel and
Jerusalem all evoke memories of the past and of the covenant heritage
of the people of God. These terms continue to be part of the heritage
of Jew and Gentile united in faith in Jesus Christ (Heb. 12:22; Gal.
4:26; 6:16).

The LORD has taken away your punishment (*verse 15*) or 'the
judgments against you'. It is the prerogative of the sovereign who
dispenses justice to extend pardon to the guilty. He has removed the
barrier in the way of their acceptance. **He has turned back your
enemy.** 'Your enemy', though singular, refers to every single one of
those who had been permitted to rise up against them as instruments
by which he gave effect to his sentence against his rebellious people.
Their enemies removed, the scattered people are restored and the LORD
is able to resume his rightful position. **The LORD, the King of Israel,
is with you.** 'The King of Israel' is emphasised by being placed first
in Hebrew. God's rule as king over his people is a fundamental
perspective of the Old Testament (Exod. 15:18; Pss. 10:16; 22:28;

24:10; 103:19), and frequently this rule is presented as being exercised through the coming Messianic king, who would be both descended from David and divine (Pss. 2:6; 45:6; Isa. 9:7; 32:1; Jer. 23:5; Zech. 9:9). Although the title 'King of Israel' now sounds directly Messianic (Matt. 27:42; John 1:49; 12:13), this was probably not intended to be a directly Messianic prophecy. It is looking forward to the coming establishment of God's rule, which is viewed as exercised directly (as in Pss. 93, 96-99) and not through a mediatorial figure. What is significant about the title here (it is not used of God elsewhere in the Old Testament) is that 'Israel' is named. What is in view is God's rule over his covenant people. Before his presence in the midst of Jerusalem had been a threat (3:5), but now it is a guarantee of the permanent security of the city (Ps. 46:5; Rev. 21:2-4; 22:3). **Never again will you fear any harm**.

On that day (*verse 16*) indicates a new start, though linked to the continuing theme (3:11). The presentation in verses 16 and 17a changes from that of the LORD as King and Judge to the related picture of him as Warrior. **They will say to Jerusalem, 'Do not fear, O Zion; do not let your hands hang limp'**. 'They will say' is literally 'it will be said'. The phrase is impersonal, and does not invite speculation as to the identity of the speakers. The message is to Zion as chosen by the LORD as his desired dwelling place (Ps. 132:13-14). Now that he is in residence there are no grounds for worry over attack from without or weakness within. Hands 'going limp' (Isa. 13:7; Ezek. 7:17) or 'hanging limp' (Jer. 6:24; 50:43) were a sign of despair and inability to resist induced by alarm and anxiety. Not letting one's hands hang limp was equivalent to 'not giving up' (2 Chr. 15:7).

The reason they have for courage and confidence is clear. **The LORD your God is with you** (*verse 17*) repeats the thought of 3:15 with the variation that **he is mighty to save**. This may also be translated 'a warrior, who gives victory (or deliverance)'. 'Mighty' refers to a warrior (1:14), to one like the valiant men who were heroes (2 Sam. 23:8), renowned for their strength and might. Of course, strength and might belong supremely to God, who is described as a mighty warrior (Isa. 10:21), as is the coming Messiah (Isa. 9:6). When God's might is awakened, then he acts to save his people (Ps. 80:2; see also Exod. 15:3; Ps. 110:5-6; Isa. 42:13). There are none who can successfully oppose his power, and so the people may rest in confidence.

The relationship between the LORD and his people is next presented as like that between a bridegroom and his bride. This bond is frequently used as a figure for that between God and his people (Isa. 54:5; Jer. 3:14; 31:32; Hos. 2:19-20; Eph. 5:25-27), just as the coming day is referred to as 'the wedding of the Lamb' (Rev. 19:7-9). **He will take great delight in you** is literally 'delight with joy', where the word 'joy' is related to 'glad' used earlier of the people (3:15). 'Delight' too may be used with God or the people as the subject. It was used by Moses to refer to God's delight in his people (Deut. 30:9). Isaiah combined it with the imagery of marriage. 'As a bridegroom rejoices over his bride, so will your God rejoice over you' (Isa. 62:5; see also Isa. 65:19; Jer. 32:41).

He will quiet you with his love would indicate quelling their fears and overcoming their propensity to restless wandering by the great display of his love towards them. However, 'you' is a supplement, and the clause could also be understood as 'he will be quiet in his love.' The LORD's great delight expresses itself both quietly and in singing. This silence is a love deeply felt, where God is absorbed in the object of its love. This is a sublime expression of the ultimate in divine love, lost in wonder over reclaimed humanity. **He will rejoice over you with singing.** One is at a loss to know which picture stretches the imagination more: God silent or God singing. 'Rejoice' (Hab. 3:18) is yet another word for joy, this time in vigorous and exuberant expression, such as the gladness of a marriage procession (Ps. 45:15).

These expressions draw from human analogies to try to express something of the LORD's delight over his saved people (Luke 15:7, 10) or at the return of the son who had been lost (Luke 15:11-32). To say that the reality is greater than these descriptions is to point, however indistinctly, to what is no doubt the unceasing activity of heaven to find out all that is entailed in the fact that God is love.

In the concluding three verses it is the LORD himself who speaks and who applies this vista of future joy to the present situation of the remnant among his people. They still had to go through the horrors of the Babylonian advance and desolation of their city as well as the deportation. Grasping what he would do for them in his power would sustain their faith in the dark days ahead as they awaited the time of his promised blessing. The repeated 'I' of these final verses shows that the emphasis is on what the LORD will do to secure the welfare of his people.

The sorrows for the appointed feasts I will remove from you (*verse 18*). The difficulties connected with understanding and translating this verse are indicated by the quite different rendering found in the

NIV margin: 'I will gather you who mourn for the appointed feasts; your reproach is a burden to you.' Both renderings speak about a coming time when the worship of the Temple would resume. At the times of the appointed feasts (Exod. 23:14-17; Lev. 23:2, 4) all Israel were to rejoice before the LORD (Hos. 12:10). But in the sack of Jerusalem the Temple was destroyed and worship ceased. Moreover many of the people were carried off into exile, where they came to realise even more bitterly how much they had lost (Ps. 137:1-6). 'Remove' is more literally 'gather'. The picture is either of the LORD gathering those who are truly sorrowful that the LORD was no longer worshipped in the Temple, and bringing them back to the land, or of gathering their sorrows so as to take them away. The Hebrew text contains the words 'They were from you', which might indicate the sorrowers as having originated in Jerusalem, or else the effective removal of their sorrows. **They are a burden and a reproach to you** is literally 'a burden upon her a reproach'. Though it is possible that the person switches quickly so that 'her' is Zion (hence NIV 'you'), it is also the case that 'her' might refer to those sorrowing as a group. Those who were mourning were experiencing the reproach or disgrace ('insults' 2:8) experienced by God's people, namely that of slavery among the heathen. The scorn of the nations added to all else that had happened to Jerusalem. But their King will remove the sentence he has imposed on them.

At the same time as the Warrior, the LORD will overcome their enemies. **At that time I will deal with all who oppressed you** (*verse 19*). The focus is on the LORD, 'Behold me!' His action is imminent; it has already started. 'Deal' does not in itself indicate the nature of the proceedings. The context makes it clear that this is in punishment. 'The oppressors' as in Isaiah 60:14 are the heathen nations who had overrun Israel.

He will provide deliverance for his people who are helpless. **I will rescue the lame and gather those who have been scattered**. This takes up the language of Micah 4:6. **I will give them praise and honour in every land where they were put to shame**. 'Honour' is literally 'a name', and this takes up the consummating promise of the covenant found in Deuteronomy 26:19: 'He has declared that he will set you in praise, fame and honour high above all the nations he has made and that you will be a people holy to the LORD your God, as he promised'. The earlier promises will be made good to the restored people. When they pondered the meaning of his word, they were not to suppose that he had set aside his purpose.

The promise is again repeated in substantially similar terms so that there would be no doubt about its fulfilment. **At that time I will gather you; at that time I will bring you home** (*verse 20*). It almost looks as if the NIV has switched the order of the Hebrew clauses, the first of which speaks of bringing and the second of which repeats the verb 'gather' from the previous verse. 'Bring' is often used in connection with the Exodus (Isa. 14:2; 43:5). 'Home' is a supplement which expresses where they were being brought to when they were gathered. 'At that time' is repeated to emphasise the certainty and simultaneity of the realisation of the promises, leading faith not to focus on the impending catastrophe that would come upon the land, but on the fact that afterwards their condition would be divinely reversed.

I will give you honour and praise among all the peoples of the earth. 'Honour and praise' reverses the order of 3:19. Notice the widening of this glory from the lands of captivity to all the earth. **'When I restore your fortunes before your very eyes,' says the LORD**. Even though it now seems remote, and perhaps impossible, it will really happen. For 'restore your fortunes', see on 2:7. 'Before your eyes' is not a promise that this will be directly witnessed by Zephaniah's generation (Deut. 1:30; 4:34; 1 Sam. 12:16). It is the remnant in their distress who are being addressed. The thought is that there will be an evident and irrefutable change in their fortunes. There will be no doubt that God had acted on behalf of his people. The scribes who put the Minor Prophets into their present order appreciated this when they placed Zephaniah directly before Haggai, which begins with the restoration of the Temple. In that there was a fulfilment of the divine promise, but the ultimate realisation awaits the new Jerusalem.

Though Zephaniah's prophecy is best known for its solemn picture of the day of the LORD (1:14-18), his theology is misrepresented unless that is balanced by the allure of this final triumph. If the grim reality of the LORD's judgment does not drive the rebellious to repentance, then the exultant celebrations may instead draw them to return to God. Who would want to miss out on all that is on offer that day? Especially as the invitation to be there is now freely extended. 'The Spirit and the bride say, "Come!" And let him who hears say, "Come!" Whoever is thirsty, let him come; and whoever wishes, let him take the free gift of the water of life' (Rev. 22:17).

Study questions: Zephaniah 3:14-20

verse 16: How should we act to prevent us from becoming ineffective through fear? (2 Cor. 4:16-18; Heb. 12:12-13)

How does Scripture employ the analogy of the bridegroom and the bride to illustrate God's relationship with his people? (Isa. 54:5; 62:5; Matt. 9:15; 22:1-14; 25:1-13; John 3:29; 2 Cor. 11:2; Eph. 5:22-33; Rev. 19:7; 21:2)

verse 17: How is God's power available to his people now? (Mark 9:1; 2 Cor. 10:4)

verse 19: What does the New Testament say about the overthrow of the enemies of the Lord and his people? (Matt. 13:41; 22:13; Luke 19:27; John 5:29; 1 Thess. 5:3; 2 Thess. 1:6-10; Rev. 21:8)

Subject Index

Index of Scripture Passages Quoted or Discussed

Christian Focus Publications publishes biblically-accurate books for adults and children. The books in the adult range are published in three imprints.

Christian Heritage contains classic writings from the past.

Christian Focus contains popular works including biographies, commentaries, doctrine, and Christian living.

Mentor focuses on books written at a level suitable for Bible College and seminary students, pastors, and others; the imprint includes commentaries, doctrinal studies, examination of current issues, and church history.

For a free catalogue of all our titles, please write to
Christian Focus Publications,
Geanies House, Fearn,
Ross-shire, IV20 1TW, Great Britain

For details of our titles visit us on our web site
http://www.geanies.org.uk/cfp

Books by Donald Bridge

JESUS - THE MAN AND HIS MESSAGE

What impact did Jesus make on the circumstances and culture of his time? What is it about him that identifies him both as a unique Saviour and the greatest example of gospel communication?

Donald Bridge challenges the way we view Jesus, and our portrayal of him to the world around us. He argues that walking with Jesus today means reading his words, welcoming the impact of his personality, embracing the provision he makes for us, and sharing his good news with others.

Donald Bridge combines a lifetime of study of the Gospels with an intimate knowledge of the land where Jesus lived and taught. He has been both an evangelist and a pastor, as well as working for several years in the Garden Tomb, Jerusalem.

176 PAGES   B FORMAT

ISBN 1 85792 117 8

SPIRITUAL GIFTS AND THE CHURCH
Donald Bridge and David Phypers

First published in the 1970s, when the Charismatic Movement became prominent in British church life, this classic study of gifts, the individual and the church has been revised and expanded in light of developments since then. The authors, Donald Bridge and David Phypers, give a balanced view of a difficult and controversial issue.

The baptism of the Spirit, with its associated gifts, is a subject which has perplexed and fascinated Christians. It is unfortunately one which also divides Christians who disagree over the extent to which gifts should appear in the Church.

Donald Bridge is an evangelist and church consultant and David Phypers is a Church of England pastor.

192 PAGES   B FORMAT

ISBN 1 85792 141 0

Reformed Theological Writings
R. A. Finlayson

This volume contains a selection of doctrinal studies, divided into three sections:

General theology
The God of Israel; God In Three Persons; God the Father; The Person of Christ; The Love of the Spirit in Man's Redemption; The Holy Spirit in the Life of Christ; The Messianic Psalms; The Terminology of the Atonement; The Ascension; The Holy Spirit in the Life of the Christian; The Assurance of Faith; The Holy Spirit in the Life of the Church; The Church – The Body of Christ; The Authority of the Church; The Church in Augustine; Disruption Principles; The Reformed Doctrine of the Sacraments; The Theology of the Lord's Day, The Christian Sabbath; The Last Things.

Issues Facing Evangelicals
Christianity and Humanism; How Liberal Theology Infected Scotland; Neo-Orthodoxy; Neo-Liberalism and Neo-Fundamentalism; The Ecumenical Movement; Modern Theology and the Christian Message.

The Westminster Confession of Faith
The Significance of the Westminster Confession; The Doctrine of Scripture in the Westminster Confession of Faith; The Doctrine of God in the Westminster Confession of Faith; Particular Redemption in the Westminster Confession of Faith; Efficacious Grace in the Westminster Confession of Faith; Predestination in the Westminster Confession of Faith; The Doctrine of Man in the Westminster Confession of Faith.

R. A. Finlayson was for many years the leading theologian of the Free Church of Scotland and one of the most effective preachers and speakers of his time; those who were students in the 1950s deeply appreciated his visits to Christian Unions and IVF conferences. This volume contains posthumously edited theological lectures which illustrate his brilliant gift for simple, logical and yet warm-hearted presentation of Christian doctrine (I Howard Marshall).

272 pages   ISBN 1 85792 259 X   large format

MENTOR TITLES

Creation and Change by Douglas Kelly (large format, 272 pages)
A scholarly defence of the literal seven-day account of the creation of all things as detailed in Genesis 1. The author is Professor of Systematic Theology in Reformed Theological Seminary in Charlotte, North Carolina, USA.

The Healing Promise by Richard Mayhue (large format, 288 pages)
A clear biblical examination of the claims of Health and Wealth preachers. The author is Dean of The Master's Seminary, Los Angeles, California.

Puritan Profiles by William Barker (hardback, 320 pages)
The author is Professor of Church History at Westminster Theological Seminary, Philadelphia, USA. In this book he gives biographical profiles of 54 leading Puritans, most of whom were involved in the framing of the Westminster Confession of Faith.

Creeds, Councils and Christ by Gerald Bray (large format, 224 pages)
The author, who teaches at Samford University, Birmingham, Alabama, explains the historical circumstances and doctrinal differences that caused the early church to frame its creeds. He argues that a proper appreciation of the creeds will help the confused church of today.

MENTOR COMMENTARIES

1 and 2 Chronicles by Richard Pratt (hardback, 520 pages)
The author is professor of Old Testament at Reformed Theological Seminary, Orlando, USA. In this commentary he gives attention to the structure of Chronicles as well as the Chronicler's reasons for his different emphases from that of 1 and 2 Kings.

Psalms by Alan Harman (hardback, 420 pages)
The author, now retired from his position as a professor of Old Testament, lives in Australia. His commentary includes a comprehensive introduction to the psalms as well as a commentary on each psalm.

Amos by Gray Smith (hardback, 320 pages)
Gary Smith, a professor of Old Testament in Bethel Seminary, Minneapolis, USA, exegetes the text of Amos by considering issues of textual criticism, structure, historical and literary background, and the theological significance of the book.

Focus on the Bible Commentaries

Exodus – John L. Mackay*
Deuteronomy – Alan Harman
Judges and Ruth – Stephen Dray
1 and 2 Samuel – David Searle*
1 and 2 Kings – Robert Fyall*
Proverbs – Eric Lane (late 1998)
Daniel – Robert Fyall (1998)
Hosea – Michael Eaton
Amos – O Palmer Robertson*
Jonah-Zephaniah – John L. Mackay
Haggai-Malachi – John L. Mackay
Matthew – Charles Price (1998)
Mark – Geoffrey Grogan
John – Steve Motyer (1999)
Romans – R. C. Sproul
2 Corinthians – Geoffrey Grogan
Galatians – Joseph Pipa*
Ephesians – R. C. Sproul
Philippians – Hywel Jones
1 and 2 Thessalonians – Richard Mayhue (1999)
The Pastoral Epistles – Douglas Milne
Hebrews – Walter Riggans (1998)
James – Derek Prime
1 Peter – Derek Cleave
2 Peter – Paul Gardner (1998)
Jude – Paul Gardner

Journey Through the Old Testament – Bill Cotton
How To Interpret the Bible – Richard Mayhue

Those marked with an * are currently being written.